T4-AHH-253

Library of
Davidson College
VOID

GREAT STORIES
FROM
GREAT LIVES

Great Stories *from* Great Lives

A Gallery of Portraits
From Famous Biographies

Edited by
HERBERT V. PROCHNOW
Author of "The Public Speaker's Treasure Chest"

HARPER & BROTHERS PUBLISHERS
NEW YORK AND LONDON

GREAT STORIES FROM GREAT LIVES

A GALLERY OF PORTRAITS FROM FAMOUS BIOGRAPHIES

3-4

SECOND EDITION

B-T

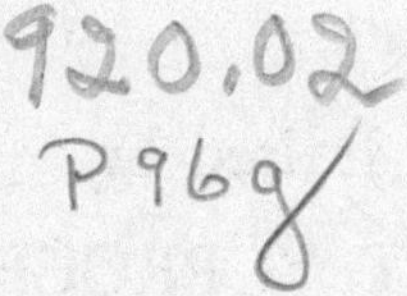

This book is complete and unabridged in contents, and is manufactured in strict conformity with Government regulations for saving paper.

TABLE OF CONTENTS

PREFACE xi

I. ABRAHAM LINCOLN: THE WAR YEARS — *Carl Sandburg* 1
Lincoln Speaks at Gettysburg

II. R. E. LEE — *Douglas Southall Freeman* 21
The Answer He Was Born to Make

III. MR. JUSTICE HOLMES — *Francis Biddle* 35
"Death Plucks My Ears"
"I Concur"
The Old Man Dozed Again

IV. BILLY MITCHELL — *Emile Gauvreau and Lester Cohen* 38
The Court Martial of General Mitchell

V. PAUL REVERE AND THE WORLD HE LIVED IN — *Esther Forbes* 48
The Ride of Paul Revere

VI. GEORGE WASHINGTON, THE SAVIOR OF THE STATES, 1777-1781 — *Rupert Hughes* 62
The Tact of Washington

VII. LOU GEHRIG, A QUIET HERO — *Frank Graham* 64
How to Pitch to Gehrig
The Day Had Come
The Shining Legacy of Courage

VIII. FANNY KEMBLE, A PASSIONATE VICTORIAN — *Margaret Armstrong* 70
Fanny Was Still Very, Very Young

IX. GRANT OF APPOMATTOX — *William E. Brooks* 78
How Grant Met His Great Day

X. I WAS WINSTON CHURCHILL'S PRIVATE SECRETARY — *Phyllis Moir* — 82
A Gift for Phrase-making
How to Make a Roast Beef Sandwich

XI. NAPOLEON — *Emil Ludwig* — 84
The Little Magician Spins His Web

XII. THE DOCTORS MAYO — *Helen Clapesattle* — 96
A Competent Surgeon in His Own Right
Great Surgeons at the Operating Table

XIII. THOREAU — *Henry Seidel Canby* — 102
On Him They Could Not Calculate
Resistance to the Power of the State

XIV. A PURITAN IN BABYLON: THE STORY OF CALVIN COOLIDGE — *William Allen White* — 108
Coolidge Does the Best Day's Work in His Life
Sadness of Farewell

XV. DISRAELI, A PICTURE OF THE VICTORIAN AGE — *André Maurois* — 121
Disraeli's Maiden Speech
Disraeli's First Speech on the Budget

XVI. ALBERT EINSTEIN: MAKER OF UNIVERSES — *H. Gordon Garbedian* — 134
The Humanity of a Great Scientist

XVII. CHARLES DICKENS: HIS LIFE AND WORK — *Stephen Leacock* — 138
Eyes That Could Not See—
Charles Dickens Visits the West

XVIII. GIANTS IN DRESSING GOWNS — *Julian B. Arnold* — 143
The First Book Printed in English
The Children of a Crowbar

XIX. MARCONI: THE MAN AND HIS WIRELESS — *Orrin E. Dunlap* — 147
The First Transatlantic Signal

XX. JEFFERSON DAVIS: THE UNREAL AND THE REAL — *Robert McElroy* — 155
A Strange Temptation That Came to Jefferson Davis
"That Is My Estate"

XXI. HEINRICH HEINE: PARADOX AND POET — *Louis Untermeyer* 158
The Tortured Wit

XXII. ALEXANDER HAMILTON, PORTRAIT OF A PRODIGY — *David Loth* 163
The Duel

XXIII. AARON BURR: THE PROUD PRETENDER — *Holmes Alexander* 171
On That Subject He Was Coy

XXIV. MASTER KUNG, THE STORY OF CONFUCIUS — *Carl Crow* 174
Confucius the Philosopher

XXV. CLARA BARTON, DAUGHTER OF DESTINY — *Blanche Colton Williams* 178
The Significance of the Treaty of Geneva
The American Red Cross Is Born

XXVI. BOLIVAR, THE PASSIONATE WARRIOR — *T. R. Ybarra* 186
"I Have Plowed in the Sea"

XXVII. THOMAS A. EDISON, A MODERN OLYMPIAN — *Mary Childs Nerney* 190
"Lights Strung on Wires Indeed!"

XXVIII. THE LIFE OF EMERSON — *Van Wyck Brooks* 198
The Moment of Inspiration

XXIX. WILLIAM ALLEN WHITE: THE MAN FROM EMPORIA — *Everett Rich* 204
What's the Matter with Kansas?

XXX. MITCHELL: PIONEER OF AIR POWER — *Isaac Don Levine* 213
"The History of the World War Was Played Out in Three Days"

XXXI. THE LITTLE GIANT, THE STORY OF STEPHEN A. DOUGLAS AND ABRAHAM LINCOLN — *Jeannette Covert Nolan* 218
When the Little Giant Held Lincoln's Hat and Cane

XXXII. GIANTS GONE, MEN WHO MADE CHICAGO — *Ernest Poole* 222
The Ravages of Scarlet Fever
The Cross-examination of Dr. Billings

XXXIII. FIGHTING ANGEL, PORTRAIT OF A SOUL — *Pearl S. Buck* 226
The Old Teacher Was Planning to Go Back

XXXIV. MR. DOOLEY'S AMERICA, A LIFE OF FINLEY PETER DUNNE — *Elmer Ellis* 237
The Satire of Finley Peter Dunne
Says Mr. Dooley to Mr. Hennessy
Mr. Dooley's Reflections

XXXV. ADMIRAL OF THE OCEAN SEA, A LIFE OF CHRISTOPHER COLUMBUS — *Samuel Eliot Morison* 239
Never Again May Mortal Men Recapture the Experience of Those October Days

XXXVI. ALEXANDER THE GREAT — *Lewis V. Cummings* 250
Alexander the Great Bequeathes an Empire

XXXVII. MOZART — *Marcia Davenport* 252
The Inspiration of Genius

XXXVIII. ISAAC NEWTON — *Louis T. More* 264
How Newton Appeared to Himself

XXXIX. OSCAR WILDE AND THE YELLOW 'NINETIES — *Frances Winwar* 265
The Repartee of Wilde and Whistler
Oscar Wilde Appraises Whistler
"And Yet They Have Not Crucified Me"
When Death Was Near

XL. PHANTOM CROWN; THE STORY OF MAXIMILIAN AND CARLOTA OF MEXICO — *Bertita Harding* 268
The Execution of Maximilian

XLI. THE LIFE OF MARGARET FULLER — *Madeleine B. Stern* 276
The City She Had Loved Was No More

XLII. WILL ROGERS, HIS WIFE'S STORY — *Betty Blake Rogers* 282
Where Will Rogers Found Humor
To Tip or Not to Tip a Soup Plate

XLIII. BENJAMIN FRANKLIN — *Carl Van Doren* 284
The Wit and Charm of Franklin as Poor Richard

XLIV. NOAH WEBSTER, SCHOOLMASTER TO AMERICA — *Harry R. Warfel* 293
He Made Words March Like Warriors Against Ignorance

XLV. FIVE AND TEN: THE FABULOUS LIFE OF F. W. WOOLWORTH *John K. Winkler* 297
Three Out of Five Failed

XLVI. LORDS OF THE LEVEE *Lloyd Wendt and Herman Kogan* 301
"We're Goin' Places, You an' Me"

XLVII. LORD MACAULAY: VICTORIAN LIBERAL *Richmond Croom Beatty* 311
"I Am of a Very Different Opinion"

XLVIII. L. EMMETT HOLT, PIONEER OF A CHILDREN'S CENTURY *R. L. Duffus and L. Emmett Holt, Jr.* 318
The Awakening of the Science of Medicine

XLIX. WOODROW WILSON: LIFE AND LETTERS *Ray Stannard Baker* 322
When Woodrow Wilson Became the Democratic Nominee for President of the United States

L. STILL SMALL VOICE *August Derleth* 336
Zona Gale's Best Novel Emerges

LI. CLARENCE DARROW FOR THE DEFENSE *Irving Stone* 343
Mr. Darrow Comments on His Own Appearance
No Further Questions
He Stays in Nights Now
Stolen Too Recently
He's Too Radical

LII. ALFRED I. duPONT: THE FAMILY REBEL *Marquis James* 346
"You Certainly Couldn't Run the Business, Could You?"

LIII. J. B. MURPHY, STORMY PETREL OF SURGERY *Loyal Davis* 357
"Look Carefully at My Kidneys"

LIV. BEAUREGARD, THE GREAT CREOLE *Hamilton Basso* 359
The Civil War Begins

LV. GROVER CLEVELAND: A STUDY IN COURAGE *Allan Nevins* 362
The Great Silver Battle of 1893

LVI. COMMODORE VANDERBILT *Wheaton J. Lane* 374
What's the Use of an Education?

LVII. GLORY-HUNTER, A LIFE OF GENERAL CUSTER — *Frederic F. Van de Water* 377
"An Example to Be Carefully Avoided"

LVIII. PASCAL, THE LIFE OF GENIUS — *Morris Bishop* 379
On That Night God Came

LIX. LIFE AND TIMES OF PIETER STUYVESANT — *Hendrik Van Loon* 391
The Last of the Dutch Strongholds in America

LX. BEYOND DAMASCUS, A BIOGRAPHY OF PAUL — *F. A. Spencer* 396
I Have Finished My Course

PREFACE

Emerson once said, "One moment of a man's life is a fact so stupendous as to take the lustre out of all fiction." If one moment in a man's life is so significant, how far-reaching in their consequences must be the great moments in the lives of great men and women.

In every life there come times of momentous decision, important turning points, tragedies, humorous situations or other experiences which are of transcendent human interest. This anthology consists of selections of such striking illustrations from great biographies. Moreover, these stories have almost invariably been chosen by the authors themselves, in other words, by those most competent and able to make the selections because of their exhaustive research in producing the biographies.

In some instances, the authors have selected delightful, thumbnail sketches, humorous as well as serious, which are revealing character studies; in other cases, they have described great, moving, historical events around which the destiny of mankind seemed to revolve. Through these pages walk faith and fear, courage and cowardice, fortune and failure. In these pages, also, men "meet with Triumph and Disaster and treat those two imposters just the same."

There are included stories of one or two lives which were in no sense illustrious or esteemed for high achievement, but were in fact sordid. If "history is," as Carlyle declares, "the essence of innumerable biographies," it is imperative that we see something of the sinners as well as the saints. But by and large, the stories are of lives which inspire us to new and greater achievement.

To the many authors and publishers who so graciously and generously contributed to this work we express our deep appreciation. Credit for the source of each selection is given in a footnote at the beginning of the passage.

Here, then, is an anthology of unforgettable stories from unforgettable biographies, written and selected by many of the most distinguished biographers of our time.

H. V. P.

I

ABRAHAM LINCOLN: THE WAR YEARS[1]

By

CARL SANDBURG

Henry S. Commager, writing in the *Yale Review*,[2] has called this four-volume biography "the greatest of all Lincoln biographies, one of the great biographies of our literature. It is great in the reflected beauty and honesty of its subject; it is great, too, in the telling. It is such a biography as Lincoln himself would have wished and would have understood, genuine, simple, broad, humane, dramatic, poetic, thoroughly American in its muscular, idiomatic words, in its humor, in its catholicity and democracy."

From this great biography and epic story of one of the most critical periods of American history, Carl Sandburg has chosen for this anthology the moving account of the address at Gettysburg.

LINCOLN SPEAKS AT GETTYSBURG

A printed invitation came to Lincoln's hands notifying him that on Thursday, November 19, 1863, exercises would be held for the dedication of a National Soldiers' Cemetery at Gettysburg. The same circular invitation had been mailed to Senators, Congressmen, the governors of Northern States, members of the Cabinet, by the commission of Pennsylvanians who had organized a corporation through which Maine, New Hampshire, Vermont, Massachusetts, Rhode Island, Maryland, Connecticut, New York, New Jersey, Pennsylvania, Delaware, West Virginia, Ohio, Indiana, Illinois, Michigan, Wisconsin, and Minnesota were to share the cost of a decent burying-ground for the dust and bones of the Union and Confederate dead.

[1] Carl Sandburg, *Abraham Lincoln: The War Years,* New York: Harcourt, Brace & Company, Inc., 1939, II, 452-477.

[2] Winter 1940, Yale University Press.

In the helpless onrush of the war, it was known, too many of the fallen had lain as neglected cadavers rotting in the open fields or thrust into so shallow a resting-place that a common farm plow caught in their bones. Now by order of Governor Curtin of Pennsylvania seventeen acres had been purchased on Cemetery Hill, where the Union center stood its colors on the second and third of July, and plots of soil had been allotted each State for its graves.

The sacred and delicate duties of orator of the day had fallen on Edward Everett. An eminent cultural figure, perhaps foremost of all distinguished American classical orators, he was born in 1794, had been United States Senator, Governor of Massachusetts, member of Congress, Secretary of State under Fillmore, Minister to Great Britain, Phi Beta Kappa poet at Harvard, professor of Greek at Harvard, president of Harvard. His reputation as a public speaker began in the Brattle Street Unitarian Church of Boston. . . . His lecture on Washington, delivered a hundred and twenty-two times in three years, had in 1859 brought a fund of $58,000, which he gave to the purchase and maintenance of Mount Vernon as a permanent shrine. . . . No ordinary trafficker in politics, Everett had in 1860 run for Vice-President on the Bell-Everett ticket of the Constitution Union party, receiving the electoral votes of Virginia, Kentucky, and Tennessee. . . .

On the basis of what Everett had heard about Lincoln he wrote in his journal shortly before the inauguration in '61 that the incoming President was "evidently a person of very inferior cast of character, wholly unequal to the crisis." Then on meeting the new President he recorded that he found him of better stuff than he had expected. As a strict worshiper of the Constitution and the Union he was drawn toward Lincoln's moderate slavery policy, writing to critics after the Administration had lost in the '62 fall elections, "It is my purpose to support the President to the best of my ability." . . . The President's "intellectual capacity" had been proved in his debates with Douglas. "He is one of the most laborious and indefatigable men in the country," said Everett, "and that he has been able to sustain himself under as great a load of care as was ever laid upon the head or the heart of a living man is in no small degree owing to the fact that the vindictive and angry passions form no part of his nature and that a kindly and playful spirit mingles its sweetness with the austere cup of public duty." . . .

Serene, suave, handsomely venerable in his sixty-ninth year, a prominent specimen of Northern upper-class distinction, Everett was a natural choice of the Pennsylvania commissioners, who sought an orator for a solemn national occasion. When in September they notified him that the date of the occasion would be October 23, he replied that he would need more time for preparation, and the dedication was postponed till November 19.

Lincoln meanwhile, in reply to the printed circular invitation, sent word to the commissioners that he would be present at the ceremonies. This made it necessary for the commissioners to consider whether the President should be asked to deliver an address when present. Clark E. Carr of Galesburg, Illinois, representing his State on the Board of Commissioners, noted that the decision of the Board to invite Lincoln to speak was an afterthought. "The question was raised as to his ability to speak upon such a grave and solemn occasion. . . . Besides, it was said that, with his important duties and responsibilities, he could not possibly have the leisure to prepare an address. . . . In answer . . . it was urged that he himself, better than anyone else, could determine as to these questions, and that, if he were invited to speak, he was sure to do what, under the circumstances, would be right and proper."

And so on November 2 David Wills of Gettysburg, as the special agent of Governor Curtin and also acting for the several States, by letter informed Lincoln that the several States having soldiers in the Army of the Potomac who were killed, or had since died at hospitals in the vicinity, had procured grounds for a cemetery and proper burial of their dead. "These grounds will be consecrated and set apart to this sacred purpose by appropriate ceremonies on Thursday, the 19th instant. I am authorized by the Governors of the various States to invite you to be present and participate in these ceremonies, which will doubtless be very imposing and solemnly impressive. It is the desire that after the oration, you, as Chief Executive of the nation, formally set apart these grounds to their sacred use by a few appropriate remarks."

Mr. Wills proceeded farther as to the solemnity of the occasion, and when Lincoln had finished reading the letter he understood definitely that the event called for no humor and that a long speech was not expected from him. "The invitation," wrote Clark E. Carr, "was not settled upon and sent to Mr. Lincoln until the second of November, more than six weeks after Mr. Everett had been invited to speak, and but little more than two weeks before the exercises were held."

On the second Sunday before the Gettysburg ceremonies were to take place Lincoln went to the studio of the photographer Gardner for a long-delayed sitting. Noah Brooks walked with him, and he carefully explained to Brooks that he could not go to the photographer on any other day without interfering with the public business and the photographer's business, to say nothing of his liability to be hindered en route by curiosity-seekers "and other seekers." On the White House stairs Lincoln had paused, turned, walked back to his office, and rejoined Brooks with a long envelope in his hand, an advance copy of Edward Everett's address to be delivered at the Gettysburg dedication. It was thoughtful of Everett to take care they should not cover the same ground in their speeches, he remarked to Brooks, who exclaimed over the length of the Everett address, covering nearly two sides of a one-page supplement of a Boston newspaper. Lincoln quoted a line he said he had read somewhere from Daniel Webster: "Solid men of Boston, make no long orations." There was no danger that he should get upon the lines of Mr. Everett's oration, he told Brooks, for what he had ready to say was very short, or as Brooks recalled his emphasis, "short, short, short." He had hoped to read the Everett address between sittings, but the photographer worked fast, Lincoln got interested in talk, and did not open the advance sheets while at Gardner's. . . .

Lamon noted that Lincoln wrote part of his intended Gettysburg address at Washington, covered a sheet of foolscap paper with a memorandum of it, and before taking it out of his hat and reading it to Lamon he said that it was not at all satisfactory to him, that he was afraid he would not do himself credit nor come up to public expectation. He had been too busy to give it the time he would like to.

The armies of Meade and Grant required attention. And there were such unforeseen affairs as the marriage of Kate Chase, daughter of the Secretary of the Treasury, at the most brilliant wedding the new Northern regime had as yet put on in Washington. . . .

And social functions aside, there were such matters as Thurlow Weed's calling on the President and outlining a plan to end the war more speedily, a plan that Weed said Stanton approved, though Seward was silent on it. Lincoln asked Weed to put it in writing. In that form it proposed that: (1) at the first military success the President should proclaim pardon and amnesty to all who had been making war on the Government; (2) during a 90-day armistice travel should be free and protected North and South; (3) all former Confederates during this armistice returning to Union allegiance should be restored to former rights; (4) at the end of the armistice the President should proclaim that as the war went on for the Union in the future "all territory, whether farms, villages, or cities, shall be partitioned equitably between and among the officers and soldiers by whom it shall be conquered." . . .

Two men, in the weeks just before the Gettysburg ceremonies, had worked on Lincoln, doing their best to make him see himself as a world spokesman of democracy, popular government, the mass of people as opposed to aristocrats, classes, and special interests. John Murray Forbes, having read Lincoln's lively stump-speech letter to the Springfield, Illinois mass meeting, wrote to Sumner on September 3, "I delight in the President's plain letter to plain people!" Forbes followed this five days later with a letter which Sumner carried to the White House and handed to Lincoln. It began with convincingly phrased praise of the Springfield letter, and proceeded into the unusual question: "Will you permit a suggestion from one who has nothing to ask for himself: one who would accept no office, and who seeks only to do his duty in the most private way possible?" With such an opening it could hardly be doubted that Lincoln read on into the next paragraphs—and read them more than once.

An aristocracy ruled the South and controlled it for war, believed Forbes, pointing to "the aristocratic class who own twenty negroes and upwards" as numbering "about 28,000 persons, which is about the 178th part of 5,000,000" whites. So Forbes urged, "Let the people North and South see this line clearly defined between the people and the aristocrats, and the war will be over! . . . If our people of the North can be made to see this truth, the rebellion will be crushed for want of Northern support, which it has had from the wolves under the sheep's garments of sham democracy, who have misled large bodies of unthinking and ignorant but generally honest Northern men."

After military successes, believed Forbes, the mass of the Southern people could be made to see this issue, "and then reconstruction becomes easy and permanent." And how could the plain people, North and South, be convinced of it in the shortest time? "Bonaparte, when under the republic, fighting despots of Europe, did as much by his bulletins as he did by his bayonets: the two went on together promising democratic institutions to the populations whose leaders he was making war upon."

"You," Forbes urged the President, "have the same opportunity, and greater; for you have enemies North and South, reading our language, whom you can teach. My suggestion, then, is that you should seize an early opportunity and any subsequent chance, to teach your great audience of plain people that the war is not the North against the South, but the people against the aristocrats."

This same idea Forbes wrote to William Evans, an English liberal, who was to call on the President. . . . And William Evans came away from his visit with Lincoln to write Forbes on November 3: "Your suggestions were duly attended to. . . . I took advantage of the hospitality afforded me to explain my views, which were in accordance with your own. . . . I did not hesitate to tell the President that had it not been for the antislavery policy of his government there would have been much greater difficulty in preventing a recognition of the Southern States."

Thus while Lincoln shaped his speech to be made at Gettysburg he did not lack specific advice that when the chance came he should stand up and be a world spokesman for those who called themselves democrats and liberals as opposed to what they termed "the aristocratic classes." . . .

Various definite motives besides vague intuitions may have guided Lincoln in his decision to attend and speak even though half his Cabinet had sent formal declinations in response to the printed circular invitations they had all received. Though the Gettysburg dedication was to be under interstate auspices, it had tremendous national significance for Lincoln because on the platform would be the State governors whose co-operation with him was of vast importance. . . .

His personal touch with Gettysburg, by telegraph, mail, courier, and by a throng of associations, made it a place of great realities to him. Just after the battle there, a woman had come to his office, the doorman saying she had been "crying and taking on" for several days trying to see the President. Her husband and three sons were in the army. On part of her husband's pay she had lived for a time, till money from him stopped coming. She was hard put to scrape a living and needed one of her boys to help.

The President listened to her, standing at a fireplace, hands behind him, head bowed, motionless. The woman finished her plea for one of her three sons in the army. He spoke. Slowly and almost as if talking to himself alone the words came and only those words:

"I have two, and you have none."

He crossed the room, wrote an order for the military discharge of one of her sons. On a special sheet of paper he wrote full and detailed instructions where to go and what to say in order to get her boy back.

In a few days the doorman told the President that the same woman was again on hand crying and taking on. "Let her in," was the word. She had found doors opening to her and officials ready to help on seeing the President's written words she carried. She had located her boy, camp, regiment, company. She had found him, yes, wounded at Gettysburg, dying in a hospital, and had followed him to the grave. And she begged, would the President now give her the next one of her boys?

As before he stood at the fireplace, hands behind him, head bent low, motionless. Slowly and almost as if talking to himself alone the words came and as before only those words:

"I have two, and you have none."

He crossed the room to his desk and began writing. As though nothing else was to do she followed, stood by his chair as he wrote, put her hand on the President's head, smoothed his thick and disorderly hair with motherly fingers. He signed an order giving her the next of her boys, stood up, put the priceless paper in her hand as he choked out the one word, "There!" and with long quick steps was gone from the room with her sobs and cries of thanks in his ears.

Thus the Kentuckian, James Speed, gathered the incident and told it. By many strange ways Gettysburg was to Lincoln a fact in crimson mist.

At the Cabinet meeting of November 17 the President requested the Secretary of War to arrange for a special train to Gettysburg. Stanton agreed, but excused himself from going, as did Welles too. Secretaries Seward, Usher, and Blair agreed to go. To Chase, who was not present, Lincoln wrote a note as though Chase might go along too, but Chase replied he had important public business. General Meade had written that duty held him with the Army of the Potomac. . . .

Thaddeus Stevens, Republican floor leader in the House, was asked if he were going to Gettysburg and said No. He was a Pennsylvania man, had at one time practiced law in Gettysburg and was then its foremost real-estate taxpayer. There might have been sentimental and practical reasons why he should go. He believed and said, however, in November of '63 that Lincoln was a "dead card" in the political deck. He favored Chase as a more thoroughgoing antislavery man for the next President of the United States, and when he heard that Lincoln and Seward were going to the dedicatory exercises, but not Chase, he clipped his words, "The dead going to eulogize the dead." Dining with the painter Frank B. Carpenter, Chase confided that Lincoln at a meeting of his Cabinet members had told them of Thaddeus Stevens's being asked by someone where the President and Seward were going.

"To Gettysburg," replied Stevens.

"But where are Stanton and Chase?"

"At home, at work; let the dead bury the dead."

William Saunders, landscape gardener and superintendent of grounds in the Department of Agriculture, called at Lincoln's request on the evening of November 17 with the plan of the cemetery he had designed. "I spread the plan on his office table," said Saunders. "He took much interest in it, asked about its surroundings, about Culp's Hill, Round Top, and seemed familiar with the place though he had never been there. He was much pleased with the method of the graves [with uniform headstones and the dead grouped by States], said it differed from the ordinary cemetery, and after I had explained the reasons, said it was an admirable and befitting arrangement. He asked me if I was going up to Gettysburg tomorrow. I told him I intended to be there and take up the plan. He replied, 'Well, I may see you on the train.' "

Also on the day of November 17 the President issued a little proclamation fixing a township line "within the City of Omaha" as the starting-point for the Union Pacific Railway. . . . The Gettysburg speech was shaping at the same time that Lincoln was preparing his annual message to Congress, assembling it in less than three weeks. In that message he would point to "actual commencement of work upon the Pacific railroad," his own act of fixing an initial point being the most tangible part of the commencement.

When Lincoln boarded the train for Gettysburg on November 18, his best chum in the world, Tad, lay sick abed and the doctors not sure what ailed him. The mother still remembered Willie and was hysterical about Tad. But the President felt imperative duty called him to Gettysburg.

Provost Marshal General James B. Fry as a War Department escort came to the White House, but the President was late in getting into the carriage for the drive to the station. They had no time to lose, Fry remarked. Lincoln said he felt like an Illinois man who was going to be hanged and as the man passed along the road on the way to the gallows the crowds kept pushing into the way and blocking passage. The condemned man at last called out, "Boys, you needn't be in such a hurry to get ahead, there won't be any fun till I get there."

Flags and red-white-and-blue bunting decorated the four-car special train. Aboard were the three Cabinet members, Nicolay and Hay, army and navy representatives, newspapermen, the French and Italian Ministers and attachés. The rear third of the last coach had a drawing-room, where from time to time the President talked with nearly everyone aboard as they came and went. . . .

"At the Calvert Street Station Secretary Seward began to get uneasy as we approached Baltimore. Upon reaching the Calvert Street Station in Baltimore all was quiet, less than two hundred people assembled, among them women with children in arms. They called for the President. He took two or three of the babies up and kissed them which greatly pleased the mothers. General Schenck and staff joined us and soon after the President went forward in the car and seated himself with a party of choice spirits, among whom was Mayor Frederick W. Lincoln of Boston, not a kinsman. They told stories for an hour or so, Mr. Lincoln taking his turn and enjoying it. Approaching Hanover Junction, he arose and said, 'Gentlemen, this is all very pleasant, but the people will expect me to say something to them tomorrow, and I must give the matter some thought.' He then returned to the rear room of the car."

An elderly gentleman got on the train and, shaking hands, told the President he had lost a son at Little Round Top at Gettysburg. The President answered he feared a visit to that spot would open fresh wounds, and yet if the end of sacrifice had been reached "we could give thanks even amidst our tears." They quoted from his unburdening to this old man: "When I think of the sacrifices of life yet to be offered, and the hearts and homes yet to be made desolate before this dreadful war is over, my heart is like lead within me, and I feel at times like hiding in deep darkness." At one stop a little girl lifted to an open window thrust a bunch of rosebuds into the car. "Flowerth for the Prethident." Lincoln stepped over, bent down, kissed her face. "You are a little rosebud yourself." . . .

At sundown the train pulled into Gettysburg and Lincoln was driven to the Wills residence, Seward to the Harper home fronting on the public square. A sleepy little country town of 3,500 was overflowing with human pulses again. Private homes were filled with notables and nondescripts. Hundreds slept on the floors of hotels. Military bands blared till late in the night serenading whomsoever. The weather was mild and the moon up for those who chose to go a-roaming. When serenaders called on the President for a speech, he made again one of those little addresses saying there was nothing to say. "In my position it is sometimes important that I should not say foolish things. [A voice: "If you can help it."] It very often happens that the only way to help it is to say nothing at all. Believing that is my present condition this evening, I must beg of you to excuse me from addressing you further."

The crowd didn't feel it was much of a speech. They went next door with the band and blared for Seward. He spoke so low that Hay could not hear him, but he opened the stopgaps of patriotic sentiment, saying in part, "I thank my God for the hope that this is the last fratricidal war which will fall upon the country which is vouchsafed to us by Heaven—the richest, the broadest, the most beautiful, the most magnificent, and capable of a greater destiny than has ever been given to any part of the human race." What more could a holiday crowd ask for on a fair night of moonlit November? Seward gave them more and closed: "Fellow citizens, good night." It was good night for him but not for them. They serenaded five other speakers. . . .

At dinner in the Wills home that evening Lincoln met Edward Everett, a guest under the same roof, and Governor Curtin and others. About ten o'clock he was in his room, with paper and pencil ready to write, when he sent a colored servant down for Judge Wills to come up. Still later, about eleven o'clock, he sent the colored servant down again for Judge Wills, who came up and heard Lincoln request to see Mr. Seward. Judge Wills offered to go and bring Seward from next door at the Harpers'. "No, I'll go and see him," said Lincoln, who gathered his sheets of paper and went for a half-hour with his Secretary of State.

Whether Seward made slight or material alterations in the text on the sheets was known only to Lincoln and Seward. It was midnight or later that Lincoln went to sleep, probably perfectly clear in his mind as to what his speech would be the next day. The one certainty was that his "few appropriate remarks," good or bad, would go to an immense audience. Also he slept better for having a telegram from Stanton reporting there was no real war news and "On inquiry Mrs. Lincoln informs me that your son is better this evening."

Fifteen thousand, some said 30,000 or 50,000, people were on Cemetery Hill for the exercises the next day when the procession from Gettysburg arrived afoot and horseback representing the United States Government, the army and navy, governors of States, mayors of cities, a regiment of troops, hospital corps, telegraph-company representatives, Knights Templar, Masonic Fraternity, Odd Fellows, and other benevolent associations, the press, fire departments, citizens of Pennsylvania and other States. They were scheduled to start at ten o'clock and at that hour of the clock Lincoln in a black suit, high silk hat, and white gloves came out of the Wills residence and mounted a horse. A crowd was on hand and he held a reception on horseback. At eleven the parade began to move. The President's horse seemed small for him, as some looked at it. Clark E. Carr, just behind the President, believed he noticed that the President sat erect and looked majestic to begin with and then got to thinking so that his body leaned forward, his arms hung limp, and his head bent far down.

A long telegram sent by Stanton at ten o'clock from Washington had been handed him. Burnside seemed safe though threatened at Knoxville, Grant was starting a big battle at Chattanooga, and "Mrs. Lincoln reports your son's health as a great deal better and he will be out today."

The march of the procession of military and civic bodies began. "Mr. Lincoln was mounted upon a young and beautiful chestnut horse, the largest in the Cumberland Valley," wrote Lieutenant Cochrane. This seemed the first occasion that anyone had looked at the President mounted with a feeling that just the right horse had been picked to match his physical length. "His towering figure surmounted by a high silk hat made the rest of us look small," thought Cochrane. At the President's right Seward and Blair rode their horses, at his left Usher and Lamon. In the next rank were six horses with the secretaries Nicolay and Hay, Provost Marshal General Fry, Lieutenant Cochrane, and military officers. Cochrane rode "a mischievous brute that required much attention to keep him from getting out of line to browse on the tail of the President's horse." The President rode "easily, bowing occasionally to right or left," noted Cochrane, while Seward lacked dignity, his trousers working up over the shoe tops to show his homemade gray socks. Seward was "entirely unconscious" that the Secretary of State looked funny—and nobody really cared. In the town of Gettysburg men with wounds still lingered in hospitals. And many flags along the main street were at half-mast for sorrow not yet over.

Minute guns spoke while the procession moved along Baltimore Street to the Emmitsburg Road, then by way of the Taneytown Road to the cemetery, where troop lines stood in salute to the President.

The march was over in fifteen minutes. But Mr. Everett, the orator of the day, had not arrived. Bands played till noon. Mr. Everett arrived. On the platform sat Governors Curtin of Pennsylvania, Bradford of Maryland, Morton of Indiana, Seymour of New York, Parker of New Jersey, Dennison of Ohio, with ex-Governor Tod and Governor-elect Brough of Ohio, Edward Everett and his daughter, Major Generals Schenck, Stahel, Doubleday, and Couch, Brigadier General Gibbon and Provost Marshal General Fry, foreign Ministers, members of Congress, Colonel Ward Hill Lamon, Secretary Usher, and the President of the United States with Secretary Seward and Postmaster General Blair immediately at his left.

The United States House chaplain, the Reverend Thomas H. Stockton, offered a prayer while the thousands stood with uncovered heads.

"O God, our Father, for the sake of Thy Son, our Saviour, inspire us with Thy spirit, and sanctify us. . . . By this altar of sacrifice and on this field of deliverance—on this mount of salvation—within the fiery and bloody line of these munitive rocks, looking back to the dark days of fear and trembling, and to the rapture of relief that came after, we multiply our thanksgiving, and confess our obligations to renew and perfect our personal and social consecration to Thy service and glory. . . . Bless the efforts to suppress this rebellion. . . . As the trees are not dead, though the foliage is gone, so our heroes are not dead though their forms have fallen —with their personality they are all with Thee, and the spirit of their example is here. It fills the air, it fills our hearts, and long as time shall last it will hover in these skies and rest on this landscape. . . ."

The chaplain prayed as a master of liturgy and a familiar of sacred literature. The *Philadelphia Press* said that with the prayer "there was scarcely a dry eye in all that vast assemblage," while the *Cincinnati Daily Gazette* reporter wrote his observation: "The President evidently united in this adjuration in all the simplicity of his soul, and the falling tear declared the sincerity of his emotions."

Benjamin B. French, officer in charge of buildings in Washington, introduced the Honorable Edward Everett, orator of the day, who rose, bowed low to Lincoln, saying, "Mr. President." Lincoln responded, "Mr. Everett."

The orator of the day then stood in silence before a crowd that stretched to limits that would test his voice. Beyond and around were the wheat fields, the meadows, the peach orchards, long slopes of land, and five and seven miles farther the contemplative blue ridge of a low mountain range. His eyes could sweep them as he faced the audience. He had taken note of it in his prepared and rehearsed address. "Overlooking these broad fields now reposing from the labors of the waning year, the mighty Alleghanies dimly towering before us, the graves of our brethren beneath our feet, it is with hesitation that I raise my poor voice to break the eloquent silence of God and Nature. But the duty to which you have called me must be performed;—grant me, I pray you, your indulgence and your sympathy." Everett proceeded, "It was appointed by law in Athens," and gave an extended sketch of the manner in which the Greeks cared for their dead who fell in battle. He spoke of the citizens assembled to consecrate the day. "As my eye ranges over the fields whose sods were so lately moistened by the blood of gallant and loyal men, I feel, as never before, how truly it was said of old that it is sweet and becoming to die for one's country."

Northern cities would have been trampled in conquest but for "those who sleep beneath our feet," said the orator. He gave an outline of how the war began, traversed decisive features of the three days' battles at Gettysburg, discussed the doctrine of State sovereignty and denounced it, drew parallels from European history, and came to his peroration quoting Pericles on dead patriots: "The whole earth is the sepulchre of illustrious men." The men of nineteen sister States had stood side by side on the perilous ridges. "Seminary Ridge, the Peach-Orchard, Cemetery, Culp, and Wolf Hill, Round Top, Little Round Top, humble names, henceforward dear and famous—no lapse of time, no distance of space, shall cause you to be forgotten." He had spoken for an hour and fifty-seven minutes, some said a trifle over two hours, repeating almost word for word an address that occupied nearly two newspaper pages, as he had written it and as it had gone in advance sheets to many newspapers.

Everett came to his closing sentence without a faltering voice: "Down to the latest period of recorded time, in the glorious annals of our common country there will be no brighter page than that which relates THE BATTLES OF GETTYSBURG." It was the effort of his life and embodied the perfection of the school of oratory in which he had spent his career. His erect form and sturdy shoulders, his white hair and flung-back head at dramatic points, his voice, his poise, and chiefly some quality of inside goodheartedness, held most of his audience to him, though the people in the front rows had taken their seats three hours before his oration closed.

The Baltimore Glee Club sang an ode written for the occasion by Benjamin B. French, who had introduced Everett to the audience. The poets Longfellow, Bryant, Whittier, Lowell, George Boker, had been requested but none found time to respond with a piece to be set to music. The two closing verses of the ode by French immediately preceded the introduction of the President to the audience:

Great God in Heaven!
Shall all this sacred blood be shed?
Shall we thus mourn our glorious dead?
Oh, shall the end be wrath and woe,
The knell of Freedom's overthrow,
A country riven?

It will not be!
We trust, O God! thy gracious power
To aid us in our darkest hour.
This be our prayer—"O Father! save
A people's freedom from its grave.
All praise to Thee!"

Having read Everett's address, Lincoln knew when the moment drew near for him to speak. He took out his own manuscript from a coat pocket, put on his steel-bowed glasses, stirred in his chair, looked over the manuscript, and put it back in his pocket. The Baltimore Glee Club finished. The specially chosen Ward Hill Lamon rose and spoke the words "The President of the United States," who rose, and holding in one hand the two sheets of paper at which he occasionally glanced, delivered the address in his high-pitched and clear-carrying voice. The *Cincinnati Commercial* reporter wrote, "The President rises slowly, draws from his pocket a paper, and when commotion subsides, in a sharp, unmusical treble voice, reads the brief and pithy remarks." Hay wrote in his diary, "The President, in a firm free way, with more grace than is his wont, said his half dozen words of consecration." Charles Hale of the *Boston Advertiser*, also officially representing Governor Andrew of Massachusetts, had notebook and pencil in hand, took down the slow-spoken words of the President, as follows:

Fourscore and seven years ago, our fathers brought forth upon this continent a new nation, conceived in Liberty and dedicated to the proposition that all men are created equal.

Now we are engaged in a great civil war, testing whether that nation—or any nation, so conceived and so dedicated—can long endure.

We are met on a great battle-field of that war. We are met to dedicate a portion of it as the final resting place of those who have given their lives that that nation might live.

It is altogether fitting and proper that we should do this.

But, in a larger sense, we cannot dedicate, we cannot consecrate, we cannot hallow, this ground. The brave men, living and dead, who struggled here, have consecrated it, far above our power to add or to detract.

The world will very little note nor long remember what we say here; but it can never forget what they did here.

It is for us, the living, rather, to be dedicated, here, to the unfinished work that they have thus far so nobly carried on. It is rather for us to be here dedicated to the great task remaining before us; that from these honored dead we take increased devotion to that cause for which they here gave the last full measure of devotion; that we here highly resolve that these dead shall not have died in vain; that the nation shall, under God, have a new birth of freedom, and that government of the people, by the people, for the people, shall not perish from the earth.

In a speech to serenaders just after the battle of Gettysburg four and a half months before, Lincoln had referred to the founding of the republic as taking place "eighty odd years since." Then he had hunted up the exact date, which was eighty-seven years since, and phrased it "Fourscore and seven years ago" instead of "Eighty-seven years since." Also in the final copy Lincoln wrote "We have come" instead of the second "We are met" that Hale reported.

In the written copy of his speech from which he read Lincoln used the phrase "our poor power." In other copies of the speech which he wrote out later he again used the phrase "our poor power." So it was evident that he meant to use the word "poor" when speaking to his audience, but he omitted it. Also in the copy held in his hands while facing the audience he had not written the words "under God," though he did include those words in later copies which he wrote. Therefore the words "under God" were decided upon after he wrote the text the night before at the Wills residence.

The *New York Tribune* and many other newspapers indicated "[Applause.]" at five places in the address and "[Long continued applause.]" at the end. The applause, however, according to most of the responsible witnesses, was formal and perfunctory, a tribute to the occasion, to the high office, to the array of important men of the nation on the platform, by persons who had sat as an audience for three hours. Ten sentences had been spoken in five minutes, and some were surprised that it should end before the orator had really begun to get his outdoor voice.

A photographer had made ready to record a great historic moment, had bustled about with his dry plates, his black box on a tripod, and before he had his head under the hood for an exposure, the President had said "by the people, for the people" and the nick of time was past for a photograph.

The *New York Times* reporter gave his summary of the program by writing: "The opening prayer by Reverend Mr. Stockton was touching and beautiful, and produced quite as much effect upon the audience as the classic sentences of the orator of the day. President Lincoln's address was delivered in a clear loud tone of voice, which could be distinctly heard at the extreme limits of the large assemblage. It was delivered (or rather read from a sheet of paper which the speaker held in his hand) in a very deliberate manner, with strong emphasis, and with a most business-like air."

The *Philadelphia Press* man, John Russell Young, privately felt that Everett's speech was the performance of a great actor whose art was too evident, that it was "beautiful but cold as ice." The *New York Times* man noted: "Even while Mr. Everett was delivering his splendid oration, there were as many people wandering about the fields, made memorable by the fierce struggles of July, as stood around the stand listening to his eloquent periods. They seem to have considered, with President Lincoln, that it was not what was *said* here, but what was *done* here, that deserved their attention. . . . In wandering about these battlefields, one is astonished and indignant to find at almost every step of his progress the carcasses of dead horses which breed pestilence in the atmosphere. I am told that more than a score of deaths have resulted from this neglect in the village of Gettysburg the past summer; in the house in which I was compelled to seek lodgings, there are now two boys sick with typhoid fever attributed to this cause. Within a stone's throw of the whitewashed hut occupied as the headquarters of General Meade, I counted yesterday no less than ten carcasses of dead horses, lying on the ground where they were struck by the shells of the enemy."

The audience had expected, as the printed program stipulated, "Dedicatory Remarks, by the President of the United States." No eloquence was promised. Where eloquence is in flow the orator must have time to get tuned up, to expatiate and expand while building toward his climaxes, it was supposed. The *New York Tribune* man and other like observers merely reported the words of the address with the one preceding sentence: "The dedicatory remarks were then delivered by the President," These reporters felt no urge to inform their readers about how Lincoln stood, what he did with his hands, how he moved, vocalized, or whether he emphasized or subdued any parts of the address. Strictly, no address as such was on the program from him. He was down for just a few perfunctory "dedicatory remarks."

According to Lamon, Lincoln himself felt that about all he had given the audience was ordinary garden-variety dedicatory remarks, for Lamon wrote that Lincoln told him just after delivering the speech that he had regret over not having prepared it with greater care. "Lamon, that speech won't *scour*. It is a flat failure and the people are disappointed." On the farms where Lincoln grew up as a boy when wet soil stuck to the mold board of a plow they said it didn't "scour."

The near-by *Patriot and Union* of Harrisburg took its fling: "The President succeeded on this occasion because he acted without sense and without constraint in a panorama that was gotten up more for the benefit of his party than for the glory of the nation and the honor of the dead. . . . We pass over the silly remarks of the President; for the credit of the nation we are willing that the veil of oblivion shall be dropped over them and that they shall no more be repeated or thought of."

The *Chicago Times* held that "Mr. Lincoln did most foully traduce the motives of the men who were slain at Gettysburg" in his reference to "a new birth of freedom," the *Times* saying, "They gave their lives to maintain the old government, and the only Constitution and Union." He had perverted history, misstated the cause for which they died, and with "ignorant rudeness" insulted the memory of the dead. . . . Its rival, the *Chicago Tribune*, however, had a reporter who telegraphed (unless some editor who read the address added his own independent opinion) a sentence: "The dedicatory remarks of President Lincoln will live among the annals of man."

The *Cincinnati Gazette* reporter added after the text of the address,

"That this was the right thing in the right place, and a perfect thing in every respect, was the universal encomium."

The American correspondent of the London *Times* wrote that "the ceremony was rendered ludicrous by some of the sallies of that poor President Lincoln. . . . Anything more dull and commonplace it would not be easy to produce."

Count Gurowski, the only man ever mentioned by Lincoln to Lamon as his possible assassin, wrote in a diary, "Lincoln spoke, with one eye to a future platform and to re-election."

The *Philadelphia Evening Bulletin* said thousands who would not read the elaborate oration of Mr. Everett would read the President's few words "and not many will do it without a moistening of the eye and a swelling of the heart." . . . The *Providence Journal* reminded readers of the saying that the hardest thing in the world is to make a good five-minute speech: "We know not where to look for a more admirable speech than the brief one which the President made at the close of Mr. Everett's oration. . . . Could the most elaborate and splendid oration be more beautiful, more touching, more inspiring, than those thrilling words of the President? They had in our humble judgment the charm and power of the very highest eloquence."

Later men were to find that Robert Toombs of Georgia had in 1850 opened a speech: "Sixty years ago our fathers joined together to form a more perfect Union and to establish justice. . . . We have now met to put that government on trial. . . . In my judgment the verdict is such as to give hope to the friends of liberty throughout the world."

Lincoln had spoken of an idea, a proposition, a concept, worth dying for, which brought from a Richmond newspaper a countering question and answer, "For what are we fighting? An abstraction."

The *Springfield Republican* had veered from its first opinion that Lincoln was honest but "a Simple Susan." Its comment ran: "Surpassingly fine as Mr. Everett's oration was in the Gettysburg consecration, the rhetorical honors of the occasion were won by President Lincoln. His little speech is a perfect gem; deep in feeling, compact in thought and expression, and tasteful and elegant in every word and comma. Then it has the merit of unexpectedness in its verbal perfection and beauty. We had grown so accustomed to homely and imperfect phrase in his productions that we had come to think it was the law of his utterance. But this shows he can talk handsomely as well as act sensibly. Turn back and read it over, it will repay study as a model speech. Strong feelings and a large brain were its parents—a little painstaking its *accoucheur*."

That scribbler of curious touch who signed himself "The Lounger" in *Harper's Weekly* inquired why the ceremony at Gettysburg was one of the most striking events of the war. "There are grave-yards enough in the land—what is Virginia but a cemetery?—and the brave who have died for us in this fierce war consecrate the soil from the ocean to the Mississippi. But there is peculiar significance in the field of Gettysburg, for there 'thus far' was thundered to the rebellion. . . . The President and the Cabinet were there, with famous soldiers and civilians. The oration by Mr. Everett was smooth and cold. . . . The few words of the President were from the heart to the heart. They can not be read, even, without kindling emotion. 'The world will little note nor long remember what we say here, but it can never forget what they did here.' It was as simple and felicitous and earnest a word as was ever spoken. . . . Among the Governors present was Horatio Seymour. He came to honor the dead of Gettysburg. But when they were dying he stood in New York sneeringly asking where was the victory promised for the Fourth of July? These men were winning that victory, and dying for us all; and now he mourns, *ex officio*, over their graves."

Everett's opinion of the speech he heard Lincoln deliver was written in a note to Lincoln the next day and was more than mere courtesy: "I should be glad if I could flatter myself that I came as near to the central idea of the occasion in two hours as you did in two minutes." Lincoln's immediate reply was: "In our respective parts yesterday, you could not have been excused to make a short address, nor I a long one. I am pleased to know that, in your judgment, the little I did say was not entirely a failure."

At Everett's request Lincoln wrote with pen and ink a copy of his Gettysburg Address, which manuscript was auctioned at a Sanitary Fair in New York for the benefit of soldiers. At the request of George Bancroft, the historian, he wrote another copy for a Soldiers' and Sailors' Fair at Baltimore. He wrote still another to be lithographed as a facsimile in a publication, *Autographed Leaves of Our Country's Authors*. For Mr. Wills, his host at Gettysburg, he wrote another. The first draft, written in Washington, and the second one, held while delivering it, went into John Hay's hands to be eventually presented to the Library of Congress.

After the ceremonies at Gettysburg Lincoln lunched with Governor Curtin, Mr. Everett, and others at the Wills Home, held a reception that had not been planned, handshaking nearly an hour, looking gloomy and listless but brightening sometimes as a small boy or girl came in line, and stopping one tall man for remarks as to just how high up he reached. At five o'clock he attended a patriotic meeting in the Presbyterian church, walking arm-in-arm with old John Burns, and listening to an address by Lieutenant Governor-elect Anderson of Ohio. At six-thirty he was on the departing Washington train. . . .

The ride to Washington took until midnight. Lincoln was weary, talked little, stretched out on one of the side seats in the drawing-room and had a wet towel laid across his eyes and forehead.

He had stood that day, the world's foremost spokesman of popular government, saying that democracy was yet worth fighting for. He had spoken as one in mist who might head on deeper yet into mist. He incarnated the assurances and pretenses of popular government, implied that it could and might perish from the earth. What he meant by "a new birth of freedom" for the nation could have a thousand interpretations. The taller riddles of democracy stood up out of the address. It had the dream touch of vast and furious events epitomized for any foreteller to read what was to come. He did not assume that the drafted soldiers, substitutes, and bounty-paid privates had died willingly under Lee's shot and shell, in deliberate consecration of themselves to the Union cause. His cadences sang the ancient song that where there is freedom men have fought and sacrificed for it, and that freedom is worth men's dying for. For the first time since he became President he had on a dramatic occasion declaimed, howsoever it might be read, Jefferson's proposition which had been a slogan of the Revolutionary War—"all men are created equal"—leaving no other inference than that he regarded the Negro slave as a man. His outwardly smooth sentences were inside of them gnarled and tough with the enigmas of the American experiment.

Back at Gettysburg the blue haze of the Cumberland Mountains had dimmed till it was a blur in a nocturne. The moon was up and fell with a bland golden benevolence on the new-made graves of soldiers, on the sepulchres of old settlers, on the horse carcasses of which the onrush of war had not yet permitted removal. The *New York Herald* man walked amid them and ended the story he sent his paper: "The air, the trees, the graves are silent. Even the relic hunters are gone now. And the soldiers here never wake to the sound of reveille."

In many a country cottage over the land, a tall old clock in a quiet corner told time in a tick-tock deliberation. Whether the orchard branches hung with pink-spray blossoms or icicles of sleet, whether the outside news was seedtime or harvest, rain or drouth, births or deaths, the swing of the pendulum was right and left and right and left in a tick-tock deliberation.

The face and dial of the clock had known the eyes of a boy who listened to its tick-tock and learned to read its minute and hour hands. And the boy had seen years measured off by the swinging pendulum, and grown to man size, had gone away. And the people in the cottage knew that the clock would stand there and the boy never again come into the room and look at the clock with the query, "What is the time?"

In a row of graves of the Unidentified the boy would sleep long in the dedicated final resting-place at Gettysburg. Why he had gone away and why he would never come back had roots in some mystery of flags and drums, of national fate in which individuals sink as in a deep sea, of men swallowed and vanished in a man-made storm of smoke and steel.

The mystery deepened and moved with ancient music and inviolable consolation because a solemn Man of Authority had stood at the graves of the Unidentified and spoken the words "We cannot consecrate—we cannot hallow—this ground. The brave men, living and dead, who struggled here, have consecrated it far above our poor power to add or detract. . . . From these honored dead we take increased devotion to that cause for which they gave the last full measure of devotion."

To the backward and forward pendulum swing of a tall old clock in a quiet corner they might read those cadenced words while outside the windows the first flurry of snow blew across the orchard and down over the meadow, the beginnings of winter in a gun-metal gloaming to be later arched with a star-flung sky.

II

R. E. LEE[1]

By

DOUGLAS SOUTHALL FREEMAN

In his official four-volume work of the life of Robert E. Lee, completed after twenty years, Douglas Southall Freeman has given us one of the great biographies of our literature.

Scholarly research, intelligent sifting of a wealth of material, careful authentication of the facts, and graceful narration combine to make this a biography of moving beauty. In this work one stands in the presence of a most distinguished figure in our national history.

In this anthology we include the dramatic story of Robert E. Lee's momentous and far-reaching decision at the outbreak of the Civil War.

THE ANSWER HE WAS BORN TO MAKE

"Our country," Lee had written one of his sons before he left Texas, "requires now everyone to put forth all his ability, regardless of self." That maxim he applied in the bewildering situation he faced when he reached home. On the Virginia side of the Potomac opinion was divided concerning the occasion for secession, but there was almost complete agreement touching the right. North of the river, just half-an-hour's ride from Arlington, cross-currents of sentiment were sweeping. In Congress and at the White House efforts were still being made to avert war; in the departments preparations were under way to face any emergency. President Buchanan was fighting to save states for the Union; General Scott and the politicians interested in the army were angling for individual soldiers whose knowledge would be useful should the conflict come. The atmos-

[1] Douglas Southall Freeman, *R. E. Lee*, New York: Charles Scribner's Sons, 1934, I. 431-447.

phere in which many officers were received by their superiors had suddenly changed. There was unconcealed interest in the probable course that would be followed by captains and colonels the prospect of whose resignation, in ordinary times, would have been heard with rejoicing because promotion would be opened to other men.

Lee was not aware of this change when he called at General Scott's office soon after he reached home. In the outer room he met his friend Lieutenant Colonel Erasmus D. Keyes, associate of his West Point superintendency, and the man whom Scott had named as his military secretary when Lee had declined that post.

The two shook hands. "Lee," said Keyes, "it is reported that you concurred in Twiggs' surrender in Texas. How's that?"

Lee became serious on the instant, but without showing any resentment of the suggestion of disloyalty, he said calmly: "I am here to pay my respects to General Scott; will you be kind enough, colonel, to show me to his office?"

Keyes said no more, but ushered Lee into Scott's room. The door was shut, and for three hours the old General and his favorite lieutenant talked together. What they said to each other, in the confidence of long and trustful association, neither ever afterwards revealed. All the evidence regarding their conversation is negative in character or is reported at second-hand. But Scott's known opinion of secession, his admiration for Lee, and his desire to assure good leadership for the army make it possible to reconstruct the substance of at least a part of what was said. Scott told Lee that he was soon to be made a colonel, and then, probably, he hinted that if he found himself too feeble to take the field he would recommend Lee as his second in command. There can be little doubt that Scott deliberately sought to appeal to Lee's ambitions, but that, knowing Lee as he did, Scott did not try to buy his allegiance with promises, which, indeed, Scott was not authorized to make. If Lee replied to Scott's overtures it was to repeat what he had said to Charles Anderson in Texas—that if Virginia seceded, he would follow her because he considered that his first obligation was to her. Scott, of course, was of a temper to argue this and probably ended a lengthy oration with the request that Lee go home, think the subject over, and await further developments. When Lee left, Scott's manner was "painfully silent." [2]

Lee went home and in agony of spirit watched the course of events. At the time of his interview with Scott, the peace conference had risen and

[2] Erasmus D. Keyes, *Fifty Years Observations of Men and Events*, New York, 1884. p. 206.

had suggested a constitutional amendment that Congress was in no mood to pass, but a different amendment, preserving slavery in the states that had it, had been approved by the House on February 28, and received a two-thirds vote in the Senate the day after Lee reached home. In Virginia, volunteers were drilling and the fire-eaters were predicting early secession, but the state convention was safely under the control of a conservative majority that was as anxious as Lee himself to preserve the Union. Virtually the only point of agreement between the radical secessionists and the Southern Whigs in the convention was that all of them were determined that Virginia would not be party to the "coercion" of any Southern state for its withdrawal from the Union. The situation in the Old Dominion seemed further stabilized by the fact that no matter what the convention did, the people of the state would be the final judges of secession. Every Virginian, however, held his breath on March 4, when Lincoln delivered his inaugural. His views on many aspects of the crisis were those of Lee. The new President was cautious in the utterances, but his announcement of his purpose to hold government property in the South and to collect taxes there was accepted by Virginians as a threat of force.

All the while Scott probably was quietly at work, seeing if he might not hold Lee to the Union. Keyes thought that Scott did not expect Lee to fight against the South, but that the General believed it possible to put Lee at the head of an army so powerful that war could be prevented. General Twiggs was dismissed from the army on March 1 for his surrender of Texas. Colonel E. V. Sumner of the 1st Cavalry was named brigadier general to succeed him on March 16. Lee was at once made colonel and was given Sumner's regiment. This commission, which was signed by Abraham Lincoln, Lee did not hesitate to accept when, on March 28, it was forwarded to him.

Between the date he was promoted and the time he received his commission, Lee probably got a letter written him on March 15 by L. P. Walker, Confederate Secretary of War. This was a direct offer of a commission as brigadier general, the highest rank then authorized, in the army the South was raising. "You are requested," the letter read, "to signify your acceptance or non-acceptance of said appointment, and should you accept you will sign before a magistrate the oath of office herewith and forward the same, with your letter of acceptance to this office." After the long years of slow promotion the honors were coming fast—a colonelcy in one army and a like offer of a generalship in the rival service, all in a breath! There is no record of any reply by Lee to this tender from the new Confederacy.

It is probable that he ignored the offer, and it is certain that he was not lured by the promise of high position. He owed allegiance to only two governments, that of Virginia and that of the Union, and there could be no thought of a third so long as these two did not conflict and Virginia did not throw in her destiny with the Confederate States.

For a few days it seemed as if the conflict of allegiance might be avoided. As late as April 3 the expectation was general that Fort Sumter would be evacuated and a clash avoided. On April 4 a test vote in the Virginia convention showed a majority of two-to-one against secession. Lee would not despair of the Union. He was for forbearance to the last, recognizing no necessity for recourse to arms. The maintenance of slavery meant nothing to him. He felt that if he owned all the slaves in the South he would cheerfully give them up to preserve the Union. He would hold to the army and to the flag as long as he could in honor do so. But during those days of suspense, Lee was confirmed in his point of view. He had been determined from the outset that he would adhere to Virginia and defend her from any foe. Now, fully, he realized that though he considered secession neither more nor less than revolution, he could not bring himself to fight against the states that regarded secession as a right. He could not think of himself as fighting with the South against the Union, unless Virginia's defense were involved, but neither, as the possibility seemed to be brought nearer, could be reconcile himself to fighting with the Union against the South. "That beautiful feature of our landscape," he said sadly one day, as he pointed to the capitol across the Potomac, "has ceased to charm me as much as formerly. I fear the mischief that is brewing there." [3]

This was Lee's state of mind when, on April 7, his old comrade of Mexican days, P. G. T. Beauregard, took a decisive step at Charleston, S. C., where he was then in command of the Confederate forces. Believing that Fort Sumter was about to be reinforced, Beauregard ordered supplies of fresh food cut off from the Federal garrison. The next day, April 8, a confidential messenger from President Lincoln announced to Governor Pickens of the Palmetto State that Sumter would be revictualed by United States ships. On the instant all the passions that had been rising since 1830 in South Carolina suddenly overflowed, and at daylight on April 12 the bombardment of Fort Sumter began. On the 14th Sumter surrendered without the loss of a single life on either side. The next day, to a nation that had gone mad, Lincoln issued his proclamation calling for 75,000

[3] Thomas B. Bryan, to whom he addressed this remark, in *Military Essays and Recollections*, 3, 14.

volunteers "to suppress combinations" and "to cause the laws to be duly executed."

The North and the South were arrayed, and blows had passed, though no blood had yet been shed—what would the border states do? What would be the action of Virginia? For the answer, Lee turned his eyes from Sumter to Richmond, where the convention was still in session. He was at a distance and knew little of the inner workings of that body. All his information was derived from the newspapers, which were too excited to be explicit.

Late on April 16, or on the 17th, he heard that the Virginia convention had gone into secret session. That was the only news from Richmond; but from Washington, on the 17th, there arrived a letter and a message. The letter bore Scott's signature and requested Lee to call at his office on the 18th. The message was conveyed in a note from a Washington cousin, John Lee. It was that Francis P. Blair, Sr., a publicist of Lee's acquaintance, formerly editor of *The Congressional Globe*, desired Lee to meet him the next morning at his house in Washington.

What was afoot now? Were the two calls related? The answer, in its entirety, Lee did not learn during his lifetime. He never realized how anxious some men high in office and influence had been to save his services to the United States army. In addition to what General Scott had done, Francis P. Blair, Sr., father of Colonel Lee's Missouri friend, Montgomery Blair, had been at work. He had been to President Lincoln, who had authorized him to "ascertain Lee's intentions and feelings."[4] Blair had also discussed the subject with Secretary Cameron and had been directed by him to make a proposition to Lee. It was to explain this that Blair had sent the message to Arlington.

Duly on the morning of April 18 Lee rode over the bridge and up to the younger Blair's house on Pennsylvania Avenue, directly opposite the State, War and Navy Building, where he found the old publicist awaiting him. They sat down behind closed doors. Blair promptly and plainly explained his reason for asking Lee to call. A large army, he said, was soon to be called into the field to enforce the Federal law; the President had authorized him to ask Lee if he would accept the command.

Command of an army of 75,000, perhaps 100,000 men; opportunity to apply all he had learned in Mexico; the supreme ambition of a soldier realized; the full support of the government; many of his ablest comrades working with him; rank as a major general—all this may have

[4] John George Nicolay and John Hay, *Abraham Lincoln. A History*, V. 4, p. 98, New York, 1890, 10 vols.

surged through Lee's mind for an instant, but if so, it was only for an instant. Then his Virginia background and the mental discipline of years asserted themselves. He had said: "If the Union is dissolved and the government disrupted, I shall return to my native state and share the miseries of my people and save in defence will draw my sword on none." There he stood, and in that spirit, after listening to all Blair had to say, he made the fateful reply that is best given in his own simple account of the interview: "I declined the offer he made me to take command of the army that was to be brought into the field, stating as candidly and as courteously as I could, that though opposed to secession and deprecating war, I could take no part in an invasion of the Southern States." [5] That was all, as far as Lee was concerned. He had long before decided, instinctively, what his duty required of him, and the allurement of supreme command, with all that a soldier craved, did not tempt him to equivocate for an instant or to see if there were not some way he could keep his own honor and still have the honor he understood the President offered him. Blair talked on in a futile hope of converting Lee, but it was to no purpose.

Bidding farewell to Blair, Lee went directly to Scott's office. He sensed Scott's deep interest in his action, and as soon as he arrived he told him what Blair had offered and what he had answered. "Lee," said Scott, deeply moved, "you have made the greatest mistake of your life; but I feared it would be so." [6]

Deep as was the difference between the two men on a public question that made personal enemies of many lifelong friends, Scott did not stop with this sad observation, but expressed the belief that if Lee were going to resign he ought not to delay. "There are times," Scott is reported to have said, "when every officer in the United States service should fully determine what course he will pursue and frankly declare it. No one should continue in government employ without being actively employed." And again, "I suppose you will go with the rest. If you purpose to resign, it is proper that you should do so at once; your present attitude is equivocal." [7]

This added a complication that Lee pondered as he left his old commander for the last time. He loved the army and the Union too well to leave either until he was in honor compelled to do so. Though willing to

[5] Robert E. Lee, [Jr.], *Recollections and Letters of General Robert E. Lee*, pp. 27-28, New York, 1905 (2nd edition, 1924, with unimportant addenda).

[6] Emily V. Mason, *Popular Life of General Robert Edward Lee*, p. 73, Baltimore, 1872.

[7] E. D. Townsend, *Anecdotes of the Civil War*, p. 29.

resign rather than to fight against the South, he had clung to the hope that he would not have to act unless Virginia seceded and the people voted affirmatively on an ordinance of secession. But Scott had now said that he should not remain in the army if he was unwilling to perform active duty. Those 75,000 soldiers, of whom Blair had talked, would not have been asked of the states if they had not been intended for early service in the field. And if they were so intended, Lee, as an officer of the army, might be called upon immediately for duty he could not conscientiously perform. Then he would have to resign under orders. That was a disgrace to any soldier.

As his brother Smith was on duty in Washington, Lee stopped to discuss this new question with him. They could come to no immediate conclusion on it and parted in the expectation of meeting again before either of them took any action. At length, over the route he had so often travelled, Lee rode out of Washington, across the bridge and up the quiet hills to the home whose white columns he could see for most of the way. He was never again to make that journey in that same fashion. The next time he was to cross the Potomac, it was to be upstream, from the South, with bands playing and a victorious, a cheering army around him.

But he did not leave his problem behind him as he turned his back on his country's capital. He carried it with him; he wrestled with it. *Was* his position equivocal? Ought he to resign at once, regardless of what Virginia did? He felt that Scott was right, but his own mind was so opposed to secession, and his devotion to the Union and to the army proved so strong, now it was put to the test, that he delayed the actual writing of his resignation, hoping against hope.

All this time he had not known what had happened after the Virginia convention had gone into secret session on the 16th. *The Washington Star* of April 18 contained an unverified report that the Virginia convention had passed an ordinance of secession and had caused three ships to be sunk at the mouth of the Elizabeth River, but *The Alexandria Gazette* of the same day contained a dispatch from Richmond, dated April 17, 5 P.M., affirming that the convention was still in secret session and that no ordinance withdrawing the state from the Union had been passed.

The next morning, April 19, Lee went into Alexandria on business and there he read the news he had hoped he would never see: Virginia had seceded! To his mind that meant the wreck of the nation, "the beginning of sorrows," the opening of a war that was certain to be long and full of horrors. But of all that he thought and felt in the first realization that his mother state had left the Union, his only recorded observation is one he made to a druggist when he went into a shop to pay a bill. "I must say," he remarked sadly, "that I am one of those dull creatures that cannot see the good of secession." [8]

If Lee had any doubt of the truth of the report in the Alexandria paper that morning, it was soon removed. That afternoon, *The Washington Star* took the news for granted. By nightfall on the 19th, Lee had no alternative to believing it. When other hopes had failed him before this time, Lee had told himself that secession could not become an accomplished fact until the voters of Virginia had passed on the ordinance of secession, as they had specifically reserved the right to do, but now Lee's judgment told him that war would not wait on a referendum. Virginia would certainly consider that her safety required the seizure of Federal depots within her borders. Had not Texas similarly provided for a referendum on secession, and had not he, with his own eyes, seen how the Texas committee of safety had committed an act of war by seizing United States property without waiting for the people to confirm or disavow the ordinance of the convention? The Federal Government, for its part, would certainly take prompt action since the state just across the river from its capital had left the Union. As one of the senior field officers in Washington, he might be summoned at any hour to defend Washington by invading Virginia—which he could not do. Duty was plain. There could be no holding back. The time had come. All the Lees had been Americans, but they had been Virginians first. From Richard the emigrant onward, the older allegiance had been paramount with each of them until the Revolution came. Had not his own father called Virginia "my native country"? In a crisis that seemed in his day to threaten the Union, had not "Light-Horse Harry" said: "Should my efforts . . . be unavailing, I shall lament my country's fate and acquiesce in my country's will . . .?" Now revolution and the older allegiance were the same. The son must be as the sire. Washington, his great model, had embraced a revolutionary cause. Dearly as Lee loved the Union, anxious as he was to see it preserved, he could not bear arms against the South. Virginia had seceded and doubtless would join the South; her action controlled his; he could not wait for the uncertain vote of the people when war was upon him. So after midnight on the 19th he sat down and wrote this letter, not more than fifteen hours after he had received positive information that Virginia had seceded:

[8] John S. Mosby, *Memoirs of* [edited by Charles W. Russell], p. 379; Boston, 1917.

Arlington, Virginia (Washington City P. O.)
20 April 1861.

Hon. Simon Cameron
Secty of War

Sir:

I have the honor to tender the resignation of my commission as Colonel of the 1st Regt. of Cavalry.

Very resp'y Your Obedient Servant.
R. E. Lee
Col 1st Cav'y.

His resignation was not prompted by passion, nor did it carry with it resentment against the Union he left. On the contrary, if there was any resentment, it was against the authors, Northern and Southern, of the consummate wickedness of bringing about division within the Union. There was a pang and a heartache at the separation from brother officers whose patriotism he had seen vindicated in the hardships of campaigning and in the dangers of battle. He was willing to defend Virginia, whatever her allegiance, but he did not desire to fight against the flag under which he had served. If he must see the Union wrecked by men who would not forbear and plead for justice through constitutional means, if he must tear himself from the service of a nation of which he had been proud, then the hope of his heart was that he might never again be called to draw a sword which only Virginia could command. It was in this spirit that he wrote farewell to General Scott, that loyal old friend, who had admired him, taught him, and advanced him. He penned this letter:

Arlington, Va., April 20, 1861.

General:

Since my interview with you on the 18th inst. I have felt that I ought no longer to retain my commission in the Army. I therefore tender my resignation, which I request you will recommend for acceptance. I would have presented it at once, but for the struggle it has cost me to separate myself from a service to which I have devoted all the best years of my life and all the ability I possessed.

During the whole of that time—more than a quarter of a century—I have experienced nothing but kindness from my superiors and a most cordial friendship from my comrades. To no one, General, have I been as much indebted as to yourself for uniform kindness and consideration, and it has always been my ardent desire to meet your approbation. I shall carry to the grave the most grateful recollections of your kind consideration, and your name and fame will always be dear to me.

Save in defence of my native State, I never desire again to draw my sword.

Be pleased to accept my most earnest wishes for the continuance of your happiness and prosperity, and believe me, most truly yours,

R. E. Lee.[9]

He came downstairs when he had finished the letters. Mrs. Lee was waiting for him. She had heard him pacing in the room above her and had thought she had heard him fall on his knees in prayer. "Well, Mary," he said calmly, "the question is settled. Here is my letter of resignation and a letter I have written General Scott."

She understood. Months later she wrote a friend, "My husband has wept tears of blood over this terrible war, but as a man of honor and a Virginian, he must follow the destiny of his state." The other members of the family understood, also. Arlington became as still and gloomy as if a death had occurred, because as one of his daughters confided to a kinswoman the following Sunday, "the army was to him home and country." Rooney, who hastened to consult his father as soon as the state seceded, was in deep depression as he saw how jubilant the people were. They had lost their senses, he held, and had no conception of what a terrible mistake they were making. Custis was no believer in secession. Had he been able to dictate policy, he said, he would have called the movement revolution and would forthwith have seized and fortified Arlington Heights.

Lee dispatched his resignation to General Scott that morning, probably by special messenger, and before night it had been forwarded to the Secretary of War.

After he had sent off the paper, he sat down to explain his act to his sister, Mrs. Marshall, and to his brother Smith. Mrs. Marshall's husband was Unionist in his sympathies. Her son Louis was now a captain in the United States Army. She herself sided with her husband and son, though she could not quite forget her Virginia uprearing. Lee took her situation into account and wrote her as tactfully as he could:

Arlington, Virginia, April 20, 1861.

My Dear Sister:

I am grieved at my inability to see you. . . . I have been waiting for a "more convenient season," which has brought to many before me deep and lasting regret. Now we are in a state of war which will yield to nothing. The whole south is in a state of revolution, into which Virginia, after a long struggle, has been drawn; and, though I recognize no necessity for this state of things, and would have forborne and pleaded to the end for a redress of grievances, real or

[9] Robert E. Lee, [Jr.], *Recollections and Letters of General Robert E. Lee*, pp. 24-25; New York, 1905 (2nd edition, 1924, with unimportant addenda).

supposed, yet in my own person I had to meet the question whether I should take part against my native state.

With all my devotion to the Union and the feeling of loyalty and duty of an American citizen, I have not been able to make up my mind to raise my hand against my relatives, my children, my home. I have therefore resigned my commission in the Army, and save in defence of my native state, with the sincere hope that my poor services may never be needed, I hope I may never be called on to draw my sword. I know you will blame me; but you must think as kindly of me as you can, and believe that I have endeavored to do what I thought right.

To show you the feeling and struggle it has cost me, I send you a copy of my letter of resignation. I have no time for more. May God guard and protect you and yours and shower upon you everlasting blessings, is the prayer of your devoted brother,

R. E. Lee.

He had left Smith Lee on the 18th with the understanding that they would confer again regarding their course of action. He therefore wrote to explain why he had resigned before consulting with him further:

Arlington, Virginia, April 20, 1861.

My Dear Brother Smith: The question which was the subject of my earnest consultation with you on the 18th inst., has in my own mind been decided. After the most anxious inquiry as to the correct course for me to pursue, I concluded to resign, and sent in my resignation this morning. I wished to wait until the Ordinance of Secession should be acted on by the people of Virginia; but war seems to have commenced, and I am liable at any time to be ordered on duty, which I could not conscientiously perform. To save me from such a position and to prevent the necessity of resigning under orders, I had to act at once, and before I could see you again on the subject, as I had wished. I am now a private citizen, and have no other ambition than to remain at home. Save in defence of my native state, I have no desire ever again to draw my sword. I send you my warmest love.

Your affectionate brother,
R. E. Lee.

Lee gave no advice to Smith regarding his own course, nor did he counsel Custis, who was as loath as he to quit the service of the United States. "Tell Custis," he subsequently wrote, "he must consult his own judgment, reason and conscience as to the course he may take. I do not wish him to be guided by my wishes or example. If I have done wrong, let him do better. The present is a momentous question which every man must settle for himself and upon principle."[10]

[10] Fitzhugh Lee, *General Lee*, p. 94, [Lee to Mrs. Lee, May 15, 1861]; New York, 1894.

When he took up his daily paper, *The Alexandria Gazette*, it was to discover that others beside himself were interested in the action he had taken. For an editorial article read as follows:

"It is probable that the secession of Virginia will cause an immediate resignation of many officers of the Army and Navy from this State. We do not know, and have no right to speak for or anticipate the course of Colonel Robert E. Lee. Whatever he may do, will be conscientious and honorable. But if he should resign his present position in the Army of the United States, we call the immediate attention of our State to him, as an able, brave, experienced officer—no man his superior in all that constitutes the soldier and the gentleman—no man more worthy to head our forces and lead our army. There is no man who would command more of the confidence of the people of Virginia, than this distinguished officer; and no one under whom the volunteers and militia would more gladly rally. His reputation, his acknowledged ability, his chivalric character, his probity, honor, and—may we add, to his eternal praise—his Christian life and conduct—make his very name a 'tower of strength.' It is a name surrounded by revolutionary and patriotic associations and reminiscences."[11]

It was not a pleasant article for a modest man to read, and it was disquieting, besides, with its assurance that some, at least, were looking to him to lead the army of Virginia, against the Union and the old flag, if war came . . . He could only pray it would not.

During the day Lee saw his neighbor and friend, John B. Daingerfield, and showed him a copy of his letter of resignation. The rest of that fateful 20th of April was doubtless spent at Arlington. Nothing of consequence occurred except the receipt, late in the evening, of a letter from Judge John Robertson, of Richmond. The judge was then in Alexandria and asked for an interview the next day. Lee set 1 o'clock as the hour and offered to meet him in town. Meantime, Lee waited and pondered. Surrounded by objects familiar through thirty years of tender association, and with his invalid wife in her chair, he must have realized that if hostilities came, war and invasion would soon bring Arlington within the lines of the Union army. The Federals could not long permit so commanding a position, so close to the capital, to remain unguarded. But in none of his letters prior to his resignation and in none of his reported conversation is there even a hint that he had any selfish regard for the fate of Arlington, either in delaying his resignation until Virginia's secession, or in deciding to leave the army when he did.

Sunday morning, April 21, dressed in civilian clothes, Lee went into

[11] *The Alexandria Gazette*, April 20, 1861.

Alexandria with one of his daughters to attend service at Christ Church. The town was wild. Overwhelmingly Southern in their sentiment, the people rejoiced at the secession of Virginia as if it meant deliverance from bondage. In their enthusiasm they fancied they were repeating the drama of 1776 and that the spirit of a Washington gave its benediction to a new revolution.

In all this rejoicing Lee took no part. His resignation was not generally known as yet, though his neighbors and friends had been waiting to see what he would do. His sorrow, his sense of the fitness of things, and his knowledge that war would be long and terrible kept him from any statement of his action. In the church, as he prayed, it must have been for his divided country. When the Psalter for the morning of the 21st day was read, he doubtless felt there was more than coincidence in these verses and the reponses:

> "13 What time as they went from one nation to another: from one kingdom to another people;
>
> 14 He suffered no man to do them wrong; but reproved even kings for their sakes. . . ."[12]

At length the service was over. The congregation stopped to talk of the inevitable theme, and then straggled slowly into the churchyard. When Lee reached the open air he became engaged in serious conversation with three men, who were unknown to the congregation and whose identity has never been established. His neighbors and friends thought the strangers were commissioners from the governor of Virginia, but it seems more probable that they were companions of Judge Robertson, who explained that the judge had gone to Washington and had been detained there but would soon arrive to keep his appointment. Lee had not been in communication with the state convention or with the governor. He had no information as to the military plans. Perhaps the visitors acquainted him with what had happened and intimated that his service was desired by his mother state, but in Judge Robertson's absence there could have been nothing official. Lee waited and chatted several hours and then, concluding that Robertson would not return, rode back to Arlington.

That evening a messenger arrived at the mansion with a letter from Robertson. He apologized for his delay and—this was the important item —invited Lee, in the name of the governor, to repair to Richmond for conference with the chief executive. Lee realized, of course, that this meant participation in the defense of Virginia, but he did not hesitate an hour.

[12] Psalm 105.

The very reason that had impelled him to resign from the United States army, his allegiance to Virginia, prompted him to sit down at once to write an answer to Robertson. Virginia's action in withdrawing from the Union carried him with her, and if she called him now it was his duty to obey. In a few words he notified the governor's representative that he would join him in Alexandria the next day in time to take the train for Richmond. There was no questioning, no holding back, no delay. The road from Arlington, though lit with glory, led straight to Appomattox. But Lee never regretted his action, never even admitted that he had made a choice. With the war behind him, with the South desolate and disfranchised, and with her sons dead on a hundred battlefields, he was to look back with soul unshaken and was to say: "I did only what my duty demanded. I could have taken no other course without dishonor. And if it all were to be done over again, I should act in precisely the same manner."

III

MR. JUSTICE HOLMES [1]

By

FRANCIS BIDDLE

Oliver Wendell Holmes was one of the most illustrious men of our time, and his life (1841-1935) covered many of the major economic and political developments of the nation for nearly a century. He was wounded in the Civil War at the battles of Ball's Bluff, Antietam, and the second battle of Fredericksburg. In 1899 he became chief justice of the Massachusetts Supreme Court, and in 1902 he was appointed a member of the United States Supreme Court.

Francis Biddle, Attorney-General of the United States, has selected three delightful character sketches and reminiscences of the late Justice Holmes which reveal his warm and gracious personality.

"DEATH PLUCKS MY EARS"

The day before his ninetieth birthday he had been to the usual Saturday conference of the Court. The night of his birthday he was to speak on the radio from his library, and there were to be tributes from the Chief Justice, the Dean of the Yale Law School, the President of the American Bar Association. As he wrote to Dean Clark, who was in charge of the program, he expected to say a few words, "mostly short ones." He had never spoken on the air before, Fanny hadn't approved; she probably wouldn't approve now if she were here, but he thought it would be fun. They were putting on a good show. He liked a good show, he thought, chuckling, liked to have the butter spread on thick, and that was all right if you remembered all the time it *was* butter.

He listened to the others before he spoke. The Chief Justice was speaking, in the rich tones he knew so well. "He has abundantly the zest of

[1] Francis Biddle, *Mr. Justice Holmes*, New York: Charles Scribner's Sons, 1942, pp. 152, 191-193, 206-7.

life," he heard the Chief say, "and his age crowns that eagerness and unflagging interest with the authority of experience and wisdom. . . . We bring to Mr. Justice Holmes our tribute of admiration and gratitude. We place upon his brow the laurel crown of the highest distinction. But this will not suffice us or him. We honor him, but, what is more, we love him. We give him tonight the homage of our hearts."

The old man was deeply moved as those who listened to him knew. He paused for a moment, then spoke quietly, rather slowly. "In this symposium my part is only to sit in silence," he said. "To express one's feelings as the end draws near is too intimate a task."

He paused.

"But I may mention," [he continued], "one thought which comes to me as a listener-in. The riders in a race do not stop short when they reach the goal. There is a little finishing canter before coming to a standstill. There is time to hear the kind voice of friends and to say to one's self: 'The work is done.' But just as one says that, the answer comes: 'The race is over, but the work never is done while the power to work remains.' The canter that brings you to a standstill need not be only coming to rest. It cannot be while you still live. For to live is to function. That is all there is in living." He paused again for a moment, and then—

"And so I end with a line from a Latin poet who uttered the message more than fifteen hundred years ago: 'Death plucks my ears and says, Live—I am coming.' "

"I CONCUR"

Before dinner, in the library, he knit his brows over a long opinion of Brandeis, filled with economic data, that Holmes knew nothing about, decorated with concise footnotes referring to trade reports, to studies of committees, to tables of figures. Beautifully clear, though, and on the bull's-eye, thought Holmes, as he leaned back in his chair. He took the opinion, and wrote on the margin:

"This afternoon I was walking on the towpath and saw a cardinal. It seemed to me to be the first sign of Spring. By the way, I concur."

THE OLD MAN DOZED AGAIN

One of the former secretaries, who was working in Washington, often came to see him, especially in the evenings, and would take his turn in reading aloud to the old man. That particular night he had begun Henry Adams' *Mont-Saint-Michel and Chartres*. He read about the *Chanson de*

Roland, how it must have been sung after Hastings, for what had happened to Harold at the battle of Hastings had once happened to Roland at Roncesvalles. The old Judge dozed—it was but a few weeks before the end—and now and then looked up to smile. Roland had been left for dead by the Saracens when they fled before the horns of Charlemagne's returning host. "Roland," the young man read, "came back to consciousness on feeling a Saracen marauder tugging at his sword Durendal. With a blow of his ivory horn—*oliphant*—he killed the pagan; then feeling death near, he prepared for it." The young man looked up. The old man sat very straight, his eyes shining with a distant fire. The reader continued: "His first thought was for Durendal, his sword, which he could not leave to infidels . . . three times he struck with all his force against the rock; each time the sword rebounded without breaking. The third time—" The old man's eyes were very bright, the fingers of his right hand, which age had never robbed of that slim and sensitive elegance, drummed a faint tattoo. He was once again at White Oak Swamp, at Antietam, on the Jerusalem Road. Again for an instant his heart had stopped as he listened for the long roll of fire from the main line. . . . And after a moment the old man dozed again.

IV

BILLY MITCHELL [1]

By

EMILE GAUVREAU AND LESTER COHEN

Billy Mitchell is the story of the life and struggles of the general who waged a long and, at the time, losing battle for his belief in the significance of the airplane in war. Many of his prophecies came true in World War II, but while he lived his views were discredited by all but a few.

Emile Gauvreau writes, "I think the second chapter of General Mitchell's own account of his court martial would be singularly appropriate for your anthology. Let Billy, God rest his brave soul, tell his own story which he left with me three months before his death. This contains the essence of his prophecy and describes his Gethsemane. I still read this prediction with a shudder and wonder how we escaped as we did after crucifying this man. I feel it is the chapter he would have chosen himself, which is the reason for my choice."

THE COURT MARTIAL OF GENERAL MITCHELL

"It was my purpose during my court martial to let the Nation know what I had discovered during my four-year tour of inspection of our air defenses as Assistant Chief of the Air Corps. In this capacity I had been as far away from my country as the Philippines and Hawaii. I had revealed my findings to my counsel, Representative Reid, an able lawyer whom I respected even though he had told the press, when taking up my case, that I was an 'extremist'. His righteous wrath was less contained than mine when he was in possession of my findings. These facts, which I had submitted to my superiors, were thrown aside. I don't think they were even pigeon-holed. Most of them were flung into the waste-basket before I was demoted and reduced to a post in San Antonio without any command,

[1] Emile Gauvreau and Lester Cohen, *Billy Mitchell*, published and copyright by E. P. Dutton & Co., Inc., New York, 1942, pp. 173-87.

much after the manner of a well-meaning cop shunted off his Main Street beat to the sticks by offended politicians.

"I remember a gasp from the court martial board when Reid referring to the report of my tour of Pearl Harbor and our Hawaiian defenses, announced:—

" 'We propose to prove that when Mitchell inspected the Hawaiian services he found not one single airplane equipped with armament, bomb racks, bomb sights or any accessories necessary to the effective operation of pursuit bombing or observation planes. In the case of the Philippines we will prove an even worse condition. It will be proved that the War Department has been guilty of almost treasonable administration.'

"As I write this a decade later, during the year 1935 which will soon have ebbed out, my latest information from Hawaii indicates that the condition of our Air Force stationed at that post has not improved to the extent that would be expected in ten years' time. We are vulnerable there because of a criminal disregard of co-ordination. Our Air Service in Hawaii has been for years nothing but a football kicked about between the Army and the Navy with an utter lack of co-operation between the military and naval commands in charge. I presented these discoveries to the War Department long ago but even to this date the reports I receive from my friends are more than disquieting. Good Christ, if people only knew! The bickerings of insect authority, the conflicting orders from Washington, the jealousies, the late hours of social life, the white uniforms in the moonlight, the gold braid, the romantic women, the caressing climate are all part of an existence to lull our men into threadbare security. I know the human equation and I know the officers' temptations. The true picture of Hawaii, now full of crawling spies, does not add any reassurance to well-informed Americans who are acquainted with Japanese cunning and treachery. Military Hawaii lives under a tradition handed down from one commanding officer to another, to be discussed years later, with a soothing nostalgia, when one returns home to the soft chairs of the Army and Navy clubs, the head resting back, the eyes closed, the jowled face smiling, the paunch expanded, the tinkling glass in hand, the toasts to Mahan. Ah, those good old days in Hawaii! Planes? Why, the Navy could clean up those little yellow-bellies before dinnertime!

"That talk will go on until we have been sent reeling from a blow delivered by our own ignored invention in the hands of our enemies, sold to them by our own betraying manufacturers wearing the decorations of the governments who would destroy us! The airplane is the seeing eye of our outposts. Reconnaissance from the air is the only means of warning

Hawaii and the Philippines of the sneaking approach of our mortal enemy in the Pacific. We should have built underground bases for planes at those strategic points ten years ago.

"A Secretary for Air, freed of the doddering Winfield Scotts of the War Department would have seen to all this. The fighting plane and the bomber, ever on the alert and in scattered formation when resting on their bases furnish the only hope of defense for Pearl Harbor. If our warships there were to be found bottled up in a surprise attack from the air and our airplanes destroyed on the ground nothing but a miracle would help us to hold our Far East possessions. It would break our backs. The same prediction applies to the Philippines, which would be at the mercy of squadrons of bombers, our warships paralyzed or scuttling for cover. Japan has known this for ten years, if we don't; and if we have to learn our lesson by such a tragedy our last battleship will have been built in less than a year after the Japanese have sprung at us. Warships will be useless without aircraft to protect them as a sky blanket. I know, because I have sunk battleships with nothing but a crate to fly me. I have preached this doctrine for seventeen years and it will be driven home in the next war when admirals, I swear, staggering on their punctured decks, stare into the sky white-faced and helpless. Then, on the doorstep of our stupidity and obstinacy may be placed the responsibility for the unnecessary loss of life to follow until we have been restored to our senses. But until that happens, untold millions of dollars will be wasted for battleships by fools in authority who persist in treating our Air Force as a step-child. There can be no better example than Hawaii of the desperate need of a separate Air Force under a single command.

"It is interesting to note, at this late date, that the report of my discoveries in Hawaii caused a flare-up just as my court martial was getting under way. Major General Charles P. Summerall, who had been selected as president of the court had been in command in Hawaii when I had made my findings of the conditions under his jurisdiction. He looked upon the criticism as a personal affront and had written a letter at the time which was in violent disagreement with my conclusions. He had denied what I had seen with my own eyes. He had opposed before the Morrow Board my recommendations for a separate Air Service and without directly identifying me had denounced me in a public address. I challenged him as a prejudiced member of the court that was to try me and with some reluctance he requested to be excused. His departure, I felt, would not have much bearing on the outcome, anyhow. The court knew from the beginning what the General Staff expected of it.

"My Hawaiian discoveries were brushed aside angrily by the men who were trying me. All they cared to establish was whether I had been guilty of breaking their gag-ruled discipline. I was bursting with my information, but I never would have broken through the entrenched forces of the embalmed heads of our Army and Navy had I not shouted it out to the public. When will these martinets ever learn that they are in charge of the *people's* army?

"It was worth the price of conviction to let the Nation know the truth, which was being choked at its source. All of it was as true in 1925 as it is now, ten years later. But even before my trial opened the General Staff had been thrown into such alarm by the recognition the news columns had given me that military publicists were appointed to visit editors and urge them to print material inimical to my own interests—which were always the country's interests. James T. Williams, Jr., editor of the *Boston American* was a notable witness who bared this chicanery.

"I was not surprised to discover that the White House had failed to produce the complete files of the Morrow report which I had hoped to use in my own defense. Vital letters from the White House to the Morrow Board were denied to me. The public probably will never know the details of those findings whose private data Coolidge kept to himself. What I received of the report was not much more than had been given to the newspapers. Wranglings in court and spasmodic objections blocked nearly every attempt on the part of my counsel to make public the conditions I wanted to reveal. But at times the prosecution was unable to keep the lid down on its skullduggery. The disaster of the *Shenandoah,* naturally, could not be ruled aside as irrelevant. My statements about it had directly involved me in the trial. The widow of the dirigible's commander, Mrs. Zachary Landsdowne, appeared shrouded in mourning to swear that an aide to Wilbur, Secretary of the Navy, had sought to influence her testimony through an acquaintance, to whitewash the catastrophe. I still feel that this was done without Wilbur's knowledge, though men as high have stooped lower.

"Commander Landsdowne had told his wife before embarking on his flight across the country that the trip was of a dangerous nature and unnecessary. He had been sacrificed with his men on a barnstorming expedition to fly over state fairs to satisfy vote-begging Congressmen. Slowly, the ghastly affair was unfolded at my trial.

"At times the purpose of my defense could not be entirely sidetracked. Rear Admiral Sims, then retired, assailed the officers in control of the Navy as ignorant and unfit and predicted that the last battleship had been built. Brigadier General Hugh A. Drum* rose to fantastic heights by angrily bellowing that to compel the evacuation of the District of Columbia by air attack, an enemy would have to drop more than 9,573,000 pounds of mustard gas, and that to place the gas, 2,000 bombers would be necessary. Major General Amos Alfred Fries was more conservative with his estimate of 1,000 bombers and twenty tons of gas. These assertions, of course, were introduced to ridicule my warnings that fleets of planes could destroy a city. Those excited men in that court room, who may survive me, are likely to see in their lifetime a corroboration of their own words, even though they were used in exaggeration.

"Fighting from my side of the barricades was an officer whose convictions and courage may help to bring our Air Force to its required strength before the next war comes upon us. He was Major H. H. Arnold, one of my boys, fearless before his bigoted superiors. He attacked bitterly the use of the obsolete planes we had to work with and produced a long list of figures showing the casualties which these machines had caused. He knew his 'flaming coffins,' still on our fields for training purposes with their murderous record of twenty-six fatal accidents and thirty-eight deaths in 1924; thirty fatal accidents and forty-five deaths during the year my trial was under way. Arnold, God bless him, spoke it all out. He produced records of the Air Service to show that 517 officers and men had been killed between 1919 and 1925. The court, in the face of this indictment of the DH's, twiddled its thumbs. It was to pay no attention to it. I pitied Arnold who had to send his men up, even in peace time, in the same suicidal crates which had killed my boys in France. My own brother died in the Air Service.

"Arnold, at the risk of his own position, defied the Morrow report with these words:

" 'To make matters worse, while we are training in obsolete planes, our service does not compare favorably with the foreign services. That is more than an opinion. Statistics show that we have only eight pursuit squadrons while England already has thirteen; France thirty and Italy twenty-two. My opinion is based on my fourteen years in the Air Service, Gentlemen. We shouldn't be in this condition.'

"But the court was more interested in a letter written on March 24, 1925 to President Coolidge by Weeks, then Secretary of War, which it produced on the eve of my conviction with the sly approval of the White House and which Major General Dennis E. Nolan, acting Chief of Staff, read to the

* In 1942 occupied with problems of New York City's air defense, blackouts and dimouts as Lieutenant General in charge of the Eastern Defense Command.

crowded room with relish and ringing tones. Its words were enough to foretell the outcome of my trial:

"'His (Mitchell's) course is so lawless, so indicative of personal desire for publicity at the expense of everyone with whom he is associated that his actions render him unfit for a high administrative position such as he now occupies.'

"General Nolan reiterated the testimony of General Staff officers that the War Department was opposed to my plan for a unified Air Service. He spoke like a trained parrot. He insisted that the present and 'satisfactory' organization of the 'Air Service branch' was directly attributed to General Pershing himself, a man who had never set foot in a plane. At least, I never met a man who saw him in one.

"I could see little use in a prepared argument which my counsel proposed to make in my defense and refused to permit him to present it. The trial had reached its farcical limits. I decided to rise in my own right and sum up the persecution in a nutshell. I remember MacArthur lowering his eyes and turning his face away. Others on the trial board, who had been my friends, bowed their heads as they sat, not in judgment, but as marionettes manipulated by the strings of the President and the General Staff determined to take me to the block. My statement may be remembered, when we have at last recognized the airplane as the greatest arm of modern warfare:

"'*My trial before this court martial is the culmination of the efforts of the General Staff of the Army and the General Board of the Navy to depreciate the value of air power and keep it in an auxiliary position which absolutely compromises our whole national defense.*'

"The curtain was coming down on the farce. I settled back in my chair like a man composing himself in an air shelter before a bombing raid. Major Allen W. Gullion had been chosen to handle the heaviest batteries in the summing up. Colonel Sherman Moreland was to assist him with a few parting shots but his face reddened with discomfiture when the crowded court room burst into spontaneous laughter upon his declaration that the obsolete DH plane, the 'flaming coffin' of the Army Air Service was 'the Cadillac of the air.' He turned about in anger, pointing at me with a trembling finger:

"'Expel from your midst anybody not meeting the requirements of patriotism!'

"I remember Gullion licking his dry lips feverishly with a darting tongue and riffling through his notes. I knew what to expect from him, an army careerist, shrewdly climbing his way up, rung by rung, from one post to the next, serving his branch of the service as a smart politician clings to his party. Those above him said he had the 'right background' and praised his adaptability. He could boast, at the time, of his professorship of Military Science and Tactics at the University of Kentucky which presumably wasted no time on the study of 'fool killers,' as airplanes were called in Professor Gullion's neck of the woods. But he has come up since then: through the General Service School, the Army War College, the Naval War College, on the General Staff Corps Eligible list, and in his back pocket an honorary degree of LL.D., from the University of Hawaii. I wonder if he remembered a word of the conditions I disclosed when he became senior judge advocate of the Hawaiian Department. Of course, it may be correctly pointed out that flying never came under his jurisdiction after he got through with me. My trial was a good stepping-stone for him and no man could have been more sure-footed when he came before the court to tell that body exactly what it expected to hear.

"'Fail to dismiss this man,' he screamed in a high-pitched voice, 'and you weaken the authority of every commissioned and non-commissioned officer in the service. Dismiss him as he deserves and you strengthen the arm of every single officer commanding a company from Marfa to Nogales; dismiss him for the sake of the young officers of the Army Air Service whose ideals he has shadowed and whose loyalty he has corrupted. Dismiss him in the name of truth, under whose aegis he has sought protection, but whose face he does not know.

"'Our soldiers are watching this case in Camp Stotsenburg, in Schofield Barracks, in Tientsin, at Governor's Island. Throw him out! We ask it in the name of the American people whose fears he has played upon, whose hysteria he has fomented, whose confidence he has beguiled and whose faith he has betrayed!

"'Is Mitchell a Moses?' shouted Gullion, the veins standing out on his temples. 'Is he a Moses fitted to lead the people out of a wilderness which is his own creation only? Is he the George Washington type as his counsel is trying to make us believe? Is he not rather of the all-too-familiar charlatan and demagogue type—like Alcibiades, like Catiline, and except for a decided difference in poise and mental powers—in Burr's favor—like Aaron Burr?'

"I heard from his companions later that Gullion had been rehearsing his speech before a mirror.

"'Dismiss from us,' he continued, his hands held up in horror with the attitude of a Bible ranter, 'this flamboyant self-advertiser, this widely imaginative, hobby-riding egomaniac, always destructive, never constructive except in wild, non-feasible schemes and never overly careful as to the ethics of his methods.'

"There was more of this. One point of Gullion's attack might have impelled me to throttle him but for the fact that I gripped my chair and held my seat. He attempted to show that my book *Winged Defense,* which had just been recently published was made up of a mass of stolen material. I was proud of that book. Years of experience from the time that Orville Wright had taught me to fly, had gone into it. But it had had a disturbing effect on the General Staff, which was ignoring every one of the warnings I had printed in it. Figuratively it had to be burned by the Army's witch doctors.

" 'He cribbed it!' shouted Gullion. 'He cribbed it, page after page!'

"This lying assault was finally stopped by Congressman Reid who said Gullion would not be permitted to try a copyright case before a court martial. My counsel was sustained, but Gullion, as though wound up for a filibuster swerved into new channels of slander. At times his words seemed to pour out of some cavernous mouth of the Dark Ages.

"Before Gullion had put down his lash, staggering to his chair, exhausted and choking with his own fury, he had flayed mercilessly, without a grain of fairness, every man who had dared to appear in my defense. Of La Guardia he said with a sneer:

" 'Here is the Congressional expert type. A man who comes here to talk about flying with fifteen or twenty hours in the air. He is beyond my powers of description. Thank Heaven he is *sui generis*!'

"It seemed incredible to believe that men with whom I had hunted and fished, with whom I had ridden at fox hunts, the friends with whom I had touched glasses at the Chevy Chase, at the Rock Creek Hunt, companions who had slapped me on the back, the friends of jolly times, were to lock themselves into a room after hearing my character torn to shreds, and come back, without being able to look me in the face, and say: 'Guilty!'

"MacArthur, whom I admired for his courage, his audacity and sincerity, surely could not be part of this! But there he was, his features as cold as carved stone. I had fought under his father, General Arthur MacArthur, in the Philippine Insurrection. We had even discussed what might

[Editor's note—Isaac Don Levine states in his book, *Mitchell: Pioneer of Air Power,* from which a selection is also included in this anthology, that an enterprising Washington newspaper reporter examined the contents of the wastebasket in the judges' chamber. He made the exciting discovery that MacArthur had voted against the sentence, and the reporter so advised Mitchell.]

be done some day if Japanese Imperialism should embark on a southward course. And here was his son, a brave soldier, appointed to strip me in mid-career, in an argument over a machine which might some day save the Philippine Islands! He is back there now (in 1935) directing the organization of the national defense of the Commonwealth Government which no battleships could protect from an air attack. Planes and nothing but planes can hold those possessions. Perhaps by this time MacArthur can see it all with an open mind. No man in his position could have a greater opportunity. Something can be learned in ten years—even by some generals.

"But MacArthur certainly had not grasped the significance of my trial in 1925. I still believe he erred honestly. Men grow in stature by admitting their own mistakes. Douglas has developed that quality. But perhaps I am a better judge of planes than of men.

"In the midst of all this clawing I still remember an unforgettable note of tenderness as my trial came to an end. My wife appeared in court and held our baby daughter for me to kiss. I recall Will Rogers, his eyes wet and blinking with anger, his lips stern, after listening to Gullion's attack.

" 'The people are with you Billy,' he said. 'Never forget that! Keep punching and we'll get somewhere. You can rope 'em.'

"Suddenly I realized it was all over. Reporters were rushing out with the news that I had been found guilty on all counts. I was sentenced to be suspended from rank, command and duty with the forfeiture of all pay and allowances for five years. The court's 'leniency' had been influenced by my military record, someone was saying.

"I stepped out of the ramshackle building into the crisp clean air. There was a low muttering in the crowded court room and friends followed me out to the street in little groups with reassuring phrases. 'It's going to be O.K., Billy'; 'You're bound to win'; 'You told 'em!'

"The holidays were approaching with their decorations and colored lights. Nothing could have been more cheerful and consoling than that trip home.

" 'Christmas in Virginia can make one forget anything,' my wife said.

"But the implications of my trial were overshadowed, in my mind anyhow, by one great event which no one seemed to associate with my predictions. It seemed to be lost in the sweep of the happenings of the times. It had taken place as my court martial approached its climax. Lieutenant James H. Doolittle, the champion aquatic aviator of the Army, had set his fourth world speed-record for seaplanes at Bay Shore Park by flying four times over a measured course at an average speed of 245.715 miles per hour. I was interested in Jimmy because, for one thing, he knew Alaska. Previously, that year, Jimmy, who was to become one of the most scientific flyers in the world, had won the Schneider Cup Race. With cool and deadly accuracy he had written in the sky the answer to my conviction!"

V

PAUL REVERE AND THE WORLD HE LIVED IN[1]

By

ESTHER FORBES

Paul Revere (1735-1818) is known by every school child as one of the patriots of the Revolutionary War. In many respects he was a jack-of-all-trades, for, among other things, he was a bell caster, silversmith, goldsmith, and powder maker as well as an engraver of copper plates. The plates for the earliest paper currency of Massachusetts were engraved by him. However, primarily this hero of the Revolutionary War lives in history because of his famous "midnight ride," and it is the highly interesting account of this ride which Esther Forbes has chosen for us from her authoritative, comprehensive, and splendidly written biography.

THE RIDE OF PAUL REVERE

Monday came taut and overstrung. At the Province House General Gage was constantly in conference with his officers. Colonel Smith was to command the eight hundred men. Pitcairn himself was to go as second in command, serving as a volunteer. Lord Percy was to bring up the reserves if necessary. General Gage "did not think the damned rebels would . . . take up arms against his Majesty's Troops." He was confident the sortie could be made, the stores destroyed, and his men brought back to Boston before any alarm roused the "countrymen" to action. Only two people were told the destination of the regulars—Lord Percy and Gage's own wife.

Tuesday was even tenser. The grenadiers and light infantry companies of the various regiments were ordered to prepare to march that night.

[1] Esther Forbes, *Paul Revere and the World He Lived In* by permission of the publishers, Houghton Mifflin Company, Boston, 1942, pp. 251-264.

Some of these men were billeted in private houses, or their women worked as servants. It was impossible to keep it a secret that they were to report for active duty. For instance, a Mrs. Stedman had hired as a housemaid the wife of one of the soldiers. As the sergeant went about rounding up his men, he could not find the husband, Gibson. He went to Mrs. Stedman and asked her to tell the man, if he turned up at her house, "he was to report himself at eight o'clock at the bottom of the Common, equipped for an expedition." Mrs. Stedman immediately sent word to Doctor Church. When Gibson arrived, she told him to prepare for the march, and "Oh, Gibson," she said, "what are you going to do?"

"Ah, Madam, I know as little as you do. I only know that I must go."

So in one way or another it might be guessed that the British were about to march. But where? Somehow Gage's secret was betrayed.

On Tuesday afternoon Gage sent out a group of picked officers. It was for them to block the roads leading towards Concord so no rebel express could ride through and warn the town. They were to pretend to be merely a pleasure party riding out to Cambridge for a dinner in the country. Their arms would be hidden by their cloaks. If questioned closely, they could admit that they were out after their own deserters. At Cambridge some of these men would turn towards Charlestown and after dark hide in the bushes to waylay any messenger who might cross the river and try to reach Concord by that route. The other officers were to do their intercepting closer to Concord. This latter is the most famous of the two groups. They were under Major Edward Mitchell. With him were Captain Lumm, Captain Cochrane, Lieutenant Grant, and one other officer—or perhaps the "sarjant" that Revere noticed. The British accounts say that all these men were officers, the Yankees call them sometimes officers and sometimes officers and their servants. These men knew Paul Revere's name, but not his face. Of these two nets spread out to catch him or any other man who attempted to go through that night, Paul Revere knew nothing. Of the third precaution all Boston knew. The man-of-war *Somerset* was moved into the very mouth of the Charles River, commanding the expanse of water any boat headed for Charlestown must cross.

The officers must have known before they left Tuesday afternoon what was their destination. Hanging about the stable, making sure for themselves that their horses were properly saddled and in top condition, talking happily about "the hell to pay tomorrow," it is likely they are the ones who let slip Gage's plans. For a groom at the Province House is said to have overheard the officers' talk. He confided in a friend of his, a fellow hostler at a near-by stable. This second boy (who had pretended to be a supporter of the Crown) then ran to Paul Revere. There was hell to pay on Wednesday and Concord was the objective.

"You are the third person who has brought me the same information," Paul Revere said, and he cautioned the boy not to say anything to anyone else. But even as the web of Paul Revere's and Joseph Warren's spy system closed about Gage's secret, the British officers were, with a pretence at nonchalance, but causing much excitement wherever they went, preparing to take their stations along the country roads to ensnare Paul Revere.

At dusk, Lord Percy left General Gage at the Province House and went quietly to the Common, where the boats were drawn up and already troops lined up waiting to embark. The townspeople stood about watching these preparations. The Earl was not recognized and listened to their comments. He heard a voice say:

"The British troops have marched, but will miss their aim."

"What aim?" asked Percy.

"Why, the cannon at Concord."

Percy went back to Gage. In some way their secret was known. The story is that Gage believed it was his American wife who had betrayed him, she being, as an early historian has it, "unequally yoked in point of politics" to her famous husband. This version seems to be gossip started by Gage's own officers, who did not like him and wanted to throw suspicion upon him and his wife.

At Joseph Warren's, the plans were perfected. As soon as it was definitely known whether the British went by land or sea, Robert Newman would be notified and the lanterns in Christ's [2] hung. This he had already agreed to do. He was twenty-three at the time. His older brother was organist at Christ's and he was sexton. He did not like the work, but had taken the job "because," as he said, "times are so hard." Not only did he have the keys to the church, but lived just across the street from it. The only drawback was that his mother's house was full of British officers billeted on the family.

These lanterns would give the warning, but no detail, of the expedition. Farther upstream the British boats would be ferrying over the troops. There

[2] Paul Revere, in the account he wrote for the Massachusetts Historical Society (1798), says the lanterns were hung in "North Church Steeple," and yet, in 1775, Christ's Church was popularly Christ's and the church at North Square "Old North." After the latter was pulled down in 1776, the nickname of "North" and "Old North" was transferred to the oldest church in North Boston, which was Christ's. Although the North Square Church has been put forward as a candidate for the lanterns, it could not have been so used. Its spire was so "stumpy," lights hung in it would not have been seen in Charlestown. Copp's Hill lay between. Paul Revere, in calling Christ's "North Church," was using the nomenclature common at the time in which he wrote, instead of when he rode.

was a chance Paul Revere could get past the *Somerset*—but only a chance. He was ready to take it.

William Dawes, the young cordwainer, would attempt to ride out through the British sentries on the Neck. He lived near North Square and his father was a silversmith. Undoubtedly Revere knew him well. He had played no conspicuous part in the brewing revolution, as had Revere, and was not a marked man, although he had recently knocked down a soldier for insulting his pretty wife. In previous years he had carried letters for the Salisbury family. "Billy" Dawes was a born actor. Later, during the siege of Boston, he used to go in and out almost at will, disguised as a drunken farmer, thoroughly enjoying himself and the risks he took. In the portrait painted of him in middle age, when he could write Major in front of his name and the proud word "merchant" after it, he is still a comical-looking fellow, with his close-set eyes, long nose, and humorous mouth. If anyone could allay suspicion of the sentries, act the part of an inebriated farmer or a half-witted bumpkin, it would be Billy Dawes. Paul Revere looked as clever as he was. Billy Dawes did not. He would have farther to go than Revere and about an equally poor chance of getting through. This he did by pretending great innocence and with the help of the sentry at the gate who was a friend of his.

Now that the troops were actually at the bottom of the Common, Joseph Warren started Billy Dawes over the Neck and sent for Paul Revere. The time had come.

"About ten o'clock Dr. Warren sent in great haste for me, and begged that I would immediately set off for Lexington, where Messre. Hancock and Adams were, and acquaint them of the movement, and that it was thought they were the objects. When I got to Dr. Warren's house, I found he had sent an express by land to Lexington,—a Mr. William Dawes." As is often pointed out, Paul Revere never got to Concord, it is noteworthy that it was only Lexington he originally started out to warn. Yet he definitely had Concord in mind as well.

The two friends parted. When, if ever, they would meet again they could not know. Joseph Warren would chance staying inside the lines a little longer for the sake of the information he might pick up. But any moment he might hear the rap on his door and see a corporal's guard, an officer with the warrant for his arrest in his hand—wanted in London for treason. Paul Revere also risked all he had and life as well. General Gage has handled the insurrection thus far with kid gloves, but no country has ever hesitated to drop with a bullet, if necessary, a man caught exciting to armed revolt.

First Paul sought out Robert Newman, who, knowing that it might be awkward for a prominent Son of Liberty and express rider to rap at his mother's door and call him out, had pretended to go to bed early, leaving the officers in the living rooms, then slipped out an upper window, over a roof, and was already in the dark street waiting for any orders. One of the vestrymen at Christ's, John Pulling,[3] went with Newman, as probably did Revere's neighbor, Thomas Barnard. The door was locked after him and the guard stood in the street as the young fellow took the lanterns from the closet and softly mounted the wooden stairs Paul Revere's feet had once known so well. Higher and higher, feeling his way in the darkness, he climbed, past the eight great bells, silent in the bell loft, until he came to the highest window of the belfry. To the north he could see, over the shoulder of Copp's Hill, the mouth of the Charles, the black hull of the *Somerset*, the glimmer of her riding lights. Beyond was Charlestown, and there he knew men were waiting, watching for his signal. He lit the lanterns, hung them, and felt his way back to the floor of the church. Probably Newman displayed his lanterns for a moment only. He certainly could not wish to warn the *Somerset*. They were out by the time Paul Revere had crossed into Charlestown. In spite of the poem, they were not a signal to Paul Revere, but from him. The Sunday before he had told Colonel Conant to watch for them. When the men in Charlestown saw "a glimmer and then a gleam of light," Paul Revere was still in Boston.

Something must have happened in the street while Newman was inside, for he dared not leave by the way he had come. Instead he climed out of a window at the rear of the church, circled about, and entered his mother's house by the roofs and the upper window. Lying awake, he might hear below him the laughter of the officers over their cards. That much of the deed was done.

Having started Robert Newman on his ascent to fame, Paul Revere went to his own house in North Square. In all directions, marching in full battle gear, small groups of redcoats were leaving their barracks and billets, heading for the Common. Troops were lined up in North Square. No one was allowed to enter it or leave. Somehow Paul Revere got through them. He put on his short surtout and heavy riding boots. Perhaps Rachel

[3] A rather weak case for John Pulling as the actual hanger of the lanterns was put forward some seventy years ago by J. L. Watson and answered most convincingly by William W. Wheildon, who goes as far towards proving Newman was the man as would be apt to be possible one hundred years after the event. The City of Boston and Christ's Church have both, after careful research, accepted Newman and left Pulling in the street guarding the tower. What Revere's nextdoor neighbor, Barnard, was doing is even vaguer, but tradition says he did something.

tried to argue him out of this dangerous ride, for he seems to have been curiously absent-minded for so competent a man. He forgot two things. His spurs and some cloth with which to muffle the oars of his rowboat. So he left the house, and his dog followed him.

Joshua Bentley, a boatbuilder, and Thomas Richardson were ready to row him across. He picked them up at some prearranged place and the three started for the part of North Boston where that winter Paul Revere had kept his boat hidden. Then the matter of muffling the oars came up. None of them wished to return to their own house, but one of them had a girl friend. He gave a peculiar whistle outside her window, at the corner of North and North Centre Streets. The window went up. There was a whispered conversation and a flannel petticoat was tossed down. Revere told his children that it was still warm when they got it. Then Revere remembered his spurs. He wrote a note to Rachel, tied it to his dog's collar. Soon the dog was back again with the spurs. This story he also told his children, but perhaps only to amuse them. So at last he was booted and spurred, but a long way yet from being ready to ride.[4]

[4] The idea that Paul Revere was the only rider out that night was so picturesquely implanted in the American mind by Longfellow in 1863 there was a natural reaction when it was learned he was by no means out alone. Although Joseph Warren officially sent out from Boston but two men—William Dawes and Paul Revere—at least three others noticed something was afoot that day in town and in a mild way did spread the alarm. These are Ebenezer Dorr, Joseph Hall, and Solomon Brown. Brown lived in Lexington, and on his way home from market noticed the little advance guard of British officers. His news resulted in the guard stationed that night about the Clark parsonage, and he and Sanderson and Loring were asked to go on to Concord and tell them there what he had seen—not that the British were marching by the hundreds, but that officers were abroad. All three of these men were picked up by Major Mitchell and were among the "countrymen" Revere mentioned as having been collected in the pasture before he himself was caught. Richard Devens had tried to get word through to Lexington as soon as the lanterns had been shown on Christ's spire. This man also seems to have been picked up, for no word of an actual expedition had come to Lexington until Paul Revere arrived. Although Longfellow made several historical mistakes, in one thing he was right. If there was room for but one man in the limits of his poem, Revere was the one to choose. He had already ridden thousands of miles as an official express. His reputation and name were well known to his friends and even enemies—like Governor Wentworth, Major Mitchell, and the two other British soldiers, Sutherland and Pope. It was he who had arranged about the signals from the spire and had already (the Sunday before) warned Concord they might be attacked and it was time to begin hiding supplies.

His part was much more active than Dawes', and (what with slipping past the *Somerset* and getting through the officers on 'Charlestown Common') much more adventurous. Neither man got to Concord. Revere was captured and Dawes fell off his horse, but by then the alarm was so general someone else would be sure to get word in time. This happened to be Doctor Prescott, for riders were setting off in all directions as soon as they heard Paul Revere's warning, at first, second, or third hand, that the British had marched. By breakfast (one notes) Private Howe found so many men on this errand that claiming to be a patriot express was the best alibi a British spy could offer. Paul Revere was well known as the principal express long before Longfellow immortalized him. . . . Dawes, who certainly did

The *Somerset* blocked the shortest route, forcing them to keep rather well out to sea. She was a great frigate of sixty-four guns and was stationed there for but one purpose—to keep men like Paul Revere in Boston. A cry to heave to or even a spatter of shot was expected. Beyond her, upstream, the British boats were going back and forth already, carrying the regulars to Cambridge.

All winter it had been abnormally warm and spring had come almost a month ahead of itself. Fruit trees were in blossom; the fields already ploughed. That night, however, was chill, and "it was young flood, the ship was winding and the moon was rising," as Paul Revere noticed. The muffled oars softly eased his little rowboat closer and closer to the Charlestown side. There had been neither hail nor shot from the *Somerset*. So he leaped to dry land close to the old Battery. Richardson and Bentley had done their work. Revere went on alone.

At Colonel Conant's he found a group waiting for him. Had they seen his signals? They had. He told them "what was acting" and learned to his surprise that the roads towards Cambridge and on to Concord were already patrolled by British officers who had left Boston in the afternoon.

Richard Devens, of the Committee of Safety, said he had left Menotomy in his chaise around sunset. And he had seen "a great number of B.O. [British officers] and their servants on horseback." As they were behaving in a suspiciously nonchalant manner and had asked where "Clark's tavern was," Devens had sent word to the Clark parsonage. It might be they were out to arrest the two rebel chiefs housed there. He knew this messenger might be picked up, as he was. Paul Revere himself might have better luck. He would need a good horse to slip through the cordon. Probably he had as fine a mount as the luxurious town of Charlestown could produce. John Larkin was one of the wealthiest citizens. It was his best horse that was now turned over to Revere. Twenty-three years later, he gratefully remembered how good, how "very good," was this Larkin horse. It would be slender and nervous in the Yankee manner, small by modern standards, surefooted, tireless. Now for the remainder of the night Revere's success, perhaps his life and the lives of others, would depend upon this horse. He would adjust the stirrups carefully to his own length, test with a forefinger the snugness of the girths. They must be tight, but not binding.

---

his share that night, seemed for a while to be destined for oblivion. At present the opposite is the danger. Realizing that he never got his dues from Longfellow, people are now saying that he really did all the work, that he got to Concord, and Revere did not, etc. Since I have begun on this book I have been asked several times if it is true that Paul Revere never took that ride at all.

The bit must hang exactly right. In that unhurried moment before mounting, he could measure the courage and stamina of his companion, catch the flash of white in the wild, soft eye, note the impatient stamp of the small hooves, feel under his hand the swelling of muscle along the neck, the strength in withers and loin, his touch and voice assuring the sensitive animal that he was his friend.

And now it was eleven o'clock. Only an hour before, he had stood in Joseph Warren's parlor knowing that the time had come. Then, by the bright cold moonlight everyone noticed that night, he swung to the saddle. Colonel Conant, Richard Devens, the light from the open door, were left behind. He eventually rode about twelve miles to get to Lexington and Concord was six miles farther on. Probably he would set a pace which he believed would last him through. With the hundreds of miles he had ridden the last few years, he would be able to judge well. Nor would he wish to fling himself headlong into any trap set for him by that advance guard of officers Devens had warned him of, with a jaded mount. For such an emergency his horse must have an extra spurt of speed left in him. That he rode the Larkin horse with more care than he does on sugar boxes, American Legion posters, copper advertisements, and all known pictures and statues is proved by the excellent condition the animal was in five hours later.

So away, down the moonlit road, goes Paul Revere and the Larkin horse, galloping into history, art, editorials, folklore, poetry; the beat of those hooves never to be forgotten. The man, his bold dark face bent, his hands light on the reins, his body giving to the flowing rhythm beneath him, becoming, as it were, something greater than himself—not merely one man riding one horse on a certain lonely night of long ago, but a symbol to which his countrymen can yet turn.

Paul Revere had started on a ride which, in a way, has never ended.

Charlestown like Boston was a promontory attached to the mainland by a slender neck. Paul Revere rode over this neck. The Charles River was on his left and the Mystic upon his right. He was now in a sparsely settled, desolate stretch of salt marsh, moors, clay-pits, and scrub. In his day this was the "common" of Charlestown and now is Somerville. Of the two roads traversing this dreary expanse, he took the one to his left which led directly into Cambridge and was the shortest way to Lexington. Only two days before he had travelled this road and knew it well.

So he rode on through the moonlight and the delicate shadows of spring trees and came to the gibbet where for twenty years Mark had hung in chains, as a horrifying warning to any other slaves who might plan insurrection against their masters. For some reason, that caused comment at the time, Mark had kept surprisingly well, but surely by now little could have been left of him but a few old bones rattling about at the bottom of his iron cage. Paul Revere noted and remembered that he reached the spot "where Mark was hung in chains." The memory of Mark may have quickened his blood, taken his thoughts back to Clark's Wharf, the apothecary shop, black Robin in his blue coat and wig. And Phillis, too. They had burned her. These two had died for petty treason. He himself rode upon high treason—armed insurrection against the King. The penalties which England could then legally inflict for high treason included the barbarous drawing and quartering. Mark's lonely gibbet might well pull his thoughts back into his youth—or forward into an unpredictable future. Luckily for him it did not make him absent-minded.

"The moon shone bright," he remembered. "I had got almost over Charlestown Common towards Cambridge when I saw two Officers on Horseback, standing under the shade of a Tree, in a narrow part of the roade. I was near enough to see their Holsters & cockades. One of them started his horse towards me and the other up the road, as I supposed to head me should I escape the first. I turned my horse short about, and rid upon a full gallop for Mistick Road." In this brief, slippery, cross-country race the heavier British charger (handsome enough for parade) was no match for the light-footed Yankee horse. Out of the tail of his eye Paul Revere could see how he was outdistancing his pursuer in three hundred yards. And next the clumsy animal had "got into a clay-pond." No shots were fired and, if any words were spoken, Paul Revere did not record them.

As the road to Cambridge was blocked, he quickly came down on that other road (now Broadway), followed the Mystic River, which he crossed, and entered Medford over a plank bridge. Here "I awaked the Captain of the minute men: and after that I alarumed almost every house till I got to Lexington."

Bells rang, drums beat—"The regulars are out!" Women gathered children and silver and fled to swamps. Men seized muskets and powder-horns. Other men mounted and rode off to other towns to carry the warning—"The regulars are out." "The horror of that midnight cry" was not quickly forgotten in Middlesex County.

Paul Revere recrossed the Mystic, went through Menotomy (as Arlington was called at that time—Lieutenant Sutherland calls it "Anatomy"), and so was back on the route he had planned to take before the officers forced him to detour. Cambridge, now behind him, did not need any express rider to tell them the British had marched. Colonel Smith had already landed his men at Phipps' farm in East Cambridge. With that curious disregard for the privates' comfort and health so many of the British officers showed, he left his men drawn up and shivering until two o'clock. They had waded up to their middles in salt water to get ashore. If only they had marched immediately, they would have been in Lexington and Concord before any sizeable force could have been raised to oppose them.

With these troops General Gage had sent his favorite spy, John Howe. The young fellow crossed with the troops to Cambridge, changed into his "Yankee dress," was given a "country horse," and told to deliver letters to certain Tories in Malden, Lynn, Salem, and Marblehead.

Close upon midnight Paul Revere came into Lexington. And here was the meeting house casting its moonstruck shadow across the Green where so soon men were to die. Close by it was Buckman Tavern from which he might have heard the voices of men, laughter even, or the clink of tankards. Captain Parker had called out the local minute men that afternoon when word first came that a handful of unexplainable British officers were abroad and might be after Adams and Hancock. It does not seem to have been known in Lexington that a considerable force of the regulars were coming until Revere arrived. As it was cold standing about outdoors, the militiamen had retired to Buckman's. The Yankee soldier had as strong a regard for his own comfort as the British officers had disregard for their men. Colonel Smith's forces freezing in their disciplined ranks in the salt marshes of East Cambridge, and Captain Parker's men so cozy and undisciplined at the same moment at Buckman's, make a characteristic contrast.

Paul Revere went straight to the Clark parsonage. There he found Sergeant Munroe and seven men guarding the house. Revere demanded to be admitted, in so loud a voice the sergeant reproved him. The ladies and gentlemen had gone to bed and had "requested not to be disturbed by any noise that night" (this sounds more like Hancock than Adams).

"Noise," shouted Revere. "You'll have noise enough before long! The regulars are out."

He knocked loudly on the door.

The Reverend Mr. Clark opened a window and thrust out his granite head. Paul Revere demanded to see John Hancock. But the clergyman, "ever deliberate and watchful," not recognizing the man in the dark, said he could not be admitting strangers at that time of night without knowing who they were and what they wanted. John Hancock had "retired to rest, but not to sleep." He recognized Revere's voice.

"Come in, Revere, we are not afraid of *you*."

So he went in and told his story. It was not merely a patrol of British officers that was out this night, but probably "over a thousand light troops." He had seen them crossing the Charles at ten. They might be here any moment now. There was no doubt but their destination was Lexington to pick up the rebel leaders, and Concord for the stores. This was thundering news and all was commotion. John Hancock would have on the finest of silk banians, moroccan slippers—elegant even when thus rudely summoned. Aunt Lydia would look even grimmer than ever with her nightclothes showing below the hastily thrown cloak. There was the minister and his wife. We can count on Miss Dolly to be pert and enchanting even if in bare feet. Sam Adams would be cheerful, self-contained, quick-witted, although reduced to a night rail.

Paul Revere asked for William Dawes, but he had not yet arrived. Although Dawes had four miles farther to ride, he had started earlier, nor had his departure been delayed by seeing about lanterns and the slow rowboat ride across the Charles River, nor did he have the cordon of British officers to penetrate.

John Hancock was demanding his sword and gun. He was determined to take his place with the minute men if they opposed the march of the British. Sam Adams tried to persuade him against such foolishness. These two men had just been elected Massachusetts delegates to the Second Continental Congress in Philadelphia. They argued about the matter, and then, half an hour after Revere, Dawes came in.

The two expresses ate and drank, and once more mounted. The countryside as well as Hancock and Adams had been warned. Three days before, Revere had got word to Concord that the British might seize the stores there and by now they were pretty well hidden. However, the two men decided to go over to Concord, alarming the minute men as they went.

As they moved out of Lexington, they were joined by Samuel Prescott, a young doctor from Concord, who had been over to Lexington courting a Miss Millikan. As it was now after one o'clock, he was hardly keeping the early hours credited to our forebears. When he heard what was happening, he offered to ride with them, for being a local man and a high Son of Liberty, he pointed out that people would "give more credit" to what he said than to strangers. Paul Revere says:

. . . . when we had got about half way from Lexington to Concord, the other two stopped at a House to awake the man. I kept along. when I had got about 200 yards ahead of them, I saw two officers under a tree as before, [not far from Hartwell Inn, South Lincoln]. I immediately called to my company to come up, saying here was two of them. (for I had told them what Mr. Devens told me, and of my being stopped) in an instant I saw four officers, who rode up to me, with their pistols in their hands & said G-D D--m you stop, if you go an inch further you are a dead Man. Immediately Mr. Prescot came up he turned the but of his whipp we attempted to git thro them, but they kept before us, and swore if we did not turn into that pasture, they would blow our brains out. They had placed themselves opposite a pair of Barrs, and had taken the Barrs down. They forced us in. The Doctor jumped his horse over a low stone wall, and got to Concord. I observed a wood at a small distance and made for that intending when I gained that to jump my Horse & run afoot, just as I reached it out started six officers, siesed my bridle, put their pistols to my Breast, ordered me to dismount, which I did. One of them, who appeared to have command there, and much of a Gentleman. asked where I came from; I told him. he asked what time I left it; I told him, he seemed much surprised, He said Sir may I crave your name? I answered my name is Revere. What said he Paul Revere? I answered yes; the others abused me much; but he told me not to be afraid, no one should hurt me. I told him they would miss their Aim. [This seems to have been a common catch-phrase that night.] He said they should not, they were only after some Deserters they expected down the road. I told them I knew better, I knew what they were after; that I had alarumed the country all the way up, that their Boats had catch'd aground, and I should have 500 men there soon; one of them said they had 1500 coming. . . . Major Mitchel of the 5th Reg't clap'd a pistol to my head and said if I did not tell the truth, he would blow my brains out. . . . I gave him much the same answers; after he and two more had spoke together in a low voice he then ordered me to mount, and the Major rode up to me and took the reins. G-D sir you are not to ride with reins I assure you; and gave them to the officer on my right to lead me. I asked him to let me have the reins & I would not run from him, he said he would not trust me. He then Ordered 4 men out of the Bushes, and to mount their horses they were country men which they had stopped who were going home; they ordered us to march. He came up to me and said "We are now going towards your friends, and if you attempt to run, or we are insulted, we will blow your Brains out." I told him he might do as he pleased.

Major Mitchell had reason to worry. They must join Colonel Smith's columns before the country was aroused and they themselves were cut off. He also wished to warn Colonel Smith that, in spite of General Gage's confidence that the "damned rebels" would not fight, it looked to him as though they would. He would now ride as fast as he could go to join the British marching out. There was no more time to bother with prisoners.

Although he had caught one of the three riders headed for Lexington, two had escaped him.

William Dawes (always the actor) made his dash for freedom, flapping his leather breeches and yelling, "Haloo, boys, I've got two of 'em." But he pulled up his horse so short, he not only fell off, but lost his watch, and presumably his horse as well. A few days later, he retraced his steps and found the watch. It was only Doctor Prescott who got through to Concord that night.

The British officers formed a circle about Paul Revere and the four countrymen. The little cavalcade "rid down towards Lexington, a pretty smart pace. I was often insulted by the officers calling me dammed Rebel, etc. etc. The officer who led me said I was in a d--m--d critical situation. I told him I was sensable of it. After we had got about a mile. I was given to the Sarjant to lead, who was Ordered to take out his pistol and if I should run to execute the Major's sentance;"

There was the soft thudding of horses' hooves, the clink of bits, spur-chains, military accoutrement. So they rode through the chilly silence of those darkest hours before the dawn. Sometimes at such an hour a cock will crow, a watch dog bark. And now there came another sound, for "when we got within about half a mile of Lexington Meeting house we heard a gun fired. The Major asked me what that was for. I told him to alarm the country."

There was no time to lose. Major Mitchell ordered the girths and bridles on the four countrymen's horses to be cut and the horses to be driven off. These men might now go home as best they might on foot. Paul asked the Major to dismiss him too. At first he would not, but admitted he could not "carry me let the consequence be what it will." More alarm guns were heard from Lexington. "The Major ordered us to a halt he asked me how far it was to Cambridge and many more questions which I answered. He then asked the Sarjant, if his horse was tired, he said yes;" Paul Revere noticed in the dark it was a small horse. "he Ordered him to take my horse.

I dismounted, the Sarjant mounted my horse, they cutt the Bridle and Saddle off the Sarjant's horse & they told me they should make use of my horse for the night and rode off down the road."

Paul Revere saw the last of the "good" Larkin horse with a British grenadier sergeant on top of him. Although the Major promised to make use of it for only the one night, it disappeared completely into the British army and that was the end of him.

VI

GEORGE WASHINGTON, THE SAVIOR OF THE STATES, 1771-1781 [1]

By

RUPERT HUGHES

The best story "in Washington's amazing and crowded career," as Rupert Hughes says, "would have to be the best dozen, hundred, or N. There are instances of his great tenderness of heart, his tears, his uproarious laughter, his blind bravery, his modesty, his fine temper, his self-forgetfulness, his profound wisdom,—no end of them. But if I must choose one, I am tempted to select an instance of his great and exquisite tact and consideration. I can imagine nothing more delicate or gracious than the incident of the memorandum he asked to have memorized and destroyed."

THE TACT OF WASHINGTON

Nothing in Washington's military career shows the kindliness of his heart and his indifference to personal autocracy more poignantly than an overlooked little memorandum that he ordered destroyed.

While Cornwallis was shackled and nagged by Clinton's minute instructions usually too late, Washington had given Greene every support in his power, but never sent him an order—only praise and sympathy.[2] Greene had undergone appalling hardships with men dropping from famine and so naked that they tied clumps of moss to their shoulders and hips to keep the muskets and cartridge boxes from chafing the skin.[3] Yet

[1] Rupert Hughes, *George Washington, the Savior of the States, 1777-1781*, copyright 1930 by Rupert Hughes, by permission of William Morrow & Company, pp. 656-7.

[2] Francis Vinton Greene, *The Revolutionary War and the Military Policy of the United States*, p. 265, New York, 1911.

[3] Major W. A. Ganoe, *History of the United States Army*, p. 76, New York, 1924.

Greene had done superb work in cooperation with Sumter, Lee, Marion, Pickens, Colonel Washington and others. On hearing that his idol, George Washington, was coming south, Greene wrote to Knox with only partial cynicism:

"We have been beating the bush, and the General has come to catch the bird." [4]

Washington, however, proved his affection secretly. Realizing that by going south he automatically superseded Greene in command and robbed him of his independence, he tried to soften the blow by a personal message sent with a letter of congratulation following Greene's success at Eutaw Springs.[5] He even went so far as to say that he was saving Greene from being superseded by Rochambeau! Not wishing to have the message run the risk of capture or publication, he instructed Colonel Lewis Morris to memorize it and destroy it. This is the message:

"Col. Morris will inform General Greene in the sincerest manner that there are but two motives which can possibly induce Genl. W—— to take the command to the southward: one, the order of C—— to repair thither; the other, the French army going there. In the last case Count R—— would command if Genl. W—— did not go in person. General Washington wishes, not only from his personal regard to Genl. Greene, but from principles of generosity and justice, to see him crowned with those laurels which from his unparalleled exertions he so richly deserves." —*Memorandum to Col. Lewis Morris, to be destroyed as soon as he has committed them to memory.* 6 October. 1781.[6]

Fortunately Colonel Morris disobeyed the order and thus preserved one of the most delicate masterpieces of tact and tenderness in the history of military command. It is difficult to imagine any of the other great generals even thinking of such a courtesy.

[4] Francis S. Drake, *The Life and Correspondence of Henry Knox*, p. 68, Boston, 1873.

[5] Worthington C. Ford, *The Writings of George Washington*, vol. IX, p. 377, New York, 1889-93.

[6] Worthington C. Ford, *The Writings of George Washington*, vol. IX, p. 378 n. New York, 1889-93.

VII

LOU GEHRIG, A QUIET HERO [1]

By

FRANK GRAHAM

This biography of one of the most famous Yankee baseball players of the last twenty years, who died at the age of thirty-eight, enables one to look not merely into the heart of a "Quiet Hero," but also into the heart of America. Frank Graham has chosen three scenes from Lou Gehrig's life which help us to understand how a nation's sport may reflect a nation's spirit.

HOW TO PITCH TO GEHRIG

On June 3, [1932], in Philadelphia, Lou performed one of the greatest feats in the long history of baseball. George Earnshaw was pitching for the Athletics and in the first inning Gehrig hit a home run. Going to bat in the fourth inning, he hit another. He went to bat for the third time in the fifth inning—and hit a third home run.

Connie Mack thought it was about time Earnshaw retired for the afternoon. Gehrig, of course, was delivering the heaviest blows but the Yankees as a team were slamming the pitcher. So Connie waved him out and called Bill Mahaffey in from the bull pen. Connie always liked Mahaffey. He thought he was a pretty smart pitcher.

"Wait, George," he said, as Earnshaw started for the clubhouse. "I want you to see how Mahaffey pitches to Gehrig."

When Gehrig stepped up to the plate in the seventh inning, Mahaffey pitched a high fast ball to him—and he hit it out of the park.

"I see, Connie," Earnshaw said. "May I go now?"

Gehrig had hit four home runs. Only twice before had a man hit four

[1] Frank Graham, *Lou Gehrig, A Quiet Hero*, courtesy of G. P. Putnam's Sons, New York, 1942, pp. 154-157, 200-204, 247-250.

home runs in a single game. Ed Delehanty of the Phillies did it on July 13, 1896, and Bobby Lowe of Boston on May 30, 1894.

And yet that day the note of frustration that so often was to be heard in the hours of his greatest triumphs was heard again. That day, in New York, John McGraw resigned as manager of the Giants and in the papers and on the radio all over the country the big news was not that Lou had hit four home runs but that the thirty-year term of the colorful and dynamic McGraw had come to an end.

That made much less difference to Lou than it did to his friends, who were chagrined that his bright achievement drew only the secondary notice of the writers and broadcasters. He was happy not so much that he had equaled a record written on the yellowing pages of the game's ancient history but that he had helped to win another game in the Yankees' pennant drive.

And so Lou and the Yankees rolled on, piling up victories, destroying the opposition of the Athletics, and at last they came to the hoped-for climax of the tussle within their own league. They won the flag. Ruppert, who did not like to finish second, had a winner again after three years of waiting. McCarthy, who liked to win as much as he did, had delivered in the second year of his service at the Stadium.

The Cubs, in a great late-season rush under Charlie Grimm, who had supplanted Rogers Hornsby as their manager, had won in the National League, and the Yankees moved to meet them in the world series. In each of their last two series, the Yankees had triumphed in four straight games. McCarthy and the players were determined to do no less. Their drive was hard and their aim was true. They smashed the Cubs—in four games.

Lou had hit .349 that year. In the world series he was terrific, hitting .529 and making three home runs.

THE DAY HAD COME

The season opened [1939]. The Yankees played eight games. They were winning, but Lou was lagging. He made only four hits for an average of .143, and he was so slow covering first base that the other players had to wait for him before making a throw. Little was said about him in the newspapers but his teammates were looking at him anxiously and the baseball writers talked about him among themselves. Nobody said anything to him about his poor playing, naturally. For one thing, he obviously was in a very bad mental state as he tried to pull himself together.

"How long can McCarthy keep him in there?" one writer asked another.

"I have an idea that when the Yankees go West, Joe will take him out. I think he just doesn't want to take him out while they are at home."

"And when he goes out . . . do you think it will be for good?"

"Maybe. Maybe if he just rests for a while, he will be all right."

The Yankees left for Detroit on the night of April 30. The next day was an off day. That day Lou spent alone, wrestling with the problem of his decline as a player, reaching a decision. McCarthy had spent the day at his home in Buffalo. When he reached Detroit on the morning of May 2, Lou was waiting for him in the lobby and went up to his room with him.

"Yes, Lou?" McCarthy said as the door of his room closed behind the boy who had carried his bags.

"I'm benching myself, Joe," Lou said.

McCarthy looked at him for a moment.

"Why?" he asked.

"For the good of the team," Lou said. "I can't tell you how grateful I am to you for the kindness you have shown me and for your patience. I've tried hard, Joe. You know that. But I just can't seem to get going, and nobody has to tell me how bad I've been and how much of a drawback I've been to the team. I've been thinking, ever since the season opened—when I saw that I couldn't start as I'd hoped I would—that the time had come for me to quit."

"Quit?" Joe said. "You don't have to quit. Take a rest for a week or so, and maybe you'll feel all right again."

Lou shook his head.

"I don't know," he said. "I don't know what's the matter with me. But I know I can't go on the way I am . . . Johnny Murphy told me so."

McCarthy frowned angrily.

"Murphy told you! I'll—"

"No, Joe," Lou said. "I didn't mean it that way. All the boys have been so swell to me and nobody has said a word that would hurt my feelings. But Johnny Murphy said something the other day that made me know it was time for me to get out of the line-up. And all he meant to do was to be encouraging."

"How was that?"

"Do you remember the last play in the game—the last game at the Stadium?"

"Yes."

"A ball was hit between the box and first base—"

"And Johnny fielded it?"

"And I got back in time to take the throw—just in time?"

"Yes."

"I had a hard time getting back there, Joe," Lou said. "I should have been there in plenty of time. And then, as I made the put out and started for the clubhouse, Johnny waited for me near the box and said:

" 'Nice play, Lou.' "

McCarthy was silent.

"I knew then that it was time to quit," Lou said. "When the boys were feeling sorry for me—"

"All right, Lou," Joe said. "Take a rest. I'll put Dahlgren on first base, but I want you to know that that's your position—and whenever you want it back, all you have to do is to walk out there and take it."

The day had come. The day when he was to fulfill a promise he had made a year before. On an August day in 1938, he had come back to the dugout after taking a swing in batting practice and hadn't gone up again when it was his turn.

"What's the matter?" a reporter had asked.

"I have a bad thumb," he said. "I think maybe the darned thing is broken."

"Are you going to stay out of the line-up?"

"I should say not! It isn't as bad as that. I can grip a bat and handle the ball all right, and there is no reason why I shouldn't play."

"You aren't thinking too much about your record, are you?" the reporter asked.

"No," he said. "I'm all right. I can play. And I'll promise you this: When the day comes that I don't think I can help the ball club, I won't be in there, record or no record."

The day had come. The record had been set at 2,130 games.

THE SHINING LEGACY OF COURAGE

The air was soft. There were blossoms on the trees and the shrubs were green and there were flowers about the doorway. In a few days it would be June. Wonder if, as he looked back across the years, he realized what a fateful month June had been in his life? He was born on June 19, 1903. As a schoolboy he had hit that home run at Wrigley Field in June of 1920. In June of 1923 he joined the Yankees and saw his name in a major league box score for the first time. On June 1, 1925, he had begun his streak of consecutive games, and on June 2, 1925, he had become the regular first-baseman. On June 3, 1932, he had hit four home runs in a game in Philadelphia. And now, in a few days, it would be June again. . . .

Eleanor didn't know that he knew he was doomed But he did. And she never let him know she knew their days together were numbered and that the numbers were dropping fast.

"There," the fellow in the press box had said that Fourth of July at the Stadium, "goes the gamest guy I ever saw."

The gamest guy had found a mate as game as he.

On the night of June 2, there was a sudden change in his condition. What Eleanor first thought was drowsiness after a day propped against the pillows on his bed reading and listening to the radio was, she quickly realized, a coma.

The doctor was at the house in a few minutes. Mom and Pop, shaken and frightened, were driving over from Mt. Vernon. Ed Barrow, roused from an easy chair in his home in Larchmont, was being whirled across the parkways by a driver who, that night, gave no thought to speed cops.

Shortly before ten o'clock, Lou opened his eyes and looked at those grouped about the bed. He seemed surprised to see them there, for they had not been there just a . . . a . . . a moment before. And then, as though he had fallen asleep again, he died. Death had brought no pain. Only bewilderment.

In newspaper offices and radio stations across the country, the report of his death came as a shock, as it did when it was announced to the public. Within an hour, messages of sympathy were pouring in on the bereaved parents and widow, and cars lined the streets about the house. The Babe and Mrs. Ruth arrived in tears.

In Detroit, Joe McCarthy stepped out of a taxicab in front of the hotel where the Yankees were staying and the manager of the hotel said to him:

"Gehrig died tonight."

Joe was shaken as though he had been struck in the face and as he walked into the lobby and saw some of the players gathered there, he saw that they knew, for they were gray and stunned. And in his room, that he had shared so long with Lou, Bill Dickey cried.

By order of Mayor LaGuardia, flags flew at half-staff in New York the next day, as the city, and the nation, mourned the death of this young man. Thousands of persons filed past his bier as he lay in state in a little church in Riverdale. The newspapers carried editorials citing his gallantry and deploring his untimely death. From the White House, from the Governor's mansion at Albany, from the homes of children who played on the sidewalks as he once had done, came expressions of grief.

He died as he had lived. Bravely, quietly. To his mother, to his wife, to all who knew and loved him, to the millions who sorrowed at his death, he left the shining legacy of courage.

VIII

FANNY KEMBLE, A PASSIONATE VICTORIAN [1]

By

MARGARET ARMSTRONG

Of the Kemble family of English actors several became famous, and among them was Fanny, who was also an author. She was one of the most colorful public figures of her time, living from 1809 to 1893. Her dynamic personality and her intelligence made her a great favorite and, fortunately, enabled her father to recoup his losses as a manager.

Margaret Armstrong has written a book of unusual literary distinction on a romantic life. She has selected for this anthology the vivid story of Fanny's triumph as Juliet when she was only nineteen.

FANNY WAS STILL VERY, VERY YOUNG

The stage of Covent Garden was enormous. Fanny stepped out into that vast emptiness and paused to look about her. Overhead, a confusion of criss-crossings cutting darkness; behind her, a confusion of meaningless shapes peering out awkwardly from another darkness; at the sides, racks of pasteboard and canvas—streets, forest, dungeons and banqueting halls—drawn away, leaving her the centre of an empty cavern. It was cold. The air smelt dusty. Her feet made no more sound than a mouse's as she crossed the smooth green baize floor. In front, a still vaster emptiness opened out; the curtain was up, the amphitheatre rose tier on tier, boxes empty, seats swathed in gray holland. No movement broke the stillness; the only light came from far above, a single ray that pricked down from

[1] Margaret Armstrong, *Fanny Kemble, a Passionate Victorian,* by permission of The Macmillan Company, publishers, New York, 1938, pp. 77-86.

some opening in the roof, alighted on the floor at her feet and spread to a round bright spot.

Fanny felt very small and young as she stood there, a new-born star told to twinkle in an empty sky with no companions to encourage her. Her father had moved out of sight; his voice seemed to reach her from miles away. But she was not frightened. The still loneliness was, somehow, inspiring, like the stillness of a mountain top. Her father bade her begin. She spoke. Her voice rang clear as a bell, soared up and out. She thrilled at the sound, rejoiced in its power, exulted in the beauty of Juliet's lines. She forgot her father, forgot herself . . .

It was over, her father kissed her. A figure emerged from nowhere, came walking in—Major Dawkins, an old friend, who had, it appeared, been listening, hidden in the back of a box. He was a critic whose opinion Charles valued. Major Dawkins said: "Bring her out at once; she will be a success." If Charles had doubted he doubted no longer; nor did Fanny's mother. There was no time to lose; if Covent Garden could by any possibility be saved—and even Charles did not believe it could be—the attempt must be made without delay. They told Fanny that she was to come out in three weeks.

Three weeks! No child of a great theatrical family really begins at the beginning; from babyhood Fanny had heard stage matters discussed and analyzed, already she knew more than any outsider could know. But this was in itself daunting for she realized what lay before her. The other members of the company were strangers, she must make their acquaintance; she must learn all the intricate stage business; learn how to carry herself towards an audience; learn how to concert her own actions with those of her fellow actors, bring out every possible effect in her own part and yet not injure theirs. When she thought of all this three weeks shrank to three hours. But it had to be done. She set herself to work like a child given a hard lesson.

To her parents, with so much to teach, the time must have seemed even shorter; but they were not dismayed. Charles, like all the Kembles, was spurred on by difficulties, and the need for haste was in itself exhilarating to her mother. Morning rehearsals began at once; and the evening brought consultations at home to decide the question of Juliet's dress. Mrs. Kemble was an authority on costume, but so was Fanny's friend Mrs. Jameson, and they did not agree. Mrs. Jameson begged for a gorgeous brocade stiff with embroidery and jewels, such as a Capulet would have worn in ancient Verona. Mrs. Kemble took a different point of view; she had no wish to return to the old way of acting historical plays in modern dress; Garrick's

Macbeth in knee-breeches and a powdered wig had been ridiculous enough, and Mrs. Siddons should not have worn a hoop as the Grecian Daughter. But she perceived technical difficulties that Mrs. Jameson did not allow for. Asked to criticize a sketch Mrs. Kemble's first thought would be: How will this dress look when it walks, runs, rushes, kneels, sits down, falls and turns its back? So now she insisted that appearance must be subordinated to action; a ruff would prevent free movement of the head and neck, and heavy sleeves ruin gesture. Moreover, the consciousness of being "dressed up" was fatal to passion, and any peculiarity of costume might easily divert the attention of the audience from Juliet herself. Charles agreed, Mrs. Jameson's drawings were put aside and Fanny was told that her Juliet would make no departure from the conventional. She was to wear a white satin ball-dress with tight bodice and full skirt, low neck and short sleeves; her thick wavy hair parted in the middle and caught into a loose knot at the back with a comb as she usually wore it. Except for a diamond girdle and a train three yards long—Mrs. Kemble realized the value of a sweeping train—she would look as Juliet was expected to look, and feel as if she were appearing at a party given by the Montagues of London rather than by the Capulets of Verona.

This decided, a still more important question remained: Romeo. Charles was Covent Garden's Romeo and extremely popular, but now the part was forbidden him; the public would not like seeing a man make love to his daughter. Various candidates were rejected. At length Charles suggested that Henry might do. Henry was too young and too cheerful and he detested acting, but a more beautiful Romeo could not well be imagined and it was hoped that his expression might soon become less cheerful as he had recently fallen in love. So Henry, to his horror, was told to study the balcony scene. The family assembled to hear him recite; their ordeal was brief. His matter-of-fact gabble, interrupted by giggles, was so absurd and the mortification that clouded his boyish face so unlike love's anguish, that a few minutes was enough. Charles smiled and flung his book on the floor. Henry, seeing which way the wind blew, clapped his arms to his sides and let out a cock-a-doodle-doo of mingled relief and triumph that sent his audience into shrieks of laughter. They laughed and laughed. And Henry was assured that he might consider himself forever immune from a dramatic career.

In the end it was decided that Mr. Abbot would have to do. The public rather liked Mr. Abbot; he was fairly good-looking though too old for the part, and knew his business. Fanny, of course, made no objection to the choice; she was too inexperienced to wish for a more passionate Romeo;

in fact it did not occur to her that Romeo was important one way or the other. But at rehearsal she discovered that Mr. Abbot was given to ranting and roaring and rushing about the stage with a violence that was disconcerting and often terrifying; for the poor man was unsteady on his feet and she feared that at any moment he might slip and fall and carry her down with him. However, she soon learned to avoid his onslaughts and the rehearsals went on without mishap.

Mr. Abbot was the weakest spot in the cast; Mr. Keely made an excellent Peter and Mrs. Davenport a perfect Nurse. Fanny's mother was to take Lady Capulet, although it was years since her retirement, for she knew that her presence would give Fanny courage, and Charles was to act Mercutio. (It became his greatest part; then and later critics agreed that "Charles Kemble's Mercutio was incomparably the best that ever trod the English stage.")

Fanny herself remained an unknown quantity. At rehearsal her performance was so uneven that no one could feel sure of her. Now and then a gesture or tone would recall her aunt, Mrs. Siddons; but such flashes of genius were rare and they came and went like fireflies. Fanny's parents realized, of course, that artistry such as Mrs. Siddons had achieved after years and years of study could not be expected and agreed that her only assets were youth, imagination and willingness to work. But when Mrs. Kemble went on to lament the child's lack of self-control as a disadvantage, Charles demurred—suppressing a smile, for self-control was not Theresa's long suit; to him, Fanny's lack of ambition seemed a more serious drawback, and he shook his head with a puzzled sigh. A Kemble who could act and did not want to was something new in the family history!

Apart from this anxiety the outlook was bright. Covent Garden's misfortunes had worried the public almost as much as they had worried Charles; theatre-goers were shocked when they saw the walls of the old play-house plastered with bills of sale, and the news that another Kemble was to appear on the stage was received with rejoicing. Enthusiasm took a practical form; several wealthy patrons of the drama started a fund to insure a handsome production of 'Romeo and Juliet'; the King's theatre gave a benefit, and the principals in the Covent Garden Company made a present of their services for the first few weeks. The advertising also was in a sense free, for the story advertised itself. It was so romantic, this story of a daughter coming to the rescue of her father like another Iphigenia! And the girl was very young, only nineteen. And very clever, a second Mrs. Siddons. As beautiful as the "Tragic Muse?" Far more beautiful! As great a genius? Far greater! Miss Fanny Kemble was a *natural* genius, entirely untrained. Entirely untrained? So much the better!—for, as usual, the public liked to believe that genius is miraculous and springs like a rabbit out of a top-hat at the bidding of some celestial conjuror. So there was much talk of Fanny's lack of dramatic training as well as of her youth and beauty; and as few people could boast of having seen her an element of mystery was added to the tale of filial devotion and all London thrilled with sentimental admiration. Everybody was urged to help the dear child, everybody wanted to. Everybody agreed with Sir Walter Scott when he wrote: "I love and honor Miss Kemble for giving her active support to her father in his need, and preventing Covent Garden from coming down about their ears."

Seats for 'Romeo and Juliet' sold like hot cakes and there was a clamorous demand for boxes, and managers of other houses began to hope that theatre-going might again become popular with the upper classes. It had not been fashionable of late, for several reasons. Most of the new plays were so poor that only a great actor like Kean could draw an intelligent audience; politics had become so absorbing that the young and ultra-modern had no time for amusement, and the wave of evangelicalism, having purified the lower orders, was washing so high that some of the very smartest people had come to perceive that the stage was wicked, that even Shakespeare smelt of brimstone and that it was a good deal safer to hear his plays read than to see them acted.

These prejudices and predilections were now forgotten. The most strait-laced could not deny that filial piety should be encouraged; the intelligentzia allowed themselves an interval of frivolity, and rank and fashion fought for the privilege of seeing Miss Kemble act. The Kembles' friends did not of course need any sentimental stimulus to rally them. Mrs. Siddons consented to honor her niece by appearing in the small stage box that had been fitted up especially for her; Mrs. Fitzgerald ordered a new purple velvet gown and notified her son Edward that he might come up from Cambridge, and the "Apostles" to a man lamented John's absence and prepared to do their best for his little sister.

But Fanny, the centre of all this emotion and commotion, remained curiously indifferent, curiously *young*. Nineteen, nearly twenty, and intellectually a woman, she faced what lay ahead of her like a docile child. She did what she was told; she spoke, curtsied, moved this way and that, smiled or wept, put on a frock or took it off, like a child anxious to please; always a little aloof, as if she were wondering what all the fuss were about. A letter to Harriet at this time is suggestive. Not until several pages had been devoted to a recent illness in the St. Leger family, the health of her own parents, and regrets that Mrs. Harry Siddons was leaving London after a long visit, did she remember to tell Harriet that the future so often discussed at Heath Farm had been decided for her; she was to go on the stage, the play was to be 'Romeo and Juliet,' she wished it were all over, and ended this brief mention with an apology; her own affairs would not have been alluded to at a time of such anxiety for Harriet but she did not want her friend to receive the first notice of her début from the newspapers.

At length the great day arrived, the twenty-sixth of October, 1829. There was no rehearsal that morning. Fanny, told to rest and keep calm, resorted to routine. Her usual hour of practicing on the piano was followed by her usual walk in St. James's Park; then she took up a book she happened to be reading, Blunt's 'Scripture Characters,' and became so absorbed that she looked up with a start when Aunt Dall came to tell her it was time to go to the theatre.

Daylight was still brightening the streets as Fanny and her mother and Dall drove to Covent Garden. A ray of sunlight shone into the carriage and touched Fanny's hair and Mrs. Kemble murmured: "Heaven blesses you, my child!" But her voice was not steady, and when they arrived she hurried off to her dressing-room afraid that her agitation might be contagious and left Fanny, still fairly calm, to be dressed by Aunt Dall.

Dall and Fanny's maid and the theatre-dresser buzzed about her, enjoying their task. Fanny stood like a lay figure while the folds of her costume were twitched and smoothed, a stitch taken here and there, a loop of hair adjusted and rouge applied. At length she was set down on a chair, with her train draped over the back, to wait. And now calm deserted her and she could no longer distract her mind with thoughts of Scripture characters; she was experiencing a new sensation, fear, and might have been waiting for the guillotine as she sat there, bolt upright, hands clasped palm to palm, heart beating in her throat. Now and then a tear would hang trembling on the long thick dark eyelashes that were her greatest beauty, and roll slowly down her cheeks. Each time Aunt Dall with a smile of pity would repair the damage to her make-up. Now and then her father would come to the door and Fanny would hear him ask: "How is she?" and each time Dall would send him away reassured. . . .

But there was satisfaction as well as anxiety in the air; it filtered backstage and reached Fanny's dressing-room. The house, they said, was jammed to suffocation; Mrs. Siddons herself had never met a better audience. The Leveson-Gowers had just come in, and the Duchess of St. Albans; Lady Dacre was already in her box; the Earl of Essex was expected. There were plenty of lesser lights such as young Mr. Wortley and the Reverend Mr. Harness and the Grevilles. Everybody was chattering and laughing. Miss Kemble was assured that she had nothing to fear . . . But Fanny did not hear these kind words, she was too far gone. She just sat and waited, numb and cold, waited for the ax to fall. . . .

At last a brisk tap at the door, a voice: "Miss Kemble called for the stage, ma'am." She stood up, Aunt Dall lifted her train, she was led to the side scene directly opposite the one where her mother stood waiting to go on. Lady Capulet advanced. A roar of applause came from the audience, Fanny sank half-fainting into her aunt's arms. The company gathered about—Charles was nowhere to be seen, he could not bear to watch Fanny's entrance. "Poor thing! Poor thing!" they murmured. Mrs. Davenport gave her a warm: "Courage, courage, my dear!" Kind Mr. Keely said in that funny voice of his: "Never mind 'em, Miss Kemble. Don't think of 'em any more than if they were a row of cabbages!" . . .

Then a voice from the stage, Lady Capulet's voice:

"Nurse!"

Mrs. Davenport waddled on. Turned, called:

"Juliet!"

Aunt Dall stood Fanny on her feet, gave her a push and sent her running straight across the stage. Stunned by the deafening applause that rose to meet her, the green baize floor seeming to heave under her feet, a mist before her eyes, she reached her mother, caught at her, and stood staring at that sea of faces. Her mother whispered—the lines came to her—she spoke. But the voice that had rung so full at rehearsal was gone. Scarcely a syllable of Juliet's lines in the first act could be heard; the audience looked pityingly at each other and clapped half-heartedly . . . The ballroom scene went better. Little by little Fanny forgot herself; the part took possession of her; at last, as she leaned from the balcony to her lover the heavenly fire flashed down and she was all Juliet. Exalted by the beauty of Juliet's words, blushing with Juliet's passion, paling with Juliet's fears, her voice rang clear as a bell,

"O, Romeo, Romeo! wherefore art thou Romeo?"

and from the top galley to Mrs. Siddons in her box the whole house knew that little Fanny Kemble was a great actress.

The applause was deafening. Young gentlemen stood on the seats and waved their hats; John's friends forgot they were "Apostles" and shouted like school-boys; young ladies clapped their gloves to shreds and flung bouquets at Fanny's feet. Here and there an elderly person might whisper that the girl could not be compared to Mrs. Siddons in talent or looks and that she was too small for tragic parts, but nobody listened to them. Most people declared that Miss Kemble was the image of her aunt—though Mr. Harness added: "Seen through the wrong end of an opera glass"—while others commented on her remarkable likeness to Malibran both in face and figure. Wave after wave of applause rose and fell, and rose again; the audience seemed as if it would never tire of demonstrating affection for the Kemble family and admiration for Fanny's genius and youth and courage . . . At last it was over. Half an hour in the greenroom of congratulations, embraces and tears of unutterable relief, and then Charles and Theresa Kemble took their child home.

Fanny was too dazed to feel any elation; the familiar streets seemed strange to her, their own house had an unnatural look, and her parents' kisses and expressions of thankfulness did not touch her; everything, she herself, seemed unreal. It was not until they sat down to supper and her father laid a little jewelled watch beside her plate that Fanny came to. A watch! She had never owned a watch—a watch was something tangible—the diligent child had been awarded a prize. Fanny laughed and cried with delight, and could not understand why Mr. Washington Irving, and the other friends who had dropped in to wish her joy, seemed amused by her enthusiasm as she kissed the little watch and declared she would christen it Romeo . . . When at length she was free to go to bed, after praying to be preserved from the many temptations of the stage she fell asleep at once; for her watch was under her pillow and she had been repaid for her weeks of hard work and even that horrible hour of stage fright seemed worth while . . . In spite of the great minds of Edinburgh, and the improving conversation of John's friends, Fanny was still very, very young!

IX

GRANT OF APPOMATTOX[1]

By

WILLIAM E. BROOKS

This character study of Grant is significant because it is essentially a study of the man. It is not an analysis of the issues of the Civil War. It is not a discussion of the economic problems of the time. It is a study of Grant, precisely that. The biography ends with Grant at his greatest, the scene at Appomattox, and it is this scene which William E. Brooks has chosen for this anthology because he believes it reveals Grant in his true light as "a modest and considerate man."

HOW GRANT MET HIS GREAT DAY

The night before . . . Lee had held his last council of war. His wagons were lost and all his camp equipage, so they sat on blankets or saddles about the fire. There were not many left: Longstreet and Gordon, Fitzhugh Lee, and Pendleton, chief of the rapidly diminishing artillery. The letters from Grant were read, the situation discussed from every angle. It was decided to make another attempt to cut through Grant's lines at daybreak, a last desperate and gallant attempt.

Colonel Newhall, of Sheridan's staff, tells the story of that last effort in his diary. As they began the attack "they gave us their best yell and pressed on faster. But not far. For the sound of this peculiar yell had hardly entered the woods, before the long lines of our infantry emerged and burst upon their astonished sight. . . . They did not even fire, palsied as they were by surprise, but rolled back like a receding wave which has spent its force

[1] William E. Brooks, *Grant of Appomattox*, copyright 1942, used by special permission of the publishers, The Bobbs-Merrill Company, Indianapolis, pp. 295-299.

against the earthworks of the shore." [2] So a white flag bore a message to Grant requesting "an interview in accordance with the offer contained in your letter of yesterday."

The man who sent the message had dressed himself with every care that Sunday morning, telling General Pendleton, when the latter expressed surprise at his appearance, "I have probably to be General Grant's prisoner and thought I must make my best appearance." [3] The day before, when he had been forced to abandon his baggage, he had kept his best uniform. This he was wearing, with a handsome sword and sash which a blockade runner had brought in, the gift of some British friends of the cause. His shining top boots were probably the only new ones left in the army. So arrayed Lee went to his last task as a soldier.

Grant had left camp that morning with no expectation that the end would come during the day, and he wore, as he had worn throughout the campaign, the rough uniform of a private soldier, only the shoulder straps showing his rank.[4] He carried no sword, and his trousers were tucked into ordinary trooper's boots, well covered with mud from his ride. In a conversation that he had after the war with Dr. Fordyce Barker he confessed his embarrassment over his shabbiness, as he remembered that once in Mexico Lee had rebuked him for his appearance, and the memory "made him uncomfortable lest General Lee should recall it also and imagine that he intended to affront him." [5] He was careful to explain to Lee before they parted that his old uniform could be explained by the fact that he had "not seen his headquarters baggage for days."

Meade's staff officer found Grant with Lee's message on the road from Farmville to Appomattox Court House, about eight miles east of the latter place. The officer brought him word also that Meade, having read the message, had granted a truce. He rode forward at a brisk trot to the little village. It stood on rising ground, and as he rode down the single street he could see the quiet host of his enemy covering the low ground at the hill's foot, while on the heights around were the Blue regiments, completely cutting off further retreat. A group of officers, headed by Sheridan and Ord, were dismounted and standing in the village street. Grant greeted them, and turned to Sheridan.

[2] Frederick C. Newhall, *With General Sheridan in Lee's Last Campaign*, p. 211, Philadelphia: J. B. Lippincott Co., 1866.

[3] Mrs. Susan Pendleton Lee, *Memoirs of William Pendleton*, p. 404, Philadelphia: J. B. Lippincott Co., 1893.

[4] *The Personal Memoirs of U. S. Grant*, II, p. 489.

[5] Thomas Nelson Page, *Robert E. Lee, the Southerner*, p. 577, New York: Charles Scribner's Sons, 1908.

"Is Lee over there?" pointing up the road.

"Yes, he is in that brick house, waiting to surrender to you."

"Well, then, we'll go over," said Grant.[6]

"That brick house" belonged to Wilmer McLean. His former home stood on the field of Bull Run, and after the battle he had moved to this little village to get away from war. But the War had overtaken him, to enact in his little parlor the last scene of the fiery drama to whose first scene he had been an unwilling witness. Lee had been waiting there, in a high-backed armchair by the window, for a half-hour before Grant came. He arose as Grant entered with extended hand, saying "General Lee." They shook hands and began talking of the days when they had met before, in Mexico. The *Memoirs* go on with the story: "Our conversation grew so pleasant that I almost forgot the object of our meeting. After the conversation had run on in this style for some time General Lee called my attention to the object of our meeting.[7]

Grant stated his terms, that Lee's army "should lay down their arms, not to take them up again" unless properly exchanged. Again the talk wandered off into other fields and again Lee had to interrupt with the suggestion that Grant write out the terms he proposed. Paroles were to be given that officers and men were not to take up arms against the United States until properly exchanged; all arms and public property were to be surrendered. "This will not embrace the side-arms of the officers, nor their private horses or baggage. This done, each officer and man will be allowed to return to their homes, not to be disturbed by United States authority so long as they observe their paroles and the laws in force where they may reside." [8]

As Grant finished writing Lee took from his pocket a pair of steel-rimmed spectacles, pushed some books aside on the table beside him, and carefully read what had been written. When he came to the last sentence he showed his appreciation and, with some degree of warmth in his manner, said: "This will have a very happy effect on my army." [9]

When Grant asked him for suggestions he pointed out that the horses of the cavalry and artillery belonged to the men who used them, and he was immediately told that the parole officers would be instructed "to let all the men who claim to own a horse or mule take the animals home with them to work their little farms." [10]

[6] Horace Porter, *Campaigning with Grant*, pp. 469-70, New York: The Century Co., 1897.

[7] *The Personal Memoirs of U. S. Grant*, II, p. 490.

[8] *The Personal Memoirs of U. S. Grant*, II, p. 491.

[9] *The Personal Memoirs of U. S. Grant*, II, p. 492.

[10] Horace Porter, *Campaigning with Grant*, p. 479, New York: The Century Co., 1897.

Then Grant asked about his need of rations, remembering that Sheridan had the cars that should have reached Amelia, and when Lee told him of this situation he gave orders that sufficient should be turned over to answer all their need.

The letters containing the terms and their acceptance were signed, the last formalities were over, and Lee left the room. He signaled to his orderly to bridle his horse, and standing on the steps of the porch he looked out over the valley where his army lay, smiting the glove he carried in his right hand on his left, in an absent sort of a way, and seeming to see nothing till his horse was led in front of him; then mounted and rode away. As he was going Grant came to the door and saluted him in silence.[11]

Grant has left us the record of his feelings as he surveyed the scene: "What General Lee's feelings were I do not know . . . but my own feelings, which had been quite jubilant on the receipt of his letter, were sad and depressed. I felt like anything rather than rejoicing at the downfall of a foe who had fought so long and valiantly."[12] And when the firing of salutes began to sound from his own lines he stopped them with the words, "The war is over; the rebels are our countrymen again; and the best sign of rejoicing after the victory will be to abstain from all demonstrations in the field."[13]

It was his day and that is how he met it, with a supreme considerateness that made the difficult task less difficult than it might have been had a smaller man controlled it. All the glory had not changed him, for once he too had been beneath the harrow, and he knew how sharp the teeth were. Grant knew something at least of what it meant to the man who was riding away, the man who after four years of valorous battle had "bent to the storm of God."

[11] Frederick C. Newhall, *With General Sheridan in Lee's Last Campaign*, p. 220, Philadelphia: J. B. Lippincott Co., 1866.

[12] *The Personal Memoirs of U. S. Grant*, II, p. 489.

[13] Horace Porter, *Campaigning with Grant*, p. 486, New York: The Century Co., 1897.

X

I WAS WINSTON CHURCHILL'S PRIVATE SECRETARY[1]

By

PHYLLIS MOIR

Here is an entertaining and distinctly human book consisting of a series of sketches, recorded with a fine sense of humor, of one of the great figures of our time.

Two selections, both of which are entertaining revelations of Winston Churchill, are given to us by Phyllis Moir. Of the second selection, the author says it is chosen particularly "because it is so typical of Churchill. He displays the same attention to detail in planning sandwiches for tomorrow's picnic as he does in planning a major piece of strategy. It is unusual to find a man with such a tremendous scope for detail."

A GIFT FOR PHRASE-MAKING

Mr. Churchill never talks for the sake of talking. If the conversation sinks to trivialities he relapses into bored silence. But he is always ready to hold forth endlessly on his favorite topics of politics, literature, journalism and Winston Churchill.

He loves especially to reminisce about his boyhood and his army days, how he was a dunce at Harrow, how he escaped from an enemy prison camp during the Boer War and how he was carried into Parliament on the crest of a journalistic scoop. I have even heard him try out on some visitor whose judgment he respected a speech or a lecture he had to deliver.

When Mr. Churchill is annoyed his wit can be sharp and merciless. At

[1] Phyllis Moir, *I Was Winston Churchill's Private Secretary*, New York: Wilfred Funk, Inc., 1941, pp. 122-123, 137-138.

a dinner party in England he once got into a heated argument with his cousin, Lord Londonderry.

"Have you read my latest book?" Londonderry asked, hoping to drive home his point.

"No," said Churchill bitingly, "I only read for pleasure or profit." A witness of this verbal encounter laughed heartily as he told me the incident.

This gift for phrase-making on the platform is matched in his private conversation by a terrifying genius for epigram. Of Ramsay MacDonald he once said, "He has more than any other man the gift of compressing the largest amount of words into the smallest amount of thought." And referring to Stanley Baldwin in the House of Commons Mr. Churchill remarked, "He used to be wiser. He used to take my advice." No wonder Baldwin dispensed with his services in the Cabinet. "I make up my mind," he complained to a colleague, explaining Churchill's exclusion from the Government, "then along comes Winston with his hundred-horse-power brain, and makes me change it."

HOW TO MAKE A ROAST BEEF SANDWICH

Mr. Churchill has a special fondness for picnics, not the rough and ready paper bag affairs, but elaborately prepared little feasts of caviar, cold game, hothouse fruits, and of course, champagne. This once gave rise to an amusing little incident which I witnessed. On one occasion at a lunch in a hotel, Mr. Churchill had as usual summoned the head waiter to plan the menu for a picnic that was to take place the next day. After selecting the main items Mr. Churchill, a precise man in all things, set about explaining how the roast beef sandwiches were to be made.

"I want some solid substantial sandwiches," he announced to the astonished head waiter, as solemnly as though he were making a statement to the House. "Get hold of a large loaf, and don't cut the slices too thin—or too thick, either. Trim the crust off the edges, and put plenty of butter on the bread. Please see to it there's enough beef for us to know it's a beef sandwich. And make certain that the beef comes clear to the edge of the bread. I don't like to bite twice into a sandwich before I can tell what's inside of it."

All this was rattled off with a very pronounced lisp, which left the unfortunate waiter completely bewildered. "Never mind," said Mr. Churchill impatiently, when he realized the man had not taken in a word. "Bring me some paper and a pencil." And then and there he proceeded to illustrate the exact size and thickness of the sandwiches with a series of quick sketches, little blueprints of gastronomical architecture.

XI

NAPOLEON [1]

By

EMIL LUDWIG

This study of Napoleon is brilliant, dramatic, and vivid. It is filled with a great treasury of quotations, letters and historical facts which enable one to penetrate deeply into the mind of the famous Corsican.

Emil Ludwig has told us that "there are in every book of mine some symbolic scenes which condense in a certain sense a whole personality in a certain epoch of his life." The scene he has chosen for this anthology is a famous interview Napoleon had with his brother, Lucien. "The conversation between the brothers," as Ludwig states in the biography, "is the most interesting of all Napoleon's recorded conversations, and has been reported by Lucien with fidelity and picturesqueness. Napoleon is there portrayed to the life."

THE LITTLE MAGICIAN SPINS HIS WEB

Lucien was now just thirty-two. It was on a December evening when he had reached the castle of Mantua, after a journey during which the dread of imprisonment, aroused by his brother's summons, had been continually present to his mind. On entering a room extravagantly lighted by numerous candelabra, he was blinded for a moment by the glare. Then he heard Rustam's voice announcing him: "Sire, your brother Lucien!"

The man to whom the announcement is made does not stir. He is seated at a large round table, which is covered by a huge map of Europe, the biggest Lucien has ever seen. Supporting his head on his left hand, with the other hand he is thrusting coloured pins into the map, pins which presumably represent army corps or whole armies. It is so many years since Lucien has seen his brother, and Napoleon has changed so much,

[1] Emil Ludwig, *Napoleon*, New York: Liveright Publishing Corporation, 1926, pp. 291-306.

that the visitor is not quite sure whether he is looking at the Emperor, and he remains motionless for several minutes. At length the man sits up, yawns, rubs his back against the chair, takes up a small bell from the table, and rings it with one strong movement. The visitor advances a step or two:

"Sire, I am Lucien."

The Emperor jumps up from his chair, dismisses the servant, and takes his brother by the hand affectionately, though with a certain amount of reserve. Lucien feels called upon to embrace Napoleon, who does not repel the advance, but accepts it with a passive coldness, as if no longer used to such intimacies. Then, taking the visitor by the hand once more, he pushes Lucien gently away to scrutinize him the better:

"So it's you, is it? How are you? How is your family? When did you leave Rome? Have you had a pleasant journey? What about the pope? How is he? Does he like you?"

Lucien notes the nervousness masked by this flood of questions, turns them off lightly, and says he is glad to find his brother in good health.

"Yes, I'm very well." He pats his waistcoat, and adds: "I'm getting fat, and I'm afraid I shall get fatter still." He looks keenly at Lucien, takes a pinch of snuff, and says: "As for you! Do you know that you are looking uncommonly well? You used to be rather too thin. Now, you are almost handsome."

"Your Majesty is good enough to make fun of me."

"No, no, it's quite true. But let's sit down and have a talk." They seat themselves opposite the huge map, the Emperor fidgets with the pins, and Lucien waits for him to begin. But, since Napoleon does not open the ball, the younger man says, hesitatingly: "Sire. . . ." At this moment, the Emperor sweeps all the pins flat, and says abruptly: "Well, what have you to say to me?"

Lucien replies that he hopes his brother has forgiven him.

"You can have my pardon soon enough. It depends entirely on yourself."

Lucien expresses his willingness to do anything compatible with his honour.

"Well and good, but what sort of things will square with your honour?"

Lucien speaks of nature and religion.

"But politics, Sire; do politics mean nothing to you?"

Lucien demurs, saying that he has retired into private life.

"It rested entirely with yourself. You could have been a king just as well as your brothers."

"Sire, my wife's honour, my children's position. . . ."

"You keep on speaking of your wife, when you know perfectly well that she has never been your wife. Is not, and never will be, for I shall never recognise her."

"Ah, Sire!"

"No, never, though the heavens should fall! Since you are my brother, I can forgive the wrong you have done me. But upon her my curse will rest!" There is a long tirade, until at length Lucien intervenes, laughing nervously, and saying:

"Moderate your words, Sire. There is a proverb: 'La processione torna, dove esce,'" and Lucien thinks it expedient to add a French translation. When Napoleon continues to talk of his brother's wife as a woman of bad reputation, and Lucien shows signs of taking offence, the Emperor tries to mollify him by admitting that these reports may be calumnious, but adds that nothing will induce him to recognise her. Besides, it is now a fundamental law, as firmly fixed as the Salic law, that no marriage in the Emperor's family is valid without the Emperor's consent. Lucien reminds him of the date of the marriage, and Napoleon answers: "Yes, but the law was passed because of what you had done!" This Napoleonic logic makes Lucien smile.

"What are you laughing at? I don't see anything laughable in it! I know what you and your wife and my enemies say about the matter. You choose your friends from among my enemies. But no good Frenchman approves of what you have done. The only way in which you can regain popular esteem is by espousing my cause, like Jerome."

Lucien, who is in the Emperor's hands, has absolutely determined to let nothing affront him. But he is spurred into opposition, springs to his feet, and does not sit down again:

"Your Majesty is mistaken! When your courtiers approve your attitude towards me as thanks for the services I was so happy to render you, they are only acting after their kind. On my side, too, my servants tell me that I am right!"—At these words, Napoleon's brow is furrowed, his eyes flash, and his nostrils work, "an unmistakable sign of rage in members of our family." But Lucien has taken the bit between his teeth, and goes on: "What ought the nation to do for me? What gratitude does it owe me? It ought to look upon me as the saviour of the man who has saved it. . . . I am proud to think that it will rather be inclined to compare me with you than with Jerome. No, Sire, public opinion, which is mightier by far than all the kings in the world, assigns every one to his true place, whatever courtiers may say."

Napoleon grows calmer. Instead of flying into a passion, as Lucien dreaded for a moment, he controls himself, and says quietly:

"Talleyrand is right. You speak of the affair with an ardour worthy of a political club. Such eloquence, Citoyen, is, believe me, long since out of fashion. I am well aware that you did me good service on the Nineteenth Brumaire; but as for having been my 'saviour,' of that proof is lacking. This much I remember clearly, that you disputed with me the unity of power which I needed for the saving of France, and that I and Joseph spent half a night before we could get you to pledge yourself to silence when these questions should be touched upon. . . . Finally, after the victory, you were inclined to oppose my personal elevation, and this conduct on your part releases me from all obligation to show gratitude.

"But you, do you owe me no gratitude? When you 'saved' me at Saint-Cloud, were not you yourself in mortal peril? I sent my grenadiers to save you from the hands of assassins. And if you, a bad brother, an unnatural brother, had really allowed that vote of my outlawry to be taken, do you imagine that I should have been such a fool as to accept the decree unresistingly? Had I not adherents enough, with God's aid, to defend this head that was destined to wear so many crowns?" He goes on to speak for a whole hour of those days, and of Corsican compatriots who had helped him; suddenly gives the conversation an intimate turn; speaks of his generals and the extent of their devotion; refers to political conflicts in which the brothers had held divergent views, and shows how his view had been right. Then he changes the subject, saying abruptly:

"Enough. That is all ancient history, like your great day of the Nineteenth Brumaire. I did not summon you that we might deliver lectures to one another." A long pause.

"Listen to me, Lucien, and weigh my words carefully, for, above all, let us avoid getting heated. . . . I am too powerful to have any desire to lose my temper. You have come to me trustfully. Corsican hospitality shall never be violated by the Emperor of the French. This virtue of our forefathers and fellow-countrymen is a guarantee for your absolute safety." The Emperor strides up and down the hall for a long time, pulling himself together, and then turns to Lucien, whose hand he takes and presses:

"We are alone here. You see? We are alone. No one can overhear us. I am wrong about your marriage. . . . Knowing your wilfulness as I did, knowing your self-love—for everything, you know, depends on self-love, which regards itself as a virtue, just as we princes dignify by the name of policy everything which turns on our passions—I ought not to have interfered with your union. People slandered your wife to me, though some ventured to speak well of her, especially Mamma, who loves her, saying she makes you happy and is a good mother. . . . Lebrun, indeed, has sung her praises, so often that Josephine once told the good fellow he must be in love with her himself. I was very much amused at my wife, who has more of a temper than people fancy. Still, I must say that Josephine never shows her claws to me! Well, I have no disrespect for your wife, but I detest her because this passion of yours for her has robbed me of the most capable of my brothers. However, her beauty will pass; you will be disillusioned; then, returning to political life, you will oppose my policy, and I shall have to take measures against you whether I like it or not; for—let me say this to you—unless you are on my side, Europe is too small for the pair of us!"

"You are making fun of me."

"No, I'm in earnest; friend or foe! It is easier for you today than ever before. You need not be surprised: there has been a change in my family policy. You will see soon enough. Your children, which hitherto I have wanted to exclude, can now be of great use to me, but they must be dynastically recognised. The offspring of a marriage I do not recognise can have no right to the throne. Tell me, then, what would you do in my place?"

Lucien advises him to make the Senate pass a simple resolution to the effect that the children come within the right of succession.

"Of course I know that I can do that, but I must not. As you said just now, public opinion has to be conciliated. What would the family, the court, France, which all watch my slightest movements, say about such a step? A recantation of that kind would do me more harm than the loss of a battle."

Lucien points out that he cannot possibly ask pardon for a marriage which had been entered into long before Napoleon's accession to the throne. "Grant my request, Sire. You will have no more faithful servant than I. All the rest of my life will be an expression of my gratitude."

The younger man goes on talking for a long time, and throughout his speech Napoleon is incessantly taking snuff, but spilling most of the tobacco, so nervous is he, growing more and more anxious; in his perplexity exclaiming at length: "Good God, you press me hard, and I am weak. But I shall not be so weak as to move the Senate to pass the resolution you ask for. I cannot recognise your wife!"

Thereupon Lucien, who is now almost beside himself, says: "Well, then, Sire, what do you really want of me?"

"What do I want? Simply that you should divorce your wife."

"But you have always maintained that we are not married, so how can we get a divorce?"

"I expected you to say that. What do you think I can mean by asking you to procure a divorce? Obviously, thereby I recognise your marriage, but not your wife. The divorce will be the best thing for your children, just like all that you have hitherto refused to do, all that I have so much wanted you to do: to annul the marriage and divorce her."

"That would be a dishonour for me and my children, and I will never do it!"

"Why is it, that with all your mother wit, you cannot see the difference between my earlier proposals and my present ones. In the former case, if your marriage had been declared null, your children would have become bastards!"

Lucien points out the difference between his children's dynastic rights and their civic rights. "You can bestow your thrones upon whom you will, Sire, for you won them at the point of the sword. But no one shall cheat my children out of their share in the modest heritage of Carlo Bonaparte, for they are as legitimate as any one else's both by canon law and by State law. The pope has even given one of my daughters the name of his mother!"

"Calm yourself! . . . Of course the divorce I ask for implies the recognition of your marriage. Nor do I wish to force an actual separation from your wife. She shall be honoured in accordance with her merits if she will make this sacrifice to my policy and to the future interests of France. I would even pay her a visit. But if she refuses, you and she will both be blamed for having sacrificed the true greatness of your children to your own egoism, and your children will curse your memory!"

Lucien answers mournfully.

"You are really incorrigible," rejoins Napoleon. "You take everything so tragically. I am not asking for any tragedies! Think it over."

After Lucien has again and again insisted upon his point of honour, and has several times wished to take leave, the Emperor once more brings up the distribution of the thrones. Eugene's position in Italy is merely provisional, and he would much rather see Lucien installed there. Napoleon complains about Hortense, too. None of them are satisfied. "Pauline is naturally the most reasonable in the matter of ambition, for she is the queen of fashion. Besides, she grows more lovely day by day. Josephine is ageing, and is greatly distressed about a divorce."

Lucien pricks up his ears. Napoleon goes on as if he were talking at random:

"Can you believe it? She always bursts into tears when her digestion is a little upset, for she fancies she is being poisoned by those who would like me to marry some one else. That is despicable. Still, in the end, I shall have to get a divorce. I ought to have taken the step long ago, and I should have had quite big children by now; for, I may as well tell you"—he speaks earnestly—"people are wrong in thinking it is my fault we have no children. I have several. Two I know of for certain." He mentions, without naming her, Leon's mother; and then, wonder of wonders, the Polish countess. "She is an exquisite woman, an angel. . . . You laugh to see that I am in love. Yes, I really am; but I never forget considerations of policy. She wants me to marry a princess. Of course, as far as feelings go, I would much rather raise my beloved to the throne. You, in your dealings with your wife, ought in like manner to be guided by considerations of policy!"

"Sire, I should act as you are doing if my wife were only my mistress."

The Emperor grows more and more animated; speaks of a fixed intention to get a divorce; deplores having given the Bavarian princess to Eugene, who does not care for her and did not choose her for himself; remarks that he might long since have had Lucien's daughter betrothed to the prince of Asturia "or some other great prince, perhaps even a great emperor. . . . Your divorce would have to precede mine, or be simultaneous. Then there would be less chatter about my divorce; for yours, in view of your obstinate refusal for so long previously, will certainly arouse more interest. Will you do me this service? I think you really ought to."

Lucien looks at him so quizzically that the Emperor is amazed, eyes his brother up and down, and says: "Why not?"

Lucien smiles at the unreasonableness of the demand. Napoleon is embarrassed, but returns to the charge. Suddenly he addresses his brother as "my dear President" (Lucien having long ago been president of the Council of Five Hundred), and adds with emphasis: "Service for service, of course—and this time you will not find me ungrateful!"

Lucien sank "into a sort of reverie, which was by no means unpleasant," so that for a few moments he hardly noticed what Napoleon was talking about. Before long he realised that the Emperor was saying, confidentially, that his only reason for wanting Lucien's divorce was that this would probably minimise the effect of his own on public opinion. Lucien, as tactfully as he could, alluded to his own advantages, pointing out that his wife was a young woman and was not barren. Napoleon took no offence. "Your wife, oh, yes, your wife, didn't I tell you? She will become the duchess of Parma, your eldest boy will be her heir, without having any claim of succession to your rights as a French prince. For this is only the first stage to which I shall raise you, until something better can be found: an independent crown."

At the word "independent," Lucien cannot restrain a smile, for he is thinking of the part his brothers have to play. Napoleon notices the expression on his face.

"Yes, independent. You will know how to reign. . . . You need only take your choice!" His eyes flash fire, and he bangs the enormous map with the flat of his hand. "I'm not talking at random. All this belongs to me or soon will. Even to-day, I can do what I please. Would you like to have Naples? I will take it away from Joseph. . . . Italy, the loveliest jewel in my imperial crown? Eugene is no more than viceroy. He hopes to become king, expects to outlive me, but he will be disappointed in this matter. I shall live to be ninety, for I cannot do with less than that for the complete consolidation of my empire. Besides, Eugene will not suit me in Italy, after I have divorced his mother. Would you care for Spain? Do you not see that it is ripe to fall into my hands, thanks to the blunders of the Bourbons you are so fond of? Would you not like to be king in the country to which you went as envoy? What would you prefer to have? It is for you to say. Anything and everything is at your disposal, if only you will divorce your wife before I divorce mine!"

Lucien is spell-bound for a time by the feverish haste with which Napoleon speaks. At last he says: "Not even your lovely France, Sire, would bribe me to this divorce; and besides. . . ." He hesitates; but the Emperor guesses his thoughts, and says dryly, with an imperious air such as Lucien has never before seen him assume:

"Do you think that you, as a private individual, are in a more secure position than I upon my throne? . . . Do you believe that your friend the pope is strong enough to protect you against me if I should seriously propose to take measures against you?" After reiterating arguments and enticements, he says in a formal tone: "You may be quite sure of this: everything for the divorced Lucien; nothing for the undivorced!"

Lucien glances at the door, as a hint to the Emperor that he would be glad to be given his dismissal; but Napoleon takes him by the hand, and says "in a vague tone, and with a demeanour which might mean anything":

"If I get a divorce, you will not be the only other one. Joseph is merely waiting for my divorce to arrange for his own. Madame Julie has been good for nothing but to bring girls into the world, whereas I urgently need boys. The only use of girls is to marry them off in advantageous alliances. Besides, your eldest girl is nearly fourteen, so you tell me; just the right age. Won't you send her to Mamma? If you do what I want, I will get Mamma to arrange something good for her. . . . You are not afraid that we shall do any harm to your spoiled darling? Tell her we shall be good friends, and that I will not pull her ears as if she were a child. . . . I need more nephews and nieces! The divorced Josephine, the grandmother of Hortense's children, will always be the enemy of my legitimate and my adopted sons." Then, murmuring as if to himself, "It must be done. I have no other way of undermining the power of Louis' and Hortense's children."

He comes back to the subject of his own illegitimate children, says he intends to adopt them, enters into details, and suddenly exclaims: "You cannot suppose that I have not the power to legitimise my natural children, just as Louis XIV. declared his bastards, the fruit of a twofold adultery, to be within the right of succession to the throne." Again he speaks of Joseph's intention to procure a divorce, and, when Lucien is sceptical, he rubs his hands delightedly, saying:

"Yes, yes! Joseph and you will both divorce your wives! We will all three get divorces, and then marry again, all of us, on the very same day!" He adds a number of quips in the like merry vein. Then, suddenly: "But why have you become so serious? One might think you a sage of classical antiquity! You must stay with me for three days. I'll have a bed made ready for you in the next room to mine!"

He presses this invitation. Lucien, who dreads his brother's blandishments, has to invent an excuse, and says that one of his children is ill.

His wife, he goes on to say, has suffered because of the Emperor's dislike; so much so, that he had been afraid at one time her anxiety and distress about the matter would be too much for her.

"Is that really so? I'm sorry. You must take care of her! Whatever happens, she must not die before you get your divorce, for if she did I should not be able to legitimise her children!"

Lucien pretends that he will think the matter over.

"That's all right. Well, well, go if you must! But be sure to keep your word!" Napoleon takes Lucien by the hand, and at the same time presents his cheek for a kiss, which is not as brotherly as it might be. Lucien departs, and when he is in the anteroom he hears the Emperor calling: "Méneval!"

Lucien quickens his steps, for again the dread of imprisonment has seized him.

No one, no historian and no imaginative writer, has ever given a more brilliant escription of Napoleon than the foregoing, penned by his brother with obvious fidelity. This evening, the Emperor is in a quandary. He wants the help of a man whom he cannot coerce, and one who in certain respects is his equal. In the light thrown by Lucien, Napoleon's character becomes positively transparent. He develops himself under our very eyes, showing us all the interplay of his motives.

He lavishes temptations in the endeavour to overpersuade his adversary. Every move is carefully thought out, that it may exercise its appropriate influence upon the ambition of his interlocutor, whom he tries to win by the studied gradations of the dialogue. The visitor finds him brooding over the map of Europe, and is greeted in a way which is to alarm and to inspire confidence by turns. The wife, the bone of contention, is first vilified and then extolled. Napoleon goes back to the phraseology of the Jacobin Club, calls his brother "citizen," pulls out one emotional stop after another. He reminds Lucien that they are both Corsicans; says with a challenging irony that Europe is too small for the pair of them; talks of Mamma and Pauline, of Joseph and Louis, using names that carry with them reminiscences of the nursery in which the Bonaparte children had played together. Thus he spins his web round Lucien.

And yet—this is the marvel—we are shown the bubbling up of his nature, the beating of his heart, the quivering of his brain. Again and ever again, imagination and passion seem to carry him beyond the limits of self-restraint. Though his brother is a declared opponent, he makes all kinds of confessions: about Josephine and the countess; about his stepchildren and his generals; about his own blunders and his new, far-reaching plans. There is a flood of confidential admissions. Why?

Because this Lucien, though an adversary, though no less gifted than Talleyrand, is a brother, and therefore, to the clannish Napoleon, is, in spite of everything, worthy of confidence. It moves us to see the way in which Napoleon detains him in private talk for hours, till midnight is long past; how he presses Lucien to stay for a few days, that they may thrash matters out; and how Lucien insists on going, not because he really needs to, but because he does not wish to bow before the force of his brother's genius. For there is a secret contest between the pair, not about love or divorce, not about honour or crowns. To-day, just as seven years before, when the younger man could not bring himself to obey the elder, the contest is between the innermost self-esteem of one rival and of the other. After all these years, in the privacy of his own thoughts Lucien is still convinced that he could have managed everything much better than Napoleon.

And yet, all the time, he loves him after his own fashion. Every word of his report betrays the obscure enmity between the brothers, the enmity that lives side by side with love. That is why he concedes nothing. The memory of the Nineteenth Brumaire has to be revived, and once more each of them is confident he was right. While these expert realists are talking, with the old phrases on their lips, the old verbiage about the greatness and the safety of France, they are really moved by nothing but their own passions. We seem to see them posturing before the crowd (a doubt seizes them—"We are alone here. You see. We are alone. No one can overhear us"); but in truth they are alone, in a strange and foreign castle, beneath huge candelabra, on which the candles are burning low.

Nevertheless, despite Napoleon's wealth and all his crowns, despite his stupendous powers of intellect and imagination, how poor a man he is, entangled in the threads of destiny, the threads which he has spun, but which are now spinning themselves in defiance of his wishes! For all his omnipotence, he is the slave of an incalculable, much-courted power, public opinion, which will not allow him to effect a reconciliation with his brother, to recognise his own children, or to marry the woman he loves. The impotence of the man of might is displayed in his own exclamations. He asseverates his power to do anything and everything—and yet he dare not do what he wants. How pleased he is with his brother, whose affairs he could manage so beautifully now that they have met after many years of separation. If Lucien would only stay with him, were it but for three days, they would certainly be able to come to an understanding. "Good God, you press me hard, and I am weak."

During this night when an emperor was offering his brother a choice among the thrones of Europe, was there not talk of the heritage of Carlo Bonaparte, a poor nobleman, on a small, out-of-the-way island? Did the Emperor of the French, who will never hear a word of his being a foreigner in France, conjure up the shade of the Corsican; was it he who evoked the penates of his birthplace for the protection of Brother Lucien, a negotiator in a hostile camp? Surely what we are recounting is a saga, told at midnight beside the fireplace in Mantua? Yes, it is the saga which the little Corsican lieutenant has woven out of the threads of his life: first a narrow band; but as he trails it after him, twists it and loops it, mixes colours and patterns, by degrees a carpet is formed; greater and more varied become the pictures produced out of the one thread, pictures of lands and thrones, of seas and men.

The whole has been woven in the most natural way in the world. Not by a miracle, but only through the working of his talents, has the man become master of men. To-night he wants to add yet another to the long list of his subjects. He has not enough time, even though he hopes to live till he is ninety. He cannot allow his brothers to have girl children, or to live with the women of their choice. But if these undesired nieces throng his stage, he must set up new nephews against them. If a wife is in danger of dying of grief, she must at least be good enough to wait until she is divorced. When the men of the family have at length forsaken the wives who are barren or can only bear daughters, then, on the same day, they will take new wives unto themselves—and all will go happily ever after. Look at him, when the conversation is drawing to a close, rubbing his hands in his satisfaction, the little magician who stands in front of his immense map. By the time he has impaled all the countries with his coloured pins, impaled them like butterflies to put away in his collection—well, by that time the candles have burned out and a large slice of to-morrow has already been devoured.

XII

THE DOCTORS MAYO [1]

By

HELEN CLAPESATTLE

Even among distinguished surgeons, this trio, the father, Dr. William W. Mayo (1820-1911), and the two sons, Dr. Charles Mayo (1865-1939) and Dr. William Mayo (1861-1939), stand as professional giants. Their magnificent achievements in medicine cover nearly a century and have transformed Rochester, Minnesota, from a small prairie city to one of the world's significant medical centers.

The biography conveys the spirit of these doctors—their struggles against great obstacles, their determination to learn the latest medical developments and the peculiar genius which enabled the father and the two brothers to make so great a contribution to their profession.

A COMPETENT SURGEON IN HIS OWN RIGHT

The chairman [Dr. William Mayo] of the state's surgeons could not admit that any operation performed by others was beyond him. In November 1888 Dr. Will was called to Kasson to examine a woman for what proved to be an ovarian tumor. Normally slight, she was now huge, and she had a nasty burn across her abdomen that she had got in reaching for something that was burning on the cookstove; her great belly had hit the stove before her hand could reach the pan. To examine her Dr. Will had her lie down on a horsehair sofa in the parlor, and as she attempted to turn onto her side at his request, the weight of the tumor upset her balance and she fell off onto the floor. Dr. Will had to call for help to get her up again.

[1] Helen Clapesattle, *The Doctors Mayo*, Minneapolis: The University of Minnesota Press, 1941, pp. 230-231, 448-449, 453-454, 457-459.

When he heard his son's report, the Old Doctor set the operation for the following Sunday morning and sent word of it to the doctors roundabout. Then he received a note from Dr. A. J. Stone in St. Paul, asking him to come up for consultation on a case there, and he left, planning to be back by Saturday night. But he did not come. Nor did he arrive on the first train Sunday morning.

By the hour set for the operation, some fifteen doctors had gathered at Mrs. Carpenter's, the patient was waiting, and with her several relatives who had left small children alone at home. They could not be asked to come back later, so taking his courage in his hands, Dr. Will told the woman *he* would do the operation if she was willing. She was, and with the assistance of Dr. Charlie, Dr. Clarke, and Dr. A. W. Stinchfield of Eyota, Will removed the tumor. It was enormous, completely filling the washtub they put it in, and the watching doctors were greatly impressed.

Although everything had gone off very well, Dr. Will spent the day wondering what his father would say. A little fearfully he went down to meet the evening train, which brought Dr. Mayo and with him Dr. Stone. Dr. Mayo had stayed over in St. Paul to assist at Dr. Stone's operation and had brought that gentleman back to watch his own, which he was planning to do the next morning. He was in high spirits, gloating a little, Will thought, over the fine case he had to show his St. Paul friend.

Hesitantly Will told them he had done the operation that morning. His father was speechless. And Dr. Stone sat down on the station steps, beat his hat against the platform's edge, and laughed till the tears came at the thought of the boy's stealing his father's big case. Then the three men went down to Mrs. Carpenter's together, saw that the patient was doing well, and took a look at the tumor in the washtub. Dr. Will always felt that on that occasion his father fully realized for the first time that his son had become a thoroughly competent surgeon in his own right.

GREAT SURGEONS AT THE OPERATING TABLE

Early in 1906 there was published in Boston a description by Dr. George N. P. Mead of a trip he had just made to the little Minnesota town. On the train he found himself one of eight doctors bound for Rochester, from California, Texas, Iowa, Kentucky, New York, and Massachusetts. Going directly to the hospital upon their arrival, they were conducted into a moderately large, well-lighted operating room, where Dr. W. J. Mayo was performing a resection of the stomach. When he had finished the major part of the procedure, he suggested that the visitors go into the next room where his brother was doing some work he was sure they would wish to see. They went reluctantly, feeling sure they could not possibly see anything as fine as what they just witnessed.

But they were quickly disabused of that notion. The younger brother was doing a thyroidectomy for exophthalmic goiter "with remarkable skill." The men watched in fascination, for the patient was stirring so restlessly that most surgeons would have stopped operating, "and would have sworn too. Not so Dr. Charles Mayo. He went right on, where a single false cut might have meant a bad case of bleeding, or the severing of a nerve and possible paralysis; he cut true, with a marvelous sureness and dexterity of touch, and the job was soon done."

The visitors spent the morning that way, passing back and forth between the two operating theaters. Dr. Will alone did ten operations, and Dr. Mead reported that together the two brothers were doing four thousand operations a year, "a total that is simply staggering."

Describing the Mayos' habit of traveling to learn any method they heard of that sounded good, which made Rochester "an almost automatic clearing house for the best work of the world's hospitals," and adding to it the thorough work of diagnosis carried on at "the Shop," the brothers' offices, Dr. Mead concluded, "It is no wonder that foreign surgeons count Rochester one of the places in America that simply must be seen." . . .

There was as much to be heard as seen in a Mayo clinic, for the brothers accompanied their operations with a running clinical commentary, reviewing the case history and the diagnosis, describing the conditions they found, and explaining what they did and why. In these talks they ranged through the whole of medical science, literature, and history, giving freely the convictions born of their wide reading and experience and, according to one listener, bringing out "points in surgical anatomy and physiology in a way so plain and forceful that one marvels at the barrenness of textbook literature on such matters."

At the operating table they illustrated with unforgettable object lessons the principles of differential diagnosis, antemortem pathology, and early surgery that filled their formal papers. No man could attend Dr. Will's clinics very often without witnessing such a demonstration as this: The history, read by the assistant while the anesthetic was given, was a classic one of "stomach trouble"—years of treatment for indigestion without relief—yet when incision brought the stomach into view it looked perfectly normal.

"You have heard the history, gentlemen, but you see this stomach. In my opinion there is nothing wrong with it; the trouble is somewhere else. If I am right in a few minutes you will notice a spasm of the pylorus." Shortly a spasm of the pyloric muscles was evident to all.

"That does not tell us where the trouble is, but it is not in the stomach. I will see if it is in the appendix." And he pulled into view a badly diseased appendix.

Then as he proceeded to remove the appendix and close the abdomen he told them of his own experience. . . .

Both men were perfectly frank about their role, constantly telling visitors where they had picked up this good thing or that. Sometimes it was from their father, often from Joseph Price, Ochsner, Murphy, or Halsted. "I used to do this differently, but Moynihan showed me his method when he was here and it was better, so I use it now," Dr. Will would say. And Dr. Charlie, "The first time I tried this operation I got stuck at this point, but Dr. George Monk of Boston was here and he told me what to do."

Many of their listeners, more used to the kind of man who "invented" some good method or instrument he had seen used in Europe, were humbled by the Mayos' simple honesty. When they spoke to the brothers about it or complimented them on their constant efforts to keep on learning from other surgeons, the answer was merely an echo from the Old Doctor: "No man is big enough to be independent of others." Or Dr. Charlie would cite the European surgeon who was doing several hundred abdominal operations a year but who never bothered to see or read what others were doing, so that he was proud of a mortality of sixteen per cent when others had reduced it to three.

Dr. Will and Dr. Charlie pretended to infallibility no more than they did to originality. In some American clinics the morning schedule would list several "abdominal operations," a vagueness that permitted the surgeon to make sure of his diagnosis while the assistant was reading the case history. The Mayos always listed a specific diagnosis, or if they had been unable to reach one they admitted it with "Explore stomach, duodenum, and gallbladder." If their diagnosis proved wrong they called for a rereading of the history and in the presence of their visitors, and sometimes with their aid, tried to discover what had led them astray.

Some surgeons, notably John B. Murphy, saved the difficult operations for doing in private, but every visitor was welcome to see any operation the Mayos did and learn from the hard luck as well as the good. Often the master was most fully revealed when things went wrong. Among Dr. W. J. Mayo's outstanding characteristics as a surgeon, next to his remarkable judgment as to how far he could go in an operation—when to go in and when to get out—was his imperturbability in a crisis.

One day he was removing a tumor of the kidney. As an upheaval of the ocean floor might render useless the navigator's charts, so the huge growth had pushed all the familiar surgical landmarks out of place and attached itself to the adjoining body parts. As Dr. Will lifted it to the surface, the largest vein in the body was ruptured; blood welled forth in a horrifying flow that would have ended life in a few minutes.

With one flash of his finger Dr. Mayo found and plugged the rent, entirely by his trained sense of touch, for the blood shut everything else from sight.

Then he said quietly to the tense watchers, "Gentlemen, I have torn the *vena cava* and it will be necessary to make another incision to repair the vein."

He stitched up the tear, made sure it was tight, and then went calmly on with the task of cutting the growth away from the tissue to which it was attached. Suddenly the tumor came loose, making a long tear in the bowel. Dr. Mayo continued talking: "This, gentlemen, is a much more serious accident than the injury to the vein. I have torn a long rent in the duodenum and if it is not made intact, the contents will leak out and the patient will live but a few days." Then slowly and carefully he sutured the torn bowel before he went on to complete the work on the kidney.

The operation took three and a half hours. At the end the spectators were exhausted by the strain and stared in awe at the outwardly unperturbed man who had carried the responsibility.

Either accident would have meant death in the hands of the average surgeon, so the men naturally watched the postoperative course of the case with great interest. There were no complications, no signs of shock, and the patient progressed smoothly to a complete recovery.

Asked one time to compare the two Mayos as surgeons, Dr. Haggard replied, "Dr. Will is a wonderful surgeon; Dr. Charlie is a surgical wonder." The amazing characteristics in Dr. Charlie were his versatility and ingenuity. Other surgeons could not get over the ease with which he turned from removing a thyroid in one case to taking out a prostate or a varicose vein in the next, always with admirable skill. To him was due the range of surgery at Rochester, which made it possible for one man to say, "If you stay here long enough you can see every operation known to surgery."

His ingenuity in devising operative procedures for the unusual case became a byword in the profession. The fellows of the American Surgical

Association met in Rochester one year and, wanting to see Dr. Charlie's peculiar talent in action, they asked Dr. Will to select some difficult case that Charlie had not examined and let them see what he did with it. As Dr. Will told the story:

> I chose the case of a woman who had been operated on seven times before coming here, and whose condition was apparently hopeless of surgical repair, and had the Fellows examine her. They all agreed that it was a case hopeless of relief, and so the whole crowd was prepared to see Charlie floored. The patient was placed before him, and when he looked at the ghastly postoperative results he whistled. Then, without apparent effort, he outlined an entirely new plan of operative treatment, which was successful, and the crowd of doctors was simply dazed.

XIII

THOREAU[1]

By

HENRY SEIDEL CANBY

Henry David Thoreau (1817-1862), an American naturalist and author, was born at Concord, Massachusetts. He believed that the less work a man did, above providing for the necessities, the better for him and society. From July, 1845, to September, 1847, he lived in a hut of his own construction on the pine slope of Walden Pond, a beautiful body of water on the outskirts of Concord. He did a little surveying, cultivated a few acres, and devoted most of his time to the study of nature and to his friends. His *Walden*, perhaps his most popular book, is the record of his two years at Walden Pond. The chief friendship of his life was that with Emerson.

Dr. Canby has produced an excellent biography which gives one a rich appreciation of the Man of Walden. He has written us that "the most famous episode in Thoreau's life is the case of his going to jail as a protest against paying a tax to support a state whose principles he didn't approve."

ON HIM THEY COULD NOT CALCULATE

Thoreau's most sensational experience was a brief but significant conflict with the political state, which has since become as famous as his plea for Civil Disobedience which inspired Gandhi's campaign in India. When young, he had been, like Emerson, of Whiggish tendencies, anti-Jackson, anti-Democratic so far as he had been anything political at all. After that curious letter in pseudo-Indian language to John, there is not the slightest indication of interest in politics as such until the slavery issue began to force itself upon his attention. He never voted. But as this issue, with all it involved for the Union and for a citizen, mounted toward an irrepres-

[1] Henry Seidel Canby, *Thoreau*, by permission of the publishers, Houghton Mifflin Company, Boston, 1939, pp. 231-238.

sible conflict, politics began, as today, to involve the least politically minded. Thoreau heartily wished that government would take care of itself while he went about his business, in which he was typically American. But government, the weak, easy-going government of the American thirties and forties, began to get itself into trouble. Pocketbooks were touched by the tariff, patriotism was involved by states' rights, conscience was stung by slavery. In its blundering action more and more interests were trampled on. Finally, government trod on Thoreau.

In 1838 he had protested a tax levied for the benefit of the established church, but was allowed to 'sign off.' That issue was dead. But in 1846 it was not so easy to be a neutral. Texas had been annexed in 1845, Polk had been elected on an imperialistic platform, the Mexican War, which in one of its aspects was a war to extend the slave-holding area into the Southwest, was formally declared on May 13, 1846. Thoreau's Abolitionist family must have been abuzz with anti-slavery talk.

In late July, when blueberries (he makes them huckleberries, perhaps to suit the altered date in 'Walden') were ripe, and men were sitting in their shirtsleeves on account of the heat, Henry walked from Walden early one evening in to Concord to get a mended shoe from the cobbler's. Shoes were always an important item in his economy. He had not paid his poll-tax for some years—for six, he said in 'Civil Disobedience' when it was published in 1849—probably not since 1843 when Alcott set the example and was arrested. Taxes, as such, he paid readily, but the poll-tax he felt to be the specific imposition of the political state—a state which, as he says in the 'Walden' version of the story, buys and sells men, and women, and children, meaning slaves. In 1846, the Mexican War stiffened his resistance. 'When a sixth of the population of a nation which has undertaken to be the refuge of liberty are slaves, and a whole country is unjustly overrun and conquered by a foreign army, and subjected to military law, I think that it is not too soon for honest men to rebel and revolutionize.' So he wrote in 'Civil Disobedience'—so he felt when they arrested him on that July evening. He had quietly declared war with the state, after his fashion, by refusing to let his dollar buy 'a man or a musket to shoot one with . . . though I will still make what use and get what advantage of her [the state] I can, as is usual in such cases.'

Was it perhaps Thoreau's unpopularity as a setter of forest fires which led the authorities to choose him as an example from among the passive resistants to the state? Did they fear that Alcott and others more important might begin stirring up trouble again because of 'principle'? At all events, he was 'seized and put into jail,' and had a most interesting night there with his cell companion, who was an alleged barn-burner, and (later) thoroughly enjoyed the idea that the poor Walden student had made the state 'run "amok"' against him, it being the desperate party which could make its will prevail only by force and with no permanent results. 'I do not hear of *men* being *forced* to live this way or that by masses of men.' Not Yankees, at least, who lived by principle—certainly not a minority made up of Thoreaus. 'I saw that the State . . . did not know its friends from its foes.'

Julian Hawthorne in his 'Memoirs' tells a different story. He reports there that Thoreau lost his temper when he was jailed. This seems to be true. Sam Staples, his jailor, interviewed many years later, said Henry 'was mad as the devil' when he turned him loose in the morning. Thoreau was a great rationalizer of his emotions when the time came to philosophize them! Unhappily, the famous story of Emerson's visit to the jail must also be rewritten. 'Henry, why are you there?' he is supposed to have said, to be answered, 'Why are you not here?' If there was such a question, it came later, after Henry's release, for Sam locked up his prisoners early, took his boots off, and wouldn't unlock them again even after the fine was paid. The phrasing also must have been different. Emerson knew precisely why he was there, since both Transcendentalists insisted upon the prerogatives of the individual in defiance of the will of the rulers of the state. That is what Henry really meant by the state—its rulers. He was not intransigent against his duties to society, but against the intransigence of rulers in what he regarded as the essential right of the individual to preserve his moral integrity. With this Emerson, of course, agreed. The issue between them—and it was real—was on what grounds a man should take his stand. Thoreau had found Alcott's previous arrest on principle a rather admirable gesture until the archangel began talking about it as if it were a revolution. Now that Thoreau was arrested, Emerson felt much the same way about him. He told Alcott in July of 1846, as Alcott records in his Journal, that it was 'mean and skulking, and in bad taste.' 'I defended it,' says Alcott, 'on the grounds of a dignified non-compliance with the injunction of civil powers.'

But Emerson's private comment was made in his Journal for the same month: 'Mr. Webster told them how much the war cost . . . and sends his son to it. They calculated rightly on Mr. Webster. My friend Mr. Thoreau has gone to jail rather than pay his tax. On him they could not calculate.' It was perhaps bad taste and a little mean for Thoreau to make an issue over a poll-tax, and thus, while great problems were being thrust upon the idealists who were on the side of the angels, to fight over a straw, and raise the question whether his friends and sympathizers, and Emerson among them, whose influence was so much greater than his own, were not also and merely stiffnecked obstructionists. Nevertheless, the state could not calculate on any subservience from Henry Thoreau.

He was in jail only one night, yet long enough for the valuable experience of seeing his townsmen from the point of view of those condemned for not conforming to the rules by which Concord lived. Then, according to Jane Hosmer, 'When his mother heard of his arrest, she hastened to the Jail, then to the Thoreau house in the Square, at which Misses Jane and Maria Thoreau then lived, and one of the latter [Aunt Maria in disguise, says Annie Russell Marble in her biography], putting a shawl over her head, went to the jailer's door, and paid the tax and fees to Ellen Staples, her father the jailer being absent.' Either Henry forbade his mother to pay, or she had not enough money at hand.

And so, by no act of his own, but unjailable again except for a new offense, Henry came out, got his shoe, and went huckleberrying, while his neighbors first looked at him and then at one another, 'as if I had returned from a long journey. . . . This is the whole history of "My Prisons."' Yet he was a little inclined to agree with Emerson that, in itself, it was not too noble a history. 'One cannot be too much on his guard in such a case,' he wrote in 'Civil Disobedience,' from which the quotations above are taken, 'lest his action be biased by obstinacy or an undue regard for the opinions of men. Let him see that he does only what belongs to himself and to the hour.' And so, having made his gesture, withheld his tax for six years, and got his reactions out of his system in a thundering essay, he paid in 1849 his poll-tax of $1.50, as the tax-book now in the Middlebury College library shows, and let the state look elsewhere for a victim!

RESISTANCE TO THE POWER OF THE STATE

'Civil Disobedience,' the lecture which Alcott liked so much, was written in 1848 as a commentary upon his jailing, of which it contains an account much more extensive than the narrative in 'Walden.' It was published in May of 1849 in Elizabeth Peabody's symposium of papers from old *Dial* contributors, called *Aesthetic Papers*, which was to be followed by others if the public responded, which they did not. 'Civil Disobedience' attracted no attention at the time, but has since gone round the world. It was Gandhi's source-book in his Indian campaign for Civil Resistance, and has been read and pondered by thousands who hope to find some way to resist semingly irresistible force.

The extraordinary effectiveness of Thoreau's essay on resistance to the power of the state is not due to any dramatic necessity in the cause that produced it. Here it has the Anglo-Saxon quality of understatement. No tyrant, no dictator, no Oriental despotism is even thought of by this Concord citizen of the most easy-going of republics. He assumes a democratic system. He assumes majority rule. He assumes a weak government, not a strong one. He does not exaggerate his act of rebellion, laughs at it a little, wonders if he has been too obstinate; then clamps down suddenly on the principle involved, which is good for all weathers. The most liberal government becomes a tyranny when it denies the right of the individual to be responsible for his intellectual and moral integrity. It can overrule him, yes, but he must somehow resist. If he is a crank, an opponent of order, which is essential to the state, if he is a self-centered egotist, he will suffer, and let him suffer. If, however, his integrity is based on values indispensable to a self-respecting man, then resistance is also indispensable, and will become a power unconquerable in the long run, even by force.

The political weakness of this argument is obvious. It leaves one of those wide margins that Thoreau liked in his thinking as well as in his life, and this time a wide margin of possible error. For if the individual is to determine his own rights, what authority is left to distingush between enlightened resistance to the rulers of a state, and anarchy, which will inevitably dissolve the state itself? Thoreau would have answered that you must have faith in man, you must believe that an intuition of what is necessary for survival is a reality in human nature. And it is the only possible answer.

But this was not the lesson which thousands have learned since from 'Civil Disobedience.' The metaphysics of politics concerns them as little as it concerned Thoreau. The conflict of man against the state is real, no matter what one thinks of its rules. It wanes, it waxes—we have reached or are nearing again one of its periodical crises. There will always be those who are faced with the sacrifice either of their just rights or their security. How can those who are determined to resist oppose, with any hope of success, a régime of irresistible force? Thoreau, writing in an America soon to be in the throes of a great rebellion, was not at that time, nor for any time, thinking of mass rebellion where motives are mixed and the objective is always power. He was concerned with the individual whose power can only be his own integrity. For him he counsels passive resistance, and this is the answer which has made his essay famous:

A very few . . . serve the state with their consciences . . . and so necessarily resist it for the most part; and they are commonly treated as enemies by it. . . .

I was not born to be forced. I will breathe after my own fashion. . . . If a plant cannot live according to its nature, it dies; and so a man. . . .

There will never be a really free and enlightened State until the State comes to recognize the individual as a higher and independent power, from which all its own power and authority are derived, and treats him accordingly. I please myself with imagining a State at last which can afford to be just to all men . . . which even would not think it inconsistent with its own repose if a few were to live aloof from it, not meddling with it, nor embraced by it, who fulfilled all the duties of neighbors and fellow-men.

And until such a state arises, he is ready to resist, when necessary, brute force. While he cannot expect successfully to oppose the force itself, his resistance may be effective because it may change the minds of the men that exercise it. And therefore it is not futile quietly to declare war upon your state.

History abundantly proves that such disobedience can be effective. There is perhaps no power in the world today able to overcome aerial bombs and machine guns but intellectual and emotional resistance in Thoreau's sense, by brave men, clear of mind, and able to endure until their conviction becomes infectious.

How would the author of 'Civil Disobedience' act if he were alive today? His revolution was a one-man revolution against a feeble state, concerned for its own prosperity. The dictatorial state, with torture at its command, and a fanaticism as strong and far less reasonable than Thoreau's presents very different problems. His answer, I should say, to the totalitarian idea would be, that such massed individuals as support these states may for the time being be impregnable, are like avalanches, which no man can hope to resist. The citizen will have to step back and, protecting integrity by any concessions possible to it, endeavor to make the nobler moral fervor prevail. But he would disobey rather than rebel, and wrestle with weakness in himself rather than use violence against the despot in the enemy. Gandhi took such a position. He struck at the pocketbook of the state, not at its armies. He refused to conform, but did not attack his rulers.

XIV

A PURITAN IN BABYLON: THE STORY OF CALVIN COOLIDGE [1]

By

WILLIAM ALLEN WHITE

William Allen White has written not only a notable and exceptionally able biography of Calvin Coolidge, but also has related the life of this "Puritan in Babylon" interestingly to the American political scene and the economic development of the nation. Excellent characterization, wit, and a wealth of facts make this biography splendid reading.

Mr. White has given us two selections: one, the story of the marriage of Calvin Coolidge and Grace Goodhue; and the other, the account of Coolidge's death and burial, which Mr. White believes "is the best writing in the book."

COOLIDGE DOES THE BEST DAY'S WORK IN HIS LIFE

The young man [Coolidge] in Northampton had realized that power in politics as an organization leader outside the office takes much time. An honest, poor man cannot afford it. So he refused reelection as chairman of the committee, but stayed on the Republican Central committee where he could have a finger in the pie. He was committed irrevocably to politics—politics for the sake of politics! He had saved a little money in his first ten years out of college. He had been elected twice to office—councilman, and city solicitor—and had served as clerk of the court. He was established as a rising young attorney, vice president of a savings bank with a wide acquaintance in his town and county. He was a poor mixer, using the word mixer to mean one who rather deliberately associates with men who have votes to give, in order to gull the voters by graces and charms of

[1] William Allen White, *A Puritan in Babylon: The Story of Calvin Coolidge,* by permission of The Macmillan Company, publishers, New York, 1938, pp. 60-66, 440-444.

manner. Yet he was a vote-getter. In the evening it was his habit occasionally to loaf downtown. He took his monthly glass of beer at the town beer gardens, stiffly and stodgily without joy in it. He sat almost silently in James Lucey's shoeshop while the loafers' parliament babbled through an evening. The Lucey friendship was one of those illogical attachments that men sometimes make; purely sentimental. Coolidge was given to these odd but genuine displays of affection. Lucey's case was classical. Lucey became attached to the youth in Coolidge's early days, gave him sententious advice, which Coolidge seemed to consider but did not. Lucey probably did teach Coolidge something about the technique of that democratic process known as "handshaking"—personal, direct vote-getting. Moreover, the shoemaker's shop was a good place in which to meet and mix with men whom Coolidge rarely met elsewhere. His barber maintained another such shop and Coolidge frequented one barbershop for nearly forty years. He had his favorite bootblack and barkeeper, he never forgot his father's old hired girl in Plymouth, nor his childhood school teacher. And through all the years while he rose to fame and power, he warmed their friendships in his heart. For after all only his face was frozen! It was said of him at the end that he was as thrifty with his friends as he was with his money. He had Jim Lucey and his first nickel at the end of his life.

Coolidge in those callow days at times might be seen sadly smoking a five-cent cigar in the drug store with the young men of his age for a few minutes after supper before hurrying to his office. Even then old settlers [2] recalled that he used to purse his mouth as though his heart were bursting with some secret sin or sorrow or as though his lips were swelling with an unrelieved chew of tobacco. But he never chewed. Neither was his heart broken. It was his way, his sad visaged demeanor. Yet withal men trusted him; probably because in a gabbling world he did not babble. He learned about men in the shoeshop, at the barbershop, around the soda fountain, before the bar of the tavern. For he was a shrewd Yankee, smarter than chain-lightning about the ways of men. He could tinker with certain cogs and levers in the human heart better than most, and not in cold blood either. For he loved his kind.

In those days his body filled out. Its gaunt gawkiness went. His face grew full but never plump. His hair was still carroty, though darkening into chestnut, and his eyes, always the beacons of his intelligence, were expressive. When he opened them they revealed a man that men could trust even if they did not return his repressed, undemonstrative love. So

[2] Conversations with the author of Coolidge's Northampton friends—Lucey, Field, Jager, et al—in 1924 and again in 1933 are authority for statements made in this chapter about Coolidge and his Northampton environment. Something of the same material is found in early biographies by Washburn, Woods, Hennessy and Sawyer.

knocking about Northampton with his heart set on two things, his account in the savings bank and his popular strength at any possible election, this Yankee tinkerer with humanity must have realized deeply and definitely how completely Theodore Roosevelt was capturing the American people. But the realization did not make him a little Roosevelt. Little Roosevelts were popping up all over the land in cities, in counties, and in states, noisy young county court-house candidates who thought they were idealists, eagerly trumpeting at the local dragons of sloth and corruption. But Calvin Coolidge was never one of those. He bided his time. He saved his money, played politics with his cards close to his vest, said little and watched.

While he was watching he met Grace Goodhue. She was a teacher in the deaf and dumb school located on the outskirts of Northampton. The teachers in the school were a few years older than the girl students in Smith College which dominated the social life of the town. The women members of the faculty of Smith College wore their stockings too blue for a young man who was as proud of his erudition as young Calvin Coolidge. His kind like to think they prefer their females dumb. Also the women in the Smith College faculty were making more money than Calvin Coolidge when he was ranging the woods looking for a mate. So he picked a teacher at the deaf and dumb school making $75.00 a month and keep, who would not put him in his scholarly place. She was a lovely creature, Grace Goodhue, then in her twenties; a graduate of the University of Vermont, but with no indigo in her hosiery. And when she, having social experience of a sorority girl in a co-educational college took a look at his obvious specifications, Calvin had no chance. He was foredoomed. Grace and Calvin met casually, went with the same boating, picnicking, dancing, whistclubbing set—not the royal families of Northampton but the young nobility and gentry on the edges of the Congregational church. Her family lived in Vermont and the awkward young statesman of Northampton did not fall under the appraising eye of his future mother-in-law until it was too late for her to stop the love affair. The mother-in-law tried vainly to postpone the wedding from June to November. Those two were never friends. But Grace Goodhue was right about Calvin Coolidge, her mother was wrong. It was love at first sight. She, however, probably saw him first. Not only was her social experience wider than his, her emotional intelligence was keener. So when her lover and her mother clashed, she followed her lover.

It is characteristic that in his "Autobiography," the page which begins with this sentence: "My earnings were such that I was able to make some small savings," is the page on which he records his first love affair. And on the next page, writing of Grace Goodhue, his first-acknowledged sweetheart, he declares:

"We became engaged in the early summer of 1905 and were married in October, 1905. . . . I have seen so much fiction written on this subject that I may be pardoned for relating the plain facts. We thought we were made for each other. For almost a quarter of a century she has borne with my infirmities and I have rejoiced in her graces."[3]

It required some emotion to pen those last three sentences nearly a third of a century after the fact! For in those three sentences are chronicled the essential details of the story of a happy, successful marriage. It was the story indeed of the woman facing one reality—the minor infirmities of an exceptional man. She understood him and still loved him. She knew he kept a mistress—politics—and that as his wife she had the deep, dependable loyalty of the man who trifles rather idly, but always turns homeward for courage, if not for wisdom, at least for solace. He was a moody man who had a cruel streak of which he was ashamed, given to tantrums when crossed, not hot tantrums but cold, peevish ones. He was the kind of man who quarrels or is irritated by one person or circumstance and "takes it out on the next person."[4] He was full of mischievous deviltries—meaningless, unimportant, which never affected his career or scarred his life. One sees them in his boyhood. They were to show up in his last days. And as a husband there was that mistress with whom he divided his talents and to an extent his income, his seven-devil lust for politics. Next to his pride in Grace Goodhue, her children, her home, his love for politics was the dominating influence in his private life.

The courtship of Calvin Coolidge and Grace Goodhue naturally was queer. Years afterward, when he was gone and her mother had been dead nearly a decade, Mrs. Coolidge, writing for a magazine[5] frankly declared that his mother-in-law and he never got on. She opposed the marriage. In the family wrangle he defeated the Goodhues and speeded up the marriage from June, 1906, to November, 1905. Before the marriage, Grace Goodhue took her gaunt, taciturn, repressed suitor up to Vermont to visit kin and friends. She remembers that he wore "a dark blue serge suit, new and perfectly tailored, and a black derby hat." And that he put a whisk

[3] "Autobiography."

[4] Frank Stearns told me this; also Frank W. Buxton; and Mrs. Coolidge reveals it plainly in her articles in *Good Housekeeping*, 1935.

[5] *Good Housekeeping*, February, 1935.

broom in the back of the buggy in which they were riding so that he could spruce up at the end of the journey. When they entered the house, and after the introductions were over, he sat on one end of a long parlor sofa, she on the other, while their friends chattered, and Calvin said nothing. "Not one word did he utter." [6] And when at last he could bear it no longer, he rose and said simply, with one of his best smiles:

"We'll be going now!"

Naturally, she was put out. And naturally, they jangled about it a little when they were riding home, and naturally, the jowering was futile. He did the same thing over and over again when he cared to. He could not help it.[7] Being what he was, profoundly loyal, he was a devoted husband; but being also self-centered, undemonstrative, reserved and like most shy men crusty and, when irritated, grumpy, he did not make her a full partner in his life. "He was not favorably impressed with my education," she wrote for *Good Housekeeping* after his death. Also she recalled that he never talked politics with her nor took her into his business confidence. If he came home moody and irritable, that was his affair. She learned to keep quiet and let him stew in his own juice. "If I had had any particular interest," she wrote about his political affairs, "I am sure I should have been properly put in my place." [8] Some men are just that way in their homes. Introverts and can't help it. Naturally Grace Coolidge, looking back at the close of a happy life which she lived gorgeously, beautifully, would write that she was always suspicious of those wives who said of their husbands, "He never gave me a cross word!" She had received her quota. Yet she never had to lie awake nights worrying over his whereabouts!

But she knew what he was before her marriage. In those days when he went to a picnic he brought more than his share of the food, and then before clearing up the debris, counted the left over macaroons and wondered what had become of one of them.[9] The other picnickers snickered. And probably Grace Goodhue realized then that she never could break his parsimonious habits. They were inbred out of a Vermont type that she understood. She accepted him as "a character," a primitive. Modern slang would call him "a sketch."

Yet he was vastly more than "a character." And shrewd Grace Goodhue sensed it. Back of his obvious gaucheries he had a mind. She recalled thirty years later that when they were married he had a small golden-oak bookcase in which five shelves were filled with standard books. The sateen

[6] Ibid.

[7] Ibid.

[8] Ibid.

[9] Mrs. Coolidge's *Home Companion* Confessions.

curtain in front of it concealed a set of Shakespeare, a history of England, a row of Kipling's poems and stories, George Ade's "Fables in Slang," "The Prince of India," a set of Hawthorne, "The Rubaiyat," Whittier's, Longfellow's, and Tennyson's poems, and a row of lexicons and grammars of the Latin, Greek, French, German, and Italian languages. And if he had a book she might be sure he had got his money's worth of it. Never was he a showoff. He told Clarence S. Brigham, of the American Antiquarian Society, that he had begun translating Dante's "Inferno" before he was married and he liked it so well that he kept right on with it and finished it afterward. A young man who will interrupt his honeymoon to translate Dante really should be allowed to count the macaroons after a picnic. His wife wrote that from the beginning he liked to read in bed, to "improve his mind"—his phrase for it. And at the head of his bed always he kept his Bible and "The Life and Letters of Charles E. Garman." She also remembered for a generation those two small paper-covered volumes of the "Inferno" on his bedside table—his escape from Northampton reality. She must have seen that bedside table and must have lifted the sateen curtain that hid those books before she married him. It is an abiding testimonial to her perspicacity that she let him count the macaroons and took him while the crowd snickered.

They had intended to take a two weeks' honeymoon. After a week in Montreal, he decided they had seen everything there was to see and she, being tactful, suggested that they come home, which they did and saved a week's spending.

Coming home they stopped in Boston and visited the State House and the governor's office in the Capitol. In one of the rooms of state was a huge chair, the governor's chair. The happy couple thought they would try it. As one of them was about to sit down, the guards came and chased them away. They remembered the abashed confusion of that incident many years.[10]

When the Coolidges came home from their economical honeymoon in Montreal, a few hundred miles from their wedding place, they went to housekeeping as soon as they could. But before they had settled down, he appeared one day with fifty pairs of undarned socks and told her when she got those done he would have some others. He had been saving them up apparently against the day of matrimony. His doctrine of work and save began early. He saved and she worked.[11] Theirs was a modest

[10] This story is found in nearly all of Coolidge's early biographies. Of course he told it in pride.

[11] *Good Housekeeping*, March, 1935.

menage. It was within their means. Here again was the shadow of his mistress, for he declared twenty-five years later: "We lived where we did that I might better serve the people." Characteristically, and this was one of his infirmities which she had to bear. After nearly a year in a boarding-house he attended to the furnishing of their home himself and took Mrs. Coolidge into it ready furnished! Two weeks later their first baby was born, eleven months after their marriage. Of this event he wrote:

"The fragrance of the clematis which covered the bay window filled the room like a benediction where the mother lay with her baby. It was all very wonderful to us." [12]

Now for the graces which upbore those infirmities: Above all, Mrs. Coolidge was amiable. She had the tolerance of an understanding heart. She could mimic her husband and did for the delectation of the family and her friends without mocking him meanly. She knew his strength and understood without blinking the facts his many minor weaknesses. Several months before their first baby came, Grace Coolidge let a fast talking frontdoor salesman sell to her "Our Family Physician" for eight dollars—a lot of money in those days for that family. When the book came she was shy about telling her husband of the purchase. The Northampton story declares that she decided to say nothing, but left it on the center table. He said nothing. But one day several weeks later she picked up the book and glancing inside found written on the flyleaf:

"Don't see any receipt here for curing suckers! Calvin Coolidge." [13]

Funny? But under the circumstances not entirely kind. Husbands have been poisoned for less. Probably she managed to get along, as most wives do who have to live with spoiled children who are essentially sound but have little soft specks here and there in the wholesomeness of their characters. She was as quick as he. She supplemented his natural shyness with a lovely candor, offset his occasional lapses into taciturnity with a gay loquacity that kept a table going when he would have let the conversation sag unwittingly perhaps if a mood was on him not caring what happened. And then above all she had faith in him. She was never jealous of his mistress. In the first years of her marriage when her children were little, she ran the house with one maid and did the washing.

Then and for years thereafter, Fred Jager, the automobile dealer, regarded the Coolidges as a good prospect. But he never could land them. Jager tried to get Coolidge to ride many times but Coolidge always shook

[12] "Autobiography."

[13] This story also is printed in "Coolidge Wit and Wisdom" by John Hiram McKee, Frederick Stokes Company, New York City.

his head and said he wasn't interested, "but Grace was. She would be glad to go." And Grace had no authority to buy. Which Jager full well knew!

Jager gave them up.[14] A car's cost was beyond the Coolidge cosmos. If the budding statesman had gone up the other route in politics, if he had not rejected reappointment to the profitable office of clerk of the court, he could have had his car and Grace would not have appeared back of the little house on Massasoit Street, Monday mornings, along the clothesline holding a clothespin in her teeth, hanging out the wash. But Coolidge knew that the money end of politics was not his vocation. Money which he venerated as a source of social and political power, he never seriously cared to acquire. But when it came his way, he saved it. Instead of taking the road to wealth, always he took the road to honors, small honors, but not financially profitable. So Grace Coolidge budgeted her household expenses well within the Coolidge income, the income of a struggling young lawyer, still a second-rate lawyer in a fourth class town. Probably his income never exceeded fifteen hundred dollars a year until he was elected lieutenant governor. He told his friends[15] that he could live in a better home if he cared to but that he wanted to be free to serve the public so that he would not be bothered with the worry of having to give up his office and come down in the world if the luck of the game of politics turned against him. He told James Lucey, the shoemaker of Northampton, that he could always sleep nights without worrying about the rent. For which the credit was not entirely his. For living within her income, running the house by keeping the family out of debt, Grace Coolidge had her full and proper share. She worked hard, kept up appearances, did her part in the town's activities, took her place alone in the Congregational church, played the game of the politician's wife, smiling the while, and knew that this man of hers with five talents of which the most shining coin was a sort of diligent honesty had to travel fast if he went up the political road. She realized that he could not climb far under the burden of debt. On the ever upward journey her shoulder was in the yoke as well as his. If there was nagging to be done she let him do it. So they were happy. For she had the priceless jewel of an understanding heart which to the end maintained for him his valiant self-respect.

SADNESS OF FAREWELL

It was a fine day, an open winter day, January 5, 1933, in Northampton. Calvin Coolidge rose, went about his daily chores, neglected to shave

[14] Letter from Jager to author, 1934.
[15] Conversation with Northampton neighbors by the author.

before breakfast. Breakfast usually punctilious—was on the tick of the tock. And at nine o'clock he went downtown to his office. He stayed there for a time, perhaps an hour, doing odd jobs, attending to the routine of his office work and business duties, then he rose and said casually to his associate that he was not feeling very well and that he thought he would go home. Just that. At home he sat down for a while, apparently reading. Mrs. Coolidge had gone into Main Street for her morning's shopping. Some casual errand attracted him to the basement. He went down, passed the man of all work there with a brusque "Good morning, Robert," and climbed the two flights of stairs to his bedroom. At noon he remembered that he had not shaved and went upstairs, took off his coat, got out his shaving tools and then—no one knows exactly what happened. When Mrs. Coolidge came in she called cheerfully to him as was her wont, but when there was no answer she went to the second floor to put away her wraps and there, face downward on the floor she found his lifeless body. He who had lived aloof, died alone.

Calvin Coolidge died the first Thursday in January and they buried him Saturday. It was a cold, dour, rainy day in Northampton, but the largest crowd assembled that Saturday that the town had ever seen. People from all over the wide Connecticut Valley motored in, and parking space, half a mile from the Edwards Congregational Church, was taken in the early morning. The Mayor announced the day before that the stores would not be closed.

"Every nickel counts," said he in a public statement. "If the business places close they might lose some sales and that is exactly what Calvin would not want."

So with Puritan thrift and to give the place a solemn air while saving the nickels, the Mayor asked the merchants to draw down the window shades. Nor did he drape the town in mourning, being frugal: "Calvin was a simple man. He would not want the people to go to all that expense," the Mayor said! So they tied crape on the City Hall.

From all over the land visitors who came thronging in, that cloudy day, saw there the bedraggled black cotton limp and listless, and a wilted flag hanging at half mast. Before nine o'clock the sidewalks on Main Street and in front of the church were packed. The windows of the stores and the high school across the street showed the buff of curious faces. Most of the seats in the church were reserved.[16] James Lucey sat in one of these—exalted in his friendship to the last. Only the galleries were free. When the

[16] The Coolidge pew well back in the Auditorium was marked and remained vacant.

doors of the church swung open it took less than a minute to jam the galleries. The crowd outside reflected symbolically the disorganization and disorder of the times. The President and members of the Supreme Court were jostled, elbowed, buffeted as the state police wangled a wedged opening for the great men to enter the church. Silk hats were knocked askew, clothing was twisted awry, and the procession of dignitaries—President Hoover, the members of the Supreme Court, the United States Representatives and Senators, the governors of adjoining states—ran a gauntlet to the church doors. As Mrs. Coolidge came in, with the Stearns family and Senator Butler, the crowd respectfully made way.

A young Congregational preacher, a few months out of college, less than half a year in Northampton, took charge of the services. He was a handsome curlyheaded boy with a voice like a bishop and he read the simple service of the democratic church.

The service opened with Handel's Largo from "Xerxes," and the church choir which Calvin Coolidge had heard so often sang "Lead Kindly Light." No eulogy was spoken. The prayer was formal and simple. Outside in the rain, which changed to snow at times, the throng stood silent when it heard the organ mourn. As Mrs. Coolidge rose to go, the organ lifted its voice in the solemn theme from Dvořák's New World Symphony, the Largo which has been given the words popularly "I'm Going Home, Going Home." The throng, hearing the dirge swell as the church door opened, made way for the Coolidges when they appeared in the street. As they entered their cars, a rift of cold New England sunlight flooded the place for a moment. But as the funeral cortège left the town, the clouds closed down. The rain began to fall listlessly.

The President and the dignitaries of the Senate and Court turned back to Washington from the church. Mrs. Coolidge and a few faithful friends, the Stearnses, Senator and Mrs. Butler, and the Coolidge family, motored behind the hearse up through Massachusetts into Vermont in a pelting rain. Yet at every farm site, village and town thousands of his New England neighbors stood uncovered, curiously, earnestly, sadly gazing at the cortège. It was afternoon when the hundred miles was spanned which separates the place where Calvin Coolidge lived for thirty years and died from the place of his birth. The funeral party was late. The afternoon was waning. Up the hill from Plymouth village the mourners came. Gathered outside the cemetery were a hundred old friends and neighbors standing under umbrellas in the sleet that was whitening the mountains.

The Plymouth graveyard rests on a terraced hillside. On the Coolidge terrace a canvas had been erected over the open grave to protect the family.

With the family standing there were Mr. and Mrs. Frank Stearns and the Butlers with Young John and his wife, and a few more intimate friends. From a vantage point just below the retaining wall of the bottom terrace a homely group of villagers watched the mourners. The weird and somber contour of a score of covering umbrellas was varied by a bright splash where a man wrapped his little boy in a yellow horse blanket. Six sturdy United States marshals in their dress uniform from the states surrounding, and of course Republicans, bore the heavy coffin to the grave. The bronze coffin carried few flowers. President Hoover's Japanese Leothe leaves lay above his predecessor's breast. The young preacher's prayer was short. Dust was consigned to dust, ashes to ashes. No band wailed, and the village watchers heard no song or psalm. There was a pause and then the clear young voice of the preacher at Mrs. Coolidge's request intoned these lines by Robert Richardson:

"Warm summer sun,
Shine kindly here;
Warm southern wind,
Blow softly here;
Green sod above
Lie light, lie light.
Good-night, dear heart,
Good-night, good-night."

For a moment the silent crowd stood, unmoving. Then the clear blast of a soldier's bugle cried taps to the lonely mountains. When the echoes had died, a strange and lovely thing happened. For a moment, scarcely more than a minute, the slanting western sun broke through the clouds, cast its horizontal light upon the hillside, then closed quickly down, leaving a lemon colored glow through the mist, brilliant like a shimmering halo. The mourners turned and went about the street and man to his long home. When they were gone the sleet fell in little gusts upon the frozen grass like grudging tears of some dejected god. Thus the earth of the hills that he loved closed over Calvin Coolidge's mortal clay. With this pale pageantry his day was done.

What of him—this rather drab, colorless figure who purposely kept drama from his life and staged himself as a primitive and solitary figure walking his appointed way to a place of power? What will be the verdict of his countrymen and of the world when the record finally closes? Of course it will be many years before the record ends. A cloud of witnesses writing their stories will appear and things unseen will become plain in another day and decade. It is too early to put a final estimate on Calvin Coolidge. But surely this much may be written—he was honest; he was cautious, but he never lacked at last for courage. He walked through the politics of his time touching elbows with the worst of his contemporaries as he met and passed them on his pilgrimage through American government from the bottom to the top. Yet he went unsmirched. He knew the obvious realities of his environment. He never blinked the sordid facts of any problem that came to his hands. Neither did he advertise those sordid facts, nor ever bewail them. He took American politics as it was, not perhaps as he would have liked it. He played the game under the established rules, with men about the table good and bad—as they came under the spotlight. He played his winning hand. He was wise according to his day and generation. His instinctive common sense was illumined by rather more intelligence than most men had with whom he gambled. He knew that politics was a cult in America, and he held no nonsense in his heart about its purification. To him that remained always "an iridescent dream." But he did, with all his heart, try to get out of the politics in which he worked, bad as it might have been, what he thought was the best for all the people. Yet he never played the demagogue. To his friends he was loyal, crabbedly cordial, and in the end always kind, whatever petty pouting he did to ease his tired nerves. To his country he gave unstinted devotion. In the terrible decade when he was in his place of greatest power, he lacked the vision to exercise the highest judgment. He was handicapped there by his background, circumscribed by his own life's pattern, his temperament, his experience as the pampered adopted child of what he felt was a benevolent plutocracy. He did not question its authority, nor its beneficence. Another wiser man coming to the helm from another ship, as for instance from business or perhaps from the academic cloister, if he had held the nation's wheel, possibly might have steered the boat from the rapids. Probably not. Such a man would have been a freak in our politics, an accident. His wisdom might have wrecked that wiser man and with him wrecked his country a few years before its debacle. Calvin Coolidge was democracy functioning at its best, which sometimes is its worst. Being what he was, he was forced, by the destiny of his own qualities, his own ideals, his high calling, into the way he took. Back of him were the urgent purposes of the American democracy, the lust for prosperity, the Hamiltonian faith that "the rich" are indeed the "wise and good," the Republican creed which identifies wealth with brains. His short, sage, oracular sentences polished like New England granite, reflected the American heart in the days when he guided the American people. But whither they would go he led them, not as a weakling, not as a demagogue, but cherishing the noblest purpose he knew, following the democratic vision of the America of his age.

Was it not well that when he laid him down to sleep his stern, scorned dying gods, the Puritan gods of things that were, rained their icy tears upon his hillside bed!

XV

DISRAELI, A PICTURE OF THE VICTORIAN AGE [1]

By

ANDRÉ MAUROIS

This biography of Benjamin Disraeli, Earl of Beaconsfield and Prime Minister of England, is historically correct, but at the same time it is as vivid as the most interesting fiction. It presents sympathetically and with keen wit and penetration the story of the almost incredible achievements of the ambitious Disraeli. In 1839, he married Mrs. Wyndham Lewis, a wealthy widow, much older than himself. In his maiden speech in Parliament he was hissed down, but by 1852 he was Chancellor of the Exchequer and in 1868, Premier. Here was a Tory in theory, a Liberal in practice, a Jewish novelist who became, impossible as it may seem, the leader of the British aristocracy.

André Maurois has given us two selections from his biography. One of these passages pictures the rather riotous scenes at the time of Diraeli's maiden speech, and the other presents an unusual description of Gladstone and Disraeli, closing with Disraeli's first speech on the budget.

DISRAELI'S MAIDEN SPEECH

At Bradenham it was possible to believe that all England was agog with the entrance of Benjamin Disraeli to Parliament. In London conversation centered rather on the young Queen, her ease of bearing, her intelligence, the affection which she seemed to feel for her Prime Minister, Melbourne. Many people too, coming back from holidays, were talking of their first railway journey; they had experienced a certain sense of danger, but soon put it out of their heads.

[1] André Maurois, *Disraeli, a Picture of the Victorian Age*, New York: D. Appleton and Company, 1938, pp. 119-131, 218-226.

Immediately Disraeli found his Wyndham Lewis "colleagues" again. Mrs. Wyndham Lewis, proud of her protégé, took him to the theatre to see Kean, in a well-heated box. He went to receive Lord Lyndhurst's congratulations, and to compliment him in his return, for this sturdy old man had just married a young girl and his sole topic was of having a son. Then Wyndham Lewis showed him the Houses of Parliament.

As the old Palace of Westminster had been partly burnt down, the Lords and Commons were sitting in temporary halls. There they were rather crowded, but Disraeli managed to make sure of a seat for himself just behind his chief, Sir Robert Peel. The latter was cordial and invited the new member to join him at a small dinner-party at the Carlton on the following Thursday. "A House of Commons dinner purely. By that time we shall know something of the temper of the House." That "we" was very acceptable. Wyndham Lewis, when he came home, said to his wife: "Peel took Disraeli by the hand in the most cordial fashion."

From the first divisions it was plain that Lord Melbourne's Whig Ministry, with the support of the Irish, was going to retain power. For a fortnight Disraeli remained a silent spectator of the debates. He had a great desire to speak, but was terribly intimidated. He saw himself set about with great men. Opposite him, on the ministerial bench, in front of the official red box, was the Whig leader, Lord John Russell, very small in his black frock-coat of old-fashioned cut, his face half hidden beneath a hat with an enormous brim, and with a stricken air, Lord John, the perfect symbol of his party, who advanced the most daring ideas in the most archaic style, and uttered the word "democracy" with an aristocratic drawl. Near him was Lord Palmerston, the Foreign Secretary, with his dyed and carefully brushed side-whiskers, Palmerston of whom Granville said that he looked like some old retired croupier from Baden, and whom the Whigs deemed vulgar, because he had not that ceremonious respect for the Crown which the Whigs had always shown, even when they were dethroning kings. Nearer to him, standing out against the massive table which separated the Ministers from the Opposition, Disraeli could see from behind the imposing figure of Sir Robert Peel, and in profile, the brilliant Lord Stanley, with his fine curved nose, his sensitive mouth, his curled and slightly unruly hair, Stanley the indolent, the disdainful, the intelligent, dressed with a carefully considered negligence that was full of lessons for Dizzy. Over by the entrance, amongst the Radicals, was his friend Bulwer; and in the midst of the Irish band, his formidable foe, Daniel O'Connell.

He was troubled also by the contrast in this assembly between the majesty of its ritual and its carelessness for appearances. Nobody listened; members chattered during the speeches and moved endlessly in and out; but the Speaker was in robes and wig, the ushers brought in and removed the mace, and a fellow-member was referred to only by the appellation of "the honorable gentleman." All these small details delighted a neophyte who had so long observed them from without. He was certain that on the day when he would rise to speak, he would commit no blunder, would address himself solely to the speaker, following the accepted fiction of the place, would call every barrister-member "the honourable and learned gentleman," every officer-member "the honourable and gallant gentleman," Sir Robert Peel, "the right honourable baronet," and Lord John, "the noble Lord opposite." Already in his thoughts, his phrases were cast in the parliamentary mould. If he became a Minister, how grandly he would strike his fist on that scarlet box! At the close of a loudly acclaimed speech, with what an air of negligence would he drop into his seat on the Treasury bench, wiping his lips with handkerchief of fine cambric! But now that he had measured at closer quarters the powerful inertia of this great body, a certain anxiety was mingled with his impatience.

In establishing the powers of the House, a discussion had opened on a subscription opened by a Mr. Spottiswoode to furnish Protestant candidates with the funds necessary to fight the Catholics in Ireland. This subscription had been extremely distasteful, not only to the Irish, but also to the Liberals, who held it to be contrary to the liberty of the electors. O'Connell had just spoken on the subject with vehemence when Disraeli rose in his place. It had been arranged that Lord Stanley should reply on behalf of the Conservatives, but Disraeli had gone up and asked for his place as spokesman, and Stanley, surprised but indifferent, had granted it.

Irish and Liberals both looked with curiosity at the new orator who now rose opposite them. Many of them had heard it said that he was a charlatan, an old Radical turned Conservative, a novel-writer, a pompous orator. It was known that he had had a violent quarrel with O'Connell, and a strong detachment of the latter's friends had grouped together as soon as Disraeli rose. On the Conservative benches, the country gentlemen examined with some disquietude this decidedly un-English face. The curls vexed them, and the costume. Disraeli wore a bottle-green coat, a white waistcoat covered with gold chains ("Why so many chains, Dizzy?" Bulwer had said to him. "Are you practising to become Lord Mayor, or what?"), and a great black cravat accentuated the pallor of his complexion. It was a grave moment and he was playing a great part. He had to show to the Liberals what manner of man they had lost in him, to the Conservatives, that a future leader was in their midst, to O'Connell, that the day of expiation was at hand. He had several reasons for confidence; his speech had been elaborately prepared, and contained several phrases of sure effectiveness; and the tradition of Parliament was such that these beginners' speeches were greeted with kindliness. "The best maiden speech since Pitt's" was the remark generally passed to the orator. Young Gladstone, for example, whom Disraeli now found again on the benches of the Commons, had delivered his five years before amid general sympathy: "Spoke my first time for fifty minutes," he had noted in his diary. "The House heard me very kindly and my friends were satisfied. Tea afterwards at the Carlton." But Gladstone came from Eaton and Oxford; he had a handsome English face, with firm and familiar features, dark-coloured clothes, and a grave manner.

Disraeli's voice was a trifle forced; its effect one of unpleasing astonishment. Disraeli tried to show that the Irish, and O'Connell in particular, had themselves profited by very similar subscriptions. "This majestic mendicancy . . ." he said. The House had a horror of long words and there was a titter of laughter. "I do not affect to be insensible to the difficulty of my position. *(Renewed laughter.)* I am sure I shall receive the indulgence of honourable gentlemen—*(Laughter and 'Question!')*; but I can assure them that if they do not wish to hear me, I, without a murmur, will sit down. *(Applause and laughter.)*" After a moment of comparative calm, another slightly startling association of words roused the storm. From the Irish group came hisses, scraping of feet, and cat-calls. Disraeli kept calm. "I wish I really could induce the House to give me five minutes more. *(Roars of laughter.)* I stand here to-night, sir, not formally, but in some degree virtually, the representative of a considerable number of members of Parliament. *(Loud and general laughter.)* Now, why smile? *(Continued laughter.)* Why envy me? *(Loud laughter.)* Why should I not have a tale to unfold to-night? *(Roars of laughter.)*"

From that moment onwards the uproar became such that only a few phrases could be heard.

"About that time, sir, when the bell of our cathedral announced the death of the monarch—*('Oh, oh!' and much laughter.)* . . . If honourable members think it is fair to interrupt me, I will submit. *(Great laughter.)* I would not act so towards any one, that is all I can say. *(Laughter and cries of 'Go on!')* But I beg simply to ask—*('Oh!' and loud laughter.)* Nothing is so easy as to laugh. *(Roars of laughter.)* We remember the amatory eclogue—*(Roars of laughter)*—the old loves and the new loves that took place between the noble Lord, the Tityrus of the Treasury Bench, and the learned Daphne of Liskeard—*(Loud laughter and 'Question!')* . . . When we remember at the same time that with emancipated Ireland and enslaved England, on the one hand a triumphant nation, on the other a groaning people, and notwithstanding the noble Lord, secure on the pedestal of power, may wield in one hand the keys of St. Peter, and—*(Here the hon. Member was interrupted with such loud and incessant laughter that it was impossible to know whether he closed his sentence or not.)* Now, Mr. Speaker, we see the philosophical prejudices of man. *(Laughter and cheers.)* I respect cheers, even when they come from the lips of political opponents. *(Renewed laughter.)* I think, sir—*(Hear, hear! and 'Question, question!')*—I am not at all surprised, sir, at the reception I have received. *(Continued laughter.)* I have begun several things many times—*(Laughter)*—and I have often succeeded at last—*(Fresh cries of 'Question!')*—although many had predicted that I must fail, as they had done before me. (*'Question, question!'*)"

And then, in formidable tones, staring indignantly at his interruptors, raising his hand and opening his mouth as wide as he could, he cried out in a voice which was almost terrifying and suddenly dominated the clamour; "Ay, sir, and though I sit down now, the time will come when you will hear me."

He was silent. His adversaries were still laughing; his friends gazed at him, saddened and surprised. During the whole of his ordeal, one man had supported him with great firmness—the right honourable baronet, Sir Robert Peel. Sir Robert was not in the habit of showing noisy approval of the orators of his party; he listened to them in almost hostile silence. But on this occasion he turned round several times to the young orator, saying "Hear, hear!" in a loud voice. When he turned towards the Chamber he could not contain a slight smile.

Lord Stanley had risen, and scornfully, without saying one single word on the incredible reception of which one of his colleagues had just been the victim, had resumed the question seriously. He was listened to with respect. Silent and sombre, Disraeli leaned his head on his hand. Once again a defeat, once again hell. Never, since he had followed the debates of the Commons, had he known of so degrading a scene. Was the life of the Cogan school going to begin again for him now in Parliament? Would he still have to fight and hate, when he desired so much to love and be loved? Why was everything more difficult for him than for others? But why, in his first speech, had he challenged O'Connell and his band?

It would be hard now to swim against the stream. Would it even be possible at all? He had lost all standing in the eyes of this assembly. He reflected with bitterness on the idea he had conjured up of this début. He had imagined a House overwhelmed by his phrases, charmed by his images, delighted by his sarcasms; prolonged applause; a complete and immediate success. . . . And these insulting guffaws. . . . Defeat. . . . O for the haven of the Bradenham woods!

A division forced him to rise. He had not heard the debate. The excellent Lord Chandos came up to him with congratulations. He replied that there was no cause here for congratulations, and murmured: "It is a reverse. . . ." "No such thing!" said Chandos, "you are quite wrong. I have just seen Peel and I asked him, 'Now tell me exactly what you think of Disraeli.' Peel replied, 'Some of my party were disappointed and talk of failure. I say *just the reverse*. He did all that he could do under the circumstances. I say anything but failure; he must make his way.' "

In the lobby the Liberal Attorney-General stopped him and asked with cordiality: "Now, Mr. Disraeli, can you tell me how you finished one sentence in your speech, we are anxious to know: 'In one hand the keys of St. Peter and in the other—'?"

" 'In the other the cap of liberty,' Sir John."

The other smiled and said: "A good picture!"

"Yes," replied Disraeli, with a touch of bitterness, "but your friends will not allow me to finish my pictures."

"But I assure you," said the Attorney-General, "there was the liveliest desire to hear you from us. It was a party at the bar, over whom we have no control; but you have nothing to be afraid of."

What was this? On others, then, impression of an irreparable collapse had not been so unmistakable as on himself? Like many highly-strung men, Disraeli picked up confidence again as quickly as he lost heart. Already the cloud of despair was lifting. Writing to Sarah on the following day, he circumscribed the extent of the disaster: "As I wish to give you an *exact* idea of what occurred, I state at once that my *début* was a *failure*, so far that I could not succeed in gaining an opportunity of saying what I intended; but the failure was not occasioned by my breaking down or any incompetency on my part, but from the physical powers of my adversaries. I can give you no idea how bitter, how factious, how unfair they were. I fought through all with undaunted pluck and unruffled temper, made occasionally good isolated hits when there was silence, and finished with spirit when I found a formal display was ineffectual." He signed it: "Yours, D.—in very good spirits."

On the same day, entering the Athenaeum, Bulwer saw old Sheil, the famous Irish member and O'Connell's lieutenant, surrounded by a group of young Radicals who were rejoicing in the Disraeli incident. Bulwer went over to them and remained silent. Suddenly Sheil threw down his newspaper and said in his shrill voice: "Now, gentlemen, I have heard all you have to say, and, what is more, I heard this same speech of Mr. Disraeli, and I tell you this: if ever the spirit of oratory was in a man, it is in that man. Nothing can prevent him from being one of the first speakers in the House of Commons. Ay! I know something about that place, I think, and I tell you what besides: that if there had not been this interruption, Mr. Disraeli might have been a failure; I don't call this a failure, it is a crash. My *début* was a failure, because I was heard, but my reception was supercilious, his indignant. A *début* should be dull. The House will not allow a man to be a wit and an orator, unless they have the credit of finding it out. There it is."

This little oration, coming from an opponent, left a shock of astonishment. The young men dispersed, rather embarrassed. Bulwer went up to Sheil and said: "Disraeli is dining with me this evening. Would you like to meet him?"

"In spite of my gout," said Sheil, "I long to know him. I long to tell him what I think."

Sheil was charming at dinner. He took Disraeli aside and explained to him that this noisy reception had been a great opportunity for him. "For," said he, "if you had been listened to, what would have been the result? You would have done what I did; you would have made the best speech that you ever would have made: it would have been received frigidly, and you would have despaired of yourself. I did. As it is, you have shown to the House that you have a fine organ, an unlimited command of language, courage, temper, and readiness. Now get rid of your genius for a session. Speak often, for you must not show yourself cowed, but speak shortly. Be very quiet, try to be dull, only argue and reason imperfectly, for if you reason with precision, they will think you are trying to be witty. Astonish them by speaking on subjects of detail. Quote figures, dates, calculations. And in a short time the House will sigh for the wit and eloquence which they all know are in you. They will encourage you to pour them forth, and then you will have the ear of the House and be a favourite."

A speech so intelligent, and showing so deep an understanding of the English, flooded the future with light for Disraeli. Nobody was more capable than he of understanding and following such counsel. He liked to fashion himself with his own hands like a work of art. He was always ready to touch up the picture. Once more he had fallen into the mistake wherewith his father had so often reproached him, that of being in a hurry, of wanting to be famous at one stroke. But he would know how to advance slowly.

A week later he rose in the midst of a discussion on authors' rights. Almost every one was inclined to give him a favourable welcome. Tories and Liberals were of one mind, that this man had been unfairly treated. That was distasteful to them. They were sportsmen; they preferred that an orator, like the game, should have his chance. A sense of shame lingered in their minds from that brutal afternoon. They were inclined to support this odd young man if he dared to make another trial. They would even put up with the excessive brilliance of his phrases and with his unheard-of images. But to the general surprise, he uttered nothing but what was commonplace and obvious, on a subject with which he was thoroughly familiar, and sat down amid general approval. The author of the project replied that he would carefully bear in mind the excellent remarks of the honourable member for Maidstone, himself one of the most remarkable ornaments of modern literature. Sir Robert Peel was strong in his approval, "Hear, hear!" and many members went up and congratulated Disraeli. An old Tory colonel came up to him and said, after some amiable growling: "Well, you have got in your saddle again; now you may ride away." To Sarah he wrote: "Next time I rise in the House, I shall sit down amidst loud cheers."

Far from having been of disservice to him, this sorry beginning had given him the prestige of a victim. Within three weeks he had acquired, in this extremely difficult assembly, a kind of popularity. He was courageous; he spoke well; he seemed to have an exact knowledge of the subjects he dealt with. "Why not?" thought the English gentlemen.

DISRAELI'S FIRST SPEECH ON THE BUDGET

Just as in Rugby football a good half-back, still keen in spite of disappointments, will pass the ball a score of times to slack three-quarters who do not even try to charge, so did Disraeli divert power into the negligent grasp of Stanley. His great task was "the education of the Party"; he had to extricate it from Protection, to raise it from a caste feeling to a national feeling, to teach it to take heed of popular comfort and of the solidity of the Empire. He put forward a bold programme to take the place of Protection, in the shape of an Imperial reform of Parliament: to admit the Colonies to a share in the administration of the Empire, to balance with their vote the democratic vote of the towns, and thus to introduce fresh elements and put an end to the absurd rivalries of Town *versus* Country, Industry *versus* Agriculture. "Romantic imaginings," thought the noble Lord, and returned to his pleasures.

But once again the ball was passed to him and the Queen summoned him to Windsor. He was now Lord Derby, through the death of his father a few months earlier. Once again he came to Grosvenor Gate and was shown into the Blue Room. This time he said to Disraeli: "You will be Chancellor of the Exchequer."

"I know nothing of finance," said Disraeli.

"You know as much as Canning knew. . . . They will give you the figures."

And next day the Ministry was formed. Such was the party's poverty in men that only three of the members of the Cabinet had already been Ministers. The Queen considered that the Ministry was composed of Lord Derby alone. And he, when asked for his views, replied "I am very well and my babes too." The Duke of Wellington had the list of new Ministers read out to him; but as he was very old and very deaf, and all the names were new to him, he kept interrupting his informant with a repeated "Who? Who?" The newspapers seized on the saying, and the Ministry came to be known as the "Who? Who?" Cabinet. As for the selection of Disraeli as Chancellor of the Exchequer, that was regarded ridiculous.

But what mattered that to him? He was like a young girl on the day of her first ball. The great old man Lyndhurst recalled to him those youthful conversations when he had expressed his desires, boyish enough in those days, and now made real. Sarah, in the depths of her rustic solitude, found herself besieged by people of the district asking for favours. The postman wanted to be transferred to the town, and spoke to Miss D'Israeli in timid, trembling tones. Dizzy went to obtain his Chancellor's robe, a robe of black silk heavily broidered with gold braid; it descended in a straight line from the great Pitt.

"You will find it very heavy," said the judge who received him.

"Oh, I find it uncommonly light," he answered.

The beginnings were none too bad. The Queen herself was amused by the reports which it was the duty of the leader of the House of Commons to address to her every evening: "Mr. Disraeli (*alias* Dizzy) writes very curious reports, much in the style of his books." Derby was well enough pleased with his crew of beginners. The House was awaiting the election. But when this was over, and it took an unfavorable turn, the unhappy Chancellor knew very well that he would not be allowed a long taste of the duties in which he found so much pleasure. Gladstone in particular had a watching eye on him.

Although neither one nor the other would have desired it, political life was slowly assuming the form of a duel between these two. To all outward appearance they were good friends. Their wives exchanged visits. Sometimes, after a somewhat lively sitting, Gladstone would even come in to say good-evening to Mary Anne. In theory the two men were Conservatives. Gladstone, with his love for indefinable shades of difference, said that he preferred to be on the liberal side of the Conservative party rather than the conservative side of the Liberal party. But their temperaments clashed and the paths of their careers crossed. Without Disraeli, Gladstone would have been the natural heir to Peel. That was the latter's opinion: "Gladstone will be the Conservative Prime Minister," he said some time before his death; and when he was asked, "What of Disraeli?" he answered, "We shall make him Governor-General of India."

Each was stern in his judgment of the other. To Gladstone, Disraeli was a man without religion and without political faith. To Disraeli, Gladstone was a man of assumed piety, who cloaked his skill in manœuvreing with feigned scruples. Gladstone had all his days lived a model Sunday-school life. At Eton he said his prayers, morning and evening. At Oxford the young men drank less in 1840 because Gladstone had been up in 1830. In Parliament he had been straight away the studious pupil, and Peel's beloved disciple. Disraeli had lived a vagabond's life, in schools and politics alike. He had known the moneylenders' parlours before those of Ministers and Bishops. Disraeli's enemies said he was not an honest man. Gladstone's enemies said of him that he was an honest man in the worst sense of the word. Disraeli's foes said that he was not a Christian; Gladstone's said that he might be an excellent Christian but that he was assuredly a detestable pagan. Disraeli had learnt his reading from Molière and Voltaire; Gladstone regarded *Tartuffe* as a third-rate comedy. The cynical Disraeli whispered in the ear of the aged and austere Mr. Bright, as he helped him into his overcoat: "After all, Mr. Bright, we both know very well what brings you and me here: ambition." Gladstone unconsciously assured himself: "Well, I do not think I can tax myself with ever having been much moved by ambition." It was said of Gladstone that he could convince others of many things, and himself of anything at all. Disraeli could persuade others, but was powerless over himself. Gladstone liked to choose an abstract principle and from that to deduce his preferences. And his tendency was to believe that his desires were those of the Almighty. He was reproached, not so much for always having the ace of trumps up his sleeve as for claiming that God had put it there. Disraeli had a horror of abstract principles. He liked certain ideas because they appealed to his imagination. He left to action the care of putting them to the test. When Disraeli changed his views, as in the case of Protection, he admitted the change and was ready to appear changeable; Gladstone fastened his constancy to blades of straw and thought that they were planks. Disraeli was sure that Gladstone was no saint, but Gladstone was far from certain that Disraeli was not the Devil.

And each misread the other. Gladstone accepted as true all the cynical professions of faith which Disraeli made as a challenge; Disraeli put down as hypocritical the phrases by which Gladstone duped himself in all good faith. Disraeli, the doctrinaire, prided himself on being an opportunist; Gladstone the opportunist, prided himself on being a doctrinaire. Disraeli affected to despise reason, but reasoned well; Gladstone, who believed himself a reasoner, acted only through passion. Gladstone with a great fortune still kept his account of daily expenses; Disraeli with his heavy debts spent his money without counting it. Both were fond of Dante, but Disraeli turned chiefly to the *Inferno*, Gladstone to the *Paradiso*. Disraeli had the name of being frivolous, but was taciturn in society; Gladstone, who was supposed to be grave, was so charming in company that to be able to go on hating him, one had to avoid meeting him. Gladstone was interested in two things only: religion and finance; Disraeli was interested in hundreds of things, religion and finance among them. Neither of the pair believed in the other's religious convictions, and there again they were both wrong. And finally, Disraeli would have been much surprised if he had known that Mr. Gladstone and his wife, when they had reason to be particularly merry, would stand in front of the fire, clasped together and swaying as they sang:

> "A ragamuffin husband and a rantipoling wife,
> We'll fiddle it and scrape it through the ups and downs of life!"

When the two rivals rose in succession on a very dark day in December 1852, for the Budget discussion, it seemed that two supernatural powers were opposing each other. Gladstone with his well-chiselled profile, his onyx eyes, his crest of black hair thrown backward with a powerful gesture, seemed like the Spirit of Ocean. Disraeli with his shining curls, his slightly stooping figure, his long supple hands, seemed rather a Spirit of Fire. As soon as they began to speak it was obvious that Disraeli had more genius, but Gladstone had assumed a tone of moral superiority which was more pleasing to the House.

Never had a Budget been attacked in Parliament as that of Disraeli was. For a whole week, night after night, it had been mocked at, made game of, scorned. All the brilliant economists in turn had demonstrated its ignorance and folly. All had ironically underlined its abandonment of Protection.

He had remained motionless, arms and legs crossed, his eyes half-closed, his pale face veiled with apathy. Were his thoughts perhaps turning to the ironical sentences he himself had hurled once against Peel? "We no longer hear much talk about the country gentlemen." Now it was to him that they were saying: "We no longer hear much talk about the famous Protection." He seemed neither to listen nor to feel. When at last he spoke, the smothered violence of his sarcasm showed that he had not been unscathed. He forced a calm, sustained tone upon himself, but from time to time there escaped a phrase of such bitter irony as to seem almost agonized. His opening—"I was not born and bred a Chancellor of the Exchequer; I am one of the Parliamentary rabble"—had strange reverberations of Rousseau, very unexpected in the leader of the Conservative party. A violent storm raged throughout the whole of his lengthy speech. The quick flashes of lightning, the roll of thunder, made a congruous setting for the diabolic figure whom his adversaries believed they were gazing upon. When Gladstone rose it was a relief. The storm had ceased. Solemn, moralizing sentences rocked the conscience very agreeably. The unctuous moderation of tone was restful.

The subtle poetry of a British Budget is perhaps the most recondite art for an unfortunate who, like Disraeli, has not been reared from infancy by the Muses of Westminster. Its mysterious but inexorable laws are such that a penny on sugar will suddenly set up a horrid dissonance (and all the old subscribers gnash their teeth and look pitifully on the new conductor of the orchestra), whereas a penny on beer would perhaps have made in their ears the most delectable harmony. The tax on malt and the naval reductions chase one another in difficult, but very strict, counterpoint, which is revealed no doubt by instinct to the born Chancellor of the Exchequer. Gladstone, a natural *maëstro* of this austere and sublime art, had no trouble in laying bare the faults of the prentice hand.

Disraeli listened, his arms still folded, his eyes very weary. From time to time he looked at the clock. In the gallery, Derby was awaiting the vote which should decide the fate of his Ministry. He listened to Gladstone attentively for a few minutes, and then let his head fall on his arm. "Dull!" he said simply.

At four o'clock in the morning the Ministry was overturned by 305 votes to 286. The taste of power had been brief. Nothing can convey the grace of Disraeli's farewells. He showed no trace of sadness, but asked pardon of the House for the unwonted warmth of his speech. Lord John congratulated him on the courage with which he had fought. And the curtain fell. That evening Gladstone noted in his journal that God knew how much he regretted having been the instrument chosen to bring about the fall of Disraeli. The man had, in all conscience, great talents. "I would only pray that they might be well used."

XVI

ALBERT EINSTEIN: MAKER OF UNIVERSES[1]

By

H. GORDON GARBEDIAN

One of the most distinguished scientists of our time, winner of the Nobel Prize, Albert Einstein is perhaps best known for his theory of relativity. But he has also made a number of other salient studies in various branches of physics.

It should be noted that Mr. Garbedian has devoted a portion of his biography to an interpretation for lay readers of the scientist's complicated theories. He has selected for this volume a passage which gives, as he says, "a picturesque portrayal of Einstein, the human being."

THE HUMANITY OF A GREAT SCIENTIST

When he [Einstein] arrived one day at Brussels on a visit to the Belgian queen, the thought that there might be a welcoming party awaiting him at the station had not entered his head, and so he failed to notice the shining limousine and the group of smartly uniformed dignitaries waiting for him. Lugging a suitcase in one hand and his violin in the other, he proceeded to walk to the castle of his hostess. The welcoming party fumed and fretted as no sign of the distinguished scientist could be found. Then they returned to the castle and informed the Queen that Einstein must have changed his mind about coming. Just then the frowning Queen noticed a dusty figure ambling up the road, whistling cheerfully. In her mood of intense displeasure, a tramp was the last thing she wanted to see and she turned to give peremptory orders to whisk him from the estate.

[1] H. Gordon Garbedian, *Albert Einstein: Maker of Universes*, New York: Funk & Wagnalls Company, 1939, pp. 172-177.

But, wait! The figure of the "tramp" had come closer now, and her Majesty's frown turned to consternation, then pleased surprise, as, calling up all her reserves of self-command she managed to stammer:

"Why, Herr Doktor Einstein! How do you do! I am so happy to see you, but why didn't you use the car I sent for you? Why did you walk all that distance?"

"Why, your Majesty, I didn't think about a car being sent for me," replied the visitor with a naïve smile. "When I got off the train, I just came out. And it was a very pleasant walk!"

Einstein could have become a very rich man in a short time if he had been willing to capitalize his fame on the lecture platform and in the newspapers. But to him an inexpensive glass dish was as good as one of silver, so why become excited about money? He believed that wealth only appealed to selfishness and always tempted its owners to abuse it. To friends who remonstrated, pointing out the good that money could do, the scientist cut in: "I am absolutely convinced that no wealth in the world can help humanity forward. The example of great and fine personalities is the only thing that can lead us to fine ideas and noble deeds. Can you imagine Moses, Jesus or Gandhi armed with the money-bags of Carnegie?"

Only one thing Einstein wanted from the world, and this, apparently, money could not buy—privacy and seclusion for a life of quiet contemplation. Probably no man was so plagued by offers of gold for newspaper articles, for public appearances, for testimonials of every imaginable article from toothpaste and shaving soap to pimple eradicators and cigars. He considered all such overtures as "corruption," and rejected them with cold disdain. To Einstein money had no lure—it was simply something to give away. At one time he was supporting 150 families in Berlin. A German journal proposed to him to reprint one of his important lectures, offering him 1000 marks for the privilege. The scientist refused. The editor persisted. It was Einstein's duty to science to permit publication, he was told, and he finally capitulated. But his consent was given on one condition. He could not, he said, accept 1000 marks for the paper. That was far beyond the true worth of the address. He would permit its publication only if the editor agreed to reduce his price to 600 marks!

The success of the German editor encouraged an American publication to approach Einstein with an offer of a fabulous sum for an article dealing with any subject he cared to discuss. The offer reduced the scientist to the point of tears. He had been insulted he told his wife.

"Does the impudent fellow think I am a movie star, or a prize fighter?" he cried.

Einstein never wrote the article. He never even bothered to acknowledge receipt of the offer. He was a scientist, a pure and honest scientist, and woe unto him who "insulted" him by treating him otherwise!

The professor never rode in a taxi, because he felt that a taxi would set him apart from the great majority of his fellow men who had to ride in street cars. When traveling, he preferred to ride third-class, and it was only after considerable persuasion by Mrs. Einstein, who always exercised a great deal of influence in worldly matters over her husband, that he agreed to compromise by riding in second-class conveyances.

It was Mrs. Einstein, an old-fashioned, modest woman, unaffected by her husband's fame, who shielded the professor from many of the annoyances of everyday life. She had charge of the family budget and she cared for the voluminous mail. With all his wizardry at mathematics, the professor could never make his bank book balance. It was she who kept the family finances straight, just as it was she who attended to the more domestic household duties. At eight o'clock each morning, as sunlight streamed into their top-floor apartment, she would turn on the water in the bathtub and call her husband. He appeared in slippers and a colorful bathrobe, played at the piano while the tub was filling, and when his wife called "Ready, Albert," crossed over to the bathroom. His wife always had to follow him to close the bathroom door—a little chore which the professor could not remember to do for himself. After a simple breakfast, he retired to his den while she sat down to sort her husband's mail according to language classifications: French, German, Spanish, Italian, Jewish, English, and so on. The mail came from all parts of the world, in all languages and in all varieties of handwriting. Some days there were several hundred letters from points as far apart as New York, Tokyo, Madrid, Moscow, Paris, London and Bombay. Mrs. Einstein went over them all, and classified them. Some she could throw away without a reply, some had to be answered immediately, others the Professor himself had to consider, while still others had to be translated or read to him.

The task of handling this correspondence required a good part of the day, and frequently the evening, too, had to be devoted by both to their mail. But Mrs. Einstein was an intelligent woman who understood that her husband, working under the strain of continued intellectual activity, required a counterpoise of fellowship and music and social fun. Friends dropped in during the evening to play musical instruments with the Herr Professor, while Mrs. Einstein bustled about smilingly to make her guests comfortable. There were visitors, too, from abroad who wished to confer with the scientist, and distinguished men and women who shared Einstein's intellectual and humanitarian interests.

Such companionship pleased the scientist greatly. He liked particularly to discuss philosophy—the teachings of Plato, Hume, Spinoza and Schopenhauer—with other intelligent men. He liked to read and discuss the writings of Tolstoy and Dostoyevsky and the skeptical works of George Bernard Shaw and Anatole France. Shaw once said that the best criticism about his *Joan of Arc* was a letter from Einstein. Gerhart Hauptmann, whose poetry Einstein regarded as the most profoundly moving of our time, became a close friend and was a frequent visitor in the scientist's home. The drama and concerts of classical music appealed to Einstein, and his wife had less trouble in coaxing him out for an evening of Bach or Mozart or Beethoven than for any other purpose. There were lighter moments, too, when intimate friends and relatives and their children dropped in for a visit. During such times, Einstein loved to play the role of the paternal uncle for the benefit of the youngsters in the party. Puffing away contentedly at his briar pipe, he would indulge in a Socratic dialogue with one of his nephews.

"I got a letter from an inventor in America this morning," he would say, "suggesting that an aviator go up above the clouds in a helicopter and wait for Europe to roll around in the natural course of the earth's revolution. He thinks he could get to Paris that way without crossing the ocean. Do you think that's a bright idea?"

"No, Herr Professor, I do not."

"But why don't you think it's a good idea?"

"Well . . . because . . . well, the helicopter is too heavy. It could not get beyond the air which it needs to support it, and . . . well . . ." (now the youngster espied a smile on the scientist's face and moved ahead more confidently) "well, of course the air is going round with the earth, too, so the man in the machine would get nowhere!"

"A very good answer," beamed Einstein. "You're a bright young man!" Then he got up and clapped the boy jovially on the shoulder, and, hand in hand, the two retired to the kitchen in complete understanding to hunt for some delicacy for the boy, and, not infrequently, for the scientist too.

XVII

CHARLES DICKENS: HIS LIFE AND WORK[1]

By

STEPHEN LEACOCK

This life of Charles Dickens (1812-1870), one of the most widely known and most beloved of all English novelists, is immensely interesting reading. Dickens's humor and the remarkable resourcefulness of his characterizations have won for him lasting esteem.

Stephen Leacock has chosen for this anthology the "account of Dickens's failure to grasp the reality of American expansion in the West." He adds, "I select it because I think I have taken more pains to bring out the point of this, than have most writers."

EYES THAT COULD NOT SEE
CHARLES DICKENS VISITS THE WEST

Thus Dickens was already "fed up" with America when he left the South. The West was to finish him.

He and his wife left Baltimore on March 23 (1842) and spent a month in travelling to the Mississippi and back. Their route lay by rail to York (in Pennsylvania), then by coach twenty-five miles to Harrisburg, and after that by water to the "far West." Here the railway had not yet reached. Travel was by canal boat and river steamer. To Dickens, the cabins of the canal boats and steamers, crowded, stuffy, and promiscuous, the everlasting tobacco-spitting, and the utter lack of privacy, made the trip almost a nightmare. He could not compare it, as the older Americans could, with the primitive transport of a generation before—the transport of the time of Abraham Lincoln's childhood. In those days the settlers

[1] Stephen Leacock, *Charles Dickens: His Life and Work*, copyright 1933, 1934 by Doubleday, Doran & Company, Inc., New York, pp. 89-96.

floated down the river in barges and flat boats, "carried" over the forest trails of the portages, and slept in rude cabins of logs and poles, one side open to the weather. To those who remembered all this, the new travel was as palatial as it was rapid—with actual shelter to sleep under, meals on real tables, so that the larger river steamers, to the rude settlers of the Western frontier, seemed glittering with luxury.

Not so to Dickens.

His sufferings began with the coach through the valley of the Susquehanna (beautiful, he admits), with twelve people crammed inside it, and on the box and roof drunken men and dirty boys. Four horses tugged the coach through the rain and mud of early spring.

Then came Harrisburg, the seat of the government, which began at once, like the Washington Congress, to spit tobacco. There was a "levee" in honour of "Charles Dickens and lady"—"with a great number of the members of both branches of the Legislature. Pretty nearly every man spat upon the carpet." "These local Legislatures," wrote Dickens to Forster, "are too insufferably apish of mighty legislation to be seen without bile."

Next came the canal boat from Harrisburg to Pittsburgh, bridging the gap from the Susquehanna to the Ohio—a marvel of convenience to people who could remember the portage days, to Dickens an awful form of travel in something between a steamer and a floating tavern.

A canal boat, floating in the dirty water of the canal—the passengers had to "fish it up with a tin ladle" to wash in—with thirty-three people sitting down to eat breakfast in the foul air of a cabin where eight and twenty men had slept on movable wooden shelves, seven and twenty of them "in foul linen with yellow streams from half-chewed tobacco trickling down their chins!" There was a bar, reeking with gin, with a barber at work shaving, and seventeen men spitting at the stove while waiting. Worse still was the fall of night. "You can never conceive," wrote Dickens, "what the hawking and spitting is, the whole night through. . . . As to having a window open, that's not to be thought of."

Here and there on the journey Dickens could see in the forests the newly made clearings and the log huts of the settlers. These his sympathetic imagination endowed with his own sensations. "Their forlorn and miserable appearance," he wrote, "baffles all description. It pains the eye to see the stumps of great trees thickly strewed in every field of wheat; and never to lose the eternal swamp and dull morass, with hundreds of rotten trunks, of elm and pine and sycamore and logwood, steeped in its unwholesome water; where the frogs so croak at night that after dark there is an incessant sound as if millions of phantom teams, with bells, were travelling through the upper air, at an enormous distance off."

This of course is Martin Chuzzlewit in the swamp settlements of the West. Anybody who knows how to compare the lot of a pioneer settler in such a cabin with that of an English factory hand or a London sempstress or a slavey in a London lodging house of the period, can measure, as it should be measured, the value of Dickens's picture of America.

From Pittsburgh the Dickenses went by river steamers to Cincinnati, to Louisville, and thence to Cairo and St. Louis. The steamers in point of accommodation were, some of them, excellent, with better cabins than the Cunard boats on the Atlantic. The hotels, too, were mostly newly built on what seemed a large and commodious scale with a certain touch of "hospitality" about them, carried down from colonial days. Dickens, in his record of discomfort, makes an honorable exception of most of them. But everywhere he complains of the utter lack of privacy, of the rude curiosity of the people pushing to get a look at him.

Everywhere he was received with acclaim, though by this time the copyright question was beginning to boil up in the press of the East, and denunciation of Dickens's "ingratitude" was finding its way into print.

At Cincinnati there was a ball given for the Dickenses by a Judge Walker and attended (according to the guest of the evening) by "a hundred and fifty first class bores." At Louisville, so runs the legend of the local press, reprinted on Dickens's second visit, the "host" of the inn offered to be of service in introducing the distinguished visitor to some of the best families of Kentucky. "When I have need of your services," answered Dickens, "I will ring for you." If it is not true, it is well found. Dickens had travelled a long way from the young radical who dreamed of Van Diemen's Land. What right, anyway, has a hotel keeper to talk to a gentleman?

Thus, pleasantly discoursing, he came to Cairo, where the Ohio meets the Mississippi—"a breeding place of fever, ague, and death, vaunted in England as a mine of Golden Hope, and speculated in, on the faith of monstrous representations, to many people ruin. A dismal swamp, on which the half-built houses rot away; cleared here and there for the space of a few yards, and then teeming with rank unwholesome vegetation, on whose baneful shade the wretched wanderers who are tempted hither, droop and die and lay their bones." "I trust," he wrote, "never to see the Mississippi again except in dreams and nightmares."

On an upper stretch of the river at that time was a little boy of six years old for whom the vast reaches of the Mississippi, moving through the forests to the distant sea, and the lights of the river steamers passing in the night, were the inspiration of a lifetime. Compare the majesty of the picture of life on the Mississippi drawn in the pages of *Huckleberry Finn* with the cramped and uninspired picture given by Dickens. It is the work of a peevish cockney travelling without his breakfast.

At St. Louis there was, to Dickens's delight, a grand hotel, the Planters' House, "as large as the Middlesex hospital." There was a large public reception spoken of as a "soirée." But for Dickens the charm of being lionized had passed. He set out on his homeward journey, travelling across Ohio by water and stage, through Columbus to Sandusky, and thence by Lake Erie to Buffalo and Niagara. His feelings and impressions as revealed in his *American Notes* are embodied in such recurrent words as tobacco-spit, swamp, bullfrogs, corduroy roads, bugs, politics. For the people he can find little praise. Those of St. Louis as seen at the soirée given for him were declared "pretty rough and intolerably conceited." But they were not as bad as humanity when seen at Sandusky, Ohio—"The demeanor of the people in these country parts is invariably morose, sullen, clownish, and repulsive. I should think there is not on the face of the earth a people so utterly destitute of humour, vivacity or the capacity for enjoyment."

Dickens passed out from the West across the Niagara frontier to Canada (May, 1842). He never saw it again.

The truth was that he did not understand the scenes he witnessed.

What was really going on was a great epic in the history of mankind. It was the advance of civilization down the rivers, and through the forests, and out upon the silent prairies of the West. The woods bowed beneath the age, the forests echoed with voices, the savannahs murmured and rustled to the touch of life. In the mind's eye one could see already the log cabins rising into cathedrals, the villages spreading into great cities, and the swamps and cane-brakes changing to the park and meadowland of a smiling civilization. It was a wonderful epic, this advance of the frontier, moving westward day by day. As beside it the ravaging conquests of early Europe, leaving a track of slaughter, seem things of horror.

But Dickens had no eyes to see it all in its true proportion. Against the crowded canal boats, the jolting stages, and frame hotels, the log shanties, and forest villages sunken in the swamps, he set the trim countryside of England, with its neat village commons and parish churches and winding roads lined with thorn hedges—the whole of it a thousand years in the making. Against the cheap frame hotel he set the gabled inns of the John Willetts that had seen two hundred Christmas fires go roaring up the chimney. He suddenly discovered that, after all, the "old Tory gentleman" whom he had denounced didn't spit on the floor, or talk through his nose, or break into the conversations of strangers; that, after all, Mrs. Leo Hunter was a lady, that Mr. Minns and his cousin were gentlemen, and that Mr. Dombey was a dignified and honourable merchant who wouldn't cheat a stranger over a swamp lot in an imaginary settlement.

So it came that Dickens's mind turned back to the England that he knew and cast out the America which he couldn't understand. The fault was his. It has been said—on a foundation difficult to prove conclusively—that Dickens had invested some of his early gains from *Pickwick* in a fraudulent land company of Cairo, Illinois, and went West partly to see the scene of his discomfiture. If so, this gave him an added bitterness against the "Far West."

In any case, there is no doubt that he saw it all with crooked eyes. Could he have seen it right, what a marvelous picture, exaggerated in detail but true in the mass, he could have made of it! Just as at the "Boz Ball" in New York, so here in the New Edens and Thermopylæs a host of "characters" were beckoning to him, like actors waiting to "come on." They were standing there in the wings waiting to catch his attention—as merry and motley a company as those of the pages of *Pickwick* itself. But Dickens, fuming and raving in the foreground over international copyright, tobacco spittle, and slavery, never knew they were there. And when he came back twenty-six years later, he was too old, too broken, too self-absorbed to care whether they were there or not. What a goodly company there was ready to his hand, with their queer clothes, their universal military rank, their magnified eyesight, their generosity, their crookedness! Dickens could *see* them, but saw them only to scoff and denounce. Measured in the same way, the people in *Pickwick* are a pack of dunderheads and fools, Pickwick himself was an amiable idiot on a string, Sam Weller was a crook, and Sam Weller's father smelt of the stable. Dickens was in a land of enchantment and never knew it.

XVIII

GIANTS IN DRESSING GOWNS[1]

By

JULIAN B. ARNOLD

In his annual review of the books published in 1942, Dr. William Lyon Phelps placed *Giants in Dressing Gowns* among the ten best. Julian Arnold writes intimately in this book of the great men and women he has known, including Grover Cleveland, Tennyson, Browning, Conan Doyle, Queen Victoria, and many others.

From this intriguing book of recollections we present two selections: one is the story of the production of the first of the countless millions of books to be printed in the English language; and the other is the discovery of cold-rolled steel.

THE FIRST BOOK PRINTED IN ENGLISH

At . . . the Huntington [library] in Southern California, I recently met two friends and at the meeting experienced that emotion of which Ruskin wrote, "it causes a curling in the cheek, and is as good for one as a week spent at the seaside." Both friends were in glass-covered cases, as behooves rare books to which their owner delighteth to do honor. One was the original manuscript of Edwin Arnold's Brahmin epic *The Song Celestial*; the other was Caxton's *Recuyell of the Historyes of Troye*. As a boy, I had watched the writing of the former; as a man, I had known the latter in London. And thereby hangs a tale.

An inconspicuous doorway in Piccadilly used to lead into a darksome burrow, lined with an infinitude of books. Upon the shelves were ranged irregular rows of volumes, flaunting their pride in vellum and tooled

[1] Julian B. Arnold, *Giants in Dressing Gowns*, Chicago: Argus Books, 1942, pp. 33-37, 154-155.

leather or screening their worth in covers tattered with the adventures of years. Here bibliophiles broke daily the tenth commandment, handling ancient tomes or desired first editions—for this was the shop of Bernard Quaritch, foremost trader in the domain of rare books and manuscripts. During the latter half of the nineteenth century, he was the world's leading authority on the valuation of libraries, and through his hands passed to collectors many of the costliest volumes in existence, from Mazarin Bibles and Shakespearean folios to age-brown fragments of classical manuscripts, the sole survivors of their lineage.

One day he showed me a pearl of great price—the first book ever printed in the English language—and I gathered that it was on its way to the Huntington Library. Its title was *The Recuyell of the Historyes of Troye*, and the sacred thing lay amongst soft wrappings in a case, like a prince in his cradle. As I gazed with reverence upon that beginning of the immense literary output of our language, Quaritch told me the story of the volume, the earliest experiment of its immortal publisher, William Caxton.

Had Caxton followed the path which his training indicated, he would probably have emerged as a millionaire-merchant and lord mayor of London—and then been forgotten. Through half his life he drove in the ruts of commerce, then suddenly hitched his wagon to the star of literature. At the time of the printing of his first book, he was Governor of the Company of Merchant Adventurers in Bruges, and in that capacity was a man of such substance that he negotiated a trading treaty with the reigning prince, Charles the Bold, Duke of Burgundy.

Now Charles of Burgundy had married Margaret of York, sister of Edward IV, King of England, and it chanced that when Caxton was attending the court of Charles the Bold, he encountered the fair Margaret who, glad of the opportunity of speaking her native English, entered into conversation with the suave Governor of the Merchant Adventurers. To her he mentioned a romance which had recently come to his hands entitled *Le Recuyell*, written in French by Raoul le Fevre, and describing the story of Troy. Margaret desired to read it but, being dubious of her knowledge of old French, asked the courtly Caxton to make for her a translation into her native tongue.

It was a simple request, but mark to what it led. Caxton began the translation in March of 1469, but it was not until September of 1471 that the finished manuscript was ready for presentation to the Duchess. Wishing to make other copies of his translation, he employed clerks for the purpose, but they proved too slow for the ardent Caxton. At that opportune hour he met Colard Mansion who showed him a document, the text of which had been impressed from wooden blocks. Caxton instantly realized the possibilities latent in the idea and agreed to finance the carving of a font of wooden letters and to provide the paraphernalia of that earliest mode of printing. In partnership with Mansion, his press was set up in Bruges in 1474, and two years later it produced Caxton's *Recuyell of the Historyes of Troye*—the first of the countless millions of books to be printed in the English language. It is a goodly sized volume, remarkably clearly impressed with ornate initials after the manner of early manuscripts.

Forsaking all else for literature, Caxton returned to England where he established his printing press at the sign of the Red Pale, within the sanctuary of Westminster. There, in the shadow of the Abbey, the shrine of the tongue which has spread over half the world, he devoted the remainder of his life to transmuting the manuscripts of his time into the form of printed books. . . .

All hail! Fair Margaret, Duchess of Burgundy, who bade the courtly William Caxton make for Your Grace a translation of Raoul le Fevre's *Recuyell*, and thereby started the mighty stream of printed English literature.

THE CHILDREN OF A CROWBAR

One busy day, an excited workman forced his way into Andrew Carnegie's office and insisted on showing to the "boss" a crowbar which he carried lovingly in his grimy hands. Vehemently Carnegie protested, and, just as persistently, the man refused to make his exit until an examination had been well and truly made of his precious crowbar. It seemed that a little while previously he had accidentally dropped the heavy tool between two mighty steel rollers in the mills and watched its safe passage under their relentless pressure. Being an observant man, he had waited until the iron had cooled enough to be handled; with his first glance at its condition, he had made a discovery of such apparent importance that he had resolved to bear it with him to headquarters.

"Of course I'll be fined for the crowbar," he said, "and maybe I'll be fired too, but I don't care. What I want you to do is to take a look at the new color and fibre of the thing, now that it's been cold-rolled. Crowbars don't look like that when they're broken, and I ought to know for I've seen plenty. But this one, when it had come out from between the rollers and cooled a bit so that I could pick it up, 'peared to me like some sort of new metal, close-grained and tough at that. Take a peek at it. Seems funny to me."

Thus urged, Carnegie complied with the wish of his employee, and at his first examination of the half-flattened instrument suddenly asked, "Have you shown this to anyone?"

"No, sir. I thought I'd just bring it to you."

"You did well, and are obviously a keen man. You won't be fired, and you won't be fined. You'll be promoted! Here's a hundred dollar note. Put it in your pocket. You'll have lots of them in the days to come—but keep quiet about this matter."

Great achievements come from little happenings; that workman rose to be one of the chief executives in the steel industry, and all the cold-rolled steel rails of the American railroads are the children of that crowbar.

XIX

MARCONI: THE MAN AND HIS WIRELESS[1]

By

ORRIN E. DUNLAP

Guglielmo Marconi (1874-1937), inventor, electrical engineer, and winner of the Nobel prize for physics, was the first to perfect the devices used in space telegraphy. To his genius is due the great scientific triumph of wireless telegraphy.

Orrin Dunlap states that he gives us the exciting story of how the first wireless signal was flashed across the Atlantic sky, because "it is not only unforgettable, but one of the great climaxes in the history of wireless, and in Marconi's life."

THE FIRST TRANSATLANTIC SIGNAL

Marconi at the dawn of a new century caught the vision of a dream. He saw men sitting on the edge of the North American continent listening to what a lambent spark was sputtering across 2,000 miles of broad, curving ocean.

New Year's Day, 1900, ushered in an electrical age of speed and scientific wonders—a Century of Progress.

The question in 1900 was, how can 20-kilowatts spread out to every point of the compass provide sufficient energy to traverse 2,000 miles in one direction? Would America and England be brought in touch with each other without the aid of the submerged cable costing from $4,500,000 to $9,000,000 or up to $2,500 a mile?

Marconi thought so, and was working feverishly toward that conclusion.

[1] Orrin E. Dunlap, *Marconi: The Man and His Wireless*, by permission of The Macmillan Company, publishers, New York, 1937, pp. 87-90, 93-99, 100-101.

The cable secluded in the bed of the sea could carry dots and dashes, but the idea that thoughts might pass through the ocean air in less than a second was something to balk human credulity.

How less tedious, less expensive it would be to utilize a free right-of-way in the heavens instead of laying a cable in Neptune's dreary sanctum? The idea had possibilities calling for a miracle man. The skeptics, of course, were countless. It was true, this man Marconi had convinced the doubting world that wireless lifted messages for short distances, but the Atlantic—well, it was much wider than the English Channel.

It was not so difficult to comprehend, in view of Marconi's achievements, that a boat 250 miles off the English coast picked up a wireless signal from the shore. But that must have been a freak of nature aided by extraordinary atmospheric conditions. So argued the die-hards. It was eight times that distance from England to America!

Marconi, a conservative scientist, knew the Atlantic project was fraught with daring—a little too much for the public mind to grasp. He realized the significance of premature announcements.

Wireless across the sea meant the very shrinkage of the earth. It meant new and revolutionary communication between every nation on the face of the globe. Wisdom called for secrecy. If the dream turned out to be a bubble it would be a matter of disappointment only to the dreamer. If successful it would be a signal of progress for mankind. So he would work quietly, unassumingly, with plans unpublicized.

He was looked upon as a modern wizard whose human traits outwardly failed to betray any eccentricities of genius. Londoners who saw him in Piccadilly or Pall Mall observed a rather sad, keen-eyed, thin-lipped young man with unlimited capacity for work and a firm faith in his own ability. His brown hair was neatly trimmed and carefully brushed; sometimes he shaved twice a day. His attire, if anything, was a little too neat for a scientist. He was fond of a fur coat and was not above afternoon tea. One who passed him in the street would class him with the average club or city man, fond of the good things in life, yet his manner and step revealed he was by no means an idler. He looked like a man faithful to friendship but one who would give it rarely.

Divested of the fur coat he looked frail. His movements were slow and direct, yet there was an odd air of diffidence very apparent when he was in the company of strangers. This shyness was emphasized if wireless telegraphy was the topic. He appeared much younger than his twenty-six years, and more than one great scientist eyed him incredulously when seeing him for the first time.

Superficially, Marconi had little to distinguish him from the average man, but closer acquaintance invariably impressed one with his tremendous energy. The doctrine of strenuous life never had a more faithful follower. He labored under high pressure and expected his subordinates to feel the same intense enthusiasm that gripped him during experimental periods. He worked by night and day when a problem presented itself.

Such was the calibre of the man intent upon transatlantic wireless; the man who was preparing for what he termed, "the big thing"—wireless between the Old and New Worlds.

Marconi, accompanied by Major Flood Page, managing director of the Marconi Wireless Company, and R. N. Vyvyan, engineer, in July 1900, went to the barren southwest tip of England and selected Poldhu, near Mullion in Cornwall, as the site for a pioneer transmitter, 100 times more powerful than any station ever built. Construction began in October.

There history would be etched electrically on the blue canopy of the globe. Professor James Ambrose Fleming of University College, London, appointed Scientific Adviser of the Marconi Wireless Company in 1899, was entrusted to design the installation. He was a specialist in high-tension alternating currents. Mr. Vyvyan was selected to supervise construction. Newspapers printed meagre reports that an Italian inventor hoped to link two far-distant points without the aid of visible wires.

The word "visible" appearing in the accounts of 1896-99 indicated the incredulity of the general public. The Gay Nineties were conservative in regard to electrical miracles; people shook their heads in doubt and wonderment....

A queer-looking structure, never before seen on the English landscape or anywhere else for that matter, was attracting attention on the forbidding rocks that jut out into the Atlantic at Poldhu. It was Marconi's latest idea of what an aerial system should comprise. There was to be a ring of twenty wooden masts, each about 200 feet high, arranged in a semicircle 200 feet in diameter, covering about an acre. It was designed as the "frame" of a conical aerial consisting of 400 wires.

By the end of August, 1901, the masts were nearly completed, but a cyclone swept the English coast on September 17; the big masts blew down like so many toothpicks after it had taken eleven months to erect them. Disappointment swept through the Marconi ranks. The engineers said it meant postponement of three months or more to remove the wreckage and build anew.

The "sister" towers on Cape Cod suffered a similar disaster a few weeks later.

Marconi was too anxious, too unconquerable a soul to permit fallen masts to get the best of him. He decided it might be possible to utilize a simpler aerial. So two poles, instead of twenty, each 150 feet high, were erected. A triangular stay was stretched between the masts and from it were suspended fifty-five copper wires. They were about a yard apart at the top and converged at the bottom, forming a fan-shaped aerial.

Everything was ready for a preliminary test.

The fiery spark crashed across the gap electrifying the makeshift web of wire and the bleak November air.

A wireless outpost at Crookhaven, Ireland, 225 miles away, heard the signals with such intensity that the engineers felt certain the power was sufficient to drive a message across the Atlantic—ten times as far as Poldhu to Crookhaven!

Marconi was sure it would. He decided to conduct the first test in Newfoundland—the nearest point in America to the Old World.

Bound on a historic journey, he sailed on November 26 from Liverpool on the liner *Sardinian*, accompanied by two assistants, G. S. Kemp[2] and P. W. Paget.

They had odd baggage for three men. Small captive balloons and a number of large kites were in the luggage. They knew the inclement weather in Canada at this season of the year and the shortness of the time at their disposal made it impossible to erect high masts to hold aloft antenna wires. But the kites and balloons might do the trick, thereby saving time and expense and possibly make history.

Undramatically, in fact, unnoticed, the trio of pioneers landed at St. John's on Friday, December 6, and the following day, before beginning operations they visited the Governor, Sir Cavendish Boyle, Premier, Sir Robert Bond, and other members of the Ministry, who promised heartiest cooperation. They cheerfully placed the resources of every department of the government at Marconi's disposal to facilitate his work.

"After taking a look at various sites," said Marconi, "which might prove suitable, I considered the best one was on Signal Hill, a lofty eminence overlooking the port and forming a natural bulwark which protects it from the fury of the Atlantic winds. On top of this hill is a small plateau some two acres in area, which seemed very suitable for manipulation of the balloons and kites. On a crag on this plateau rose the new Cabot Memorial Tower, erected in commemoration of the famous Italian explorer John Cabot, and designed as a signal station. Close to it there was

[2] Mr. Kemp was one of Marconi's most valued electricians and his diary of wireless was a great asset to Marconi when in court fighting patent litigation and infringements.

the old military barracks, then used as a hospital. It was in the forum of this building that we set up the apparatus and made preparations for the great experiment.

"On Monday, December 9, we began work. On Tuesday we flew a kite with 600 feet of aerial as a preliminary test, and on Wednesday we inflated one of the balloons, which made its first ascent during the morning. It was about fourteen feet in diameter and contained about 1,000 cubic feet of hydrogen gas, quite sufficient to hold up the aerial, which consisted of wire weighing about ten pounds. After a short while, however, the blustery wind ripped the balloon away from the wire. The balloon sailed out over the sea. We concluded, perhaps the kites would be better, and on Thursday morning, in spite of a gusty gale we managed to fly a kite up 400 feet.

"The critical moment had come, for which the way had been prepared by six years of hard and unremitting work, despite the usual criticism directed at anything new. I was about to test the truth of my belief.

"In view of the importance of all that was at stake, I had decided not to trust entirely to the usual arrangement of having the coherer signals record automatically on a paper tape through a relay and Morse instrument, but to use instead a telephone connected to a self-restoring coherer. The human ear being much more sensitive than the recorder it would be more likely to hear the signal.

"Before leaving England I had given detailed instructions for transmission of a certain signal, the Morse telegraphic 'S'—three dots—at a fixed time each day beginning as soon as word was received that everything at St. John's was in readiness. If the invention could receive on the kite-wire in Newfoundland some of the electric waves produced, I knew the solution of the problem of transoceanic wireless telegraphy was at hand.

"I cabled Poldhu to begin sending at 3 o'clock in the afternoon, English time, continuing until 6 o'clock; that is, from 11:30 to 2:30 o'clock in St. John's."

As the hands of the clock moved toward noon on Thursday (December 12, 1901), Marconi sat waiting with the telephone receiver held to his ear. It was an intense hour of expectation. Arranged on the table were the delicate instruments ready for a decisive test. There was no calibrated dial tuner to facilitate adjusting the circuit to a specific wave length. In fact, the wave of Poldhu was not measured. There was no device to measure it. Professor Fleming thought there should be some method of measuring wave length but he had yet to invent his cymometer or wavemeter.

The length of Poldhu's wave was a guess. There was nothing precise or scientific about tuning. But based on the fact that the aerial was 200 feet high and that it was linked with a series coil or "jigger," Professor Fleming estimated the wave length was not less than about 3,000 feet or 960 meters.

Marconi had to hunt for the wave.

A wire ran out through the window of Cabot Tower, thence to a pole and upward to the kite which could be seen swaying overhead. It was a raw day. A cold sea thundered at the base of the 300-foot cliff. Oceanward through the mist rose dimly the rude outlines of Cape Spear, the easternmost point of the North American continent.

Beyond rolled the unbroken ocean, nearly 2,000 miles to the coast of the British Isles; wireless might leap that in one ninety-third of a second! Across the harbor the city of St. John's lay on the hillside. No one had taken enough interest in the experiment to go up through the snow to Signal Hill. Even the ubiquitous reporter was absent.

In Cabot Tower, the veteran signalman stood in the lookout's nest scanning the horizon for ships, little dreaming that mysterious waves might be coming out of the sky from England.

Wireless was ready for the crucial test. Its destiny was at stake. So was Marconi's. Everything that could be done had been done. The receiving outfit was as sensitive as Marconi could make it; he had faith that these instruments would pick up the faintest trace of a signal.

Marconi listened and listened. Not a sound was heard for half an hour. He inspected the instruments. They looked perfect. Had something gone wrong at Poldhu? Had some mysterious force led the signals astray? Was the curvature of the globe a barrier? All these things flashed through his mind, coupled with the fact that it was almost fantastic to believe an unseen wave of intelligence could cross through the ocean air and strike such a slender target as a copper wire. It seemed incredible. It would be so easy for the message to travel off in some undesired direction.

Marconi knew, however, if the signal went east, north or south it would also go west and to that wire antenna dangling from the kite.

Without warning there was a sharp click in the earphones. What caused it? Was some stray static playing a prank? Indeed not! Marconi had at last found the right tuning adjustment to put him in touch with Poldhu!

"Suddenly, at about 12:30 o'clock, unmistakably three scant little clicks in the telephone receiver, corresponding to three dots in the Morse code, sounded several times in my ear as I listened intently," said Marconi, in recounting the day. "But I would not be satisfied without corroboration.

" 'Can you hear anything, Kemp?' I said, handing the receiver to him.

"Kemp heard the same thing I did, and I knew then that I had been absolutely right in my anticipation," recalled Marconi. "Electric waves which were being sent out from Poldhu had traversed the Atlantic serenely ignoring the curvature of the earth, which so many doubters considered would be a fatal obstacle. I knew then that the day on which I should be able to send full messages without wires or cables across the Atlantic was not very far away. Distance had been overcome, and further development of the sending and receiving instruments was all that was required."

Wireless had flashed across the Atlantic's sky like "some meteor that the sun exhales."

Again and again Marconi and Kemp listened to be sure there was no mistake. Paget was called in. He listened but heard nothing; he was slightly deaf. What Marconi and Kemp heard must have been Poldhu. There was no other wireless station in the world to send that pre-arranged signal. And a marvel was that it was noon time; it would have been so much easier to perform the feat at night when darkness aids the flight of long-wave wireless. Marconi was not aware of that.

It was mid-afternoon. The kite gyrated wildly in the gale that swept in from the sea. The antenna failed to maintain the maximum altitude and the fluctuating height naturally influenced reception. The wind tugged and tugged at the kite, finally at 2:20 o'clock the antenna was lifted within range of the repetitious dots. And that gave further verification.

At dusk the inventor and his companions went down the hill toward the city sparkling with lights. He made no statement to the press. In fact, he felt rather depressed because he had not intercepted a continuous stream of signals. Possibly the stress of the preceding days had something to do with his disheartened feeling.

It is said that a secret is no longer a secret if more than one person holds it, but that night three men kept a secret from the world. And what they harbored was front-page news—news that would find a place in history books.

They went to sleep dreaming of what they had heard and in hope that a new day would put the stamp of success on their work by further verification. It almost seemed too true for them to believe their own ears. They would listen again for the three elusive dots.

They were up on the hill early the next morning, anxious to lend an ear to space at noon, for that was the appointed time for Poldhu to broadcast.

The signals came on schedule but were not quite as distinct as the day before. The changing weather on a 2,000 mile front could make a radical difference in behavior of the waves. There was no doubt, however, that wireless had spanned the Atlantic. Nevertheless, the modest inventor hesitated to make his achievement public, lest it seem too extraordinary for belief.

Finally, after withholding the news for two days, certainly evidence of his conservatism and self-restraint. Marconi issued a statement to the press, and on that Sabbath morning the world knew but doubted. . . .

The scientific world was mindful that Marconi had never released a statement in public until absolutely certain of the facts. He never had to withdraw a notice as to his progress. As soon as the significance of the event was realized star reporters and special magazine writers rushed northward from New York to get the story from the lips of the inventor.

He told them it cost $200,000 to get the three dots across the Atlantic! To Marconi there was nothing problematical about the future; he had spanned the Atlantic. He had upset the calculations of mathematicians.

XX

JEFFERSON DAVIS: THE UNREAL AND THE REAL [1]

By

ROBERT McELROY

Comprehensive research, impartiality in judgment, and a scholarly understanding of the subject by the author make this full-length biography of the president of the Confederacy an exceptionally able study.

Robert McElroy presents two selections from his work which reveal something of the mind and character of Davis. Of the second story, Dr. McElroy states that it "shows, more personally, what manner of man Davis was."

A STRANGE TEMPTATION THAT CAME TO JEFFERSON DAVIS

Temptations come to statesmen in strange guises, and during the early summer of 1862, one of the strangest possible temptations came to Davis. Major Walker Taylor, a cousin of the first Mrs. Davis, appeared at Richmond, with a daring scheme to capture Lincoln and bring him South, and Colonel William Preston Johnston, Davis' aide-de-camp, gives us an account of the interview between him and Davis:

" 'Well, Walker,' said Mr. Davis, affably, 'what is it?' 'Mr. Davis, I want to bring Lincoln a prisoner to you in this city.' 'Nonsense!' said Davis, 'How can such a thing be done?' 'Just as easily,' said Taylor, 'as walking out of this town. I came across the Potomac at no great distance from Washington, and while I was there (in Washington) I watched Lincoln's habits closely and know his outgoing and incoming. I tell you, sir, that I can bring him across that river as easily as I can walk over your doorstep.'

[1] Robert McElroy, *Jefferson Davis: The Unreal and the Real*, New York: Harper & Brothers, 1937, I, 344-345, II, 504-505.

" 'How could you do it?' said Mr. Davis. 'Lincoln,' replied Taylor, 'does not leave the White House until evening, or near twilight, and then with only a driver, he takes a lonely ride two or three miles in the country to a place called the Soldiers' Home, which is his summer residence. My point is to collect several of these Kentuckians whom I see about here doing nothing and who are brave enough for such a thing as that, and capture Lincoln, run him down the Potomac, and cross him over just where I crossed, and the next day we will have him here.'

"Davis shook his head and said: 'I cannot give my authority, Walker. In the first place, I suppose Lincoln is a man of courage. He has been in Indian wars, and is a Western man. He would undoubtedly resist capture. In that case you would kill him. I could not stand the imputation of having consented to let Mr. Lincoln be assassinated. Our cause could not stand it. Besides, what value would he be to us as a prisoner? Lincoln is not the government. He is merely its political instrument. If he were brought to Richmond, what could I do with him? He would have to be treated like a magistrate of the North, and we have neither the time nor the provision. No, sir, I will not give my authority to abduct Lincoln'."

"THAT IS MY ESTATE"

As news of disaster after disaster arrived, Davis retained not only his courage, but his calm and his cheerful exterior. Clark declared: "I saw an organized government disintegrate and fall to pieces little by little, until there was only left a single member of the Cabinet, his private secretary, a few members of his staff, a few guides and servants, to represent what had been a powerful government. . . . Under these unfortunate circumstances, his great resources of mind and heart shone out most brilliantly. He was calm, self-poised; giving way to no petulance of temper at discomfort; advising, consoling, laying aside all thought of self; planning and doing what was best . . . for our unhappy and despairing people, and uttering words of consolation and wise advice to every family where he entered as guest." One story of many which survive illustrates both his generosity and his financial condition after his guarded treasury had been disbursed. He stopped at a little cabin on the roadside and asked a woman who stood in the doorway for a drink of water. She turned to comply with his request, and while he drank, a baby barely able to walk crawled down the steps toward him. The mother smiled. "Is this not President Davis?" she asked. "It is, madam," he answered. She pointed proudly to the child. "He's named for you." The President drew a gold coin from his pocket and handed it to the mother: "Please keep it for my little namesake and tell him when he is old enough to know." As he rode away with Reagan, he added, "The last coin I had on earth, Reagan. I wouldn't have had that but for the fact I'd never seen one like it and kept it for luck."

His luck had left him before this generous impulse took his lucky coin, but he added, cheerfully, "My home is a wreck, Benjamin's and Breckinridge's are in Federal hands, Mallory's residence at Pensacola has been burned by the enemy, your home in Texas has been wrecked." He paused and drew from his pocket-book a few Confederate bills: "That is my estate at the present moment."

XXI

HEINRICH HEINE: PARADOX AND POET[1]

By

LOUIS UNTERMEYER

In the preface to this biography, Louis Untermeyer says "that in Heine I first recognized that combination of the trivial and the elemental, the juxtaposition of the romantic and the realistic, which seems to me the enriching power of poetry—at least the poetry to which I devoted myself."

This biography of the illustrious lyric poet, Heine, is written with deep understanding and genuine sympathy, and it discloses many entertaining and enlightening facets of his restless life and paradoxical personality. The selection chosen gives us flashes of Heine's wit even in the face of impending death.

THE TORTURED WIT

1844-1847

By February, 1846, Heine's physical condition was dreadful. His left eye was closed; there was no sensation in his lips. "I kiss, but I feel nothing," he wrote Lasalle. "Part of my tongue is paralyzed, too. Everything I eat tastes like earth." In September he wrote Campe, "My speech-organs are so crippled I can hardly articulate; for four months I have been scarcely able to eat because of the difficulty of chewing and a complete loss of taste. My frame has shrunk; I look like a wizened one-eyed Hannibal. . . . I know I cannot be saved, but I expect to hang on another miserable two or three years.[2] Death, between you and me, is the least thing to fear. It is dying which is terrible, not death—if there is such a thing as death. Death may be the final superstition." On October 19, 1846, he wrote to Heinrich

[1] Louis Untermeyer, *Heinrich Heine: Paradox and Poet*, New York: Harcourt, Brace and Company, Inc., 1937, pp. 302-308.

[2] Actually Heine lived until 1856, almost ten years more.

Laube. "I am happy that you are coming here. Do not delay your visit too long, for though mine is a lingering illness, there may be a sudden change, and in that case you would arrive too late to argue with me about immortality, the Fatherland, Campe, and other vital issues. Indeed, you might find me singularly silent. This winter at least I will be at Faubourg Poissonière, No. 41; if you do not find me at this address, look for me in the Montmartre Cemetery, not at Père Lachaise—it is too noisy for me there."

These are characteristic utterances. Facing dissolution and impending death, never for a moment free of pain, Heine's wit never deserted him. It was a sardonic humor, even (though not unnaturally) perverse; the wit was twisted and tortured, but it would not die.

The deathless and contradictory quality of that wit has impressed commentators of every persuasion. It is the basis of Matthew Arnold's and George Eliot's essays on the poet; it is the chief exhibit of Sigmund Freud's *Der Witz und seine Beziehung zum Unbewussten* ("Wit and Its Relation to the Unconscious"), in which there are more than twenty-five references to Heine. Heine knew that wit, like art, was by nature heretical; but his was a particularly Jewish wit, the humor of antitheses, of the incongruities of beauty and misery, perfection and terror. It was peculiarly Jewish, too, in its self-mockery; a kind of self-beating which anticipates the enemy's blows, and so becomes hardened to flagellation. But it is most characteristic in the way in which the tragic is suddenly turned into the ridiculous. Heine, like Santayana, saw the world as a perpetual caricature of itself, a mockery and contradiction of what it pretends to be. Heine had been mortally hurt by its pretenses and hypocrisies, and wit was his chief weapon against the pompous dignities which were scarcely less hateful and harmful than the indignities. Wit was the clown's bladder that Heine whirled about, but when a head was struck the bladder somehow acted like a bludgeon. Heine, who had whined and wept without relief, found a kind of comfort in bursts of rankling laughter; he was willing to seem ridiculous if he made the enemy suffer from ridicule. Employing this seemingly foolish plaything Heine challenged authority, rebelled against the established injustices, stopped his opponents with his unexpected foolhardiness, and saved his hide, as well as his soul, through critical derision.

It was a much-belabored hide, and there were times Heine felt it scarcely worth saving. "What good will my reading do me," he exclaimed one day, looking up from a pile of medical books, "except that I will be able to give lectures in heaven on what the doctors do not know about my disease." "Can you hiss today?" anxiously inquired one of his doctors—*siffler* meaning to expel air sharply, to whistle or to hiss. "Alas, no," Heine wheezed disconsolately, and then brightening, "except at one of Scribe's comedies." Grimly he played variations on the theme. "Is your illness really incurable?" he was asked. "Heavens, no," he answered lightly enough. "Some day I shall die of it." Or "My constitution is even worse than the Constitution of Prussia." Perhaps most famous of Heine's mordant rejoinders is his response to the person who, during Heine's last hours, hoped God would forgive the dying man. "Of course he will," Heine answered comfortably, "*c'est son métier* [that's his profession]."

Forgiving was not Heine's business nor his specialty. "My nature is the most peaceful in the world," he wrote with deceptive mildness. "All I ask is a simple cottage, a decent bed, good food, some flowers in front of my window, and a few trees beside my door. Then, if God wanted to make me completely happy, He would let me enjoy the spectacle of six or seven of my enemies dangling from those trees. I would forgive them all the wrongs they had done me—forgive them from the bottom of my heart, for we must forgive our enemies. But not until they are hanged!" . . . .

It is Freud . . . who points out the catharsis obtained by the Jew's unrestrained laughter at his plight, his ability not only to endure degradation and hopelessness but to make fun of his own misery. It is not a general *Weltschmerz* but a racial torture which makes Heine jest ironically in such poems as "The New Jewish Hospital in Hamburg" and again in "The Baths of Lucca" when he writes, "Do not talk to me about the Jewish religion; I would not wish it on my worst enemy. It isn't a religion, it's a misfortune." Later, referring to the Jews as "the dough from which gods are kneaded," he said, "If the Jews were finally extinct, and it became known that a single survivor of the race still existed somewhere, I believe men would travel a hundred miles to touch his hand, a hand that is despised today." And it was as a Jew and a rebel that he wrote, "My favorite God is Christ—not because He is the legitimate scion of a Father-God who ruled before him, but because, though He was born a Dauphin-Prince of Heaven, He has democratic sympathies and does not enjoy Court functions; because He is not the God of aristocratic, crop-headed theologists and pedants, but a simple God of the people, a Citizen among citizens."

It was against disparagement that Heine directed his shafts, as one who shoots first because he is afraid of being hit. And it was against the high and mighty ones that the barbed arrows were aimed. They usually went home. Once when Baron Rothschild complained to Heine that his house was overrun with poets and painters, saying, "What shall I do with these shiftless artists! I can buy them by the dozen!" "No doubt," Heine replied.

"But when they are bought, how are you going to sell them at a profit?" At another time the same Rothschild made the mistake of telling Heine he had learned that the muddy Seine was quite pure at its source. "Yes," Heine smiled, "and your father is known to have been an honest man." With the Rothschild dinner parties in mind Heine said that the Italian *Lacrymae Christi* got its name from the tears Christ shed to see the rich drink the best wine while the poor went hungry and thirsty. But it was not alone upon the Jewish millionaires that Heine took vengeance. "The Hanoverian aristocracy are asses," he wrote, "asses who talk only about horses."

Heine's personal thrusts were equally keen and devastating; he could inflict mortal wounds with one phrase between the ribs. He said of Hartmann, a minor poet who considered himself irresistible, "All the women fall in love with him—all except the Muses." Of Léon Halévy, brother of the musician who wrote *La Juive*, "He is as dull as if his brother had composed him." Of Hugo: "Hugo is the perfect Egoist—or, rather, he is a Hugoist." Of an actor: "He was so lean that his full face looked like a profile." Of Alfred de Musset: "Everyone has some weakness, and Musset is vain. Vanity is one of his four heels of Achilles." Of a German savant: "He studied night and day, fearing that, years later, some worms might find an idea missing in his head." Of a woman he disliked: "She is like the Venus de Milo in so many ways. She is unbelievably old; she has no teeth; and her body is covered with yellow spots." Of the French Academy: "The Academy is a nursery for decrepit men of letters entering their second childhood. It is a great philanthropic institution, suggested possibly by the Hindoos who provide hospitals for old and helpless monkeys."

But Heine was not always savage. Often he delighted in wit as "a playful judgment," to borrow a phrase from Kuno Fischer's *Über den Witz*. The surprising play of words and ideas was often so sudden that the hearer is momentarily baffled. Freud devotes many pages to an analysis of the following anecdote: While Heine and the French poet Soulié were gossiping in a Parisian *salon* there entered a money-king who was sometimes compared to Midas, and not only because of his love of gold. He was immediately surrounded by a group of admirers who fawned upon him. "See," said Soulié, "how the nineteenth century worships the Golden Calf." "Oh," said Heine, with a rapid glance at the object of adoration, "surely he is older than that!" Sometimes the wit was critically just, as when he wrote of Börne's lack of aesthetic feeling: "He was like a child, who, touching a Greek statue, is insensible of the glowing beauty, and complains that it is cold."

Sometimes the wit was mock-apologetic, as when Heine replied, upon being asked why he continually ridiculed Massmann and his poetry, "I am too old to get new fools; I live by the old ones—and Massmann is a safe annuity." . . . Often, however, it was irresponsible play for its own sake, the fun of displacement, the pleasure of arresting the too casual reader with ingenuities and insolences. "Nature, like the poet, can produce the greatest number of effects with the smallest amount of material: one sun, some trees, flowers, water, and love. And if the last is missing then the sun is only so and so many miles in diameter, the trees are so much fuel, the flowers are labeled according to their stamens, and the water is wet. . . ."

Cruel, flippant, subtle, violent, self-defensive, delicately couched and bitterly delivered, the wit proceeded from the droll to the outrageous. It had vitality, but it was not the humor of health. Nor could it be. Already in 1846 Heine knew he was a dying man.

XXII

ALEXANDER HAMILTON, PORTRAIT OF A PRODIGY[1]

By

DAVID LOTH

Few men in the early history of the United States left a record of greater achievement for the public good than Alexander Hamilton. Brilliant, eloquent, courageous in the expression of his convictions, Hamilton made a deep impress upon the life and development of the American nation.

This biography tells the story of Hamilton's life (1757-1804) from his clerical work in a West Indian business to his death at the age of only forty-seven in the famous duel at Weehawken, New Jersey, with Aaron Burr, Vice-President of the United States.

David Loth states that he selected the story of the duel because he thinks it is "one of the best incidents in Hamilton's life since nothing was so characteristic as his leaving it."

THE DUEL

"Is the Vice-President sunk so low as to submit to be insulted by General Hamilton?"

The sneer, directed at both men with impartial venom, came from the scabrous James Cheetham, a Jeffersonian newspaper hack who had learned the art of political journalism from Cobbett. But Cheetham relied upon the bludgeon rather than the lash, a typical example of his reportorial style being his charge, during the campaign, that the brothels of New York were filled with the unhappy victims of that wholesale seducer, Aaron Burr.

[1] David Loth, *Alexander Hamilton, Portrait of a Prodigy*, Philadelphia: J. B. Lippincott Company, 1939, pp. 296-305.

A gentleman of Burr's quality could not with propriety notice officially what such trash might say. Nevertheless, as the Vice-President contemplated his political future in the early summer of 1804, he was as cast down as was possible for that gay and sanguine temperament. The hatred of Jeffersonians and Hamiltonians pursued him with a violence that was in some respects flattering, but just at this time, defeated and a little sore, he was in no humor to appreciate the subtle compliment.

He was accustomed to the vigorous blows exchanged in the political arena, but since he himself did not indulge in personal abuse, he did not tolerate it in his equals. He had known well enough for years who his real enemy was in New York; he had heard hints without being able to put a finger on anything definite of how that enemy habitually reviled him. And at last he fell across a statement, not very precise but still something in black and white that warranted a demand for explanations. On June 18, therefore, Hamilton in the quiet of his retirement, received this curt note:

"Sir: I send you for your perusal a letter signed by Charles D. Cooper, which, though apparently published some time ago, has but very recently come to my knowledge. Mr. Van Ness, who does me the honor to deliver this, will point out to you that clause of the letter to which I particularly request your attention. You must perceive, sir, the necessity of a prompt, unqualified acknowledgement or denial of the use of any expressions which would warrant the assertions of Dr. Cooper."

With such sharp courtesy did duels begin, and as Hamilton read the lines under the solemn stare of Lawyer William Van Ness, Burr's devoted friend, he could not miss their import. He managed to preserve the glacial calm proper under the circumstances, even as he read on in the Doctor's letter the paragraph to which Van Ness now sternly pointed:

"General Hamilton and Judge Kent have declared in substance that they looked upon Mr. Burr to be a dangerous man, and one who ought not to be trusted with the reins of government. I could detail to you a still more despicable opinion which General Hamilton has expressed of Mr. Burr."

Two days went into the composition of a reply, more time than had been lavished on many numbers of *The Federalist*, but this was a delicate task. The dilemma was inescapable. Behind the comparatively mild words of Dr. Cooper lay the complex difficulties of the Code of Honor. If Burr really meant to press the issue, there was no alternative between the duel and ignominy in the eyes of gentlemen. It would be easy enough to repudiate Dr. Cooper, but that would hardly satisfy the conventions of the code. Burr would undoubtedly demand some comprehensive and public statement repudiating also any personal remarks on which Cooper's opinion could have been founded. Recalling the highly insulting phrases of some of his letters, Hamilton knew he could never give his opponent an honest and satisfactory answer. A lie, even if he had been willing to manufacture it, would only make him ridiculous and infamous among those who had received his confidences.

All the same, Hamilton did not want to fight. His aversion to dueling, which had kept him from calling out Monroe, had become a passionate distaste since poor Philip[2] had fallen. But between refusing to send a challenge and refusing to accept one was a gulf which his pride would not permit him to bridge. All he could do was attempt by his pen to avert the penalties of the sword—or rather of pistols.

The careful circumlocutions of his reply to Burr were in odd contrast to that gentleman's plain language. With considerable skill, Hamilton played with the meaning of "despicable" and "more despicable" as applied to unspecified opinions. He hoped that Burr would agree with him after mature reflection. He went over the difficulties of deciding just what he was supposed to disavow, adding:

"I deem it inadmissible, on principle, to consent to be interrogated as to the justness of inferences which may be drawn by others from what I may have said of a political opponent in the course of fifteen years' competition."

This was highly reasonable. The only trouble with it was that it missed the point, as Burr did not fail to see at once. The Vice-President did not care about Hamilton's views on the justness of other men's inferences. He wanted a disclaimer of what Hamilton himself would consider "despicable" references. If none had ever been meant or uttered, it was easy—and no more than fair—to say so. On this point they haggled painfully, stilted expressions of their antipathy passing between them in the hands of solemn, formal, meticulously garbed and meticulously spoken friends who bowed low, said little and never smiled. Pertinacious as a skillful cross-examiner must be, Burr pressed for a direct answer. Had General Hamilton impugned his honor or not? Desperately the squire of the Grange juggled and parried, but there was no escaping that remorseless question, and he had no intention of making a flat statement.

Within a week the business had passed into a still more formal phase.

[2] Philip Hamilton, the eldest son of Alexander Hamilton, was killed in a duel at Weehawken in 1801.

Van Ness had assumed the burden of Burr's correspondence. Major Nathaniel Pendleton, a trusty ally, wrote for Hamilton. The emissaries were no more successful in reaching an agreement than their principals, and on June 27 Van Ness ended the unsatisfactory fencing with a direct challenge.

"I shall want a little time to make some arrangements respecting my own affairs," Hamilton said in accepting, and the day was set for July 11.

For the first time in his life, the veteran of the raid on Trenton and the storming of a Yorktown redoubt had an opportunity to display his physical courage to the full. In the Revolution he had looked gaily at danger, for that was the price of fame. There had been, too, the odd exaltation that comes upon many men when facing peril with their fellows. This meeting with Burr was altogether different, thoroughly distasteful, unaccompanied by the hope of glory or the inspiration of idealism. He must go forth toward a death that would prove nothing, benefit no one and add no luster to the name of Hamilton.

He met the test. With complete calm he went about his business, played with the children, bantered Betsey about her domestic preoccupations, jested with his friends. Son James, wrestling with the problem of a speech he was to deliver at Columbia, appealed for help, and one morning his father, as willing a ghost writer for his children as for Washington, left him a draft with this note:

"I have prepared for you a Thesis on Discretion. *You may need it.* God bless you."

He himself needed fortitude as well as discretion for display in public. The day after the duel was definitely arranged, he presided over the Cincinnati's Fourth of July celebration at Ross's Hotel, where, the minutes relate, "a number of appropriate toasts were drunk and the evening spent in that harmony and social glee, which has ever distinguished the Society on that auspicious day."

As the wine flowed and conversation rang through the hall, smoke rising in clouds and laughter punctuating with festive hilarity some rather feeble jokes, the President General was the merriest in a merry throng. His effervescent spirits were commented upon, and the former officers agreed that political reverses had not soured his temper. They called on him for song, and as he rose, flushed and smiling, the still reddish hair brushed back from the still youthful face, they broke into cheers. Then the pleasant tenor, wandering off key at intervals, rose above the smoke and chatter:

"We're going to war, and when we die
We'll want a man of God nearby."

The singer's head was thrown back, his lips twisted in a faint grin even as he sang, the slender hands waved graceful accompaniment. A few feet away only one of his old comrades in arms was grave, expressionless among those smiling listeners. Elbow on table, cheek on hand, Colonel Aaron Burr stared solemnly at the life of the party. The black eyes never winked, the normally cheerful countenance was almost glum. Even after the song ended, his neighbors noticed that their usually garrulous fellow was rather silent. They forgot about him for a while, and when they looked for him again, he was not there. Colonel Burr, wonderful to relate, had gone home early.

Hamilton stayed to the end, but his next week was not filled with fun. He was extremely busy putting his clients' business in order, getting papers together, preparing cases to be tried by others, writing notes. As for his own affairs, he could only shake his head over them. He had supposed himself, what with his western lands and the Grange, to be worth the tidy sum of $10,000. But as he sat writing in the privacy of his study after Betsey and the children had gone to bed, he totted up the various sums he owed and "am pained to be obliged to entertain doubts, whether, if . . . the sale of my property should come to be forced, it would even be sufficient to pay my debts."

The short July nights hardly gave him time for all he had to write. There were letters to clients, letters to creditors, letters to friends, and one painful letter to Betsey, who would never understand why he had to go out and get himself killed just like Philip in a senseless quarrel of men. Often he rose from the desk to pace the floor, muttering to himself as once he had muttered under the trees on Batteau Street thirty summers ago. The man's problems gave more cause for muttering than the boy's had ever done. For he hated to leave his children, and for once tenderness and affection broke through the bonds he had imposed upon himself, and the pen that was more at home in the hot strife of politics or the cool mazes of finance traced for Betsey gentle, simple words of love from the man who appreciated her qualities if he could not match her devotion.

He had public duties, too. There must be left behind a reasoned statement of the motives that impelled him to accept a challenge in spite of religious, moral, personal, private and public reasons for declining. He numbered them, and went into some detail to refute them. His future usefulness "whether in resisting mischief or effecting good . . . would probably be inseparable from a conformity with public prejudice in this particular." To emphasize his disinclination, he left on record the statement that he intended to throw away his first fire to give "opportunity to Col. Burr to pause and reflect."

There were other letters on his financial condition and apologies for extravagance at the Grange—"To men who have been so much harassed in the base world as myself it is natural to look forward to a comfortable retirement." There were letters on public affairs and in the last of all, a note to Theodore Sedgwick on July 10, he made his final assault upon the spirit of secession and the spirit of democracy.

"I will here express but one sentiment," he wrote, "which is, that dismemberment of our empire will be a clear sacrifice of great positive advantages without any counterbalancing good, administering no relief to our real disease, which is *democracy*, the poison of which, by a subdivision, will only be the more concentrated in each part, and consequently the more virulent."

That was his political testament. His personal testament, leaving what he had to leave along with good advice and the hope that his debts would be paid by his wife and children, was drafted more easily. (Not far away Burr was making the same sort of will, for he too had debts to bequeath and the urgent hope that Theodosia would display "a little more perseverance, determination and industry in the cultivation of her mind.") Hamilton, at least, could mention his wife's prospects as a daughter of Philip Schuyler—an allusion "that venerable father, I am sure, will pardon. He knows well the nicety of my past conduct." On that note the busy pen became still—its work when published read "like the confessions of a penitent monk" to Burr—and for a few hours the writer slept.

The dawn was misty, the sun a red blur low over Brooklyn when Hamilton passed toward the river through the quiet city, cool in the early summer morning. Pendleton and the botanical Dr. Hosack were with him on the trip by barge to Weehawken, where Philip had fallen, and as they approached the rocky shore, covered with trees and shrubs, they could see Burr and his second were before them. The sun had risen clear of the haze now, and the air was warmer as the little party—leaving the doctor in the boat, for he must know nothing officially of the illegal enterprise on which they were bound—climbed slowly to a broad shelf in the steep slope. Only a few yards long and less than half as wide, the ledge presented a level stretch of grass overhung with rocks and trees.

The preliminaries were soon arranged. The ground was measured, the pistols loaded, the seconds conferred briefly. Pendleton won the choice of position, and Hamilton found himself standing at the northern end of the confined space, back to a huge boulder, weapon in hand, gazing out across the river where little waves danced in the sun. He could see for miles, beyond where the masts of a dozen ships swayed at anchor in the harbor, beyond the sloping lawns and gardens, beyond the tiny houses of the city to the misty outline of Staten Island, a purplish blotch of color swelling up from the lower bay. It was his city, his home, and between him and the glorious panorama of the summer landscape stood the dark, menacing form of Aaron Burr. A voice was saying something about making ready, a slow firm voice it was, and two motionless, slim, black figures confronted each other across twenty feet of dew-freshened grass.

"Present," said the voice.

Burr's arm rose with slow deliberation, it seemed to the watchers. The man was calm as on the day when he had carried Montgomery's body through the British fire at Quebec. Then in the silence the shot roared harshly on that rocky slope. A second roar, prompt as an echo, replied as the other pistol spoke sharply, and Hamilton, drawing himself up on tiptoe, crashed forward on his face. His arm, too, must have been raised, perhaps involuntarily, for Van Ness saw a leaf, severed from the top of a tree by the bullet, fluttering to the ground.

For a split fraction of a second, that falling leaf was the only movement on the ledge. Then three men burst into rapid action. Burr moved impulsively toward his fallen adversary. Van Ness leaped to intervene, while Pendleton ran to kneel beside his friend. Dr. Hosack and the bargemen were scrambling up the rocks, and Burr's second, screening his principal with an umbrella from identification, led him away into obloquy and ostracism to embark on strange adventures, suffer tormenting tragedies and close thirty years of wandering in a shabby old age.

There was still life in the quiet figure on the turf. With infinite care they carried him to the boat, laid him tenderly on cloaks spread in the bottom and pulled like mad for the New York shore. Before they reached it, Hamilton was conscious, and that he really had fired involuntarily through a merely convulsive movement was evidenced by his remark on the trip across the river.

"Take care of that pistol," he murmured. "It is undischarged and still cocked; it may go off and do harm."

He had already assured Dr. Hosack in his confident way but in a weak voice that the wound was mortal, and as they neared the Manhattan shore he whispered:

"Let Mrs. Hamilton be immediately sent for—let the event be gradually broken to her, but give her hopes."

They bore him to William Bayard's house in Jane Street, and sent for Betsey and more doctors. But there was nothing anyone could do. A little laudanum scarcely eased the intense agony of thirty hours broken only by brief intervals of merciful unconsciousness. The bullet had broken a rib, passed through the liver and was resting against the spine. He lay there in the big square room on the second floor, quiet and uncomplaining, and never saw the red sun of his morning go down in festal glory behind the green of Castle Point. But he breathed and suffered through the night, surrounded by a wife and friends so distracted they forgot to treasure for posterity the few broken words he could still utter.

The sun came up again to find him living yet, and in torment. It was July 12, 1804, and as the room grew hot with the glare of summer and the faint scent of Bayard's flowers wafted in at the open windows, the painful twitchings of the man on the bed relaxed, the low moans of agony ceased. Betsy sobbed among her weeping children, spent with grief, while the callous Gouverneur Morris, cynic and roué in whom some doubted the existence of a heart, went groping down the stairs, reeling, blinded by his tears. Alexander Hamilton, who had closed his career at thirty-eight, was dead at forty-seven.

XXIII

AARON BURR: THE PROUD PRETENDER [1]

By

HOLMES ALEXANDER

In any list of the most colorful figures of early American history, Aaron Burr (1756-1836) would have to be included. He enlisted in the Revolutionary War as a private and was advanced until he became a lieutenant colonel. He was at Valley Forge and made a brilliant record at the battle of Monmouth.

Burr's success in politics was rapid, culminating in his election as a United States senator from New York and later as Vice-President under Jefferson. Burr and Jefferson each had an equal number of votes for the Presidency in the Electoral College; Jefferson was chosen President by the House of Representatives on the thirty-sixth ballot, and in accordance with the Constitution at that time Burr became Vice-President. In 1804 he was nominated for governor of New York, and it was during this campaign that the argument arose between Burr and Hamilton which resulted in a duel and in Hamilton's death. After Burr retired from the Vice-Presidency, he journeyed to the Southwest and was accused of the intention of invading Mexico to establish an empire including a part of the United States. He was arrested for treason and taken to Richmond, Virginia, for trial, but following an investigation before Chief Justice Marshall the prosecution was dropped.

In the passage which follows we witness the death scene of the proud Burr.

ON THAT SUBJECT HE WAS COY

Easily the most succinct pronouncement Aaron Burr ever made on himself was an epigram he turned while lying in Mrs. Newton's [who operated a boarding house] basement. He had just finished reading that

[1] Holmes Alexander, *Aaron Burr: The Proud Pretender,* New York: Harper & Brothers, 1937, pp. 354-356.

celebrated passage in *Tristram Shandy* where Uncle Toby catches a fly and puts it out the window, saying: "Go, poor devil, get thee gone. . . . This world surely is wide enough to hold both thee and me." The Colonel closed the book and mused aloud:

"If I had read Sterne more and Voltaire less I should have known that the world was wide enough for Hamilton and me."

He was eighty years old in February of 1836. That spring Mrs. Newton moved to another house, but Mr. Burr did not accompany her. He had himself transported over the bay to the village of Port Richmond on Staten Island. The change was partly to be near some of his Edwards cousins, but "mainly," said the local undertaker with whom Mr. Burr struck up a ghostly friendship, "to escape the importunities of certain well-meaning revivalists and other ministers who sought to convert him." . . . He could not shake off the sightseers, the clergymen, the phrenologists. "The parsons . . . came at first day after day until he finally refused to converse with them at all." "That chap . . . with a carpet bag who began to come down here regularly by the last boat" turned out to be a representative of the firm of Fowler & Wells, Phrenologists. They could afford to wait, these patient stalkers. A last-breath conversion or a death mask of the mysterious head. Precious things, these. Worth waiting for.

But Mr. Burr had become most stubborn about dying. The summer passed into September and still he lingered, a scarcely perceptible bulge under the bedclothes, a fleshless skull that showed an awed gazer "eyes . . . the keenest and most magnetic I ever saw in a man's head." Everything was ready and waiting except the corpse. Mr. Buell, the undertaker, stood loyally at hand. In New York, Swartwout and others organized a pilgrimage "to pay the last honors to Pompey." At Princeton permission had been given to use the graveyard. But Mr. Burr kept peering up from bed with those sardonic lips still capable of a smile or quip.

"Go to hell," he advised the maid who was puttering about the room.

"Colonel, I've been there and seen the old man, and he says he has only room for you."

He "laughed heartily" at that.

Dr. Hosack, who had attended Hamilton's last gasps, informed Mr. Burr that the time was nigh.

"He's an infernal old fool," wheezed the Colonel to Adrian Verplanck, who happened to be in the room. "Open that drawer. . . . Do you see a letter on that box? . . . It is from a lady and she says she will call on me today. Anyone who thinks I will die with such an appointment doesn't know Colonel Burr."

"Twenty-four hours at the fartherest," said the physician.

"Doctor, I can't die. I shan't die. My father and mother and grandparents and uncles and aunts were all pious and godly people; they prayed for my conversion a thousand times, and if God be a hearer of prayers, he is not going to let me die until their prayers are answered. It is impossible that a child of so many prayers will be lost."

"Mr. Burr, you are already dying."

This was a cue for the Reverend Mr. Vanpelt whom the Edwards relatives had posted at the bedside. He stepped forward.

"Colonel . . . your time with us is short."

"I am aware of it," said Aaron Burr.

The Reverend Vanpelt warmed to his task. "In this solemn hour of your apparent dissolution . . . let me ask you how you feel in view of approaching eternity; whether you have good hope, through grace, that all your sins will be pardoned . . . for the sake of . . . our Lord Jesus Christ?"

"On that subject I am coy," said Aaron Burr and died on Wednesday the fourteenth of September in 1836.

XXIV

MASTER KUNG, THE STORY OF CONFUCIUS [1]

By

CARL CROW

Confucius, the great sage of China, whose clan name was K'ung, lived from about 550 B.C. to 478 B.C. His professed disciples amounted to perhaps 3,000 with seventy or eighty he called "scholars of extraordinary ability." Several were men of distinction among the statesmen of that day, and they spoke of Confucius as the greatest of mortal men. He made no claim to Divine revelations, but was concerned largely with man and his duties in society.

Carl Crow's book gives an enlightening account of the economic, political, and social conditions of the time and a delightful version of Master Kung's life, interlarding it all with amusing anecdotes, epigrams, and humor. In the passage which follows we see the distinguished Chinese philosopher as he taught those about him.

CONFUCIUS THE PHILOSOPHER

Master Kung kept his disciples under rigid mental discipline. He was careless or indifferent regarding their gratuities of fees, or food or clothing but would waste no time with a stupid pupil. A few for that reason gained a questionable fame for they are known to history only because of the humiliating reproofs the Master gave them. According to his own statements he made no attempt to sugar-coat the pill of learning. He once said in effect that in his teachings he would present one corner of a proposition and if the student could not from that construct the other three corners he bothered no more about him. No doubt that was his theory but his disciples were warmly attached to him and he was warmly

[1] Carl Crow, *Master Kung, the Story of Confucius*, New York: Harper & Brothers, 1938, pp. 205-215.

attached to them and some of the least brilliant followed him for years, so in his teachings he was not so strict as this theory would indicate. He had no charity for sloth and laziness which he looked on as a contemptible weakness. He caught a lazy disciple asleep in the sun and cried out to the others:

'Rotten wood cannot be carved, a wall of dirty earth will not receive the trowel! What is the use of my trying to teach this fellow!'

He was by no means an ascetic and enjoyed a good meal and the glow of alcohol as well as any man but these were trivialities as compared to the more important things of life. But he was constantly impressing on his disciples the sacrifices that must be made in the name of scholarship and told them:

'The scholar who cherishes the love of comfort does not deserve the name of scholar.'

While he was quick to rebuke his disciples for silly questions and stupid comments, their unquestioning acceptance of his teachings brought equally prompt condemnation.

'Hui gives me no assistance,' he said of one of them. 'There is nothing that I say in which he does not delight.'

The Master was probably as fortunate in his involuntary selection of disciples as they were in their carefully considered selection of a master. Many of them were men of but little less than his own age who proved, by their later careers, the brilliancy of their minds and the soundness of their characters. The questions they put to him were not the idle inquiries of immature schoolboys but the earnest questionings of men who were able to feel a serious concern over the troubled period in which they lived and by their urgent questioning stimulated the mind of the Master. It is significant that his most notable and most discussed sayings are embodied in his informal conversations with his disciples and not with his more formal discourses to dukes, viscounts, barons and others who often asked for his advice.

One day a disciple approached him with an inquiry regarding a strange new ideal of human conduct which Lao-tsze, the philosopher he had met at Loyang, had proposed and which was being seriously considered in some quarters.

'What do you say,' asked the disciple, 'about the idea that injury should be recompensed by kindness, that one should return good for evil?'

To Master Kung's logical mind there could be but one answer to a theory of this kind, which he rejected at once as vain idealism.

'If you returned kindness for injury, and good for evil,' he replied, 'what would you return for kindness and what for good? No! Recompense injury and evil with justice! Recompense kindness with kindness, good with good!'

A disciple on another occasion asked for a word which might serve as a general rule of conduct throughout life. The Master selected the word which has been translated as 'altruism' and then amplified its meaning by saying:

'Do not unto others what you would not have others do unto you.' . . .

It would of course be possible to fill several not uninteresting pages with quotations from the wise common-sense advice which Master Kung gave to his disciples but a few examples will suffice:

It is bootless to discuss accomplished facts, to protest against things past remedy, to find fault with bygone things.

Men's faults are characteristic. It is by observing a man's faults that one may come to know his virtues.

The scholar who is bent on studying the principles of virtue, yet is ashamed of poor clothing and coarse food, is not yet fit to receive instruction.

When you see a good man, think of emulating him; when you see a bad man, examine your own heart.

Without a sense of proportion, courtesy becomes oppressive, prudence degenerates into timidity, valour into violence, and candour into rudeness.

Though in making a mound I should stop when but one more basketful of earth would complete it, the fact remains that I *have* stopped. On the other hand, if in levelling it to the ground I advance my work by but one basketful at a time, the fact remains that I *am* advancing.

A great army may be robbed of its leader, but nothing can rob a poor man of his will.

To take an untrained multitude into battle is equivalent to throwing them away.

It is harder to be poor without murmuring than to be rich without arrogance.

Hopeless indeed is the case of those who can herd together all day long without once letting their conversation reach a higher plane, but are content to bandy smart and shallow wit.

The serious fault is to have faults and not try to mend them.

Men's natures are all alike; it is their habits that carry them far apart.

Men who are of grave and stern appearance, but inwardly weak and unprincipled—are they not comparable to the lowest class of humanity—sneak thieves who break into the house at night?

Your goody-goody people are really the ones who are the thieves of virtue. . . .

One of his human vanities which has been shared by most men was a conceit that he could appraise the character of men—not only of the great men of the past but of living men of lesser importance, including his disciples. He was constantly studying the characters, not only of the people about him but of historical personages, and his appraisals were in most cases surprisingly accurate. He was rather dogmatic about this and like all others who try to accurately calculate such an uncertain and variable factor as human character, he sometimes went wrong. With experience he grew more discreet.

'At first,' he said, 'my way with men was to hear their words and give them credit for their conduct. Now my way is to hear their words, and look at their conduct.'

He did not believe that a man could conceal his character. One of his disciples was of such an unprepossessing—not to say stupid—appearance that the Master did not expect even mediocre achievements from him yet he turned out to be one of the most brilliant of the band and later founded an important school of disciples of his own. Another disciple who gained great fame and who is accorded high honours in the Confucian temples was distinguished for little except his own unswerving loyalty and the Master's favouritism. When the high honours which had been heaped on this disciple were called to the attention of a dour old scholar, the latter made a remark over which other Chinese scholars have chuckled for centuries.

'It only goes to show,' he said, 'how far a horse fly can travel on the tail of a horse.'

XXV

CLARA BARTON, DAUGHTER OF DESTINY[1]

By

BLANCHE COLTON WILLIAMS

Here is a biography of the founder of the American Red Cross, based on a collection of letters and other documents which have been hidden since 1904 in a secret closet, and which were finally turned over to Blanche Colton Williams. The documents are now deposited in the Library of Congress and may not be used by any other author until 1950.

Clara Barton, who lived from 1821 to 1912, was a heroic and significant national figure. During the Civil War she distributed supplies for wounded soldiers. In the Franco-Prussian War, she assisted in organizing military hospitals. After years of work, her efforts to organize the American Red Cross were successful in 1882. She was the first president of the American Red Cross and held that position until 1904.

The passages which Blanche Colton Williams has chosen for us indicate the courage, persistence and self-confidence of Miss Barton in her struggle to attain her objective. Miss Williams states that the first passage "shows a turning point in Miss Barton's career—the greatest turning point. The second reveals her triumph in obtaining our adhesion to the Treaty of Geneva."

THE SIGNIFICANCE OF THE TREATY OF GENEVA

[While Clara was with the Uptons, of the United States Consulate in Switzerland, her friend Dorence Atwater's post as Consul to Seychelles was abolished. Immediately, she wrote to her most influential friends, urging Atwater's retention or transference.] Pending their replies, Clara rode, gathered flowers—between the leaves of her diary of that eventful 1870, poppies and pansies crackle and fall to dust—visited and was visited, dined at hotels and studied the organizations of Switzerland.

[1] Blanche Colton Williams, *Clara Barton, Daughter of Destiny,* Philadelphia: J. B. Lippincott Company, 1941, pp. 159-165, 265-268.

Dr. Appia had asked at their first meeting why in her opinion the United States had not acceded to the Treaty of Geneva.

"What is the Treaty of Geneva?" she asked in wonder.

"You have never heard of the Red Cross?" he parried.

"Only since hearing you are a member of the International Committee."

"And you have not yet been told of Henri Dunant?"

"I am deplorably ignorant."

"I should like to begin at the beginning, and prefer to bring with me books and documents." When he came again, he held her rapt with the story of the Genevan youth who became a banker and industrialist and, by chance, saw the Battle of Solferino, eleven years ago, "the most murderous blood-bath of the century," and with a selflessness the greater in being spontaneous gave unwearying labor to relieve suffering on the field where suffering was greatest. He told her how Henri Dunant toiled day and night for seventy hours as if in a dream.

"No one knows that toil better than I," she said, while Appia picked up one of the small volumes he had brought.

"Dunant," he continued, "was nervously shattered"—Clara nodded; that she could understand—"but recovered and returned to his banking. But unable to forget the soldiers covered with blood, swarming with flies and maggots, he wrote his experiences in *Un Souvenir de Solferino*. And then," Appia said surprisingly, "I met him." He, too, had been at Solferino but as a medical observer and chiefly in hospitals where he distributed linen bandages, and so had not then crossed Dunant's path. They did not exchange experiences until a year or so ago, after Victor Emmanuel awarded to them both the Order of Saints Moritz and Lazarus . . . "In this little book," he held up the *Souvenir*, "lies the origin of the Red Cross. You have observed our national flag?"

"A white cross on a red ground. Very beautiful, Dr. Appia."

"The Red Cross flag reverses it: red on white. But I go on," and he read from the close of Dunant's work, " 'Would it not be possible, in time of peace, to form relief societies for the purpose of having care given to the wounded in wartime?' "

Laying aside the booklet, Appia resumed: "Dunant closes with a number of illustrations of men and women who have given themselves to saving men on the field and in hospitals; of those in recent years he mentions Florence Nightingale."

Remembering the many times she had been compared with the Lady of the Lamp, Clara smiled.

"He will yet know of you, Miss Barton. It is but a little while that I have known of your service on the field."

Mr. Dunant not only would know of her but would exchange letters with her and send her books, with his compliments.

"And from that sentence the Red Cross grew?" she brought him back to the narrative.

"I approach that Treaty," he smiled, "but would ask you to read for yourself much more than I can tell you now. Dunant's idea was, you must know, that these relief societies in each country should have as members of their governing board those men enjoying most honorable reputation and highest esteem. The committees would appeal to all who could philanthropically devote themselves in any emergency to the work of relief, which would bring aid to the battlefield and take care of the wounded in hospitals."

"Isn't it much like our Sanitary Commission—this plan?"

"I grant you, yes. But you were not one nation working with a confederacy of nations. From the time the *Souvenir* was published, to be reprinted again and again, this idea of a brotherhood spread. Victor Hugo wrote Henri, 'You are arming humanity and serving freedom.' Ernest Renan told him, 'You have created the greatest work of the century.' But I pass on to M. Gustave Moynier."

"I have heard of him. A resident of this city?"

"A lawyer, yes. President of the Geneva Society for Public Welfare. A great organizer, a practical man, whereas Henri is a visionary. Opposites, each complemented the other. Seven years ago, Mademoiselle, in February, 1863, those two men, with Dr. Maunoir, General Dufour, and myself—we five only—founded the Red Cross, on the principle advocated by the *Souvenir*. By this time, Henri was insisting that the powers among nations must recognize an international code to be determined by a covenant. We would, of course, have the movement centralized here, would have it international, and free from all partisanship."

He looked at the vibrant small woman, whose eyes reflected his own zeal. At the woman of whom Martin Gumpert would write, long after, "She traveled for her shattered health to Europe, never suspecting that there in the meantime a work had begun that would henceforth fill her whole life, and to which . . . through the founding of the American Red Cross, she was to render immortal services."

"I cannot tell you now of all our labors, how Dunant gathered names for founding Central Committees, how we feared he had gone too far in his now famous circular—"

"Circular?"

"Secretary of the Geneva Conference, Dunant published it on his own authority. Briefly, every European Government would give the National Committee organized in every European capital its protection and patronage. The governments would declare the military sanitary personnel, and all persons connected with it, as neutral persons. In time of war, further, the governments would facilitate dispatch of materials for the personnel, and donations which the Societies would send to the war-stricken countries. Our Committee wished that the International Conference should study the means whereby this humanitarian work—that of the Red Cross, as it is now known—might be realized with regard for customs and laws of the various nations. The Conference would also like to investigate how effective aid could be rendered to either army without avoiding suspicion of espionage."

"A great purpose, Dr. Appia! If we had but had such an organization behind us in our Civil War . . ."

"Ah, but we were not fully organized until 1864! Henri concluded his circular in the hope that European governments would give their delegates to the Conference all necessary instructions. We were all busy getting representatives to the Conference. How many nations were represented, think you?"

Clara would not venture to say . . . Three or four, perhaps, she was guessing.

"Sixty-two delegates from sixteen nations came, in addition to delegates from certain welfare societies. We were in conference from the 26th to the 29th of October, 1863. Moynier has become our President, I should have told you; he is suited to handling masses of men."

"And your part, Dr. Appia?"

"In the Danish war of 1864 I was again in the hospitals, but I was back for the Geneva Convention of August 8th, that year."

"You invited no delegate from my country?"

"Your Mr. Charles S. P. Bowles came as representative of your Sanitary Commission——"

Neither he nor Clara then knew or for some time later that Bowles, who was appointed Foreign Agent in Europe of the United States Sanitary Commission, discussed the Geneva Congress with Seward, Secretary of State. Seward declared that while our United States held itself aloof from European congresses or compacts of political nature, it had nevertheless sent delegates to a number of congresses in Europe, some of which he listed. The Congress now proposed to be held at

Geneva, however, was for modifying the International rules of war, and if we participated would involve our signing while in the midst of a civil war. Sending a delegate empowered to act for our government was "nearly or quite impossible." Seward added, however, that the United States stood ready to treat with anyone, or with all other Powers individually, for the accomplishment of the grand objects of the Geneva Congress, "or even to adopt later the Treaty stipulations which shall wisely emanate and result from that Congress. The government wishes to act as a free agent, with option in these premises, and in its own good time."

So it was that Bowles was sent to Geneva not as national delegate but as partly official observer.

"A Mr. George C. Fogg, your Minister at Berne, also came as informal representative. He had just come from his work, in the United States, with Sanitary Commissions and spoke to us of that work."

Clara nodded, full of memories.

"In short, Mademoiselle, your own Sanitary Commission explained by Minister Fogg proved that our plan was not impossible. His rooms at the Hotel des Bergues became the rendezvous of delegates when the Congress was not in session. His diagrams, medals, photographs, his clear expositions—all swayed the delegates in the right direction."

"So we had something to do with the outcome, after all? And what was that outcome?"

"Certain delegates signed the Treaty of Geneva, as it is called, a Treaty you must study fully to evaluate but which, in general, provides for security of hospitals in which the wounded may be collected; they shall be held neutral and be respected by belligerents. All persons employed in the care of the wounded in these hospitals—surgeons, nurses, chaplains, attendants—shall be held neutral. When not required for the wounded, they shall be conducted under escort to rejoin their posts, not permitted to roam free under cover of neutrality. Field hospitals shall not be subject to capture. All who entertain and care for the wounded in their houses shall have military protection. By the Treaty, any signatory power is bound to give required care and treatment to all sick and wounded who fall into their hands, and to return them ultimately to their own country and friends."

"And why did you call your organization the Red Cross?"

"To secure the neutralization of hospitals and materials and nurses engaged in the services of the wounded, a common sign was needed and established. Out of compliment to the Swiss Republic, you have guessed, we reversed the colors of our insignia."

"How many governments signed?"

"On August 22, 1864, twelve. Delegates from your country, from England, Sweden and Saxony were without requisite power to sign."

"And since then?"

"Nine others by the end of 1867. The Papal State entered in 1868."

"And why have we not signed?" Clara was troubled, not grasping the application of the Monroe Doctrine.

"Why, indeed?" Appia extended his hands and let them drop. "Perhaps you will take up the question with your government?"

"Perhaps, when I return. I must study the subject, you will agree." He put into her hands all the important documents bearing on the Treaty of Geneva, the establishment of the Red Cross. "Your Dr. Bellows has been unsuccessful," he added.

"The Head of our Sanitary Commission?"

"The same."

She opened her eyes and wondered more than ever.

THE AMERICAN RED CROSS IS BORN

Out of friendly interest or urged by remarks of rival organizations, Secretary Blaine now inquired about "the foreign decorations of Miss Barton." She delivered to his secretary three insignia of the honors conferred: the Iron Cross of Merit (1873), the Gold Cross of Remembrance (1871), and the Red Cross of Geneva (1871) "placed upon my neck by the Grand Duchess of Baden." She would be with the Grand Duchess, she added, for she had promised to spend alternate winters there, but for constant occupation in trying to secure the adoption of the Treaty of Geneva. She mentioned her book of one hundred pages or so, then in press, explaining the subject, origin, and history of the Red Cross, a work of which she had ordered 5,000 copies for gratuitous circulation. She informed him of four societies: the National, at Washington; the locals at Dansville, Rochester, and Syracuse, which had sent thousands of dollars to the hungry, thousands of garments to the naked in the burned fields of Michigan, an estimated total relief of $80,000.

She still met suspicion and strong opposition from the Blue Anchor, which tried by every means to obtain for itself governmental approval. Those who had been her friends, even, were indifferent or "too busy." "I do not believe," she wrote, "any member of my Society will be of any help to me in this hard work . . ." After she had been present at the trial of Guiteau, where she was treated with marked courtesy and seated inside the rail, she saw Senator Lapham and asked him to take charge of the Treaty in the Senate. Of one thing she was certain: as soon as the Treaty was ratified, she would resign from Red Cross affairs. Her financial agent reported an increase in her holdings. "I can live where I please—Washington, Oxford, Dansville. It has been my part to do the work of the Treaty; somebody else can continue."

Senator Lapham, sympathetic, told her everything was "hung up" at the State Department; but when she hastened there, she heard surprisingly, "All is well." On December 10, 1881, Blaine had written the President of the United States, Chester A. Arthur, deeming it unnecessary "to enlarge upon the advisability of the adhesion of the United States to an international compact at once so humane in character and so universal in application." Two days later, President Arthur transmitted to the Senate this report of the Secretary of State, with accompanying papers. The same day, the 47th Congress, First Session, acknowledging his message, referred it to the Committee on Foreign Relations and ordered it printed, 3,000 copies. By January, 1882, Clara wondered what could have happened.

"The Treaty is ready," said Frelinghuysen, the new Secretary of State. "Unsigned documents are usually not to be shown, but we should like to know whether this is what you desire," and he handed her a volume of unbound parchment.

With trembling hands, she opened the book and read from beginning to end. In truth, as William E. Barton remarks, "It was a great and solemn document such as she had never before handled; and her life and her hope were bound up in it." Clara, herself, wrote, "How long a cry I indulged in I do not know."

After awhile, Frelinghuysen asked very gently, "How does it suit you?"

"All I could have hoped for," she smiled through tears, "but I am ashamed to have done so badly, myself."

"That," laughed the Secretary, "is all right."

At the end of the document were the formal words of ratification with blank spaces for the signatures of the President and the Secretary of State.

"When will they sign?" Clara wondered.

"Any time, now." . . .

In February, the Senate Foreign Relations Committee unanimously approved the Treaty. March 16th was a "sad day," wrote Clara—and even as she made the entry, came a note from Lapham in the Senate Chamber. He had the gratifying privilege of informing her of the ratification, that afternoon, by the Senate, of the Geneva Convention. "I had the injunction of secrecy removed so that it could be published at once," he concluded. "*Laus Deo!*"

Clara laid down the letter and wiped her eyes.

Depressed by jealousies and dissensions, she called a meeting for reorganization of the Society in its now National status. Men and women of importance in Washington joined and in becoming charter members raised the spirits of the National President. Now, toward the end of March, 1882, had arrived the season of the Mississippi overflows, drowning livestock, sweeping away houses, annihilating inhabitants of inundated regions. Perhaps she had better not resign: calls for relief were clamant enough this spring.

Upon receipt of Senator Lapham's note, Clara cabled President Moynier. On March 24th he wrote, after informing his colleagues of the International Committee, that he might thank her in the name of all. Commending her zealous perseverance, he asks her to present the United States President with their congratulations, and awaits notice from the Government of its decision. "It is your Society alone and none other that we will patronize, because it inspires us with confidence."

As a testimonial of gratitude for services already rendered, the Committee sent Clara one of the medals struck off in 1870 in honor of the Red Cross. Of small intrinsic value, it was their only means of recompensing "the most meritorious" of their assistants. She would please regard it as only a simple memorial, a proof of esteem and gratitude.

Clara's final goal was reached on July 26, 1882, when President Arthur issued a Proclamation the intent and purpose of which was to ratify fully and without challenge the adhesion of the Government to the Treaty of Geneva.

XXVI

BOLIVAR, THE PASSIONATE WARRIOR [1]

By

T. R. YBARRA

Mr. Ybarra, a native of Caracas and related by a collateral branch of his father's family to one of Bolívar's aides, has written a biography of the great Venezuelan patriot which is chronologically and geographically accurate.

Simon Bolívar, soldier and statesman, was born in Caracas, Venezuela, in 1783 and died in 1830, at the age of only forty-seven. But into those forty-seven years he crowded the action, achievement and thrills of a century. He was the founder of Greater Colombia, and from the component parts of his Colombia four free republics have been formed—Colombia, Panama, Venezuela and Ecuador. Bolivar was the hero of more than 200 battles, and was dictator-president of the nation whose name (Bolivia) was adopted while he lived. He has been called the George Washington of South America and was officially invested with the title of *Libertador* of all the countries whose independence he obtained from Spain through revolutions he led.

"I HAVE PLOWED IN THE SEA"

Simon Bolívar was now no longer Dictator-President of Colombia, no longer President of Peru or of Bolivia, no longer general-in-chief of armies marching to create new nations in the New World. He was simply a citizen of Venezuela, and that land, having broken away from the great triple republic of Colombia, established by him on the ruins of Spain's South American Empire, now spurned him and forbade him to set foot on her soil.

When he turned over the Presidency and walked out of the Presidential Palace at Bogotá as an ordinary citizen, he was not only ill and dejected

[1] T. R. Ybarra, *Bolívar, the Passionate Warrior,* New York: Ives Washburn, Inc., 1929, pp. 350-363.

but well-nigh penniless. . . . His dejection grew steadily deeper. Every report he received from the lands he had liberated bore out the truth of his despairing words "Those who worked for South American freedom have plowed in the sea!"

Everywhere the common welfare was being sacrificed to personal ambitions. Each leader pursued his own unscrupulous ends, without regard to his country. South America's long history of turbulence, instability and bloodshed was beginning. Nobody had a thought any more for La Gran Colombia; they had not even waited for Simon Bolívar's death to tear it to pieces. . . .

And the Congress of Panama?—that splendid vision which had come to him of a League of American Nations banded together for mutual welfare, for exchange of constructive ideas between the free republics of the American continent, a League destined to make the Old World respect the New and the New respect itself—what of the Congress of Panama? Dead at birth! Laughed at, spurned, by those whom it was to protect, as the insane dream of a lunatic!

"I have plowed in the sea!" Well might Simon Bolívar, in the black bitterness of disillusionment, repeat over and over again those words. . . .

December, 1830.

Vainly searching for health—panting, coughing, spitting blood—Simon Bolívar drags his weary steps to the port of Santa Marta, on the Caribbean coast of New Granada. There, he knows, the climate is better than at Cartagena. It may help him.

He makes the journey by water. So weak is he when the vessel reaches Santa Marta that he has to be carried ashore. Still there are a few loyal friends with him—General Montilla, General Silva, Andrés Ybarra, the aide wounded at Bogotá by Bolívar's would-be assassins: and a few more. Señor Mier, a resident of Santa Marta, enrolls himself among the last men loyal to the Liberator by offering him hospitality at his country place, San Pedro Alejandrino, just outside Santa Marta.

It soon becomes clear to those around him that the Liberator's days are numbered. In haste, they summon physicians—Dr. Révérend, a Frenchman settled at Santa Marta, and the surgeon of a United States gunboat which happens to be in the harbor. The two examine the patient, look at each other, gravely shake their heads.

"Send for a priest!"

On the tenth of December the last rites of the Roman Catholic Church are administered to Simon Bolívar. He lies on his bed, or propped up in a chair, now listless, now with his brain spurred to feverish activity. He is deathly white; his frame, never more than puny, has wasted almost to a skeleton. An old, broken man—yet in age only forty-seven.

The tireless brain still functions—again and again he addresses those about him.

"What brought you to America?" he suddenly asks the French doctor.

"The wish to find liberty."

"Did you find it?"

"Yes, General."

"You have been more fortunate than I, Doctor! So far I have not found liberty!"

One day, feeling better, he dictates a farewell to the citizens of the republics to which he has brought independence. Faithful friends, having written down his words, gather around the dying man; one of them reads aloud what he has dictated. The last words are: "If my death should bring union, I shall go down with a tranquil mind to my grave!"

Bolívar listens, hollow-cheeked, sunken-eyed, huddled together in an arm-chair. At first he shows no emotion. But when he hears the words "my grave" he suddenly cries, in tones of ghastly hoarseness:

"Yes, my grave! That is what my fellow citizens have presented to me. But I forgive them. If only I might carry to the grave with me the consolation of knowing they are united!"

The Seventeenth of December.

"How is the Liberator?" asked General Montilla of Dr. Révérend.

"I do not think he will live through the day."

Silent and tearful, some of the dying man's friends gather around his bed. He is already delirious. Toward noon the doctor sees that the end is a question of minutes. Going to each of Bolívar's friends, scattered about in the villa of Señor Mier, the Frenchman tells them:

"Gentlemen, if you wish to witness the Liberator's last moments of life, make haste!"

All crowd about the death-bed.

Simon Bolívar lies in his death agony. At one o'clock he draws his last breath.

When Doctor Révérend, asked by Bolívar's friends to lay out the corpse, begins his sad task, he finds that the nightshirt which the Liberator was wearing when he died is torn. The Frenchman is beside himself with indignation. He exclaims:

"Not even as a corpse will I allow Simon Bolívar to wear a torn garment! If there is not a better one for him here, I shall send to my house for one of my own!"

General Silva, one of the friends who had stood by the death-bed, hurries to his room, returns in a few minutes with another nightshirt. In that garment Dr. Révérend lays out the corpse.

Thus died Simon Bolívar the Liberator—the man who freed four countries and founded a fifth, the victor in a score of furious battles, whose exploits had made him famous all over the universe and brought him a place of honor, rivaled by few, in the august list of the apostles of liberty—in exile, under an alien roof, clad in a borrowed nightshirt. . . .

No one man could bring into being the United America founded on the splendid international ideals which shone brightly in his dreams, and few men are endowed with the sort of soul to make even dreaming such a thing possible. Simon Bolívar had such a soul. His dreams may have been extravagant, but they were glorious: they may have been mad, but they were beautiful.

Before he died he knew that what he had dreamed could not become fact. Long before he lay on his melancholy death-bed at Santa Marta he knew that the superb dream-structure which, throughout his life, had shimmered in glory before his eyes, was a thing of air and illusion and evanescence.

"I have plowed in the sea!"

Simon Bolívar was a dreamer in his youth and in his maturity, in poverty and in prosperity, in misfortune and in power: all his life he nourished himself on dreams, and he lived long enough to know that his dreams were only dreams.

But—*he dreamed*! All honor to him!

XXVII

THOMAS A. EDISON, A MODERN OLYMPIAN [1]

By

MARY CHILDS NERNEY

After two years of research among the treasures at Menlo Park, while the great inventor was still there, Miss Nerney produced this biography of Edison. It gives an intimate portrayal of Edison's personal charm, his constant experimentation and his almost incredible capacity for work. He was born in 1847 and by the time of his death in 1931 had lived to see the remarkable contribution which he had made to human welfare and progress.

Miss Nerney comments regarding the selection which she has given us from her biography, "Focussing, as it does, upon the two most important achievements of his career—his lamp and his central system—this passage suggests the quality and range of the inventor's genius and the vast scale of his operations. For, in developing his incandescent electric light and his central power system, Edison had to cope with problems of finance, of science, of engineering, of materials. His world-wide hunt for a filament, the skepticism of public and press, the alarm of investors in gas over the portent of a competitive industry, the sleepless ordeal of endless experiments, were but incidents in the drive of this young man, who at only 31, was setting the stage for the coming age of light and power."

"LIGHTS STRUNG ON WIRES INDEED!"

Edison started his drive to subdivide the electric current in the fall of 1878. In his earlier experiments with the incandescent light he had tried a number of materials for a filament, including carbon. He now concentrated on platinum, organizing a search for this metal by questionnaires and agents that ranged from Mexico and Canada to the Pacific Coast and

[1] Mary Childs Nerney, *Thomas A. Edison, a Modern Olympian*, New York: Random House, 1934, pp. 79-90. With the permission of Mary Childs Nerney, copyright owner.

even overseas. A favorite of Edison's among these agents was Frank A. McLaughlin, a mining prospector and promoter, who contributed some of the "atmosphere" to Menlo Park in the early days. "Platina," as they called it, was the first apple of discord that fate let fall in the path of the young inventor who started to sift the river bottoms, not for gold, but for the platinum he hoped to find with it.

"A wild hunt," remonstrated some of his associates, a comment the inventor took lightly while he broadcasted circulars for the precious metal. "I shall require large quantities of it in my new system of electric lighting," he said naïvely. Meanwhile his friend, Professor Barker of the University of Pennsylvania, with whom he advised on the scientific aspects of his search, warned him against "the indiscriminate examination of rocks" and cautioned that he did not know of any localities in the United States where platinum could be found in paying quantities. In short the world output was limited. The young experimenter drove ahead.

By the time Edison had applied for his first lamp patent in October, 1878, money had melted away like the platinum filaments. To proceed he had to have capital. It was then, October 17, 1878, that Lowrey's group formed a syndicate with an authorized capitalization of $300,000 and made $50,000 of this available for research. With these preliminaries arranged, the Old Man and his tribe started to make a great magic. The setting sun left them at their benches and its first rays found them swaying on their feet, since none might sleep out of his turn. One of them, assigned to keep a careful tally of the hours off, would make his rounds, touching each man on his shoulder when his time came to snatch a little rest. They dropped down on benches or anywhere they could. When their four hours were up, around came the monitor on the minute to wake them up. . . . A favorite retreat of the inventor, when he did not sleep on top of his desk, was a cupboard under the stairs among the scrubbing pails and the dust brooms.

As a result of these experiments by April, 1879, he had applied for a number of lamp patents in most of which platinum was a feature. He had spent a great deal of money and had nothing to show for it but a lamp that was short lived and so expensive to make that it was commercially impractical. To his fundamental principles already mentioned, however, he had added that of an hermetically sealed and exhausted all glass globe. But he could not dodge the truth that platinum was a failure, that even if successful as a filament it would not do, since there was not enough of it in the world to make it a commercial possibility. So he gave it up and began to think about nickel. He did more: he abandoned his experiments on the lamp and went back to other inventions. Perhaps he felt that he was "going stale" on the electric light problem.

Great was the consternation of his financial backers. The faithful Lowrey, "friend Lowrey," was at hand, however, to prevent what might have been a breach. It was he who had first interested J. P. Morgan in the young inventor and who later engineered his great legal contests. Better than anyone who knew the Edison of those early days, he seems to have grasped the quality of his genius. Tactfully he explained to this doubtful group of business men what the young inventor had so often said to him about no experiment being a failure. "It always proved something." Persuasively he brought out that "no great end could be obtained without considerable doubt and tribulation," that this was just the time when they "must all stand by the inventor and the enterprise." Morgan listened but said nothing. But he continued to stand by for, like Lowrey, he could recognize genius.

"Be sure you are right about nickel and everything else before having anybody know much about it," cautioned Lowrey, while he threw in a word about the possibility of their having been rash in putting up such expensive buildings so soon. He urged the inventor to "give confidence for confidence," to express himself freely when he came to a difficulty, while he assured him that such a course would not prejudice them toward his plans by making them lose courage at the wrong time. Lowrey's fine understanding and unwavering faith are one of the brightest spots in the inventor's life which was notable for distinguished friendships. Serving, however, as envoy plenipotentiary between Edison and Morgan was like being entrepreneur between the Mountain and Mahomet so far as covering the linear distance between them was concerned. He could not move the mountain to Menlo, that is, not easily. He could not beguile young genius away from his experiments. Nor could he often make the trip himself, caught as he was in the emergencies of a large legal practice. He hesitated to ask Upton to come in because that would take him away from Edison. But somehow he managed, and another $50,000 was advanced for more experiments. It was at this time that Robert L. Cutting, Jr., one of the incorporators who had just read J. W. Starr's scientific account of his failures objected, saying:

"I have read Mr. Starr's book and it seems to me that it would have been better to spend a few dollars for a copy of it and to begin where he left off, rather than to spend $50,000 coming independently to the same stopping point."

"No," said Edison, "I don't think the incandescent light will ever be found that way. It's not a matter of beginning where Starr left off, because I believe the incandescent light lies somewhere between his beginning and his stopping point—that he passed over it. So have I. That is why I want to go back after it again."

In the fall of 1879, Edison began to think again about his lamp, led to it by one of those curious circumstances that mark the path of the inventive genius. Sitting one day in his laboratory absently rolling a bit of lamp black and tar for his carbon transmitter button between his fingers, the thought occurred to him to try carbon again for a filament. It had the high resistance necessary; rods of carbon, however, he had proved, did not last at high incandescence. Why not go to the other extreme then and employ a carbonized substance of minute diameter? But what? It should be not more than one sixty-fourth of an inch in diameter, about six inches long and "U" shaped in order to reduce the size of the glass globe in which they were to operate.

Cotton sewing thread! That might turn the trick! It was a bold thought consistent too with the open-mindedness that drove him back on his own track to carbon, and consistent too with the man who, one day squandering a fortune to sift the river beds of California for platinum, on the next would give it up for something he could find at home in mother's workbasket.

Then began "the Great Thread Tournament"! It was a task requiring the fortitude and the patience of an Edison and the delicate fingers of a Batchelor. Bit by bit they broke off the thread, carbonizing the tiny lengths, until they had used up almost an entire spool. They kept at it all one night, all of the next day and all of another night, only to have the filament break after they got it out of the mold and before they could get it down to the glass blower's, where it had to be fastened into a bulb; as delicate an operation as removing the carbonized thread from the mold. Back at it they went, snipping off more thread, stoking the furnace, gently withdrawing the mold from the fire, waiting several hours for it to cool, holding their breath while they opened it, balancing it delicately as they carried it down to old Boehm to fasten it into the glass bulb. Finally they succeeded in sealing a carbonized length into a bulb. After connecting the bulb with the wires of a generating machine and with an air pump to exhaust the air, they turned on the current. A steady light met their unbelieving gaze. For forty hours they watched this glow. Edison then speeded up the current to see how much the filament would stand—the new light flared up suddenly and went out.

They had subdivided the electric current. The pundits who had held it was against the law of conservation of energy were wrong. Rather it was a beautiful illustration of the transformation of energy, or would be, by the time the genius of an Edison and his gifted assistants should have done with it. Years afterward the inventor in refusing to grant interviews on the nature of electricity put the matter characteristically when he advised his editor correspondent: "Send your reporter down to the cellar and tell him to interview the coal pile."

The gifted Upton put it more scientifically when in his article on the subject he wrote: "Mr. Edison's system of lighting gives a completed cycle of change. The sunlight, poured upon the rank vegetation of the carboniferous forests, was gathered and stored up, and has been waiting through the ages to be converted again into light. The latent force accumulated during the primeval days, and garnered up in the coal beds, is converted, after passing in the steam engine, through the phases of chemical, molecular, and mechanical force, into electricity, which only waits the touch of the inventor's genius to flash out into a million domestic suns to illuminate a myriad homes."

A haggard man stumbled home in the early dawn shuffling the autumn leaves as they whirled down the windswept lanes of Menlo Park. He had won; he had invented a practical incandescent lamp; now he must make it a commercial success. He knew that thread was not the right filament and that he had to work out and apply the details of a whole system. As yet he had demonstrated only principles. He threw himself down in his clothes and slept for twenty-four hours.

Edison started his hunt for another filament by carbonizing everything within range of his imagination from celluloid and cork to fishline and woodsplints, not omitting even hairs from the red beard of his friend MacKenzie, the Mount Clemens station agent, who now paid long visits to Menlo. Finally he chose paper (bristol board) after proving that it would burn several hundred hours. His application for a patent on his lamp with a paper filament, which he filed on November 4, 1879, was granted on January 27, 1880, No. 223,898, the basic lamp patent.

Edison had a lamp that would burn, but the public—and particularly the scientists—were skeptical of his achievement. After the phonograph, the prestidigitator of Menlo Park might pull any kind of bunny out of his sleeve. Even so, the claim that a lighting system to illuminate great cities could be developed from a loop of charred paper fastened in a glass globe suggested hocus-pocus rather than science. It was too simple to impress the popular mind—and then there were the investors in gas. What was to become of their billion and a half, they whispered, if Edison should be right? Well, he shouldn't be—not if they could help it.

Quite as fundamental to his new lighting system as a successful lamp was a generator. "His first experiments in machines for generating the electric current did not meet with success. His primal apparatus was in the form of a large tuning fork, constructed in such a way that its ends vibrated with great rapidity before the poles of a large magnet. These vibrations could be reproduced with comparatively little power. Several weeks of practice proved, however, that the machine was not practical and it was laid aside." There followed a number of dynamos leading to the "Faradic Machine" (named in honor of Faraday), with which he was to make his first successful demonstration; "long-legged Mary Anns" was the less classic name by which these "Z" type dynamos came to be known.

Edison decided to give a public exhibition and made his announcement through Marshall Fox, his reporter friend, one who, in Newark, had held him suspect as a genius. Fox got a scoop for his paper, the New York *Herald*, on the story—and incidentally came near losing his job thereby. The Managing Editor, Thomas B. Connery, did not see the story until it was in type. He then tore into the City room and, thrusting the offending sheet under the nose of the City Editor, Albert E. Orr, shouted: "How did that stuff get into the paper, Mr. Orr? Lights strung on wires indeed! You've made a laughingstock of the *Herald*! Oh, what will Mr. Bennett say?"

A special train ran down from New York to Menlo Park the night of December 31, 1879, carrying guests who came by invitation. The Pennsylvania Railroad had to continue these trains for several days to accommodate the crowds that wanted to see the new wonder with their own eyes —sixty lights strung on wires overhead and connected with wires covered with asphaltum that ran along the ground in wooden troughs. Some of the houses at Menlo, too, were lighted with the new lamps. As their inventor watched his glowing lamps swinging in the trees on that snowy New Year's Eve he knew that his hardest work was still before him. For, if laymen found the idea of the incandescent lamp too novel for practical consideration, Edison's idea of a central station for the distribution of light and power was startling, even to some of those closest to him. Explaining his idea to Johnson, he ended by inquiring: "Do you catch on with your intellectual grippers?"

"Holy Jesus," was Johnson's reply, "this is a great thing you have got onto now!"

While working out his plan for the demonstration of his central system in a thickly settled area—New York was finally chosen—Edison continued his search for a filament for his lamp. Picking up a bamboo fan in his laboratory one day, he happened to think that bamboo might furnish the material he sought. For him, to think was to act, and he immediately started agents off to the ends of the earth with orders to bring back, or to send back, samples of all kinds of bamboo—or of a better fiber, if they could find one. Samples by mail and samples by the bale poured into Menlo Park. The story of this hunt is another Arabian Nights' tale that will "keep children from play and old men from the fire" long after Aladdin and his magic lamp are forgotten. Moore, who found the most satisfactory fiber, went to China and Japan; Brauner to Brazil; Segredor to Cuba, where he died of yellow fever; MacGowan, who had the most lurid adventures of them all, survived the horrors of the wilds of Ecuador, Peru, and Colombia, only to disappear in the streets of New York, never to be heard from again.

Hanington went to Uruguay, Paraguay, and Argentina; Hamilton and Payne to Florida, to the West Indies, and to South America; while Ricalton, a New Jersey schoolmaster, went around the world. Whatever of glamour or of glory their adventures may have held for these crusaders of science—and if a man dropped out there were a dozen eager to take his place—their sole significance to Edison was to get the best possible fiber for his lamp. He met Ricalton upon his return after a year of absence with the laconic greeting "Did you get it?" They might even be forgotten. One man, stranded in Mexico, so the story goes, wrote to the Laboratory for money. But dollars were scarce around Menlo Park just then, and, none being forthcoming, the man sold his horse and saddle and managed to reach Chicago on the proceeds. There a friendly stranger advanced the funds to get him home.

As a result of these trips into far places of the world a Japanese farmer settled down to grow bamboo for Edison in Japan, and to improve its quality. This marvelous grass furnished the most satisfactory filaments for his lamps for a number of years. In the end he discarded it for a manufactured cellulose, but not until he had tested some six thousand species of plants and vegetable fibers. He spent ten years and $100,000 on this bamboo marathon—and wily nature gave him the answer in his laboratory.

It is not within the scope of this narrative to detail the separate inventions that led up to Edison's triumphant demonstration of his central system in New York—his improvements on the contemporary dynamo; his creation of the Jumbo dynamo—since no dynamo then existed that could carry the steady current needed for the electric light; his evolution of the principle of "large, direct, connected units" of power; his feeder and main systems, as simple as a tree trunk and its branches; his running the wires underground instead of overhead. His interminable experiments, his flashes of genius brought forth the details of his system: the electrolytic meter, the switches, fuses, sockets, the service boxes, and tubes (conduits), to mention only a few. Those who cherish the idea that inventions spring in full panoply from the brain of their creator like Minerva from the brow of Zeus, should follow, step by step, this gigantic undertaking which laid the basis for the age of light and power. It was the greatest achievement of his career, for it gave scope for all of his unique gifts—originality, universality, detail, superhuman patience and physical endurance, brilliance and fortitude, intuition and practical application, continuity and drive.

XXVIII

THE LIFE OF EMERSON [1]

By

VAN WYCK BROOKS

This study is, in the words of Van Wyck Brooks, "a biography of an inner life." It is a different type of biography, a series of portraits of Emerson's thinking, his spirit and his nobility. Unquestionably it is one of the notable biographies of recent years.

As an American poet and essayist, Emerson (1803-1882) brought to his work qualities of independence, love of freedom, virtue, sincerity, and a strict adherence to high ideals. His writing contains many epigrams and his style is brilliant. He was a Puritan in spirit perhaps, but he had the vision of a poet.

THE MOMENT OF INSPIRATION

He knew and would know no such thing as haste in composition. Well said Simonides: "Give me twice the time, for the more I think the more it enlarges"; and he who found himself hurried and gave up carrying his point, even for once, wrote in vain. Goethe had the *urkräftige Behagen,* the stout comfortableness, the stomach for the fight, and he would have it, too! It was true that every writer was a skater and had to go partly where he wished and partly where the skates carried him. True that a thought he had once believed so happy often turned out to be nothing but empty words. While it glittered newly before him he fancied he had chipped off a scale of the universe; then he came again to the record a few months later and it seemed the merest tinsel. But certain things he could do to control his style, keep it hard and firm, hard but light and elegant as Landor's. He could cancel every "very," and every "intense" and "ex-

[1] Van Wyck Brooks, *The Life of Emerson,* published and copyright by E. P. Dutton & Co., Inc., New York, 1932, pp. 143-152.

quisite," avoid the fat of the language, and all such terms as "Yes, to a certain extent," "as a general thing." (Had he used "grim" too often? A mannerism, perhaps; and that would never do.) He could keep to the Saxon forms and eschew the ponderous Latinisms; he could make every word cover a thing. And what compensations there were for all his difficulties! A new phrase at times was like a torch applied to a train of powder—it awakened so many thoughts. And sometimes in making a sentence he felt himself launching out into the infinite and building a road into Chaos and Old Night.

But how control his moods? They never believed in one another. One state of mind was never able to remember, was unable even to conceive of another state. Life was a flash of light, then a long darkness, then a flash again. To-day the electric machine would not work, not a spark passed; and presently the world was all a cat's back, all sparkle and shock.

Mysterious, ungovernable, these periodic motions of the soul. There were fortunate hours when things sailed dim and great through his head, hours when the right words came spontaneously like the breath of the morning wind, when he could not sit in his chair for the joy that brought him bolt upright and sent him striding about the room, when he had not the composure to set down the thoughts that thrilled him. His intellect was so active that everything ran to meet it. He was like the maple trees in the spring when the sugar flows so fast that one can not get tubs enough to contain it. And then came hours of pain, sterility, ennui, and he sat out the day and returned to the necessities of the household doubting if all this waste could ever be justified. No child passing the house on his way to school, no boy carrying a basket, but gave him a feeling of shame and envy. He was on the brink, it seemed, of an ocean of thought into which he could not swim. And sometimes the ocean itself seemed a mirage.

Was persistence enough, at such times, mere brute sitting, day after day, in the face of his own skepticism? It was true that the mood returned, sooner or later, always, and life had a grip again and the hours a taste. How cheering were those anecdotes of old scholars and poets, Niebuhr, for instance, whose divination came back to him after years of eclipse, and George Herbert who, having lost the muse in his youth, found himself later, "after so many deaths," living and versing again. He had known such minds himself, minds like those pear-trees which, after ten barren seasons, burst into a second and even more vigorous growth. But was there no way of domesticating these high states of contemplation and continuous thought? The rich veins of ore were always there, could he only command the shaft and draw them out. Writing was his metre of health, and success in his work was food and wine, fire and horse and holiday. Were there no tonics for the torpid mind, no rules for the recovery of inspiration?

Alas, neither by land nor by sea could one find the way to the Hyperboreans! But one thing was certain: his talent was good only as long as he worked it. If he ceased to task himself he had no thoughts. That was the value of the journal he kept so faithfully: every day he collected the disjointed dreams, the reveries, the fragments of ideas, the drupes and berries he found in his basket after endless and aimless rambles in woods and pastures. It was the hive in which he stored his honey, cell by cell, as the bees in his brain distilled it. A treasure, this journal, for a desultory mind; many were its uses. He could no more manage his thoughts than he could manage thunderbolts; but once he got them written down he could come and look at them every day and grow accustomed to their faces, and, by and by, discovering their family likeness, he could pair them and range them better and join them in the proper order. By this means, too, he could convert the heights he reached into a table-land. A fact that was all-important a month ago stood here along with one that was equally important a month before, and next month there would be another. Here they all occupied but four lines, and he could not read these thoughts together without juster views of each than when he read them singly. His journal was indispensable, for what was written was the foundation of a new superstructure, a guide to the eye for still another foundation. Every thought he expressed was a cube, and every cube a candidate for the mosaic of his essays. And if the results were precious, so was the habit. Work, of all tonics, was the most effective, and this was the most inviting form of work.

No doubt, but for work itself what were the best conditions? The free mind was the fruit of an austere law: it had to be reconquered day by day, it subsisted in a state of war and belonged only to those who fought for it. But how conduct the fight, how prepare for it? What were the omens, and how was he to read them? How coax and woo the strong instinct to bestir itself and work its miracle? The ancients were masters of this art: what was it Plato said about living out of doors and simple fare and gymnastic exercises, and Pythagoras, of the use of certain melodies to awaken in the disciple now purity, now valour, now gentleness? For every constitution there were certain natural stimulants, just as there were natural poisons, and the problem was to find these, to know them, and to regulate one's life accordingly.

For himself, he had such low animal spirits that he could not stand an extravagant, flowing life. He regretted it as much as he regretted the shortness of an American scholar's day. He marvelled at the constitution of the Germans, with their twelve, fourteen, sixteen hours of work. He loved in others the generous, spontaneous soil that flowered and brought forth fruit at all seasons. But he had to consult the poorness of his powers; he had to be content with moderate, languid actions. If he had obeyed his irregular impulses, established half the relations his fancy prompted, he would not have been followed by his faculties; he would certainly have died of consumption in six months. Parties disqualified him, and so did arguments. There were those who, disputing, made him dispute, and nervous, hysterical persons who produced the like symptoms in himself.

The one good in life was concentration, the one evil dissipation. What untuned him was as bad as what crippled or stunned him: domestic chores, even correcting proof-sheets, even packing a trunk. And talking about himself—how empty it made him feel! And being praised—a pest, the worst of all spoil-thoughts. (One turned around to look at oneself and one's day was lost in personal considerations.) And manual labour untuned him. (Did they fancy that the greatest of arts, the subtlest and most miraculous, could be practised with a pen in one hand and a crowbar or a peat-knife in the other?) Trifles? A grasshopper was a burden. It was all very well to talk of a life taken as it comes. Thoreau, with his tough grain, knew the weight of these feathers in the scale: He had found that the slightest irregularity, were it only the drinking of too much water on the preceding day, disturbed the delicate poise that composition demanded. Carlyle knew this too, with his room on the top floor, high above the orbit of all housemaids: he could hope there for six years of history. And George Sand knew it, humouring her love of heat. Was the steel pen a nuisance? Try the quill. For himself, he pounded so tediously on that string of the exemption of the writer from all secular tasks because his work needed a frolic health to execute.

Plenipotence of health; for health was the first muse, comprising the magical effects of air, landscape and exercise upon the mind. And silence was the second. How true was Fra Angelico's remark that "he who practised the art of painting had need of quiet, and should live without cares or anxious thoughts"! How like his own the experience of that old Chinese painter who wrote: "Unless I dwell in a quiet house, seat myself in a retired room, with the windows open, the table dusted, incense burning, and ten thousand trivial thoughts crushed out and sunk, I can not have good feeling for painting or beautiful taste, and can not create the Yu." Proclus was right. "How can the soul be adjacent to the One, except by laying asleep the garrulous matter that is in her?"

His own primal rule was to defend the morning, to keep all its dews on, to relieve it with fine foresight from any jangle of affairs. A stroll in the orchard first, in spring and summer, attuned him for the day. But he knew many other stimulants, many other provocative influences. A Greek epigram at times, a verse of Herrick, a glance at the mottoes in some novel of Scott, a page from the Neo-Platonists. Nectar, opium, these latter, as he let sail before him the pleasing and grand images of these gods and demoniacal men. He heard of rumours rife among the azonic gods, of demons with fulgid eyes, of the unenvying and exuberant will of the gods, of the aquatic gods and the Plain of Truth, the meadow, the paternal port. What pictorial distinctness!—as if the gods were present. "This is that which emits the intelligible light that, when it appeared, astonished the intellectual gods and made them admire their father, as Orpheus says." What rhetoric! These rare, brave words filled him with hilarity and spring. His heart danced, his sight was quickened, he beheld shining relations between all things. He was impelled to write, he was almost impelled to sing. (Read Proclus much and well if you wish to grow handsome!)

No need to tell this man the secret that beside the energy of his conscious intellect he was capable of new energy by abandonment to the nature of things. The perfection of writing was when the animal thought, and a little wine and good food furnished some elemental wisdom, and the fire, too, as it burned on a winter's day; for he fancied that his logs, which had grown so long in the sun and wind at Walden, were a kind of muses. Why should one spare any stimulant, any purgative, that brought one into a productive state, to the top of one's condition? How easily, alas, one lapsed into flesh and sleep!

Health, south wind, books, old trees, a boat, a friend—auspicious all; and the fair water that Demosthenes drank. There was inspiration for Emerson in any assertion of the will, in a glance at the first proposition of Political Economy: "Everything in the world is purchased by labour, and our passions are only causes of labour." Then walking had the best value as gymnastics: with the first step over the threshold of his study he would suddenly get a spontaneous perception of his subject more just and searching than hours of toil had given him. The sight of a man of genius filled him with a boundless confidence in his own powers; and certain trifling expedients sometimes served. Writing letters, for instance. When thoughts refused to come and the gift of the happy phrase, the bright image, seemed to have vanished forever, he would begin to write to some friend, and behold, there he was, floating off on the most cordial tide of expression. And the power of the fetish was not to be despised. Handel always composed in court dress, and Machiavelli, before sitting down at his writing-table in the evening, threw off the garments of the day and arrayed himself in his robe of ceremony. Was there not some virtue in this association? Some virtue in his own coat, made for him in Florence, which he wore when he wrote his essay on Michael Angelo?

As a final strategem, for perfect seclusion, he would go to a hotel: in summer, some country inn, in winter the American House in Hanover Street. Even in Concord, even on his little farm, there were always distractions, running feet in the halls, a leak in the roof, a disaster in the garden. The day was cut up into short strips, and the world seemed to be in a conspiracy to invade him, to vanquish him with details, to break him into crumbs and fritter his time. Friend, wife, child, fear, want, charity, all knocked at his door at the critical moment, rang alarums in his ear, scared away the muse and spoiled the poem. (And the carpenters, the masons, the tradesmen. Did they think a writer was an idler because he worked with invisible tools, worked to invisible ends?) Then a few days in Boston, at Nantasket Beach, in the mountains, made all the difference. No distractions there, no visitors. Not an insect's hum to shake the quiet hours.

The moment of inspiration—he was its reverent slave. He watched and hailed its aurora from afar.

XXIX

WILLIAM ALLEN WHITE: THE MAN FROM EMPORIA[1]

By

EVERETT RICH

During the McKinley-Bryan presidential campaign in 1896 both the Populist and Democratic parties supported Bryan. William Allen White, a young conservative who a few months before had bought the Emporia, Kansas, *Gazette*, in opposing the Populists wrote a fiery editorial, "What's the Matter with Kansas?" The editorial brought him immediate fame and established him nationally in three fields, literature, journalism, and politics. White's notable activities since then have been too varied and too numerous to enumerate, but he is best known as the editor of the Emporia *Gazette*, a small-town paper, which for nearly a half-century he has refused to leave despite all efforts to lure him away.

The story which Everett Rich has taken from the biography, to use his own description, "contains one of the most famous editorials ever written in America. And it is further unique in that it brought a young editor into immediate national prominence which he held on to as tenaciously as a cat holds on to a rug when one tries to pull the cat across it backward by the tail."

WHAT'S THE MATTER WITH KANSAS?

The Kansas political campaign of 1896 was the last spasm of a dying revolution. The genesis of the political turmoil lay in the economic predicament of the farmer. In 1890 three-fourths of Kansas farms were mortgaged, and on these mortgages the farmer was struggling to pay an average annual interest of 9 per cent. In many cases, the face of the mortgage was as much as the value of the land. Lyon County, regarded as one

[1] Everett Rich, *William Allen White: The Man from Emporia*, copyright 1941 by Everett Rich, and reprinted by permission of Farrar & Rinehart, Inc., publishers. pp. 83-92.

of the most prosperous in the state, had a total mortgage indebtedness of $5,588,600 against a valuation of $6,493,491. From 1880 to 1890 approximately 450,000 mortgages were written on Kansas property, and about one-third of these "were foreclosed or the property deeded to the holder of the mortgage without legal proceedings." In the first six months of 1890 more than 10,000 farms were either foreclosed or transferred to the mortgage holder to save the expense of foreclosure. In Reno County foreclosures reached the staggering figure of 426 in a single term of court. Farmers, attempting "to hang on" and ever looking forward to higher prices, had plunged farther and farther into debt. To pay interest and taxes, they had had to borrow on their chattels at an annual rate of from 40 per cent to 375 per cent. At the same time, they were burning their corn because they could not exchange it for coal except at a loss, and burying their eggs because they were not worth hauling to market.[2]

Suffering from these and a hundred other ills, real or imaginary, farmers, laborers, and merchants were in the right psychological state to listen to any Messiah who promised to lead them out of their economic wilderness. And saviors, both men and women, arose by the score. Mary Elizabeth Lease electrified her listeners by telling them that they should "raise less corn and more Hell"; Jerry Simpson rode to national fame by championing the "single tax," attacking the "grain gamblers," railroads, and kindred groups and organizations; and the names of a half-dozen others became household words throughout the nation. Under the inspiration of these leaders the discontent solidified itself in the form of the Populist Party, and the campaign of 1890 had all the earmarks of a religious reawakening. Tens of thousands flocked to the party gatherings where every man under the influence of a political revivalist became his own authority on the railroads, trusts, finance, taxation, and other topics of the hour.

Attended as it was by religious hysteria, the Populist movement attracted to its ranks the lunatic fringe in politics. On this aspect of the movement, the Republican Party centered its major attack. Without seriously attempting to answer the arguments of the Populists, the Republicans reviled and ridiculed the party by picturing it as a conglomeration of ignoramuses, half-wits and crackpots. The nation at large, out of sympathy with the movement, accepted the vilification at face value. "Sockless" Jerry Simpson is a case in point. Simpson, far from being the clod-hopper of popular imagination, was a cultured gentleman and "of more than usual sense for an American congressman." [3] He was not only a serious student of econ-

[2] Statistics are from William E. Connelley, *History of Kansas*, II, 1135 ff.

[3] William Allen White, *The Editor and His People*, New York: Macmillan, 1924.

omics, but widely read in both American and English literature. He had come to Kansas with fifteen thousand dollars; and after seven years of farming, his money was gone and he was city marshal of Medicine Lodge at forty dollars a month. Throwing over his marshal job, he became the farmers' candidate for Congress against James P. Hallowell, a Civil War colonel, a successful lawyer, a congenial spirit, and an eloquent speaker, "known among his friends as 'Prince Hal.'" Simpson, in attacking Hallowell, compared his own lowly estate with that of his opponent's and asserted that Hallowell wore silk underwear. "I can't represent you in Congress in silk underwear," he said; "I can't afford to wear it." Victor Murdock, then a young reporter, substituted "socks" for "underwear" and in reporting the speech quoted Simpson as saying, "Prince Hal wears silk socks: I don't wear any."[4] Murdock's story was accepted as true, and within a week everywhere Simpson was spoken of as "Sockless" Jerry or "Sockless" Simpson. Later, William Allen White added Socrates, and Simpson "came to be known throughout the length and breadth of the land as the 'Sockless Socrates from Kansas.'"[5]

By 1894, Kansas Populism was definitely on the decline. The Populist Party, which had swept the Republicans from office, had failed to alleviate the general economic suffering. As a consequence, its leaders had fallen out, and were calling each other names. But because the economic situation remained essentially unaltered, the forces of discontent needed but one clear strong voice to rally them. In 1896 the magnificent voice of William Jennings Bryan captured the remnants of this once powerful organization as he earnestly pleaded for the free coinage of silver, and every man became an authority on the currency.

Day by day as the McKinley-Bryan campaign progressed, the young editor of the Emporia *Gazette* laid his offering on the Republican altar. By every rule of self-interest he should have been writing editorials extolling Bryan and denouncing the Republican McKinley. But for some indefinable reason, he thought of himself as a member of the privileged class. When the Populists marched up and down Emporia streets waving banners, "Abolish Interest and You Will Abolish Poverty," he did not see his newspaper profits going to pay the interest on a mortgage—he saw red. Preaching that sort of thing was "lunacy"; it was "anarchy." In unqualified terms he told his readers just that; and for his pains the Populists taunted him

[4] Victor Murdock, *Folks,* p. 103, New York: Macmillan, 1941. Sometime before Murdock had tried unsuccessfully to dub an Oklahoma reformer, named Daniels, as a sockless statesman. Daniels was not wearing socks when Murdock saw him, but Simpson was.

[5] William E. Connelley, *History of Kansas*, vol. II, p. 1168, Chicago and New York: American Historical Society, 1928.

with "Silly Willy" and drew a picture of the *Gazette* as a jackass and put it into their procession.

For White the silver issue in the 1896 campaign was but ostensibly the question at stake. The real issue was, "Shall American institutions, as they have been since the beginning, stand, or shall they be changed?"[6] The cardinal principle on which the American government had been founded was that "the state should give every man protection in his right to enjoy 'life, liberty, and the pursuit of happiness.' " Beyond the protection of the citizen "in his enjoyment of peace" the state had no right to interfere. The American way was "hands off," taking the part of neither the weak nor the strong. What had grown up in the West in recent years was the "un-American doctrine of state paternalism."

It is claimed by these doctors that when one man is weak, when he fails to get on in the world, when he finds himself at the bottom of the heap, the state should help him up. The believers in the new creed hold that it is the duty of the state to check the accumulation of one man's wealth and to end another man's poverty. They say that the man with the large fortune and the man who commits a crime are both subjects for state interference. They say that the man who is without means is the nation's ward, that he should be protected against the "oppression of wealth."

To White such a theory of government was neither American nor democratic; it was European and socialistic. The true American theory, as conceived by "the fathers" and as embraced by the Republican Party, says to the weak man:

. . . "Be strong or go under." It says to the strong: "Only be fair and keep within the law." It says to the poor: "There is no way on earth to get rich except by frugality, good management, and industry." The Republican party, speaking for the old-fashioned, sturdy Americanism, says to the man who asks that the state shall step in and relieve him of his burden: "You had an equal opportunity with your fellows. You had as good an education, as good a body, as fair a start; if you are behind and the other man is ahead, the thing for you to do is to catch up. We can't stop him. He is running his own race; if he is violating no law we shall let him go ahead—the faster he goes the better."

Furthermore, the Populists and their whole infernal lot, who were now attacking the foundations of the government, were the same party "which sympathized with treason in '61," . . . "abused Lincoln for upholding the government by continuing the war," and "defied the troops of the United

[6] The quotations which follow immediately are from "The Sweep of It," Emporia *Gazette,* August 11, 1896.

States in Chicago." It now "silver plates a revolution, and calls to its aid all the forces of failure, of jealousy, of malice and sectional hatred to accomplish its dangerous scheme. It rallies state's rights under Altgeld, revolution under Tillman, despair under Peffer, anarchy under Debs, greed of office under Gorman, and all the wild, remorseful emotions of men who have failed in life under Bryan."

But though the young editor was writing as if the fate of the nation were in the balance, he planned to go on a vacation in the very midst of the conflict. Regardless of the threat to the nation, the intensity of a political campaign has never interfered with William Allen White's chucking the whole thing if he decided to do something else. Thus it was that while he was opposing the Fusion Party[7] most vigorously, he set August 15 as the date of his departure for Colorado, where he was to join Mrs. White for a short vacation. Early that Saturday afternoon as he was returning from the post office with an arm load of letters and exchanges, a Populist stepped up to him and began to ply him with questions on a silver argument which he thought White could not answer. White, annoyed at the interruption, was further irritated when a crowd gathered, which applauded everything his opponent said and jeered all his responses.

Any Saturday afternoon crowd in Emporia in August is largely made up of farmers and "town men of leisure," whether it be in 1896 or at the present time. And in August, 1896, in the midst of a prolonged drought with the thermometer standing at 107 degrees, wheat selling at 40 cents, corn 16, butter 10, chickens 8 if dressed, eggs 6, steers 3, hogs 2½, and the city without a street force because of no money—their political sympathies emphatically did not coincide with those of the editor of the *Gazette*.

They were naturally for Bryan and the vigor of the campaign in the *Gazette* together with the easy, innocent looking face of its youthful editor, gave them a notion that it would be a lot of fun to play horse with him on the street, which they proceeded to do. A crowd of them, 15 or 20, surrounded him and played froggy-in-the-meadow politically with the young smarty, guying him and reviling him and provoking him to language. But somehow his language got jammed. The madder he got the more he sputtered and the less he spoke, and his face lost all expression except its color. He looked as featureless and as mad as a freshly spanked baby in the combat area, and finally, with his arm full of mail, stalked proudly down the street with a number of thoughts corked up to him.[8]

[7] The Populists and the Democrats had endorsed the same roster of candidates.
[8] Emporia *Gazette,* August 16, 1926.

When White did reach the *Gazette,* he found the printer "howling for more copy for the editorial page." Glancing at his watch to see how much time he had left to catch the train, he plunged into writing, all hot and angry. Sentences "simply rolled off" his pen; and as the pages were completed, the printer took them one by one "hot off the griddle."[9] That evening Democrats and Populists were treated to "What's the Matter With Kansas?" another tirade of "Silly Willy's":

Today the Kansas department of agriculture sent out a statement which indicates that Kansas has gained less than two thousand people in the past year. There are about two hundred and twenty-five thousand families in the state, and there were about ten thousand babies born in Kansas, and yet so many people have left the state that the natural increase is cut down to less than two thousand net.

This has been going on for eight years.

If there had been a high brick wall around the state eight years ago, and not a soul had been admitted or permitted to leave, Kansas would be a half million souls better off than she is today. And yet the nation has increased in population. In five years ten million people have been added to the national population, yet instead of gaining a share of this—say, half a million—Kansas has apparently been a plague spot, and in the very garden of the world, has lost population by ten thousands every year.

Not only has she lost population, but she has lost money. Every moneyed man in the state who could get out without loss has gone. Every month in every community sees some one who has a little money pack up and leave the state. This has been going on for eight years. Money has been drained out all the time. In towns where ten years ago there were three or four or half a dozen money lending concerns stimulating industry by furnishing capital, there is now none, or one or two that are looking after the interests and principal already outstanding.

No one brings any money into Kansas any more. What community knows over one or two men who have moved in with more than $5,000 in the past three years? And what community cannot count half a score of men in that time who have left, taking all the money they could scrape together?

Yet the nation has grown rich, other states have increased in population and wealth—other neighboring states. Missouri has gained over two million, while Kansas has been losing half a million. Nebraska has gained in wealth and population while Kansas has gone down hill. Colorado has gained every way, while Kansas has lost every way since 1888.

What's the matter with Kansas?

There is no substantial city in the state. Every big town save one has lost in

[9] *Harper's Weekly,* XLVI (February 1, 1902), p. 155.

population. Yet Kansas City, Omaha, Lincoln, St. Louis, Denver, Colorado Springs, Sedalia, the cities of the Dakotas, St. Paul and Minneapolis and Des Moines—all cities and towns in the West have steadily grown.

Take up the government blue book and you will see that Kansas is virtually off the map. Two or three little scrubby consular places in yellow-fever-stricken communities that do not aggregate ten thousand dollars a year is all the recognition that Kansas has. Nebraska draws about one hundred thousand dollars; little old North Dakota draws about fifty thousand dollars; Oklahoma doubles Kansas; Missouri leaves her a thousand miles behind; Colorado is almost seven times greater than Kansas—the whole West is ahead of Kansas.

Take it by any standard you please, Kansas is not in it.

Go east and you hear them laugh at Kansas, go west and they sneer at her, go south and they "cuss" her, go north and they have forgotten her. Go into any crowd of intelligent people gathered anywhere on the globe, and you will find the Kansas man on the defensive. The newspaper columns and magazines once devoted to praise of her, to boastful facts and startling figures concerning her resources, are now filled with cartoons, jibes and Pefferian speeches. Kansas just naturally isn't in it. She has traded places with Arkansas and Timbuctoo.

What's the matter with Kansas?

We all know; yet here we are at it again. We have an old moss-back Jacksonian who snorts and howls because there is a bathtub in the statehouse; we are running that old jay for governor. We have another shabby, wild-eyed, rattle-brained fanatic who has said openly in a dozen speeches that "the rights of the user are paramount to the rights of the owner"; we are running him for chief justice, so that capital will come tumbling over itself to get into the state. We have raked the old ash heap of failure in the state and found an old human hoop skirt who has failed as a business man, who has failed as an editor, who has failed as a preacher, and we are going to run him for congressman-at-large. He will help the looks of the Kansas delegation at Washington. Then we have discovered a kid without a law practice and have decided to run him for attorney-general. Then for fear some hint that the state has become respectable might percolate through the civilized portions of the nation, we have decided to send three or four harpies out lecturing, telling the people that Kansas is raising hell and letting the corn go to weeds.

Oh, this is a state to be proud of! We are a people who can hold up our heads! What we need is not more money, but less capital, fewer white shirts and brains, fewer men with business judgment, and more of those fellows who boast that they are "just ordinary clodhoppers, but they know more in a minute about finance than John Sherman"; we need more men who are "posted," who can bellow about the crime of '73, who hate prosperity, and who think because a man believes in national honor, he is a tool of Wall Street. We have had a few of them—some hundred and fifty thousand, but we need more.

We need several thousand gibbering idiots to scream about the "Great Red Dragon" of Lombard Street. We don't need population, we don't need wealth, we don't need well-dressed men on the streets, we don't need cities on the fertile prairies; you bet we don't! What we are after is the money power. Because we have become poorer and ornerier and meaner than a spavined, distempered mule, we, the people of Kansas, propose to kick; we don't care to build up, we wish to tear down.

"There are two ideas of government," said our noble Bryan at Chicago. "There are those who believe that if you just legislate to make the well-to-do prosperous, this prosperity will leak through on those below. The Democratic idea has been that if you legislate to make the masses prosperous their prosperity will find its way up and through every class and rest upon us."

That's the stuff! Give the prosperous man the dickens! Legislate the thriftless man into ease, whack the stuffing out of the creditors and tell the debtors who borrowed the money five years ago when money "per capita" was greater than it is now that the contraction of the currency gives him a right to repudiate.

Whoop it up for the ragged trousers; put the lazy, greasy fizzle who can't pay his debts on the altar, and bow down and worship him. Let the state ideal be high. What we need is not the respect of our fellow men, but the chance to get something for nothing.

Oh, yes, Kansas is a great state. Here are people fleeing from it by the score every day, capital going out of the state by the hundreds of dollars; and every industry but farming paralyzed, and that crippled, because its products have to go across the ocean before they can find a laboring man to work who can afford to buy them. Let's don't stop this year. Let's drive all the decent, self-respecting men out of the state. Let's keep the old clodhoppers who know it all. Let's encourage the man who is "posted." He can talk, and what we need is not mill hands to eat our meat, nor factory hands to eat our wheat, nor cities to oppress the farmer by consuming his butter and eggs and chickens and produce. What Kansas needs is men who can talk, who have large leisure to argue the currency question while their wives wait at home for that nickel's worth of bluing.

What's the matter with Kansas?

Nothing under the shining sun. She is losing wealth, population, and standing. She has got her statesmen, and the money power is afraid of her. Kansas is all right. She has started in to raise hell, as Mrs. Lease advised, and she seems to have an over-production. But that doesn't matter. Kansas never did believe in diversified crops. Kansas is all right. There is absolutely nothing wrong with Kansas. "Every prospect pleases and only man is vile."[10]

In the meantime, William Allen White had boarded the Santa Fé and was proudly bearing the proofs of a little collection of short stories to

[10] Emporia *Gazette,* August 15, 1896.

Mrs. White that they might read them together. So completely had he forgotten the incidents of the afternoon that not even the name of the Populist who provoked the editorial remained in his memory. His temperature, like that of his state which by Monday had broken to 71 degrees in Emporia, had burned itself out. Thus closed the first chapter of "What's the Matter With Kansas?"

The second chapter opens in Chicago. Paul Morton, vice president of the Santa Fé, "happening to meet Herman Kohlsaat, publisher of the Chicago *Times-Herald*, told him he had just read an editorial in a little Kansas paper giving a striking picture of conditions which, Morton said, Chicago and the East ought to know about."[11] Kohlsaat asked Morton to send him the paper, and he reprinted the editorial in both the *Times-Herald* and *Evening Post*. By way of Chicago the piece reached New York, where the *Sun* reprinted it. Then the Republican national committee began turning copies out in 100,000 lots, as the Republican press throughout the country broadcast the editorial to their countless readers. White, vacationing in the Colorado mountains, was totally unaware that he had caught the popular imagination. By the twenty-seventh of August, he, back in Emporia, had learned that Mark Hanna was using his "wail of woe" as a campaign document, and banteringly asked his readers if that ought to "be good for the post office."[12] A month later, although the Republican national committee was to distribute a million copies during the campaign, White had not yet seen a single reprint from that source.

Yet long before this date White knew he was standing on the threshold of fame. Kohlsaat wrote him that "the article has attracted more attention than anything that had been published during the campaign." Tom Reed, Speaker of the House of Representatives, wrote that he had "not seen as much sense in one column in a dozen years."[13] Every reputable Republican paper in towns of 50,000 or more had reprinted the editorial. Exchanges were pouring in; letters from individuals and McKinley clubs were sending money and asking for thousands of copies. Edition after edition had to be printed. Eight years later with McKinley in his grave, with Roosevelt in the White House, and with White totally reversed in his political attitudes, on the average from two to three letters a week were still dribbling in asking for copies.[14]

[11] Mark Sullivan, *Our Times*, vol. I, p. 138, New York and London: Charles Scribner's Sons, 1931.

[12] Emporia *Gazette*, August 27, 1896.

[13] Emporia *Gazette*, September 25, 1896.

[14] Emporia *Gazette*, August 15, 1904.

XXX

MITCHELL: PIONEER OF AIR POWER [1]

By

ISAAC DON LEVINE

To Americans the name of Billy Mitchell stands for the man who had the courage to fight for his convictions regarding the importance of the airplane in modern warfare. In another selection in this anthology there is a vivid description of Mitchell's court-martial for the ideas he held.

Isaac Don Levine has chosen the passage which follows from his scholarly biography "because this incident was not only a turning point in the course of the first World War, but also in the life of Billy Mitchell. It was the first great test confronting Mitchell in the war, and it was really on this occasion that he became America's first flying general."

"THE HISTORY OF THE WORLD WAR WAS PLAYED OUT IN THREE DAYS"

On Bastille Day it seemed as if the zero hour had come. Mitchell was in Paris making a last-minute attempt to get a supply of new airplanes to the front. The Germans had moved up masses of troops to various positions. While the Allied commanders did not know exactly where the enemy would strike, it was believed that the drive would be directed at the peak of the salient on the Marne.

The evening of the 14th Mitchell was having a late dinner in Paris. He was joined by Donald Brown of the Red Cross. He expected to drive back to his headquarters at Haute Feuille. At ten minutes past midnight of July 15 the nothern sky was lit up with great flashes and the rumbling of the distant heavy artillery could be heard. "I was certain that the main

[1] Isaac Don Levine, *Mitchell: Pioneer of Air Power*, New York: Duell, Sloan and Pearce, Inc., 1943, Reprinted by permission of the publishers, pp. 119-124, 126-127.

attack of the Germans was being launched," he jotted down in his diary, and invited Brown to join him if he wanted to see "the greatest battle in history."

A little before three o'clock in the morning Mitchell, driving at breakneck speed, reached headquarters. "The whole sky was lighted up by the flash of the artillery on both sides," he noted. "Rockets and signals were appearing everywhere; searchlight beams were sweeping the skies; the buzz of airplanes going and coming, and the noise of the bombs dropping, covered the whole line."

Mitchell began to issue orders disposing of his forces for action by daylight when Major Gerard, with his aide, coming from army headquarters, were announced. The two French air officers were in a very perturbed state. No one was as yet certain where the main blow would strike. The Germans were pressing the sector of the 3rd French Army along the Marne, where the Americans were entrenched at Château-Thierry, as well as that of the 4th French Army toward Rheims and the Champagne. The plan was clearly to drive south and enflank Paris, only forty miles away from the apex of the salient. It now appeared that the French air division, due to a confusion in orders, was not ready to meet the enemy that morning, and it was proposed to have the American and British squadrons patrol the skies immediately. Mitchell saw no advantage to the plan, feeling certain that it would lead to heavy and unnecessary losses. He proposed instead that a reconnaissance mission be carried out over the active front to find out what the enemy was doing. Major Gerard agreed and left.

Mitchell decided to do his own reconnaissance. He lay down and snatched a few minutes of sleep. He possessed all his life this capacity to concentrate and relax at will. Before daybreak the commanding officer of the American air force was winging his way alone over the inferno below and across the salient held by the Germans. Underneath the ground troops were putting up terrific resistance. Everybody was sure that all the bridges across the Marne had been destroyed, and the word had gone out that the enemy must not cross the river.

Mitchell flew straight north. He had climbed high and except for general artillery fire, he saw no unusual troop movements in the center of the large pocket which formed the Château-Thierry salient. He then turned and flew up the Marne where the American sectors began. In the vicinity of Jaulgonne he spotted a few Fokker planes whose pilots either did not see him or ignored him. He swooped down low as he approached a turn in the Marne. It struck him as strange that the roads did not gleam with their usual whiteness. Suddenly he beheld east of Dormans five bridges spanning the river. It did not seem possible. Observing no German planes overhead, getting no attention from any of the enemy anti-aircraft guns, Mitchell descended to within 500 feet of the ground. "The whitened roads were green with thousands of German troops driving on toward the Marne with the steadiness and determination of a huge caterpillar," Major Elmer Haslett wrote in his chronicle of this singular flight in his *Luck on the Wing* immediately after the war.

The masses of stalwart German troops were streaming toward the five bridges, which turned out to be pontoons. Having made this discovery, Mitchell flew on in the direction of Rheims. Here a crucial battle was going on. The American infantry of the 3rd Division was endeavoring to stem the onslaught. Enemy planes were beginning to swarm in the sky. After reaching the field of the 1st Pursuit Group safely, Mitchell ordered an aerial attack upon the bridges and rushed over to the headquarters of General Liggett to report his observations. He immediately made a similar report to Major Gerard of the 3rd French Army. And then he climbed into his car and drove to the headquarters of General Foch, where he went at once into conference with his friend Major Armengaud, general staff liaison officer of aviation.

The Germans were pouring across the Marne, and it was clear that there would be no holding them back by frontal counter-attacks. Mitchell proposed that the enemy's great supply base at Fère-en-Tardenois be subjected to a massed attack from the air by all the available bombardment and pursuit units. This was approved. "It was quite evident," he recorded, "that, as the Germans were attacking at the head of the salient of which the base was formed by Soissons on one side and Rheims on the other, if we could get in from either side of the base, we could turn the whole German position and if successful, attack them in the rear and perhaps destroy their whole army. It was the best chance that presented itself during the war and Marshal Foch was not slow to avail himself of it."

Word had spread along the front that an American pursuit plane had flown over the enemy lines and discovered the location of the bridges over which the Germans were sweeping across the Marne. "This flight by a pursuit plane and the resulting information was, I think, unquestionably one of the greatest flights of the entire war," wrote Haslett. "I did not learn until several days later who the aviator was. No one seemed to know, nor could we find any record on the regular reports." According to Haslett, Mitchell, whose aide he became after the Armistice, had scribbled a little note before leaving his headquarters on the solo mission and left it for his chief of operations, Captain Phil Roosevelt. The message said that in the event he did not return by eight o'clock that morning, Major Brereton should be notified to take command of the American air force at the front. Roosevelt had been out all night, and the note never reached him, as Mitchell returned in time to retrieve it.

"It was singularly fortunate that the man who undertook this hazardous mission was a rare tactician and strategist," concludes Haslett. "He realized the awful truth where the ordinary airman would not have conceived the possibilities of such a situation. He knew that the biggest German Army ever concentrated was on the move in a final effort to intimidate and conquer the world. And when the flyers found out who had made that mysterious flight, our morale was strengthened one hundred per cent." The airmen gloried in having a chief of such fighting caliber.

Mitchell was strenuously at work on the forthcoming aerial assault on the base at Fère-en-Tardenois. In the meantime Colonel Hartney's 1st Pursuit Group was in the air nearly all the time. "I shall never forget July 15, 1918, as long as I live," he writes. "It seemed as if the whole German army, in desperation, simply hurled itself at our part of the lines." In Berlin there was jubilation as reports from the front told of the German troops marching on the way to Paris.

On July 16, at noon, British and American air squadrons launched a combined attack, bombing and blowing up a number of ammunition dumps. The Germans were taken completely by surprise by this attack in broad daylight, according to Mitchell, and were put on the defensive in the air, having to assemble unexpectedly a large force to protect their bases in the rear. The British suffered a loss of twelve planes in the operation.

"We had found the Achilles heel of the German position north of the Marne and had seized the initiative in the air," Mitchell rejoiced. "It is the first case on record where we, with an inferior air force, were able to put the superior air force on the defensive and attack whenever we pleased, without the danger of the Germans sending great masses of the pursuit aviation over to our side of the line. What we could do if we had one thousand good airplanes instead of a measly two hundred and fifty!"

In spite of this, with the Allied line broken in the center, Berlin was sure of having virtually achieved victory. But Mitchell's flight was beginning to affect the German prospects. Foch was already setting the stage for a surprise move, the most decisive one in the war. In the night, in complete darkness and secrecy, American and French divisions were being shifted to the vicinity of Soissons, the dormant northern flank of the salient. In the daytime, to mislead German aerial observers, troop movements were instituted in the direction of Rheims, to simulate the rushing of reinforcements there and to divert attention from the concentrations going on at the opposite flank. Mitchell was massing his air forces to support the scheduled surprise blow at the base of the salient.

"It was an operation fraught with the greatest importance for the Allies," commented Mitchell. "If it succeeded, the Germans would have to retire from the Château-Thierry salient." And that would spell the loss of Germany's last chance on the Western front. . . .

There was elation at Foch's headquarters, and with good reason, more than anyone could realize at that moment. The tide of the whole war had been turned. Up to July 16 the Allies had been on the defensive for nearly four years. From now on the Germans would be on the defensive. Mitchell was received with beaming faces when he went down to headquarters. Major Armengaud told him that all the data gathered by the American airmen had proved correct, indicating the exact point of attack and, within a few hours, its exact time. "We are now sure that the Germans are on the run," chronicled Mitchell.

He won recognition for his own historic flight. On November 7, he was awarded the Distinguished Service Cross "for extraordinary heroism in action" displayed on several occasions, one of the instances cited being "a flight in a monoplane over the bridges which the Germans had laid across the Marne during July, 1918, which led to the first definite reports of the location of these bridges and the subsequent attack upon the German troops by our air forces."

That the tide had turned by July 18 was fully realized in Berlin, too. The German Chancellor subsequently revealed that on July 15 he was convinced that "before the first of September our adversaries would send us peace proposals. On the 18th even the most optimistic among us knew that all was lost. The history of the world was played out in three days."

During these three days the American troops, some 275,000 strong, heroically stepped into the breach and helped break the German tide. The enemy was finally sent reeling back and the Marne salient, with its threat to Paris, wiped out.

XXXI

THE LITTLE GIANT, THE STORY OF STEPHEN A. DOUGLAS AND ABRAHAM LINCOLN[1]

By

JEANNETTE COVERT NOLAN

Being little more than five feet in height (contrasted with Lincoln's six feet, four inches), with a large head, and a great chest and shoulders, Stephen A. Douglas became known popularly as "The Little Giant."

Born in Vermont, Douglas moved to Jacksonville, Illinois, in 1833, at the age of twenty. In 1841 he was a judge of the Illinois Supreme Court. In 1843 he was elected to the United States House of Representatives, and in 1847 to the United States Senate, defeating Abraham Lincoln. He is perhaps best known for his famous debates with Lincoln.

In the Presidential election of 1860, Douglas ran against Lincoln, but despite his defeat strongly supported Lincoln and advocated the maintenance of the Union. He died in June, 1861, shortly after the outbreak of the Civil War.

Jeannette Covert Nolan has given us a striking scene of the gallant Little Giant at Lincoln's inauguration.

WHEN THE LITTLE GIANT HELD LINCOLN'S HAT AND CANE

"The prospects are gloomy, but I do not yet despair. . . . We can never acknowledge the right of a state to secede."

Thus wrote Douglas.

Lincoln had been elected, but he had not the confidence of all the people, nor, indeed, of all the members of his own party. A good man,

[1] Jeannette Covert Nolan, *The Little Giant, the Story of Stephen A. Douglas and Abraham Lincoln*, New York: Julian Messner, Inc., 1942, pp. 249-253.

perhaps—though no one knew much about him. In this Douglas could be of assistance. He knew Lincoln. From the floor of the Senate he asked that the country have faith.

South Carolina seceded.

It was wrong, Douglas said, unlawful, criminal. "*Are we prepared for war?* I do not mean that kind of preparation which consists of armies and navies and supplies, and munitions of war; but are we prepared *in our hearts* for war with our own brethren and kindred? I confess I am not."

Mississippi seceded, Florida, Alabama, Georgia. Louisiana and Texas would surely follow.

Why not an eleventh-hour compromise? Douglas implored. "I never intend to give up hope of saving this Union so long as there is a ray left."

But the South was obdurate. This Union talk was "the merest balderdash."

Bidding farewell to Springfield, Lincoln had started eastward, speaking along the way at Indianapolis, Cincinnati, Cleveland, Pittsburgh, Harrisburg. He had been warned that he might be mobbed in Baltimore. Rather against his will, he put on a disguise of felt hat, pulled down over his eyes, and a large, enveloping shawl, and let himself be smuggled through that city and into Washington.

His intimates were distressed at this unseemly entrance into the capital, and his critics charged him with being an undignified weakling.

"No," Douglas said to one of these critics. "No, he is not that, sir; but he is eminently a man of the atmosphere which surrounds him. He has not yet got out of Springfield, sir. He does not know that he is President-elect of the United States, sir; he does not see that the shadow he casts is any bigger now than it was last year. It will not take him long to find it out when he has got established in the White House."

Adele hurried to call upon Mrs. Lincoln, offering hospitality and friendship; and the press everywhere commented upon the graceful little act. How like Adele Douglas! Mrs. Lincoln seemed a bit dazed by her sudden transition from Illinois housewife to the place as First Lady of the land. She was the same Mary Todd she had always been: petulant, erratic, sharp-tongued, overeager. It would be well, said Washington society, for her to have as mentor a woman so poised and experienced as Mrs. Stephen A. Douglas.

Three days after Lincoln's arrival, Douglas went to see him. For hours they were deep in conference. When Douglas rose to leave he took Lincoln's hand and gazed steadfastly up at him.

"You and I have been for many years politically opposed to each other, but in our attachment to the Constitution and Union we have never differed—in this we are one—this must and shall not be destroyed."

Tears glinted in Lincoln's eyes. "God bless you, Douglas. . . . The danger is great but with such words and such friends why should we fear? . . . With all my heart I thank you. The people with us and God helping us, all will yet be well. God bless you, Douglas, I can't forget it."

As the door closed, Lincoln murmured, "What a noble man Douglas is!"

Thereafter the two were often closeted together. Every ray of hope for compromise had now been extinguished, but Douglas was resolved that no one should doubt his complete allegiance to the new President.

"I shall attend the inauguration," he said. "I shall be there, and if any man attacks Lincoln, he attacks me too!"

The day dawned cloudy but not chill, and by noon the weather was like summertime. Washington was full, and in distant areas of the city were United States troops, ready if the ceremonies should be menaced.

A military escort went to fetch Mr. Lincoln from his hotel, with Mr. Buchanan stepping out of the carriage, where the liveried coachman sat on the box. Mr. Buchanan greeted Mr. Lincoln, both got into the carriage, the band played *Hail, Columbia*, and mounted soldiers formed a parade which wound along Pennsylvania Avenue toward the Capitol.

The Diplomatic Corps and the Justices of the Supreme Court, headed by Chief Justice Roger Taney, were congregated in the Senate chamber; at ten minutes past one, Mr. Buchanan and Mr. Lincoln were ushered in. Then the company filed out to the platform erected over the east Capitol steps. Lincoln was introduced to the vast crowd.

He was awkwardly holding in his hands his brand-new silk hat and the huge, gold-headed cane presented to him for this historic occasion. For an instant he seemed not to know what to do with these fineries; he stared at the rickety little table before him and seemed uncertain.

But someone near him came to his rescue. Smiling, Stephen Douglas came forward, to relieve him of hat and cane, to stand stanchly, comfortingly close to him as he began his speech.

Fumbling in his pocket, Lincoln drew out his spectacles and clamped them on his nose, read from a manuscript.

He would not, he said, interfere with the domestic institutions of the South, or with any of the safeguards of the Constitution, but he believed in the Union. By his reasoning, a state could not possibly secede from the Union, which had been created to endure forever. An attempt at such desertion must be viewed as insurrection or, if on a large scale, revolution.

His purpose as President would be to see that all the laws of the Union were executed in all the states. "We are not enemies, but friends. We must not be enemies. Though passion may have strained, it must not break our bonds of affection. The mystic chords of memory . . . will yet swell the chorus of the Union, when again touched, as surely they will be, by the better angels of our nature."

He was visibly affected, his voice strange, throbbing with feeling. When Chief Justice Taney administered the oath of office, Lincoln's palm smote, firm and flat, upon the Bible.

He turned, and Stephen Douglas was there beside him. Their hands clasped.

"Mr. President, I congratulate you. I am with you now, and to the end."

In the evening occurred the Inaugural Ball, and Senator Douglas had the honor of taking in Mrs. Lincoln. Her dress was blue and she had thrust a feather into her hair. She was flushed and happy. Perhaps she thought of other balls when Stephen Douglas had walked beside her, danced with her. He was his usual self tonight, immaculately groomed, courteous—the gallant Little Giant.

Within six weeks, the cannon of the Southern general, Beauregard, had fired upon the United States garrison at Fort Sumter and civil war was a fact.

XXXII

GIANTS GONE, MEN WHO MADE CHICAGO [1]

By

ERNEST POOLE

From Ernest Poole's superb biographical sketches of the pioneers who made Chicago, we present two selections from the life of the distinguished Chicagoan, Dr. Frank Billings. Mr. Poole's book is filled with a series of fascinating portraits which give one a new sense of appreciation of the men who helped so substantially to build this great city of the Middle West.

THE RAVAGES OF SCARLET FEVER

Frank Billings was born on a Wisconsin farm, back in 1854. There he grew to be huge and strong, working from daybreak and into the dark, with ax or scythe or with heavy shoulders braced to meet the bound and bite in the soil of an old-fashioned plow. In the evenings he read by the light from the hearth. He made up his mind that he wanted to teach; and to earn the money for normal school, he hired out to a farmer, who paid him $20 a month because he found the young giant was able to do the work of two men. For three years he taught in frontier schools, but a book that he read on anatomy set him dreaming of a doctor's career, so he saved and bought a drugstore and ran it till he had money enough at last to come to Chicago in 1878.

At the college soon to be known as the Northwestern Medical School, eking out his expenses by tutoring, he worked so well that on graduation he won the highest available prize, first place as intern in the immense Cook County Hospital. He rode the ambulance for a year, then served three more at his school as demonstrator in anatomy. The laws of that

[1] Ernest Poole, *Giants Gone, Men Who Made Chicago*, New York: Whittlesey House, McGraw-Hill Book Company, Inc., 1943, pp. 293-295, 299-300, 308-309.

time made it so hard to get bodies for dissection that "body snatching" was common practice among the wild young medical students. Billings himself in his student days had taken part in such gruesome exploits, and of one of them I was given this account by a doctor friend:

On their way out to Potter's Field, in a wagon on a cold winter night to get a body buried that day, in front of a lighted saloon they spied the wagon of their rivals, the Rush Medical boys, who had beaten them to the field and had stopped on their way back for a drink, leaving the rigid dead man propped up on the driver's seat. Quickly Billings and his friends transferred him to their wagon and it started back for town, leaving Billings behind as rear guard in the dead man's place on the driver's seat. When the Rush Medical boys came out and one climbed up beside Billings, he said suddenly: " . . . Boys, this stiff don't feel cold as he ought to be!"

"And neither would you be yourself, if you were burning in hell as I am!" said Billings in sepulchral tones. Out of the wagon tumbled the boys, and roaring with laughter he drove it away.

But that had been back in his student days; and rebelling against conditions which drove students to such grim jobs, young Billings now gathered a group of anatomists like himself, who rallied physicians all over the state in a movement which led to a law allowing medical schools the use of unclaimed bodies in public institutions and so advanced the research work which was later to save numberless lives.

Having earned enough to go abroad, he spent a year of hard study in Vienna, Paris and London. He grew interested in the new science of bacteriology for which Pasteur had battled against the standpatters; and on returning to Chicago, Billings worked in a laboratory for which he had brought equipment from France. Other physicians brought to him specimens for analysis; and his experiments caused such a stir that, when the august American Medical Association met in Chicago in 1887, Billings was asked to exhibit cultures of disease-producing bacteria. So new was this part of their science to the physicians of those days that in introducing Billings the venerable chairman apologized for giving fifteen minutes of their valuable time to talk about "a mere medical fad!" The germ theory a fad—less than sixty years ago! But the young iconoclast worked on, and gained such standing that in a few years he was elected president of the Chicago Medical Society. . . .

The rich could take him or leave him. They took him and kept him. Some became his cronies, and they drank and sang and played poker together when they could crowd in the time. But never forgetting the work of his life, he got from them huge sums with which to advance human welfare all over the West. A great beggar and a keen judge of men, he knew when to bide his time; but if he decided the moment was ripe, he would leap like a tiger on his prey. After pulling one rich patient through a serious illness which left the magnate meek as a mouse, Billings asked for his backing in a big research project. The man offered him $1,000.

"Wait a minute," Billings said, and he talked until his listener said he would give $4,000. "Now, wait a minute!" Billings replied. "You don't seem to have any idea of how important a job this is or what it may mean to people all over the face of the earth! It's a hundred times more important than you seem to realize!"

"But, my God, Frank!" his patient cried. "That would make it $400,000 for me to give!"

"Now you're whistling!" Billings said, and he got from his patient just that amount!

"The good that he did by such appeals can never be known," one doctor said. "You can doubtless remember the ravages of scarlet fever when you were a boy. Mothers dreaded it like the plague, for their children died of it like flies. If today it is no deadly scourge so long as it has proper care, the mothers should give thanks to Frank Billings; for when Harold McCormick and his wife, John Rockefeller's daughter, lost their small son through scarlet fever, in his memory Billings induced them to found the McCormick Institute for Infectious Diseases, which in later years led to the discovery of the scarlet-fever germ."

THE CROSS-EXAMINATION OF DR. BILLINGS

Toward the end of his career, he was called to testify in court as to whether a former woman patient of his had been sane when she made her will. Not only the judge but both lawyers were patients of Billings and knew him well. One of them, John Hamline, had played golf with him for years; but when Hamline rose in court to cross-examine him, he glanced in a puzzled way at a card and said:

"Billings—Billings. Is that the name?"

"It is, sir."

"Ah, now I have it. You're a physician, I believe."

"I am."

"Frank Billings?"

"Yes, sir!"

"Ah." John Hamline's face grew suddenly stern. "Dr. Billings, did you attend Marshall Field?"

"I did."

"What became of him?"

"He's dead."

"What's that? I'm a little deaf, sir. Will you please repeat your reply?"

"I said he's dead!"

"Poor fellow. Ah. Dr. Billings, was George M. Pullman your patient?"

"He was."

"Is he living?"

"No, he's dead."

"Repeat that, please!"

"I said, he's dead!"

"Did you take care of Philip Armour?"

"I did."

"Where is he now?"

"He's dead!"

"Merciful God!" The lawyer named three more rich men who had died of old age; and when he got the same reply, he threw up his hands in disgust. "That's all! I'm through with the witness!" he said. And while the whole court roared with laughter, Billings gave his tormentor a look that said: Through with me, are you? Damn your eyes, wait till next time I get *you* in bed!

XXXIII

FIGHTING ANGEL, PORTRAIT OF A SOUL [1]

By

PEARL S. BUCK

This biography of Pearl Buck's father is a companion volume to her biography, *The Exile*, of her mother, Carie. It is written with the beauty and literary charm which invariably characterize her work.

Here is the portrait of austere and stern Andrew, the father, with his unshakeable faith in the rightness of his principles and with his untiring labors as a missionary in China.

In the dramatic passage which Pearl Buck has selected for this anthology, we see Andrew, the old teacher, as he is affectionately called by the natives, courageously wait for death with his family in the raging storm of a great revolution in China.

THE OLD TEACHER WAS PLANNING TO GO BACK

But he was not yet to have peace for his work. While he had been living out his zestful days, another storm was rising out of the south, the storm of China's last and greatest revolution.

He had not paid much heed to it. There had been so many wars and revolutions in his day and he had long since refused to go away because he heard a war was threatening. Nobody would hurt him, he always declared. So he had stayed when others fled, coming and going in his usual routine, waiting, perhaps, on the side of a street for an army to march by, but granting no further concession to the eternal upset of China's political life.

And the sight of his tall, white-haired figure coming and going as usual gave the common people comfort and a sense of stability.

[1] Pearl S. Buck, *Fighting Angel*, New York: The John Day Company, copyright 1936, by Pearl S. Buck, pp. 271-289.

"Has the Old Teacher gone?" they asked each other.

"No, he has not gone," was the answer, and they settled themselves again. "If the Old Teacher should go, we would not know where to hide ourselves," they used to say.

But then he never went. And he pshawed the idea that this revolution was different from any other. When people talked of the new Bolshevik influence he refused to grant it importance. Bolsheviks were only people, after all. Besides, "the Chinese will never put up with them," he used to say with confidence. It was one of the secrets of his immense serenity that he always firmly believed anything he said himself.

So as the new revolution swept up from the south and knotted itself into central China and expanded again down the Yangtse River, Andrew regarded it without fear and indeed this time with something of indifference. He had seen so many revolutions come and go, leaving nothing but waste behind, that he had no great optimism. Besides, his mind was turning more and more away from the affairs of men to the one great central meaning of his life, his own work. He had a full sense now of the few years left him, and nothing must turn him aside from that work. He did not hear then the rising of any storm. When news filtered through the countryside of a murdered Catholic priest, he remarked calmly, "Well, he was a Catholic, and they don't like Catholics, I suppose."

When the foreign consuls began to send out warnings, urging women and children and old people to go to Shanghai, since no one could foresee exactly what turn the approaching revolutionary armies would take, it did not occur to him that he could possibly be included among them. What! He run with the women and children?

But then the white people were all sharply divided. Some of them felt no good could possibly come of the new movement, led as it was by the young Western trained Chinese and aided by the Bolshevists. There were others who believed in it and still more who did not know what to think or do. The news of the treatment the white people were receiving in the revolutionary territory was disconcerting, but one could get no proofs or confirmation and mad rumor is at its maddest in China, the land of many tongues and boundless prejudices among men of all colors.

Carie's daughter took sides with the revolutionists. Sun Yat-sen she had admired since her childhood. Carie had taught her that. "Something will come from him," Carie used to say in her tones of confident prophecy, although he was a fugitive most of her life. So when Andrew said he would not go away as the revolutionary armies approached, Carie's daughter made no demur.

Then there came that morning when the consular advice was very strong indeed, amounting as nearly to a command as the representative of a democratic nation may go, that all Americans, women and children and those who were aged must go away, because of reports of serious anti-foreign action on the part of the revolutionists. They were very near then, those armies. One could, if one listened, hear the sound of distant cannon. And the final contingent of those white people who had decided to leave were going that day. It was the last chance, and if it were refused, there would be no other. All who stayed must stay through to whatever the end would be, because the crisis of battle was near, and the great city gates would be locked, and none could go out or come in until it was known who were the victors.

Carie's daughter took thought that morning. She believed in the revolutionists, but there might be a rabble after the battle. She thought of her small children, of her sister who had taken refuge with her from a city in the far interior already held by the revolutionists—that narrow escape had not been very promising. And there was her sister's child, too. Well, they could manage with the children, but what of Andrew? He could not walk far or endure hardship any more now. She begged him to go to certain safety.

But Andrew when compelled against his will had a trick of falling ill. It was not conscious pretense—it was an actual disturbance caused by the distress of not having his own way. When she went upstairs to call him to get ready to go he lay there on that narrow iron bed of his, the sheet pulled up to his chin.

"I'm ill," he said very faintly. "I couldn't possibly go."

She looked at him, knowing him, and that there was no persuading him.

"Then we all stay together," she said, and went away and closed the door.

Through that whole day the sound of the guns grew louder and the echo more hard against the rocks of the mountain. By afternoon the city gates were already locked, and there was a strange tense stillness everywhere. Shops were closed, and the streets were empty. People sat behind closed doors, waiting for no one knew what. They had done the same thing many times before, and even the children had been through wars. But this time it was different. One heard such things—the laborers, servants, apprentices, the poor who lived in the mud huts—they were all full of a strange excitement. No one knew what to expect.

In the empty streets Andrew's rickshaw passed as usual, his puller trotting along in the old frock coat. It was March and the air was still keen. Andrew preached that night in one of his street chapels, but almost no one was there to hear him and those who were hurried away quickly into the darkness. He came home to find the whole house alight and a steady stream of Chinese neighbors pouring into the gates. The cellars were full of unknown and poor people taking refuge. It had always been safe in the foreigners' houses before. In no war since 1900 had the foreigners been attacked—the foreigners had gunboats and treaties to take care of them. It was all familiar enough to Andrew. He sat in the living-room with the family and their Chinese friends. Only the unknowing children were asleep.

"This floor seems to seethe," he said. "The cellars are so full." Then he said, "I'm glad I stayed. One must share the life of those one has chosen to be one's own people."

Midnight came on and still there was no news and nothing could be seen in the darkness, and there was only the constant roaring of cannon to be heard. He was very tired. "Since I can't settle any of the fighting, I think I'll go to bed," he said at last with his dry smile. And so he went upstairs to lie and listen to the cracking guns. Near dawn there was a sudden silence and before he could wonder what it was he fell asleep.

It seemed no different from other days, that revolutionary dawn. He woke and the March sun filled his room, and from downstairs came the clatter of breakfast dishes and the smell of bacon and coffee. There were no more guns. Everything was over. He did not need to miss a single day of work. He got up, bathed in the shower he had rigged up for himself out of a small tin tub and the nozzle of a flower sprinkler and dressed carefully and went downstairs, very cheerful and triumphant, to the usual seven o'clock breakfast. They were all waiting for him, children and grandchildren, and Carie's daughter was gay over the first daffodils of spring from her garden. She had run out before breakfast and cut them and they were on the table.

"Prophetic daffodils!" she said. "I'm glad they waited to open until today."

Everything was all right, they said. The revolutionists had won, the city gates were open, the city had surrendered and was quiet. The Chinese had all gone home to breakfast, and the house was normal again.

"How silly to have gone away!" they told each other over bacon and eggs.

"Wars are all about the same in my experience," said Andrew in great content.

It was a cheerful meal, and afterwards the men hurried off to eight o'clock classes, and Carie's daughter tucked Andrew's lap robe about him in his rickshaw and put a small red rosebud she had grown in a window pot into his buttonhole. Red was for the new day.

He could choose the road through the city or the back road through the hills. This morning he chose the hill road. The air was fresh and sharp and sweet, and the sunshine was warming.

But he had scarcely set himself to enjoy it when he heard his name shouted loudly, over and over. He looked about, but no one was near. Indeed, when he came to think of it, he had seen no one upon the road. Usually it was busy with farmers carrying their baskets of early fresh vegetables on their shoulders to the city markets, or the road was dusty with the feet of donkeys, carrying bags of rice crossed upon their backs. There had been no one.

Then he saw one of the servants from the house running after him, shouting to him. The rickshaw puller halted and the man came up panting. He was the color of cheese and his mouth was so dry he could scarcely speak.

"Old Teacher—Old Teacher—come back!" he panted. "They are killing the foreigners!"

"I don't believe it," said Andrew.

"It is true. One of them is dead already. They shot him in the street. Your elder daughter beseeches you to return."

"I won't," said Andrew. "I have work waiting for me. Go on!" he said to the puller, but the servant laid hands on the shafts.

"She said if you would not come I was to lift you and carry you back, though you struck me for it."

"As for me," said the puller, "I will not pull you on and have your blood on my body."

They had him helpless.

"Go back, then," said Andrew grimly.

It was not the first time he had had to think of being killed. The sunshine was grey to him. No one knew what this day would be—perhaps the end—and his work was not done.

When he reached the house they were gathered on the doorstep waiting for him. They had run out of the house just as they were, without coats and hats. In ten minutes the whole world had changed. The gayety of the breakfast table, the warm security of the house, were now as though they never had been.

"Here he is!" the servant shouted, and the puller lowered the shafts and he stepped out.

"What does all this mean?" he demanded.

"We must hide!" Carie's daughter cried to him.

Hide! All these little children! Besides, he hated the thought of it.

"We'd better go decently into the house and pray," he said.

"We can't delay," she replied. "The revolutionary armies are against us. They've killed the two Catholic fathers already, and Jack Williams!"

Before he could argue with her the servants came wailing and running toward them, and there were neighbors slipping in at the gate secretly.

"Hide—Hide!" they begged him. "The foreigners' houses are no safety today."

"Where can we hide?" Carie's daughter cried.

The Chinese looked at each other. Who indeed dared to take the burden of these white people? If they were found in a man's house he would be killed and all his children. There was no use to die foolishly.

All the time a strange horrible uproar had been gathering out of the streets. It was the sound of a mob. There was no time to be lost. But there was nowhere to go. The white people looked at each other. This land had been home to them, for Andrew since his youth, for his children and their children since they were born. But suddenly, in an hour, it was home no more. Their house could not shelter them, no gates, no walls could make them safe.

A small stumpy blue-clad figure came running in the back gate as fast as her bound feet would let her. It was only a woman, a common peasant woman whom Carie's daughter had given food in a famine in the north country, and who in another famine had come south to find her again. Carie's daughter had not rejoiced to see the woman, penniless, half-starved and pregnant. But she took her in because she had a silly soft heart, and she let the baby boy be born there and took care of him to keep him from the tetanus by which the woman had lost every other child she had, and took care of him again when the woman once let him get nearly burned to death. She had not been at all pleased to do it, and had scolded the stupid grateful mother for her stupidity, and when the woman's husband wandered down from the north to hunt his wife she had been thankful to find him a job as a farm laborer and so get them all off her hands. But the baby grew into a chubby brown little boy, and it was nice to see him alive.

This woman, then, came running in. Her husband was away all day, and her little room empty, she said, and Carie's daughter and all her family were to come and hide there. It was only half a tiny hut, really, and no one would think of looking among mud huts. She was tugging at them, she had Carie's daughter's hand, and she pulled Andrew's sleeve, and picked up the smallest yellow-haired child, and started out of the gate and across the fields, and so they followed her.

In the packed silence of the tiny hut they sat down, some on the board bed, some on a bench, and she shut the door silently.

"This is a safe place," she whispered through the cracks. "There are so many children in these huts that if a little foreign child cries it will not be known."

But none of the little foreign children cried that live-long day. There were two little girls and a little boy, none of them yet five years old, a lively, noisy trio on other days. Today, in the darkness, in the strange howling roar outside, they sat perfectly still upon their elders' knees, knowing somehow in what peril they were.

As for Andrew, he could not believe this was the end. All day he sat without a word, among his children and grandchildren. But no one spoke. Each of them was busy in himself. Andrew was thinking back over the years. "Not so much thinking," he wrote afterwards, "as letting the pictures of what had gone drift across my mind. Often I thought I was somewhere else." And one of Carie's daughters sat thinking of her unborn child and wondering if he would now live to be born. And the other sat looking at her two little girls and thought steadfastly how when the hour came she must be strong and before she died herself she must see them dead first, though she did it herself, and not leave them in the hands of the soldiers.

The strange hours passed. The servants stole across the fields with loaves of bread under their coats and a bottle of boiled water and a tin of milk for the children. Every now and again the door opened and the face of a Chinese friend would appear. Only there was always that moment of fear—was he a friend? Who could tell in this day? But they were friends, and they came in to knock their heads before us, and to beg us to take heart because they were doing all they could with the revolutionary leaders to intercede with them for our lives. And at noon the door opened again and a kind unknown motherly Chinese woman came in with bowls of hot rice gruel and told us to eat and not fear—that no one in all the little cluster of huts would tell that we were there. They had threatened even their children, she said. "I told my little devil I would beat him to death if he told," she said to comfort us. And the day mounted to noon.

The noise outside the hut increased. Andrew had heard that noise before—the noise not of angry people but of people in greed, of poor people who see what they have coveted now within reach. There was the sound of thudding upon wood, of a gate being crashed in, the sounds of feet running across ground, of wooden doors splintering, and then the howling of greed again.

"They've got in the house," said Andrew suddenly.

The hut door opened as he spoke and the two Chinese came in who had been interceding with the revolutionary leaders. They fell on the earthen floor before Andrew.

"Forgive us," they said, "we cannot save your lives. We have done all we can, but there is no longer hope."

And rising and bowing, they went away, their faces the color of clay.

For two hours Andrew and his children sat waiting, expecting every instant to see the door open and soldiers rush in. But it did not open. And outside the din went on, the shouting and the howling. The hut was lit with firelight now—they were burning the foreigners' houses. There could be only a few minutes left. Each in his own fashion took leave of life and earth and thought of how to die proudly before an enemy race, and Andrew bowed his head. The children were alseep in our arms, heart-breakingly precious because it was the last time. The next moment—in an hour at most—it would be finished for us all.

Then across the horror and the din there came a terrific thunder. The hut shook and the children woke. Again it came, again and again, such thunder as none of us had ever heard before. Our ears were stopped with the noise. We stared at each other, asking—it was not thunder from heaven—not this regular repeated roar.

"Cannon!" cried one of the men.

Andrew shook his head. "The Chinese have no such cannon," he shouted above the din.

"American-British cannon," the other shouted back.

Then we remembered what we had all forgotten—there were American, English and Japanese gunboats in the river seven miles away. They had opened fire on the city. We were in a fresh danger. We might be blown to pieces by our own guns. But instantly we were all relieved—it would at least be a clean death, quick and clean—no torture at the hands of Chinese soldiers.

Suddenly it was over. All noise ceased. The guns stopped, and there was silence, a strange, sudden complete silence. There was no more sound of shouting, no more howling, no more screeching of wrenched and breaking wood. Only the sound of crackling flames went on and the dark little hut was brighter than any day could light it.

Andrew stood up and looked through the tiny window and across the hills. He pressed his face against the hole, staring at something.

"They are burning the seminary buildings!" he whispered. And he sat down and covered his eyes with his hands. His work was gone again . . . .

There was nothing to do but wait now. Someone would come and tell us what to do. It was a long and dreary waiting, the hardest of the day. None of us could guess what the bombardment meant or what the silence. Was the city laid waste under those mighty guns and were we only left alive? No one came near.

Late that night the door opened. There stood two of our Chinese friends, with a guard of soldiers.

"We have come to take you to a safe place," they said gladly.

But the soldiers made us halt. They were in a strange uniform and surely there never was so villainous a guard. Their faces were jeering and flushed, and their features swollen as though they were drunken. They stood there, leaning on their guns, the light of the torches on their wicked, mocking faces. We shrank back. Commit the children and Andrew to these?

"But these are the same soldiers who have been attacking us all day," Carie's daughter protested.

But there was no other way.

"It is your only chance," our friends urged us. "All the white people are gathered in the big laboratory in the university. We will take you there."

So one by one, Andrew first, we filed out of the tiny hut, eight feet by ten, where we had lived for thirteen hours, three men, two women and the three little children. Those three great tall men! Carie's daughter never thought them so huge before that day.

Across the dark fields we went, past smoking and charred ruins of what only that morning had been cheerful American homes, to the black pile of the university buildings. Once a little weary child, stumbling, fell against a soldier and he turned with a snarl that made the heart stop.

But the child's mother cried out, "She did not mean to push you—she is only three years old!" and the soldier went on with a grunt.

So at last we reached the gate of the university. There stood another guard of revolutionary soldiers, the same dark, jeering, evil-looking men. They laughed as we came by and seized their guns and shook them to frighten us. But not even a child cried—they only looked, wondering, having been taught all their small lives to like the Chinese and call them friends. So the dreary little procession entered the building and filed upstairs in the darkness.

There in the big laboratory we found gathered over a hundred white people, men, women, and children, nearly all Americans. Seven had been killed since dawn, but all these others had hidden somehow and been hidden by Chinese friends, and had been rescued after much hideous experience at the hands of mobs and soldiers. We had been very fortunate, we found afterwards. Few of the other white people had not had to face their enemies in one way or another. But the dreadful day was over, and now the darkness covered them and they were trying to rest. Yet at every fresh entrance they cried out to know who was there and if they were safe. One by one all through the restless night, the white people came in, some wounded, some beaten, but no more dead. But no one knew what the dawn would be, for the city belonged to the revolution now.

All through the next day we waited, gathered together in the big room. It was not a sad day, though no one knew what its end might be. We organized ourselves, distributed what food there was, and attended to those who were ill and wounded or had newborn babies. And there were those Chinese working for us. They came and went, bringing food and clothes and bedding. They came weeping and begging forgiveness, and telling us that the dead were decently buried. They brought us toothbrushes and towels and coats, for the March wind was piercingly cold and the buildings were unheated, and the soldiers had robbed us of warm outer garments.

All of us were homeless and penniless, and we did not know whether or not we were yet to be massacred, and there were among us the widowed and those young mothers of newly born babies and women who had suffered such indignity at the hands of mad soldiery as cannot be told. But somehow the day was not sad. We were not friendless. There was not one of us who had not friends among the Chinese and these risked their lives to bring us comfort. For after we went, if ever we were to go, their names would be upon a proscribed list of those who had helped foreigners, and who were "running dogs of the imperialists."

In the afternoon the order came from the guard for us to move out, and go down to the bund seven miles away and get on the American and English battleships in the harbor. We were hurried out by the same wicked-looking soldiers into the street and in broken-down carriages, or on foot or however we could, the march began. At dusk we rounded the road to the river and there, alight from stem to stern, the battleships lay waiting. American marines, American sailor boys, were standing on the bund and they hurried forward and helped old men and women and children into the dories, and then there was the rush of the dark water about the boats, the heave and sweep of the swelling current, the black precipice of the ship's side and the swinging ladderway, and at last the firm deck beneath the feet. Hearty voices cried out, "You're on American territory now—cheer up!" "Supper's waitin'!"

But it was all a daze—the crowded cabins, the small saloon, the pots of hot food on the table, soup and baked beans and stew, ladled out by shouting, joking sailors. Food and sleep—and oh, the heaven of safety! Women who had not wept once, who had stood up to pillage and cruelty and death, could not keep from weeping, and brave little children who had stood straight and defiant beside their parents before the guns of the soldiers, cried endlessly about nothing.

As for Andrew, he disappeared from the table and Carie's daughter went out to find him and see how he did. He was standing by the ship's side, staring across the water to the dark city. There was not a light in it, but he knew where it lay, for dim against the sky he could see the crest of the mountain, and the city walls curled about the mountain's foot.

"What are you thinking?" she asked.

"I was just planning about going back," he said quietly. He did not turn or say anything more, and she left him there, gazing into the dark city. Going back! Of course he would be thinking of nothing else.

XXXIV

MR. DOOLEY'S AMERICA, A LIFE OF FINLEY PETER DUNNE [1]

By

ELMER ELLIS

Finley Peter Dunne (1867-1936) was an American journalist, born and educated in Chicago. He became internationally famous because of a series of humorous sketches in Irish dialect which he contributed to the daily papers. These stories were satirical and amusing reflections on social and political topics of the day as expressed principally by a character Dunne created called Martin Dooley, a pleasant but shrewd philosopher.

Many of Mr. Dooley's expressions will probably live permanently, although the source may be forgotten. Who does not recall his comment, "The Supreme Court follows the election returns" or perhaps the less well-known one, "A fanatic is a man that does what he thinks th' Lord wud do if He knew th' facts iv th' case."

From Mr. Ellis' biography of the famous originator of the colorful Mr. Dooley, there are given here three brief humorous observations.

THE SATIRE OF FINLEY PETER DUNNE

In the locker room at the National Golf Links after a round of golf, one of the foursome passed some uncomplimentary remark about the manner in which Dunne's girth was increasing with age. Dunne agreed: "My fat is piling up under my belt, while yours goes under your hat." Once he entered one of his clubs just in time to help to his feet an elderly doorman who had tripped on the entry rug and sprawled on the floor. "You'll have

[1] Reprinted from *Mr. Dooley's America, A Life of Finley Peter Dunne*, by Elmer Ellis, by permission of and special arrangement with Alfred A. Knopf, Inc., New York, 1941, pp. 275, 292, 309.

to be more careful, old man," Dunne warned, "or you'll be mistaken for one of our members."

SAYS MR. DOOLEY TO MR. HENNESSY

"We're a great people," said Mr. Hennessy, earnestly. "We are," said Mr. Dooley. "We are that. An' th' best iv it is, we know we are."

MR. DOOLEY'S REFLECTIONS

"Th' further ye get away fr'm anny peeryod th' better ye can write about it. Ye aren't subject to interruptions be people that were there." . . . "Many a man that cudden't direct ye to th' dhrug store on th' corner whin he was thirty will get a respectful hearin' whin age has further impaired his mind."

XXXV

ADMIRAL OF THE OCEAN SEA, A LIFE OF CHRISTOPHER COLUMBUS [1]

By

SAMUEL ELIOT MORISON

Samuel Eliot Morison, professor of history at Harvard, prepared for writing this monumental two-volume biography by following the routes of Columbus' voyages in sailing vessels, which compared in both size and rig to those used by Columbus. In this excellent study one finds the unusual combination of an author's rich marine experience, a delightful prose style, competent scholarship, and documentation based upon four and a half centuries of references.

The selection which Dr. Morison has made describes the most wonderful experience perhaps any seamen have ever had in world history—when the ocean for the first time gave up the secret that had puzzled Europeans since they began to ask what lay beyond the western horizon's rim.

NEVER AGAIN MAY MORTAL MEN RECAPTURE THE EXPERIENCE OF THOSE OCTOBER DAYS

Sun set under a clear horizon about 5.30, every man in the fleet watching for a silhouette of land against its red disk; but no land was there. All hands were summoned as usual, and after they had said their evening prayers and sung the *Salve Regina* "which all seamen are accustomed to say and sing in their own fashion," Columbus from the sterncastle made his men a little speech, reminding them of the grace Our Lord had shown them in conducting them so safely and prosperously with fair winds and a clear course, and in comforting them with signs of better things to come; and he urged the night watch to keep a particularly

[1] Samuel Eliot Morison, *Admiral of the Ocean Sea*, by permission of Little, Brown & Company and the Atlantic Monthly Press, 1942, Boston, I, 294-308.

sharp lookout on the forecastle, reminding them that although he had given orders to do no night sailing after reaching a point 700 leagues from the Canaries, the great desire of all to see land had decided him to carry on that night. Hence all must make amends for this temerity by keeping a particularly good watch, and looking sharp for land; and to him who first sighted it he would then and there give a silk doublet, in addition to the annuity of 10,000 maravedis that the Sovereigns had promised. The gromet then sang his little ditty for changing the watch and turned the *ampolleta*, boatswain Chachu bellowed out the Castilian equivalent to "Watch below lay belo-o-w!" and the men took their stations with eyes well peeled.

During the eleven and half hour since sunrise, with a brisk trade wind and the heaviest following sea of the entire voyage, the fleet had made 78 miles, an average of almost 7 knots. At sunset it breezed up to gale force, until the vessels were tearing along at 9 knots. At the same time Columbus ordered the course changed from WSW back to the original West. Why he did this, nobody has explained. I suspect that it was simply a desire to prove that he was right. He had begun the voyage by steering a course due west for Japan, and so he wished to pick up land on a due west course. I have known commanders, good seamen too, who are like that. Or the change may have been just a hunch. If so, it was a good one, for the WSW course would have missed Guanahaní, and put the fleet next day in a dangerous position with the long shelterless shore of Long Island under its lee. Common prudence would have made Columbus heave-to for the night, since shoals and rocks invisible by moonlight might lie ahead. *María's* pilot, Peralonso Niño, is said to have so advised him; but the Captain General felt that this was no time for common prudence. He had promised the men to turn back if land were not made within three days, and he intended to make all possible westing in this gale of wind. So the signal was made for *oeste*!

Anyone who has come onto the land under sail at night from an uncertain position knows how tense the atmosphere aboard ship can be. And this night of October 11-12 was one big with destiny for the human race, the most momentous ever experienced aboard any ship in any sea. Some of the boys doubtless slept, but nobody else. Juan de la Cosa and the Pinzons are pacing the high poops of their respective vessels, frequently calling down to the men at the tiller a testy order—keep her off damn your eyes must I go below and take the stick myself?—pausing at the break to peer under the main course and sweep the western horizon, then resting their eyes by looking up at the stars. Consultation as to whether or not to shorten sail; Martín Alonso perhaps confiding to pilot Cristóbal García that he doesn't like carrying sail this way in a gale of wind with possible shoals ahead, but if that crazy Genoese can carry sail we can carry sail; *Pinta* can stand it better than that Galician tub, and heave-to quicker if anything shows up, and I want one of you men of Palos to win that *albricias*, d'ye see? Lookouts on the forecastles and in the round-tops talking low to each other—Hear anything? Sounds like breakers to me—nothing but the bow wave you fool—I tell you we won't sight land till Saturday, I dreamt it, and my dreams—you and your dreams, here's a hundred maravedis says we raise it by daylight. . . . They tell each other how they would have conducted the fleet—The Old Man should never have set that spritsail, she'll run her bow under—if he'd asked my advice, and I was making my third voyage when he was playing in the streets of Genoa, I'd have told him. . . . Under such circumstances, with everyone's nerves taut as the weather braces, there was almost certain to be a false alarm of land.

An hour before moonrise, at 10 P. M., it came. Columbus, standing on the sterncastle, thought he saw a light, "so uncertain a thing that he did not wish to declare that it was land," but called Pedro Gutiérrez to have a look, and he thought he saw it too. Rodrigo Sánchez was then appealed to, "but he saw nothing because he was not in a position where he could see anything." One guesses that Rodrigo was fed up with false alarms, and merely stuck his head out of the companionway to remark discouragingly that he didn't see nothing; no, not a thing. The light, Columbus said, "was like a little wax candle rising and falling," and he saw it only once or twice after speaking to Gutiérrez.

At this juncture one of the seamen named Pedro Yzquierdo, a native of Lepe, thought he saw a light and sung out, *"Lumbre! tierra!"* Pedro de Salcedo, Columbus's page-boy, piped up with "It's already been seen by my master," and Columbus, who heard the cry, snubbed the man with, "I saw and spoke of that light, which is on land, some time ago."

What was this feeble light resembling a wax candle rising and falling, which Columbus admits that only a few besides himself ever saw? It cannot have been a fire or other light on San Salvador, or any other island; for, as the real landfall four hours later proves, the fleet at 10 P. M. was at least 35 miles off shore. The 400,000 candlepower light now on San Salvador, 170 feet above sea level, is not visible nearly so far. One writer has advanced the theory that the light was made by Indians torching for fish—why not lighting a cigar?—but Indians do not go fishing in 3000 fathoms of water 35 miles offshore at night in a gale of wind. The sentimental school of thought would have this light supernatural, sent by the Almighty to guide and encourage Columbus; but of all moments in the voyage, this is the one when he least needed encouragement, and he had laid his course straight for the nearest land. I agree heartily with Admiral Murdock, "the light was due to the imagination of Columbus, wrought up to a high pitch by the numerous signs of land encountered that day." Columbus admitted that only a few even thought they saw it. Anyone who has had much experience trying to make night landfalls with a sea running knows how easy it is to be deceived, especially when you are very anxious to pick up a light. Often two or three shipmates will agree that they see "it," then "it" disappears, and you realize that it was just another illusion. There is no need to criticize Columbus's seamanship because he sighted an imaginary light; but it is not easy to defend the fact that for this false landfall, which he must have known the next day to have been imaginary, he demanded and obtained the annuity of 10,000 maravedis promised by the Sovereigns to the man who first sighted land.[2] The best we can say in extenuation is to point out that glory rather than greed prompted this act of injustice to a seaman; Columbus could not bear to think that anyone but himself sighted land first. That form of male vanity is by no means absent from the seafaring tribe today.

At 2 A.M. October 12 the moon, past full, was riding about 70° high over Orion on the port quarter, just the position to illuminate anything ahead of the ships. Jupiter was rising in the east; Saturn had just set, and Deneb was nearing the western horizon, toward which all waking eyes were directed. There hung the Square of Pegasus, and a little higher and to the northward Cassiopeia's Chair. The Guards of Polaris, at 15° beyond "feet," told the pilots that it was two hours after midnight. On speed the three ships, *Pinta* in the lead, their sails silver in the moonlight. A brave trade wind is blowing and the caravels are rolling, plunging and throwing spray as they cut down the last invisible barrier between the Old World and the New. Only a few moments now, and an era that began in remotest antiquity will end.

Rodrigo de Triana, lookout on *Pinta's* forecastle, sees something like a white sand cliff gleaming in the moonlight on the western horizon, then another, and a dark line of land connecting them. "*Tierra! tierra!*" he shouts, and this time land it is.

[2] The sum was considerable, equivalent to ten months' pay of an able seaman. The Sovereigns raised it in a manner characteristic of the day, by a special tax on the butcher shops of Seville. Columbus assigned the annuity to Beatriz Enríquez before departing on his Fourth Voyage, and she continued to draw it after his death.

Martín Alonso Pinzón, after a quick verification, causes a lombard already loaded and primed to be fired as the agreed signal, and shortens sail in order to wait for the flagship. As soon as *Santa María* approached (remembered *Pinta's* steward many years later) Columbus called out, "Señor Martín Alonso, you have found land!" and Pinzón replied, "Sir, my reward is not lost," and Columbus called back, "I give you five thousand maravedis as a present!"

By Columbus's reckoning the land was distant about 6 miles. The fleet had made 65 miles in the eight and a half hours since sunset, an average better than 7½ knots; according to our reckoning they were very near latitude 24° N, longitude 74° 20′ W when Rodrigo sang out. . . .

This first land of the Western Hemisphere sighted by Columbus, or by any European since the voyages of the Northmen, was the eastern coast of one of the Bahamas now officially named "San Salvador or Watlings Island." Other candidates there have been for this honor; the Grand Turk, Cat Island, Rum Cay, Samana Cay and Mayaguana. But there is no longer any doubt that the island called Guanahaní, which Columbus renamed after Our Lord and Saviour, was the present San Salvador or Watlings. That alone of any island in the Bahamas, Turks or Caicos groups, fits Columbus's description. The position of San Salvador and of no other island fits the course laid down in his Journal, if we work it backward from Cuba.

San Salvador is a coral island about 13 miles long by 6 wide; the 24th parallel of latitude and the meridian of 74° 30′ West of Greenwich cross near its center. The entire island, except for a space of about 1¾ miles on the west or leeward side, is surrounded by dangerous reefs. By daylight Columbus's fleet must have drifted to a point near the Hinchinbrooke Rocks off the southeastern point. Making sail and filling away, they sought an opening through the reef barrier where they might safely anchor and send boats ashore. And the first gap that they could have discovered, one easy to pick out with a heavy sea running, was on the western shore about 5 miles north of Southwest Point. Here, rounding a prominent breaking ledge now called Gardiner Reef, the caravels braced their yards sharp and entered a shallow bay (Long or Fernandez), protected from winds between N by E around to S by W. Off a curving beach of gleaming coral sand, they found sheltered anchorage in 5 fathoms of water.

Somewhere on this beach of Long or Fernandez Bay took place the famous Landing of Columbus, often depicted by artists, but never with any respect for the actual topography. Las Casas's abstract of the Journal, and Ferdinand Columbus, who had the Journal before him when he wrote the biography of his father, are the unique sources for this incident. Fitting together the two, we have this description:—

Presently they saw naked people, and the Admiral went ashore in the armed ship's boat with the royal standard displayed. So did the captains of *Pinta* and *Niña*, Martín Alonso Pinzón and Vicent Yáñez his brother, in their boats, with the banners of the Expedition, on which were depicted a green cross with an F on one arm and a Y on the other, and over each his or her crown. And, all having rendered thanks to Our Lord kneeling on the ground, embracing it with tears of joy for the immeasurable mercy of having reached it, the Admiral arose and gave this island the name *San Salvador*. Thereupon he summoned to him the two captains, Rodrigo de Escobedo secretary of the armada and Rodrigo Sánchez of Segovia, and all others who came ashore, as witnesses; and in the presence of many natives of that land assembled together, took possession of that island in the name of the Catholic Sovereigns with appropriate words and ceremony. And all this is set forth at large in the testimonies there set down in writing.[3] Forthwith the Christians hailed him as Admiral and Viceroy and swore to obey him as one who represented Their Highnesses, with as much joy and pleasure as if the victory had been all theirs, all begging his pardon for the injuries that through fear and inconstancy they had done him. Many Indians having come together for that ceremony and rejoicing, the Admiral, seeing that they were a gentle and peaceful people and of great simplicity, gave them some little red caps and glass beads which they hung around their necks, and other things of slight worth, which they all valued at the highest price.

At this point Las Casas begins to quote the *palabras formales* (exact words) of the Admiral, as we may now fairly style Columbus. So we may gather, as well as words can convey, the impression made by this branch of the American Indians, on the vanguard of the race that would shortly reduce them to slavery, and exterminate them:—

In order that we might win good friendship, because I knew that they were a people who could better be freed and converted to our Holy Faith by love than by force, I gave to some of them red caps and to some glass beads, which they hung on their necks, and many other things of slight value, in which they took much pleasure; they remained so much our friends that it was a marvel; and later they came swimming to the ships' boats in which we were, and brought us parrots and cotton thread in skeins and darts and many other

[3] These declarations are unfortunately lost. Columbus perhaps had learned from the Portuguese the protocol that he always followed in taking possession; henceforth, for over a century to come, a notary, pen, paper and inkhorn were a prescribed part of an explorer's equipment.

things, and we swopped them for other things that we gave them, such as little glass beads and hawks' bells. Finally they swopped and gave everything they had, with good will; but it appeared to us that these people were very poor in everything. They go quite naked as their mothers bore them; and also the women, although I didn't see more than one really young girl. All that I saw were young men, none of them more than 30 years old, very well made, of very handsome bodies and very good faces; the hair coarse almost as the hair of a horse's tail and short; the hair they wear over their eyebrows, except for a hank behind that they wear long and never cut. Some of them paint themselves black (and they are of the color of the Canary Islanders, neither black nor white), and some paint themselves white, and others red, and others with what they have. Some paint their faces, others the whole body, others the eyes only, others only the nose. They bear no arms, nor know thereof; for I showed them swords and they grasped them by the blade and cut themselves through ignorance; they have no iron. Their darts are a kind of rod without iron, and some have at the end a fish's tooth and others, other things. They are generally fairly tall and good looking, well made. I saw some who had marks of wounds on their bodies, and made signs to them to ask what it was, and they showed me how people of other islands which are near came there and wished to capture them, and they defended themselves. And I believe and now believe that people do come here from the mainland to take them as slaves. They ought to be good servants and of good skill, for I see that they repeat very quickly all that is said to them; and I believe that they would easily be made Christians, because it seemed to me that they belonged to no religion. I, please Our Lord, will carry off six of them at my departure to Your Highnesses, so that they may learn to speak. I saw no beast of any kind except parrots in this island.

Saturday October 13: At daybreak there came to the beach many of these men, all young men as I have said, and all of good stature, very handsome people. Their hair is not kinky but loose and coarse like horsehair; and the whole forehead and head is very broad, more so than any other race that I have seen, and the eyes very handsome and not small, and themselves not at all black, but of the color of the Canary Islanders; nor should anything else be expected, because this is on the same latitude with the island of Ferro in the Canaries. Their legs are very straight, all in a line; and no belly, but very well built. They came to the ship in dugouts which are fashioned like a long boat from the bole of a tree, and all in one piece, and wonderfully made (considering the country), and so big that in some came 40 or 45 men, and others smaller, down to the size that held but a single man. They row with a thing like a baker's peel and go wonderfully [fast], and if they capsize all begin to swim and right it and bail it out with calabashes that they carry. They brought skeins of spun cotton, and parrots and darts and other trifles that would be tedious to describe, and gave all for whatever was given to them.

In his Letter to the Sovereigns, which was promptly printed at Barcelona and widely distributed throughout Europe in a Latin translation, Columbus lays stress on the gentleness and generosity of the natives:—

They are so ingenuous and free with all they have, that no one would believe it who has not seen it; of anything that they possess, if it be asked of them, they never say no; on the contrary, they invite you to share it and show as much love as if their hearts went with it, and they are content with whatever trifle be given them, whether it be a thing of value or of petty worth. I forbade that they be given things so worthless as bits of broken crockery and of green glass and lace-points, although when they could get them, they thought they had the best jewel in the world.

Unfortunately this guilelessness and generosity of the simple savage aroused the worst traits of cupidity and brutality in the average European. Even the Admiral's humanity seems to have been merely political, as a means to eventual enslavement and exploitation. But to the intellectuals of Europe it seemed that Columbus had stepped back several millennia, and encountered people living in the Golden Age, that bright morning of humanity which existed only in the imagination of poets. Columbus's discovery enabled Europeans to see their own ancestors, as it were, in a "state of nature," before Pandora's box was opened. . . .

These Indians of the Bahamas, and indeed all whom Columbus encountered on his First Voyage, belonged to the so-called Taino culture of the Arawak language group. Their ancestors had emigrated to the Antilles from the mainland of South America, and within a century of Columbus's voyage had branched out from Haiti, overrunning Cuba, Jamaica, and the Bahamas, pushing back or enslaving an earlier and more primitive tribe known as the Siboney. The Tainos were fairly advanced in civilization, growing corn, yams and other roots, making cassava bread from yucca, spinning and weaving cotton, making a fine brown pottery adorned with grotesque heads, and various ornaments and utensils of shell, living in huts made of a wooden frame and palm thatch. The broad, low forehead that Columbus remarked was due to a process of artificially flattening the skulls of infants, by pressing them between boards.

Columbus's frame of reference, it is interesting to note, was partly African and partly classical. He expected to find kinky-haired blacks such as he had encountered on the coast of Guinea, because Aristotle taught that people and products on the same latitude were similar; but he reflected that being on the same latitude as Ferro—a mistake of 3° 41′—it was not surprising to find them of the same brown color as the Guanches, the primitive inhabitants of the Canaries. The word that he used for their canoes *almadias*, was what the Portuguese used for the dugouts of West Africa; and the trading goods that he brought, Venetian glass beads, brass rings, red caps, and the small round bronze bells used in falconry, were exactly what the Portuguese had found to be in most demand among the Negroes.

Although the Tainos had driven back the primitive hunter folk, their only weapon, a short spear or dart with a fish-tooth or fire-hardened wooden point, was insufficient to cope with the Caribs, who occasionally raided them from the Caribbee Islands. Much less were they prepared to resist domination by the Spaniards. And it is clear from the concluding sentences of Columbus's Journal for October 12 that on the very day of discovery the dark thought crossed his mind that these people could very easily be enslaved. On October 14 he noted, "These people are very unskilled in arms, . . . with fifty men they could all be subjected and made to do all that one wished." It is sad but significant that the only Indians of the Caribbean who have survived are those who proved both willing and able to defend themselves. The Tainos, whom Columbus found so gentle and handsome and hospitable, are long since extinct.

Guanahaní, the native name of this island, means the *iguana*, a reptile now extinct there. Columbus described it as "very big and very level and the trees very green, and many bodies of water, and a very big lake in the middle, but no mountain, and the whole of it so green that it is a pleasure to gaze upon." The island is honeycombed with salt lagoons, the largest of which is only a few hundred yards from the beach where Columbus landed; and the highest hill on the island is only 140 feet above sea level. Later, after exploring the northern part, Columbus noted groves of trees, the most beautiful he had ever seen, "and as green and leafy as those of Castile in the months of April and May." Visitors to San Salvador and the other Bahamian Islands find Columbus's descriptions of nature extravagant, and are inclined to accuse him of laying it on thick to impress the Sovereigns.

Any land looks good to seamen after a long and perilous voyage, and every woman fair; but Columbus's description of the Bahamas was not extravagant for 1492. At that time they were highly fertile and covered with a dense growth of tropical hardwood, which the Indians had cleared but slightly to plant gardens. In the late eighteenth century, the English colonists (many of them loyalist refugees from the United States) caused a large part of the forest to be cut down in order to grow sea-island cotton. This exhausted the soil, and hurricanes stripped the island at not infrequent intervals. When cotton culture ceased to pay, the fields were abandoned, and today such parts of the islands as the Negroes do not use for their potato patches and pasturage are covered with a scrubby second growth and ruins of old plantation houses. Large trees for making dugout canoes of the size that Columbus described no longer exist. Near an inland lagoon of San Salvador we were shown a surviving grove of primeval forest which for lushness and beauty merits Columbus's praise, and this grove harbors a variety of tropical woodpecker that must once have had a wider forest range. Skeletal remains of other birds which could only have lived among dense foliage have been discovered on the island by naturalists.

All day Saturday, October 13, the caravels lay at anchor in Long Bay with a swarm of canoes passing back and forth, while the Spaniards in turn took shore leave, wandered into the natives' huts, did a little private trading for the curios that all seamen love, and doubtless ascertained that the girls of Guanahaní were much like others they had known. Columbus, who ever had an eye for "improvements," reported that he found "a quarry of stones naturally shaped, very fair for church edifices or other public uses." Three centuries elapsed before anyone thought to build a church at San Salvador, and then it was found easier to fashion the soft coral rock into rectangular blocks; the outcrop that Columbus saw at Hall's Landing just north of his landing place, partly under water and curiously split into squares like flagstones, is still unquarried.

The Admiral was busy gathering such information as he could from signs and gestures; his Arabic interpreter was of no use in this neck of the Indies. On Saturday night he decided that no time must be lost, he must press on to Japan. But first San Salvador must be explored. On Sunday morning the three ships' boats took the Admiral north along the leeward coast "to see the other side, which was the eastern side, what was there, and also to see the villages; and soon I saw two or three, and the people all came to the beach, shouting and giving thanks to God. Some brought us water; others, things to eat. Others, when they saw that I did not care to go ashore, plunged into the sea swimming and came aboard, and we understood that they asked us if we had come from Heaven. And one old man got into the boat, and others shouted in loud voices to all, men and women, 'Come and see the men who come from Heaven, bring them food and drink.' Many came and many women, each with something, giving thanks to God, throwing themselves flat and raising their hands to Heaven, and then shouting to us to come ashore; but I was afraid to, from seeing a great reef of rocks which surrounded the whole of this island, but inside it was deep and a harbor to hold all the ships in Christendom, and the entrance of it very narrow."

This was the place now known as Grahams Harbor, formed by the reefs that surround the island coming together in an inverted V. At three or four places the reefs rise high enough to form cays, and beside one of these on the western side, Green Cay, is a good boat channel with 7 feet of water. Here, rather than the alternate High Reef channel, which is difficult for a stranger to find, was probably where the boats entered. "Inside there are some shoal spots," Columbus correctly observed, "but the sea moves no more than within a well." The smooth water inside these coral-reef harbors is always a pleasant surprise to mariners.

Glenn Stewart's yacht lay quietly and safely in Grahams Harbor during a heavy norther in January 1930.

Columbus's boats rowed across the harbor, about two miles to the eastward, where they found a rocky peninsula that thrusts out from the northern side of San Salvador, half of it almost an island, and "which in two days could be made an island," suitable for a fortress. Since Columbus's visit the sea has here broken a narrow channel that one can wade across at low water. Someone, probably the English, took up Columbus's suggestion that the place was a natural fortress, for Dr. Cronau found an iron cannon there in 1891. After inspecting the harbor the boats returned to the vessels at their anchorage in Long Bay, a row of some twenty miles going and coming; and in the early afternoon the fleet made sail for Cipangu.

So ended forty-eight hours of the most wonderful experience that perhaps any seaman have ever had. Other discoveries there have been more spectacular than that of this small, flat sandy island that rides out ahead of the American continent, breasting the trade winds. But it was there that the Ocean for the first time "loosed the chains of things" as Seneca had prophesied, gave up the secret that had baffled Europeans since they began to inquire what lay beyond the western horizon's rim. Stranger people than the gentle Tainos, more exotic plants than the green verdure of Guanahaní have been discovered, even by the Portuguese before Columbus; but the discovery of Africa was but an unfolding of a continent already glimpsed, whilst San Salvador, rising from the sea at the end of a thirty-three-day westward sail, was a clean break with past experience. Every tree, every plant that the Spaniards saw was strange to them, and the natives were not only strange but completely unexpected, speaking an unknown tongue and resembling no race of which even the most educated of the explorers had read in the tales of travelers from Herodotus to Marco Polo. Never again may mortal men hope to recapture the amazement, the wonder, the delight of those October days in 1492 when the New World gracefully yielded her virginity to the conquering Castilians.

XXXVI

ALEXANDER THE GREAT [1]

By

LEWIS V. CUMMINGS

In his life of Alexander the Great, Mr. Cummings presents a well-documented, thorough and learned study of the first world conqueror. Biography, history, geography, and the science of military strategy are combined in this work to give a remarkable picture of a conquering war machine and its leader.

Alexander the Great, son of Philip and King of Macedon, lived only from 356 B. C. to 323 B. C., but in those few years he established himself as one of the most unusual characters of all history. At the age of thirteen he was a pupil of Aristotle, and at twenty he came to the throne of Macedon. One after another he extended his conquests until he was the ruler of a vast empire stretching from the Ionian Sea to the Indus River with plans for the consolidation of what was essentially the entire civilized world. One language and a common civilization were his goals. While in Arabia on an expedition in 323 B. C., he contracted a fever and died. His body was taken to Alexandria, Egypt, which city he had founded during his conquests. The great empire he had built was divided among several rulers.

The short but dramatic passage describing the last moments before his death reveals a profound understanding of what confronted the empire he had built.

ALEXANDER THE GREAT BEQUEATHES AN EMPIRE

Perdiccas, standing close to the sick-bed, doubtless recognizing that death was very near, bent over and spoke to Alexander, and the latter weakly handed him the imperial seal ring. Perdiccas bent lower, and asked to whom he wished to leave the throne. No doubt in that one last lucid

[1] Lewis V. Cummings, *Alexander the Great,* by permission of the publishers, Houghton Mifflin Company, Boston, 1940, pp. 452-3.

moment Alexander achieved a higher degree of understanding than he had ever known before, an understanding which is given to many only when it is too late. Around his dying bed were grouped his officers, hard, unrelenting, avaricious, and power-mad men whom he himself had trained in their way, waiting only for his death to begin rending the empire. Perhaps, too, he could already see the glittering armies going forth to tear it apart; to hear the shouts and screams of men locked in deadly battle; and the snarl and howl of the jackal and hyena over the battlefield afterward. And he knew to whom the sovereignty would fall at last. His answering whisper, "Kratisto," "To the strongest," was hardly audible. At sunset on June 13, 323 B.C., the conqueror breathed his last.

XXXVII

MOZART[1]

By

MARCIA DAVENPORT

The fire of genius animated Wolfgang Mozart (1756-1791), composer, almost from the day of his birth. When only three years old his father began to teach him minuets on the clavier. Other child prodigies may have equaled this accomplishment, but the peculiar genius of Wolfgang was his native urge to compose, which was evident at only four years of age. At six he composed his first published work. His title of "musician of musicians," given by Gounod in 1882, was won not simply because of his early brilliance, but because his marvelous powers steadily grew, two of his greatest compositions being produced in the last year of his life.

At the age of fourteen he went to the Sistine Chapel in Rome to hear Allegri's famous *Miserere*. Later he wrote the entire composition from memory, to the complete amazement of everyone who heard of it. The composition was guarded as a secret and even the singers were forbidden to transcribe it on pain of excommunication.

One of his masterpieces was *Figaro* and two of his greatest compositions, *The Magic Flute* and the *Requiem*, were written, as indicated, in the last year of his life. Mozart's extant works have been catalogued in 626 items, starting with minuets composed at the age of four and ending with the *Requiem*. At his death he was buried in a pauper's mass-grave, these graves being dug up every ten years. No one left a cross or a marker and thus his grave is now unknown. "But," in the words of Marcia Davenport, "the music is alive."

The author has written the life of this genius with a sprightly charm and a sympathetic appreciation that Mozart himself would have loved. Marcia Davenport says of the selection she has made for us from her splendid book, "it is full of episode and colorful characterizations and anecdotes. It concerns the period in Prague when Mozart was writing *Don Giovanni* with Lorenzo da Ponte. Its mood is very gay." In 1787 Mozart and his wife, Constanze,

[1] Marcia Davenport, *Mozart*, New York: Charles Scribner's Sons, 1937, pp. 282-304.

visited Prague as Count Thun's guest. It was decided then that he should compose this opera, which he did for the small amount of only 100 ducats (about $228). Thus *Don Giovanni* was given to the world.

THE INSPIRATION OF GENIUS

The best of ham, beer, and music have always delighted visitors to Prague; Wolfgang was never an exception. How he had loved it last January when he was there as Count Thun's guest! Now, in September, he and Constanze started off in the highest spirits. The coach clattered along between golden harvest fields and steep reddening hills, stopping to change horses in little villages where women with gay skirts tucked up over their ample hips pounded linen at the town pump. . . .

Soon they saw once more in the distance the soft haze that has ever embraced Prague; then they recognized the needle-spires of St. Vitus; then the yellow-grey masses of old houses clustered on the Moldau, and the steepled towers of the Karlsbrücke. Presently they rumbled throught scattered outskirts, and into the heart of the old town, pulled up with a great clatter, and jumped out to greet the excited Bondini, who rushed about chattering in Italian to Wolfgang, and in German to the porters struggling with the luggage. According to his contract as manager, he had found them good rooms, he said, in the Three Golden Lions on the Kohlmarkt; a nice, comfortable inn, right in the centre of town, near the opera house, and close to all the good *Bierstuben* and *Weinkellern*—with a wink at Wolfgang.

"Come along now, come up and see the pleasant apartments I have for you, get settled quickly, we have much to do, everyone is wild to see *Kapellmeister* Mozart again, everybody wants to drink your health—*Evviva il grande Maestro*!"

They swarmed up the dark stairs after Bondini jabbering and waving his arms. The rooms were pleasing, a good-sized drawing-room and a smaller bedroom with windows on the curve of the street. Until recently these same rooms were, appropriately enough, the offices of the Prague Philharmonic Orchestra. Everyone bustled around, Wolfgang grinning and rubbing his hands, Constanze exclaiming, Bondini throwing coppers to the gasping porters. Finally the boxes were unstrapped and opened, some of the travel-dust hurriedly washed off, powder dabbed on Wolfgang's head—"Come on," Bondini cried, "hurry, we have much to do. You, *Signora*," with a low bow, "will surely be glad of a short rest and an opportunity to unpack the many baggages—" and throwing an arm across Wolfgang's thin shoulders, he dragged him, shouting, out of the room and down the stairs, and onto the street and into the arms of Prague, waiting in the coffeehouses to cheer the little wizard from Vienna and drink his health to three times three.

Meanwhile, northward in the dark mountains near Teplitz, there sat, in the library of the ancient Bohemian castle of Dux, seat of the Counts Waldstein of Wallenstein, a tall old man with flabby yellow skin—once the warm olive of the Venetian—a few stumps of bad teeth, and two black eyes like half-live coals. The librarian had a big writing-table in the window-embrasure of the immense room. All around him, reaching to the vaulted, whitewashed ceiling, were ranks of bookshelves, painted white, and filled with the coffee-cream vellum and golden leather of beautifully bound tomes. These the old man was obliged to arrange and catalogue. But those mountains of mussed papers on his table, the reams strewn about the floor, are not the orderly notations of a cataloguist; they are the memoirs of Giacomo Casanova de Seingalt, now in his sixty-third year.

He had been Count Waldstein's librarian for three years, a position he held because he was penniless and pathetic, and because Waldstein had a kind heart and a sense of humor. He was willing to subject his household to the rages of the impotent old diavolo for the privilege of having his still brilliant conversation at table and in the library. Casanova's memories were lurid, if his actions could no longer be, and his tastes unchastened. . . .

Small wonder that as soon as he had his manuscript of *Isocameron* (*I Piombi*)—the famous Escape from the Leads—ready, in October, he should vent his excitement . . . in a profane tantrum, command a place in the post-chaise, and, spluttering and wheezing, showering Venetian curses, hoist himself into it and hasten the grouchy coachman on to Prague. In Prague was the printer who was to bring out *I Piombi*; in Prague there were loose and witty women (though he could only gaze), and music, and fast society, and gaming tables (for which he had no money); and in Prague, when he reached there, was his old crony, Lorenzo Da Ponte—just arrived from Vienna with an unfinished libretto. He had to come to wind it up, and "superintend rehearsals" with Mozart. . . .

Lorenzo had arrived a few days after Wolfgang and had found rooms, not without suggestions from him and Bondini, in the Platteis, a big lodging-house on the Ferdinandstrasse. Its rear rooms opened on the little curving street which runs from the Kohlmarkt to the Martinskirche, and on which the Three Golden Lions faces. Thus Lorenzo, who had two fine French windows, could go out onto his balcony, cup his hands, and shout to Wolfgang, whose windows were directly opposite; they could almost clasp hands across the street. They used this convenience joyously. Passersby beneath saw the long, dark face and black hair leaning over the railing to shout bawdy jokes, or indulge in raucous but good-natured disagreement about the *Don* with the thin fair face and sandy hair hanging out of the Golden Lions casement.

Then this childish amusement would succumb to man-sized thirst, and Lorenzo roar that they should stop acting like nincompoops: "Come downstairs *subito*, Wolfgang, we will go and have a glass of punch, or two or three, and ho! for the great Da Ponte and great Mozart, and ho! for the brave Prague players, and *bravo! Il Don Giovanni*, that would make them both famous, *per* Dio, you see if it wouldn't!"

So they would meet at their street doors, and cock their tricornes on the sides of their pigtailed heads, and throw up their chins, and slap each other on the shoulders, and link arms, and swagger off to the coffeehouse, where the whole room would stand and cheer when Mozart hove into the doorway, and the blind harpist on the step instantly strike up *Non più andrai*, everybody singing in chorus, and coppers clinking at the old beggar's feet.

Then—was it possible? Could the old man sitting stiffly alone at a corner table be whom he looked? Could that thin face, that sloping forehead, and those blazing eyes belong to anyone else? Never, impossible! Of course, it cannot be—but it is—è Giacomo! è Casanova! Oho, my old friend Da Ponte—*benvenuto, saluti*—ah, a happy day for all, a happy day indeed. Embraces, salutes, exclamations.

"Here is Mozart, Casanova. Mozart, the composer who wrote *Figaro* with me, you know, the great Mozart. *Cavaliere* Casanova de Seingald—*Kapellmeister* Mozart. Boy, a bottle of your best Orvieto!" "And cheese, Lorenzo!" "*Si, si, si, formaggio*, here boy, bring cheese, and bread, and ham. Ha, ha, ha, ha"—slapping their thighs, offering snuff, black eyes snapping and broad throats warming with wine.

"But what are you doing here?" "And what are *you* doing here?" both questions at once, and Casanova's interest rose when Lorenzo said:

"An opera. A new opera, Giacomo, better even than *Figaro*. We are writing it for Prague, for Bondini at the opera here. The première is soon. Wolfgang here has done fine work, and I—I am not so clumsy. The plot? *Basta*, we have a fine plot—*il Don Giovanni*, the Spanish legend, a mighty stallion that, a fellow worthy of yourself. In fact, Giacomo, now that I think of it"—Lorenzo's eyes dilated and he brought his palms together with a triumphant smack—"but Casanova, he *is* yourself! Wolfgang!," swinging about in his chair, "Wolfgang, *pizolo mio*, here is Don Giovanni!

Ah, you will help us, Giacomo! And we have no problems, no troubles, all is merry as the marriage bell!". . .

Prague saw the three roisterers parading the tiny cobbled streets—huge, toothless Lorenzo, with his booming laugh, senile Casanova with sparks of old fire in his eyes; between them, Wolfgang, trotting along in a vacuum of bliss and ideas, a quiet little man, looking up at each in turn to catch the last outrageous remark and cap it with some *Salzburger dreckiger Witz* that made them pound his slight back and bellow with joy. They drank rivers of wine and punch and beer, widening the circle to include Bondini, Strobach, the orchestra conductor, Franz Duschek, Guardassoni, sometimes young Count Thun, sometimes anybody, sweeping the town in a whirl of enthusiasm for themselves and everything they did, and always to the strains of *Figaro*, which pursued them everywhere. The Bohemians adored Mozart, and from the depths of his heart he wrote his greatest opera for them, fired by the unique experience of being wholly appreciated for the only time in his creative life. . . .

The triple carousal did not last long; Lorenzo had been only a week in Prague, when he received a furious letter from Salieri ordering him back to Vienna to finish the libretto for *Tarar*. Disgustedly he admitted he would have to go; he would miss the première of *Don Giovanni*, and what was much worse, he had the book all ready except for one scene, the confused result of their reluctant cutting when they saw how their original plans would exceed any practicable length. This was Leporello's aria in the second act, after the sextet and recitative, where the rascal has to get himself and his master out of a nasty hole, soothe Masetto, who has been beaten by the disguised Don, attend the perpetually outraged feelings of Donna Elvira, and get off the scene as quickly as possible. Lorenzo had brought things to a pass where radical action was necessary; now he was faced with the possibility of leaving poor little Wolfgang in the lurch. This he could not do. Calling on Mary and the saints, he sat in a wineshop with Casanova and gnashed his teeth. What in the world should he do? He couldn't leave it unfinished, he had no time to write any more poetry. He was stuck, he was worried. Of course, a light broke. Hadn't Casanova been free with good suggestions? Hadn't he added some rich touches to the wonderful seduction scene at Don Giovanni's ball?

"Here," Lorenzo shouted suddenly, seizing some paper, "here, what am I thinking of, half-wit that I am! You do it, for God's sake"—sweeping aside protests—"you know what to do, you know the fix Leporello is in. Ah, Giacomo, for the love of Jesus, get him out of it—write this scene for me!"

Casanova was vain of his literary ability, and certainly no man could call himself a great lover who was not something of a poet. All we know is that, not many years ago, in some of Casanova's effects discovered at Schloss Hirschberg in Bohemia, were found two sheets of paper, not titled, but without doubt the ones on which he sketched his plans for extricating Leporello. Later, when Lorenzo had time, he worked those ideas into his book. Alternative version of this theory is that Da Ponte never asked Casanova, of whom he was said to be envious, to help him. But after Lorenzo had returned to Vienna, Casanova went to Bondini and Mozart, criticized Da Ponte's libretto, and tried to have himself commissioned to rewrite it. Failing in that, he did revise the one scene that was causing trouble.

However, regardless of who was responsible for it, Wolfgang was inspired by the crafty succession of lies to put the whole thing into a racy burlesque in G major, which, when Leporello—the greatest of nature's rogues—dolefully accuses the Don, "*l'innocenza mi rubo, l'innocenza mi rubo*" (depraved my artless mind!) suddenly drops to a ridiculous, hollow A minor. And, as if to complete the confusion, there are some modern performances from which the whole aria, *Ah, pietà*! *Signori miei*! is omitted altogether, making no sense out of Leporello's antics. But plenty of chuckles went the rounds of Prague about it, while Lorenzo, back in Vienna, finished a forgotten piece for a forgotten composer, and missed the opening of *Don Giovanni*, the most unprecedented triumph in the annals of the Prague opera. . . .

Franz and Josefa Duschek were unusual in many ways. They gave friendship freely. They were both fine artists—he a pianist, she a soprano—who had the extraordinary good luck to own a charming villa, the Bertramka, at Koschirsch, a suburb just over the Moldau from the city. When every town in Europe had its quota of musicians, not one of whom lived more securely than in some meagre lodging, a couple who had the means to own a delightful country place and keep open house in it were the good angels of the whole profession. . . .

The yellow house is on the side of a high hill overlooking the sharp spires and massive walls of Prague; a typical eighteenth-century villa set in the midst of a green garden and dark old trees, and so built on the side of the slope that a long, smooth grass terrace in the rear is level with the raised drawing-room. The terrace is laid out between the vineyard hills, and surrounded on three sides by thick groves of maple, chestnut, and locust trees. The fourth side is open over the valley, with a stucco balustrade forming an outdoor room where the guests sat waiting their turn at the bowling-games on the grass, or looking down at the comfortable activities of the little farmyard just below.

All day long the house and grounds rang with the exuberant noises of musicians making holiday; somebody playing harpsichord duets in one room; four slightly drunk and very mellow fiddlers practicing quartets in another; Josefa prancing about her household duties with her cap on one ear, singing a new aria at the top of her voice. Franz sat on the terrace with Strobach and Guardassoni, who had run over from the opera house for the afternoon. Each had a long cool pipe and a fine stein of Pilzner. Constanze strolled along the garden paths with Ponziani, the first Leporello, laughing at his sallies; and in a corner by the balustrade, at a little table on the paving, with a glass of punch at his elbow, and the wind ruffling his hair, Wolfgang, scribbling away as hard as he could, tossing off sheet after sheet of even, beautiful manuscript.

Whenever one of the men summed up a lady in a savory phrase, Wolfgang roared with the rest and threw in a word to increase the laughter. Then he grinned and drove his scratchy quill more furiously. When he came to the end of a line, he flapped over the sheet—no more paper.

"Stänerl," he called, turning around in his chair, "go in and bring me more paper."

"You haven't any more like that, it hasn't come from town."

"Well, then, *Potz sapperment*, bring me anything you can find!"

The paper she brought was another size, the staffs ruled by different measure. What of it, Wolfgang shrugged, plunging his quill in the ink again.

They had come out to stay at the Bertramka about the time Da Ponte had returned to Vienna. Here with the Duscheks were all their friends, gay parties, and no expenses, with two delightful rooms at their disposal at the far end of the house. Each room had a big porcelain stove, of which they were glad when the first frost nipped the hilltop, but Wolfgang spent almost all his time on the terrace. He loved company and particularly the Prague company. Bowls were played all day long and Wolfgang joined every game, leaving his manuscript with a stone on it to keep the pages from blowing away while he took his turn, then dashing back to his little table to write another line or two. Letter-perfect, complete, he set down the marvellous score of *Don Giovanni*. He had hardly a note on paper when they moved to the Bertramka, yet every day, all day, once he had started, he wrote in never-to-be-revised perfection melodies and harmonies that bewildered their first hearers with their loveliness, humor or grandeur. As he finished each part, he sent it off to the singer who was to learn it, and rushed along to the next.

Of course, his whole score stood, "though it be long, complete and finished in my mind," and the time having come to write it down: "I take out of the bag of my memory, if I may use that phrase, what has previously been collected into it in the way I have mentioned. For this reason the committing to paper is done quickly enough, for everything is, as I said before, already finished, and it rarely differs on paper from what it was in my imagination."...

Don Giovanni was written in the midst of the things Wolfgang loved best in the world; company, chatter, punch, games, dancing—the weeks at the Bertramka were a festival of happiness.

Wolfgang had small inclination to stop merrymaking in the interests of serious rehearsal, though the Bertramka was crowded daily with singers, all being coached by the great Mozart himself—who would leave them with their mouths open when his turn came in the bowling-game. However, he was moved to write Jacquin that "there is no such able personnel here as at the theatre in Vienna, so that the opera cannot be learned in a short time"—and the next week, "—a further delay has been occasioned by the illness of one of the singers. As the company is so small, the impressario is obliged to take all possible care of his people, for fear lest some unforeseen indisposition should put him in the most awkward of all awkward situations—that of not being able to stage anything at all!" The company was not only smaller than at Vienna, but not so fine—Teresina Bondini, the manager's wife, either could not or would not grasp the full significance of Zerlina's distress, and more than once Wolfgang gnashed his teeth and swore under his breath, *um Gottes Willen,* if I only had Kelly and Benucci and Storace to sing this opera instead of these bumpkins . . . ! "And there are constant delays here because the singers (being lazy) will not rehearse for opera, and the *entrepreneur* (being anxious and fearful) will not force them to do so. . . ."

However, on the 22d of October, the cast was summoned to the theatre for the first stage rehearsal. Only one week was allotted for this work, and Wolfgang labored hard and honorably to whip them into shape. Signora Bondini was his despair—she would not scream behind the locked door as Lorenzo had decreed, and short of hiring some ruffian to double in reality for the Don's fictitious rape, Wolfgang was at his wits' end for a way to teach her. Finally, getting the orchestra started on the scene, he sneaked back to the wings and at the proper moment crept up and pinched her so hard in a vulnerable spot that she screamed like a stuck pig. "*Ah, brava, Signora!*" he cried, "at last you've learned it. Now continue, gentlemen."

He found the orchestra far superior to the singers, so superior, indeed, as to be able to appreciate the real meaning of his ideas. They fell in, too, with his peculiar habits of composing, one of which was not to include the brass and drum parts in the original score. One day he finally wrote down the missing parts from memory and brought them in with him, handing them to the players as he said, "Gentlemen, pray be particular at this place"—marking it—"as I believe you will find four bars too many or too few." He was quite right. Another feat of that uncanny memory—to carry the trombone parts, so integrally important in the serious themes, in his head as parts of the whole, and draw them out without the slightest confusion.

But even the serious business of rehearsing could not stop the progress of his holiday, and on the evening of October 28th the Duscheks had a large and very gay party. Wolfgang was, of course, the life of it, dancing to the music of *Figaro*, rushing to the clavier to extemporize a *Deutscher Tanz*, circling the rooms with upraised glass to clink with every well-wisher in the house; and there were many, for the première of *Don Giovanni* was scheduled for to-morrow, the 29th. As it grew late, Duschek, Guardassoni, and Bondini became more and more uneasy, stealing nervous glances at each other, and following Wolfgang's prancing feet with worriedly raised eyebrows. Finally Duschek cornered him and said:

"You know, Wolfgang, this is all very well, but the première is to-morrow and you haven't a note of your overture on paper." Wolfgang shrugged and waved his hands.

"I'll have it done," he said.

"Yes" Bondini put in, "*you* have it done already—in your head—but how is the orchestra going to play it from your head? I know you, Mozart."

Guardassoni looked his grimmest, and the three finally prevailed on Wolfgang. He sighed, and gazed wistfully around the roomful of happy people, shook his white pigtail, and folded his hands meekly.

"Very well," he said, "find Stanzi and tell her to make me some punch and bring it to me in my room. And good-night," he added sourly. "Enjoy yourselves."

When Constanze brought the punch, he was seated at the table scribbling hard.

"Come here, Stänerl," he said, reaching for her hand and kissing it, "and sit right here beside me. I'm terribly sleepy, I don't know how I'll stay awake. Now sit here, little Stanzi-Marini, and for God's sake keep me awake—talk to me, darling, or say verses, or something."

So she sat down and began to tell him silly stories, chattering as conscientiously as Scheherezade while he dashed off the hollow, portentous chords of the Andante. His whole overture was as perfect in his memory as the rest of the score he had already written out; the problem was only to keep awake, oh, just to keep awake! Constanze's chatter helped, but the punch made him sleepy; every time she paused his head drooped, his eyelids twitched together, the pen started slipping in his fingers. At three o'clock his chin fell on his breast. Constanze saw he could not go on; she got up, put her arms around him, and propelled him to the couch.

"Only an hour, Stänerl, promise. Only one hour, or I won't get through," he mumbled. "You won't let me sleep longer?"

She promised, but had not the heart to wake him in one hour, so she let him sleep until five o'clock. Then he got up and scribbled so furiously that at seven Constanze could send for the copyist. With a great groan of relief, Wolfgang flung himself into bed.

That evening, all streets in Prague led to the yellow opera-house. From the great mansions on the avenues, coaches full of ladies in brocades and jewels, their mountains of white hair glistening with flowers and aigrettes, their escorts gorgeous in velvet and jewelled swords, rolled into the narrow square to the great entrance for boxholders. The good townspeople, brushed and scrubbed, poured into pit and galleries. Even from wretched holes and evil-smelling warrens, hordes of poor but true Bohemians flocked to pay their coppers for a seat somewhere, anywhere, a place under the eaves where they could perch and hear their own new opera. Close to the stage, a box was reserved for the loyal, excited group from the Bertramka. Here were good Franz and Josefa with Constanze between them, and all the other friends who had surrounded Wolfgang and made his working weeks so uniquely happy. The orchestra filed in and took their places shortly before seven. There was a slight hush as the huge audience waited for the conductor; he should appear at once. But he did not. Many a similar occasion would have elicited hisses and catcalls, but they waited patiently for a long twenty minutes. Finally there was a stir at the little door under the stage; that would be he. But no, it was a house attendant, with his hands full of papers. Constanze, white and nervous, could not restrain a faint smile. The boy was bringing in the overture parts, still wet with ink and sticky with sand, and distributing them to the players, who had never seen them before. The copyist had not done as brilliant a rush job as the composer, but when the parts were arranged on the desks, the little door did open for Wolfgang, pale and damp of forehead, but forcefully reassured by a thunder-clap of applause. He bowed, took his place at the clavier and picked up his baton. The first stern, full, unearthly chord flowed out to the tense ears of Prague, then the second. At the resolution into D major, with its enchanting succession of prophetic themes, the house moved as if to break into applause, and the overture subsided in a wave of uncontrolled enthusiasm. With the curtain going up and the violins settling into Leporello's air, Wolfgang winked at the *Konzertmeister* and said out of the side of his mouth, "A good many notes fell under the desks, to be sure, but it went off damn well, just the same."

Posterity has heard finer performances, technically, than Bondini's company gave in Prague that night. But what those singers lacked in voice and training they made up in their magnificent spirit. With the divine inspiration of Mozart himself at the clavier, and with the advantage, not only of having been trained by him, but of being able to watch him as they brought his great work to life in his own hearing, they sang and played like genii. He was deeply moved. He knew the eternal worth of *Don Giovanni*, and the wiser among the players and audience knew it too. At the utterly sublime climax of the first act, where Don Giovanni's ball is the setting for one of the finest scenes in any opera, the house burst into roars, cheers and bravos.

At the end of the opera, Wolfgang had purposely abandoned in the music all the rough comedy Da Ponte had intended for his *dramma giocoso*, and flung himself passionately into the wild, terrifying punishment meted out to the frightened but always noble reprobate. The solemn, other-worldly notes of the ghostly Commendatore, alternated by stormy, sweeping, chromatic minor scales—the consuming fires of hell and the wails of the damned—gripped and dried every throat in the house, caused eyes to bulge from stinging sockets, breath to come fast and loud. When it was over, there was a moment of tense, pregnant silence; then the graceful white-and-gold interior came suddenly alive. The house was shaken to its cellars by such an overwhelming torrent of applause, shouts, and cheers as it has never sheltered since. In the street outside, the ovation sounded like the reverberation of a battle. Trembling, still bewildered at the violent return to a world of people from his own world of sound, Wolfgang was hoisted onto the stage to take the bows with the deliriously happy singers. Again and again the little man with the plain face and insignificant body was cheered, blessed, and pelted with flowers. Cries of speech, speech, punctuated the salvos of applause and yells of *Viva Maestro*! Someone pushed him, and hesitantly, Wolfgang took a step forward. He stretched out his little white hands in their best lace ruffles, looked for a moment down into the cheering mob. Then, from an overflowing heart, that had known the chill depths of indifference, and would know them more bitterly still, with tears running down his cheeks, he said, *"Meine Prager verstehen mich."*

Special Note: In 1787 Prague was a provincial capital of the Austrian Empire, and as such, its streets and landmarks bore German names which I used, for accuracy's sake, in this text. In any and all references to modern Prague, I would use the Czech names of its streets and landmarks. Their only correct and legitimate nomenclature is Czech, and has been Czech since the founding of the Czechoslovak Republic in 1918.

M.D., 1943.

XXXVIII

ISAAC NEWTON [1]

By

LOUIS T. MORE

Isaac Newton (1642-1727), English physicist and natural philosopher, and one of the world's great scientific geniuses, matriculated at Trinity College, Cambridge, on a poor man's scholarship. His great discoveries—his work in optics, the invention of fluxions or the infinitesimal calculus, and the law of gravitation for which he is perhaps best known—were made before he was twenty-five years old. With the exception of his optical experiments, they were not announced to the world or perfected until twenty years later in the immortal *Philosophiae Naturalis Principia Mathematica* (1687).

Dr. More has combined his thorough knowledge of mathematics, chemistry, physics and history to write this authoritative work. In the brief quotation which follows there is some indication of the reason for Isaac Newton's genius.

HOW NEWTON APPEARED TO HIMSELF

However Newton may have regarded himself in comparison with other men, he was piously humble in the presence of the mystery of God and the universe. Just a little while before his death he said: "I do not know what I may appear to the world; but to myself I seem to have been only like a boy, playing on the sea-shore, and diverting myself, in now and then finding a smoother pebble or a prettier shell than ordinary, whilst the great ocean of truth lay all undiscovered before me."

[1] Louis T. More, *Isaac Newton*, New York: Charles Scribner's Sons, 1934, p. 664.

XXXIX

OSCAR WILDE AND THE YELLOW 'NINETIES[1]

By

FRANCES WINWAR

This biography of one of the leading advocates of the decadence of the "yellow nineties" bears the clear imprint of Frances Winwar's excellent literary craftsmanship. In this story Oscar Wilde lives with all his unusual strength and tragic weakness, with all his humor and wit. The account of the trials, Wilde's life in prison, and his final degraded years is candid but moving in its understanding of Wilde's career.

Oscar Wilde (1856-1900), born in Dublin the son of a famous Irish surgeon, was educated at Oxford, where he graduated with honors. In 1879, living in London, he became the leader of a so-called aesthetic movement. Even in college he looked with scorn on manly sports, wore his hair long, and professed great emotions on the subject of "art for art's sake"—an idea J. M. Whistler, the famous artist, was promoting. Wilde soon became widely known through his poems, his charming fairy tales, his great success as a dramatist with *Lady Windermere's Fan* and other works. In 1895 he was convicted of a serious moral offense and was sentenced to two years' imprisonment at hard labor. In prison he wrote *A Ballad of Reading Gaol*, a poem of strength, and *De Profundis*, an account of some of his prison experiences and a kind of *Apologia*. His comedies were clever, and he possessed wit and epigrammatic brilliance.

THE REPARTEE OF WILDE AND WHISTLER

Once at an exhibition of Whistler's "arrangements" an art critic, seeking to impress the painter, flung the words *good* and *bad* at the canvases with a temerity that made the wiser gasp. Whistler did not fail them.

[1] Frances Winwar, *Oscar Wilde and the Yellow 'Nineties*, New York: Harper & Brothers, 1940, pp. 50-51, 142, 204-205, 362.

"My dear fellow," he flashed upon the hapless Humphry Ward. "You must never say this painting's good or that bad! Good and bad are not terms to be used by you. Say I like this and I don't like that and you'll be within your right. And now come and have some whiskey. You're sure to like that."

Wilde who was standing by rashly exclaimed: "I wish I had said that."

"You will, Oscar, you will!" darted the Butterfly, exploding into his triumphant "Ha! Ha!" He felled his victims with the prowess of the little tailor in the story. Only they were men, not flies, and they could come back at him.

Oscar enjoyed these encounters which caused him to be talked about, although he preferred it when he had the last word. Forbes-Robertson who had stood with him at the gangplank to welcome Sarah Bernhardt and, less extravagant, had given her a gardenia, loved to tell one of Wilde's retorts. A squib in one of the papers had it that Whistler and Wilde had been seen at Brighton talking as usual about themselves. Whistler, seizing the opportunity, sent Wilde the cutting with the comment: "I wish these reporters would be accurate; if you remember, Oscar, we were talking about me." Immediately Wilde rejoined with the wire: "It is true, Jimmie, we were talking about you, but I was thinking about myself."

OSCAR WILDE APPRAISES WHISTLER

"That he is indeed one of the greatest masters of painting, is my opinion. And I may add that in this opinion Mr. Whistler himself entirely concurs."

"AND YET THEY HAVE NOT CRUCIFIED ME"

Wilde would have wanted life to be a road pleasantly shaded against inclemency, opening out, as one advanced, more and more glorious prospects. Even though his two heroes, Christ and Bonaparte, had taught him that in the one case the end was Calvary and in the other the rock where the Eagle rotted in chains, he deluded himself with the hope that with him it would be different. He, the Lord of Life, would carve his way to the summit where Beauty lay revealed. He would not know defeat. Nevertheless, in the depths of his being an obscure fear gave warning. He heard it in his rare silences; sometimes it spoke to him through his own mouth in allegories that held meaning through indirection. What crown of life excelled the crown of martyrdom? Christ without His thorns, Bonaparte without his chains—would they have lived on to tenant the souls of men forever?

"Now when the darkness came over the earth," a prophetic Wilde would speak, "Joseph of Arimathea, having lighted a torch of pinewood, passed down from the hill into the valley. For he had business in his own home. And kneeling on the flint stones of the Valley of Desolation he saw a young man who was naked and weeping. His hair was the colour of honey, and his body was as a white flower, but he had wounded his body with thorns and on his hair he had set ashes as a crown. And he who had great possessions said to the young man who was naked and weeping, 'I do not wonder that your sorrow is great, for surely He was a just man.' And the young man answered, 'It is not for Him that I am weeping, but for myself. I too have changed water into wine, and I have healed the leper and given sight to the blind. I have walked upon the waters, and from the dwellers in the tombs I have cast out devils. I have fed the hungry in the desert where there was no food, and I have raised the dead from their narrow houses, and at my bidding, and before a great multitude of people, a barren fig-tree withered away. All things that this man has done I have done also. And yet they have not crucified me.' "

WHEN DEATH WAS NEAR

Even in the nearness of death Wilde's brillance was not quenched. When to please him one night they brought him the iced champagne he loved, he said with a glimmer of the irresistible Oscar, "I am dying beyond my means."

XL

PHANTOM CROWN; THE STORY OF MAXIMILIAN AND CARLOTA OF MEXICO [1]

By

BERTITA HARDING

Bertita Harding has written a vivid account of the attempt of Napoleon III to rule Mexico through the Austrian archduke Maximilian. By scholarly research she has been able to present not only a fascinating and authentic picture of the social background of mid-nineteenth century Mexico, but also a clear insight into the character and motives of Maximilian and Carlota. The story of Maximilian's early life and marriage with Carlota, his brief and disastrous reign, Carlota's return to Europe and Maximilian's death are all told in a most readable style in this rushing narrative. The particular passage which Bertita Harding has selected for this anthology is the dramatic story of Maximilian's death at Querétaro, Mexico.

Maximilian (1832-1867) was born in Vienna and was the brother of the Emperor Francis Joseph. He was responsible for the growth of Trieste as a naval center and was governor general of the Lombardo-Venetian kingdom in 1857. He married Princess Charlotte [Carlota], daughter of King Leopold of Belgium. In October 1863 a deputation from the Mexican Assembly of Notables offered him the crown of Mexico which had been created by French armed intervention. He accepted and landed in Vera Cruz in May 1864. In June he entered Mexico City to be crowned Emperor. He attempted energetically to consolidate his dominions, but his efforts failed. Financially and politically he was dependent upon France. When French troops were withdrawn from Mexico following a protest from the United States, Maximilian lacked support. The Empress Charlotte returned to Europe to enlist the assistance of Napoleon and the Pope; she failed, and the strain proved so great that she lost her mind.

[1] Bertita Harding, *Phantom Crown; The Story of Maximilian and Carlota of Mexico*, copyright 1934, used by special permission of the publishers, The Bobbs-Merrill Company, Indianapolis, pp. 322-330.

Although Napoleon's agents made repeated efforts to obtain Maximilian's escape, he refused to save himself. With his principal officers, he was finally courtmartialled, convicted and shot by the forces of President Juárez, despite pleas for clemency from four nations.

THE EXECUTION OF MAXIMILIAN

During the last week a false report had been spread, to the effect that the Empress Carlota had died at Miramar. Maximilian wrote at once to the Austrian Minister, Baron von Lago:

> Only a moment ago I learned that my poor wife has been released by death from her misery. Such tidings, however much they may tear my heart, give boundless consolation to me, for I have now only one wish on earth, that my body may find burial beside the remains of my wife. With this mission, dear Baron, I entrust you as representative of Austria.

In another part of the letter he emphasized a point which caused him grave concern. "I am expecting you," he wrote, "to spare no effort in saving all Austrian officers and recruits still in Mexico, so that they may return at once to Europe."

As the time grew shorter the rumor concerning Carlota's death was denied and Maximilian, plagued with uncertainty, addressed a parting note:

> My beloved Carla! If God should allow you to regain your health, so that you may read these lines, you will learn how cruelly fate has dealt me blow after blow without respite since the day of your departure. Disaster has dogged my steps, breaking all my hopes! Death seems a happy solution. I shall go to my end as a soldier, a sovereign defeated but not dishonored. . . . Then, if your own distress becomes too great to bear, and God calls you to join me soon, I shall bless the hand which has been so heavy upon us. Farewell, Charlotte!
>
> Maximilian.

He spent the fifteenth of June writing from dawn till dusk, remembering all his close relatives and friends. That night, looked upon as his last on earth, he did not go to bed but engaged in final preparations. Taking stock of his personal effects, the Emperor distributed a few trifles among his followers. Basch was to have the scarf-pin sent by Franz Joseph to Miramar in those far-off days when the Archduke Maxl had needed a little prodding. . . . A pair of cuff-links went to Blasio, while the brushes and all remaining articles were to belong to the Salms. It was not until morning that the prisoner fell asleep.

Late the following day he was roused by a voice announcing that the execution would take place at three o'clock in the afternoon. An armed official stopped before each of the condemned men's cells and recited the sentence, after which the army chaplain, Padre Soria, appeared with censer and chalice. The Church offered redemption through the last sacraments, confession and holy communion. Maximilian accepted these ministrations with outward calm. Only a characteristic habit of stroking his chin betrayed that he labored under a nervous strain.

The small span of life which was now left him stretched out interminably. With sharpened senses the prisoners anticipated the striking of the fatal hour. At last a clock in a remote belfry chimed three, and Maximilian rose from his cot. He planted himself in the doorway of his cell, waiting five minutes, ten, half an hour. Why didn't they come? He felt he could not bear the torture. Time hung over him in an agony of suspense.

The bell in the tower rang out four o'clock and from somewhere there came the echo of a paternoster. Maximilian recognized the voice. It was Mejía, praying. Mejía was in no hurry. There was something that held him to life; something he would not explain.

The Emperor groaned in respair. Why couldn't they make an end of this? Had Latin procrastination combined with Indian lethargy to lend an added edge to his suffering? Surely the *mañana* habit did not make a fitting taunt for those awaiting death.

Footsteps sounded in the courtyard below. Now they approached, and in another moment General Riva Palacio stood in the corridor, jerking his arms and waving a piece of paper. It was a message from San Luis Potosí.

"*Die Begnadigung*," murmured Maximilian. ("The pardon!")

A faint radiance sparkled in his eyes and slowly lighted up his wan face. Suddenly the Emperor realized how fiercely he clung to earth, how desperate was his own love of living. Pride of origin and regal poise faded into nothingness beside that indestructible force—man's instinct for self-preservation.

Palacio had guessed Maximilian's meaning and shrugged apologetically. "No pardon," he announced, shaking his head, "but the execution will be postponed for three days, because the wife of Comrade Mejía is in childbed. The prisoner will be allowed to visit his son."

"*Alabado sea Dios*!" finished the prayer from the next cell.

The time that followed was the most difficult of all. A restlessness filled the little town of Querétaro. Every one had misunderstood the telegram, and every one believed that Juárez, relenting at last, chose this devious way of granting mercy in order to save his own integrity before the law. Even the Liberal chieftains, Escobedo and Corona, were certain of Maximilian's imminent release. So were the remaining prisoners, who vaticinated thereby their own salvation. Felix Salm-Salm felt especially cheerful. He was already wondering where in the world a man could find another war. He had taken up heroism as a career.

At the old inn the diplomatic representatives, far less hopeful, were gathered in conclave. Their interview with Juárez had been fruitless. Neither the Indian President nor his Minister, Lerdo, was accessible to persuasion or bribery. The present delay in the execution plans might be puzzling but by no means reassuring. Baron von Magnus, the most skeptical of the group, dispatched a long telegram to San Luis Potosí. It ran:

> On June sixteenth the condemned men have, figuratively speaking, already been led to their death. I beseech you, in the name of humanity and of Heaven, to give orders that their lives shall not again be threatened, that they shall not be forced to die a second time. And I repeat once again the assurance that my sovereign, his Majesty the King of Prussia, and all the monarchs of Europe related to the imprisoned Prince by the tie of blood—namely, his brother, the Emperor of Austria; his cousin, the Queen of Great Britain; his brother-in-law, the King of the Belgians; and his cousin, the Queen of Spain; as well as the Kings of Italy and Sweden—will readily agree to give his Excellency Señor Benito Juárez all guaranties that none of the prisoners will ever return or set foot on Mexican territory.

Baron von Lago also translated and passed on a message he had just received from Vienna. It appeared that at the eleventh hour, realizing his brother's danger, the Emperor Franz Joseph had reinstated Maximilian as heir presumptive to the Austrian throne. He now hoped that this measure would safeguard, if not Maximilian's position, at least his person, since it was unthinkable that a ranking member of a ruling house could be executed in cold blood by a foreign power. But Juárez was a son of the New World, which he considered far older than the Old, and he was totally unhampered by dynastic feeling. Furthermore, he refused to be cowed by the information that Maximilian was the "Cousin of Europe." On the contrary, it had been imprudent of Magnus and Lago to call the Indian's attention to this fact. Juárez was beginning to believe that the slightest move of his little finger would be heralded around the earth. It was a most satisfying thought.

A telegram from Maximilian himself, asking that he alone be allowed to pay the penalty, while Miramón and Mejía returned to their families, met with equal cynicism. As for his two countrymen, Juárez would teach them the rewards of treason. No particular triumph in that. But the Hapsburg scion begging for favors—here was historic justice! Among Maximilian's ancestors was Charles V, white scourge of the Aztecs, while behind Juárez loomed the shadow of the Lord Motecuhzoma, whose name signified "Severe Man." . . . In the teeth of all the tyrants everywhere the dusky patriot would do this deed which was to him a sacred duty. He would do it and fear no one.

There were no replies to Magnus, Lago, or Seward in Washington (who had finally contrived a circumspect and polite letter). Maximilian of course expected none. He had already appealed to the Hofburg for a pension to be provided for the widows of his companions in death. It was the least that Austria might do, to acknowledge their sacrifice.

And so the morning of the execution arrived. During the night, while the prisoners slept, Maximilian had an extraordinary caller. General Escobedo, Commander-in-Chief of the garrison, stole into the convent to ask forgiveness for the ignoble part he must play. The Emperor was touched.

"*Un abrazo, amigo,*" he said hoarsely, and the two men held each other for a brief second.

Escobedo's throat tightened so that he could not answer. To ease the strain Maximilian began to rummage among his effects, until he came upon a faded photograph of himself in coronation regalia (which he never actually wore). After inscribing the print he handed it to his captor.

The general left. But as he passed Mejía's cell a pang of self-reproach shot through him. In some earlier revolution he and Mejía had fought on the same side, and the latter had saved Escobedo's life. It was a debt, never repaid, which long pre-dated Maximilian's arrival.

Mejía stood erect behind the bars and he now saw Escobedo pass. In the gloom their eyes met. The Liberal commander stopped.

"I can save you, Tomás," he whispered, "if you are willing to escape alone. It was I who obtained the delay, that you might know your child."

Mejía flushed. "And the Emperor? And Miramón with his torn face?"

Escobedo made a sign of protest. "I can not help them too, without exposing us all. Besides, they would not survive the hardships—"

"*Gracias, mi jefe,*" said Mejía without further interest. "I have seen my son. Now let me die with his Majesty."

Sick at heart, Escobedo departed.

It was three o'clock in the morning. The prisoners finished dressing, while at one end of the long corridor the priest Soria reappeared, wearing biretta and alb. He trundled a small campaign altar and began at once to read a low mass, gazing the while with pity upon his sparse congregation.

While the monstrance was being raised during the consecration of the Host, Maximilian and his companions dropped to their knees to receive the blessing.

After the service the Emperor drew his wedding-ring from his right hand. He turned to Doctor Basch with a confused expression.

"Carla—" he began. Then: "Is there still no confirmation?"

"None, your Majesty." But a physician's faith in palliatives caused Basch to imply that the Empress had preceded her husband in death. This was the only real service he could now render the doomed monarch.

"Then—take it to my mother," Maximilian said, handing Basch the ring. "*Sie sollen ihn meiner Mutter bringen.*"

A scapulary and a rosary which the kindly Father Soria had given to the Emperor were also destined for Vienna. But the small medallion of the Madonna—Eugénie's present, which was to have brought him luck—Maximilian bequeathed to the Empress of Brazil.

"She will need it," he said reflectively.

He turned now to Miramón and Mejía. "Are you ready, gentlemen? Have we done with everything?"

He clasped both generals and the members of his following in turn. To the former he said: "We shall meet again in another world."

A detachment of infantry clattered through the passage. The officer in command announced that no foreigners were to accompany the Emperor from now on. This was a blow to Prince Salm-Salm, who continued to nurse mad schemes of possible escape during the drive to the scene of death.

Maximilian descended the stairs. He was in uniform. He wore a single order, the Golden Fleece. On reaching the street his eyes blinked at the unaccustomed brightness, for the sun was already high in the heavens.

"What a glorious day," he exclaimed. "I could not have chosen one better on which to die."

From far off there came the blare of a cornet. Maximilian turned to Mejía.

"Tomás, is that the signal for the execution?"

"I can not say, Sire; this is the first time I am being executed."

A smile from his master rewarded the brave cynic. Three carriages had meanwhile driven up and the condemned men climbed into them. Surrounded by a cavalry escort the procession started through the town, the firing squad marching at the rear. Even now the revolutionaries were taking no chances; a melodramatic dash for freedom would have ended in carnage.

But Maximilian had no such thought. He rode through the deserted streets resigned at last to his fate. The citizens of Querétaro did not see him pass, for the hour of the execution had been kept secret. Only here and there did a pair of dark uncomprehending eyes stare behind shuttered windows after the swift cavalcade.

At a safe distance a cloaked figure darted along, uttering strange Magyar sounds. "*Boldog Istenem*! [Good God!] I didn't believe it could come to this. I didn't believe——"

It was Tüdös, the cook, who had hovered about the Capuchin convent these many days and nights, waiting for his master. No one knew the black-haired, swarthy Hungarian, and no one stopped him now as he followed the gloomy train to the Hill of the Bells.

As the carriage neared the edge of the town a childlike wraith ran screaming from a doorway. It was Mejía's wife, with her newly born infant at her breast. She caught up with the vehicle which bore her husband away. Clutching one of the mudguards she let herself be dragged along until a sharp bayonet broke her grip.

Tomás Mejía saw her fall, and a great terror engulfed him. All his gallantry, his Indian fortitude—which was not unlike that of Juárez—suddenly withered. He felt the sickness that comes with a brutal blow in the stomach. On arriving at the foot of the Cerro he was almost insensate with grief and had to be lifted from the carriage.

The spot where Maximilian had been taken prisoner was chosen as the site of his immolation. With princely bearing, although his features had blanched at Mejía's agony, the Emperor walked uphill. Beside him went Miramón, equally staunch, for Miramón remembered that he had once ruled Mexico.

When they were near the top the firing squad lined up on three sides of a square opposite a low adobe parapet. The prisoners were stationed with their backs against this improvised elevation which had been constructed during the siege as a breastwork, guarding more important fortifications on the summit. In a mumbling monotone the firing parties were told off.

At this point a significant precaution appeared necessary. Obviously the troops could not be trusted, for the commandant in charge now read aloud to them a scathing pronunciamiento, threatening instant death to any one who raised a hand to save the Emperor. In the morning stillness four thousand soldiers, encamped at the foot of the hill, heard the message and pondered its meaning.

From the church of San Felipe Neri a bell rang out seven o'clock. Maximilian was asked if he had anything to say. He nodded. Walking up to the firing squad he distributed a few gold coins among the men, begging them to shoot well and not to aim at his head. In the event of his body being returned to Europe, he wanted to spare his relatives the sight of gory disfigurement. Had Juárez been present, this ultimate fastidiousness in the face of death would have drawn a smirk of derision from his impassive Indian countenance.

The soldiers, on the other hand, seemed abashed by an avowed emotion. A young captain stepped forward, stammering an excuse. The Emperor interrupted him.

"I understand, *amigo*," he said simply; "it is your duty."

And now he saw the faithful Tüdös crouching behind the wall, his nervous fingers clawing at the unbaked clay. The presence of the servant, the last and only being out of a dear past, comforted Maximilian.

"Eljen Császár, veled!" cried the Hungarian. ("Hail Emperor, farewell!")

They embraced. Maximilian was unable to speak. A cold sweat had broken out on his face. He wiped it and, almost absently, left his hat and handkerchief with Tüdös, to take home. Yes, Tüdös was going home. But he, the gay, the urbane Maxl of other days, was not. He would never again need a hat....

The world was a great riddle. As if dazed, the Emperor took his place beside Miramón and Mejía. Before him lay the hamlet of Querétaro, drowsing peacefully in the sun. Looking up at a Mexican sky of ineffable blue, he made his last speech, in the best Spanish he had ever used:

"*Muero por una causa justa. Perdono á todos y ruego que todos me perdonen. Espero que mi sangre corra por el bien de esta tierra. Viva México!*" ("I die in a just cause. I forgive all, and pray that all may forgive me. May my blood flow for the good of this land. Long live Mexico!")

He had finished. The officer in charge raised and lowered his sword, while a volley of shots rang out. Maximilian collapsed, badly wounded. He had fallen face downward, and now they heard him groan: "*Hombres!* [Men!]"

Some one ran up to the twitching body and turned it over. The Emperor was still alive. Again, without a word, the officer swung down his blade. He was indicating the heart. Now a single shot was fired, which scorched Maximilian's tunic as it killed him. The servant Tüdös threw himself upon his master to extinguish the smoldering flames.

XLI

THE LIFE OF MARGARET FULLER [1]

By

MADELEINE B. STERN

In this biography Madeleine Stern reinterprets the life of brilliant but eccentric Margaret Fuller (1810-1850), a notable American woman and author. Miss Stern describes also Miss Fuller's part in the liberal movement in America in the first half of the last century. The book is particularly interesting because it has dramatically recreated striking episodes in Margaret Fuller's career, of which the one here given is a splendid example.

The years 1844-46, when she lived in New York and wrote brilliant essays on art and literature for the *Tribune*, were the most productive in Margaret Fuller's life. In 1846 she went to Europe, and while residing in Rome, married Giovanni Angelo, Marquis Ossoli. She was a friend of Mazzini, Italian liberal. During the Italian revolution of 1848 she worked in Roman hospitals, and when Rome fell, she and her husband fled with their infant son to the mountains. Garibaldi, famous Italian liberal, gave heroic but ineffectual service in this struggle to free Italy. In 1850, when Margaret Fuller and her husband and child sailed for the United States, they were drowned in a storm off the New York coast. Her history of the Italian revolution was lost with her.

Miss Stern gives the following reasons for her choice of this selection from the book: "First, the passage represents the type of biographical writing in which I most ardently believe, that is, the integration of details of background with the life of the character. The struggle for Roman liberation played an important part in Margaret Fuller's life and therefore its course must be interwoven with her career. Secondly, the fall of Rome was most significant for Margaret Fuller. She had found herself in participating in the struggle for liberation, and the failure of that cause involved a personal defeat."

[1] Madeleine B. Stern, *The Life of Margaret Fuller*, published and copyright by E. P. Dutton & Co., Inc., New York, 1942, pp. 459-464.

THE CITY SHE HAD LOVED WAS NO MORE

The bells had tolled away a whole month by the time Margaret learned that Garibaldi had returned to Rome on the last day of May and Lesseps had signed an agreement with the Triumvirs, assuring them that the French would protect Rome against Austria and all the world. The barricades were stronger than ever in the streets, but Margaret saw that the soldiers were less pre-occupied with military affairs than with sitting next to the market-men shelling peas. Rome was disturbed the next day to hear that Oudinot had repudiated Lesseps' armistice, but the General had, at least, made a gentlemanly agreement not to attack the place until Monday, the fourth of June. There would be a few more days of peace, Margaret thought, while Garibaldi's men were stationed on the west bank. Garibaldi himself was ill, but there was no great need of vigilance since the city would have all of Sunday to prepare for the attack. If the soldiers insisted on shelling a few more peas, there surely was no necessity of denying them their enjoyment.

At four in the morning of Sunday, June third, Margaret was awakened from sleep in her room on the top floor of the Casa Diez by the noise of sappers' picks and guns, rolls of cannon and volleys of musket fire. She quickly looked out of the window in the direction of the Porta San Pancrazio and saw the smoke of the discharges, the flash of the bayonets. With her glass she could see the men—orderlies dashing about to search, no doubt, for their regiments, armed civilians pushing their way across the bridges among cheering crowds, the bright red tunics and round hats of Garibaldi's Legion filing toward the Porta San Pancrazio, and the infamous French, their gun barrels flashing in the early morning sunlight. Now Margaret walked out to the loggia to hear the bells clanging from every campanile, the drummers beating the alarm, the distant sounds of the *Marseillaise* that the bands played to shame the French with the irony. On the hilltop she saw the balcony of the Corsini crowded with French soldiers while Garibaldi sat on his white horse, sending up division after division to dash at the garden gate. Through the narrow passageway Margaret watched Manara's men rushing up the slope under a storm of bullets, while the distant cries of *Avanti! Avanti!* echoed over the ringing bells and drumbeats.

The sun rose higher in the skies and the sultry noon settled over the city. Margaret stood silent on the loggia, holding her glass to see the wounded slung in scarfs or rolled back through the streets on hand-barrows, to see the dead piled in the open loggias near the Villa. All day long the heavy cannonade boomed through the city, musket answering musket with fire and smoke. Then she saw the gunners, the infantry, mobs of citizens and artists flooding through the Porta San Pancrazio, sweeping along in a dense mass to the Villa. The Corsini was a ruin of charred debris, bodies and arms. Through the trees Oudinot's army flashed, regiment behind regiment, till the pines threw long shadows in the dusk. After the last gleam of light flickered over the city Margaret turned from the loggia, wondering what the outcome had been, wondering where Giovanni was in all the tumultuous city, dreading to think that perhaps he too might lie among the heaps of the dead.

Not until later did she learn that three hundred Italians lay dead or wounded, that Giovanni had escaped, but that the French had captured the Valentini and the Corsini, and were besieging Rome. The city was afire with bursting rockets. Day after day shells flew over the Janiculum, shattering the *Trastevere* below. Now Margaret learned the distinction between the two-handled bomb and the hollow grenade. She could not laugh when the Italians greeted the bursting shells with cries of *"Ecco un Pio Nono!"* For the Villa Borghese, the villa of Raphael, was laid waste, and the trees cut down at the Villa Albani. Burnt was the Villa Salvage, with all its fine frescoes, and the banks of the Tiber were shorn of their trees. Garibaldi still sat on his horse in his short white poncho, smoking his cigar through the day, but the French light cavalry in their little *kepis* were sweeping over the Campagna, cutting off the convoys from Rieti, and in the courtyard of the Fate-bene Hospital one of their rockets had burst.

The wounded men called to Margaret as she entered the hospital, saying that they did not want to die like mice in a trap. Now that the bombardment continued incessantly she spent seven or eight hours a day at the Fate-bene or the Pellegrini, comforting the wounded students from Pisa and Pavia, Padua and Rome. She had learned much from Princess Belgiojoso, who had given up a distinguished Paris salon to serve the Republic, and who now sat long nights at the bedside of the dying poet Mameli, reading Dickens to him by the light of a little oil lamp. Every day Margaret watched the carts of the wounded, dreading to find in one of them the face she knew so well. As she moved about the wards where fair young men were bleeding to death, she felt herself a Mater Dolorosa. The woe of all the mothers who had borne these men was hers; in twenty years her own son might be thus cut down. The men themselves seemed even braver now than on the field. She saw one in his narrow bed kissing the pieces of bone that had been extracted from his arm, hanging them round his neck as relics and mementos. She wept sometimes when she could not relieve the pain of the suffering, and one crippled young man, seeing her in tears, clasped her hand whispering, *"Viva l' Italia." Cara bona donna*, they called her. God is good; God knows, they said. And one soldier remarked to her joyfully as she sat near his bed, "Think that I can always wear my uniform on *festas* just as it is now, with the holes where the balls went through, for a memory." The sturdy Garibaldians spoke to her of their chief and she in turn brought them books or told them the news of the day. In the Pope's Palace on the Quirinal she walked with the convalescents, one with his sling, another with his crutch, while the gardener played the waterworks for the soldiers and gathered flowers for her, their friend. As she walked through the wards before returning home the men raised themselves on their elbows to catch a last glimpse of her, calling out, "When will the Signora come again?"

She came as often as she could, for now she had few friends in Rome, save Giovanni, whom she could not see frequently. Sometimes she carried to him a concealed basket of provisions which he promptly shared with his comrades. Margaret sought him out at his post, finding him exhausted and faint for want of rest, but still resolute in his determination to follow Mazzini's ideals. The wall that he defended was stained with blood. Giovanni showed her pieces of a bomb that had burst at his side, and she saved a bit of it as a relic. Whenever he could, he came to her, to comfort her, to get the handle of her parasol mended, to speak of the hospitals and the wounded. But he could not leave his post for long, and she dared not stay with him, nor had she the heart to leave him. Their little hurried notes were all that remained now, and she left word for him at the Casa Diez, telling him when she would return, thanking God that he was still alive. He answered dashing off a line to the Casa, begging her not to overwork, and to take care of herself for little Angelo's sake.

It was hard that she could not see the baby during the siege. Every dreadful possibility now arose in her mind as an actuality. He would be hurt by the Croats, the house would be burned over his head, and if he escaped how would they get the money to buy his bibs and primers? Every day in the burning sun she waited among the crowds at the post office for letters about him, letters that demanded money for the care of the child. Amid the roar of the bombardment she heard his voice, crying for her, the helpless moan that musketry could not drown nor cannon stifle.

So from day to day she lived, wondering as the moon rose that she had survived another sunset. The few letters that drifted in from America filled her with nostalgia, with a desire to escape to the peace of her home. Ellen was living with her mother at Manchester and Richard had married Sarah Batchelder. He sent money to Margaret and she longed to see him and her mother once again. At first, before the French had arrived at Civita Vecchia, Margaret had thought she would never find a tranquil abode in her family. She was caught in such a net of ties that she despaired of going back; America was so far away that return seemed impossible. But now she wanted to go home for the baby's sake, and in one of her hurried notes to Giovanni she told him so, begging that if ever he loved another he would think first of Angelo.

Her hopes had been raised so high before that first dreadful Sunday in June. Rome's future and her own were linked together in an indissoluble tie. Rome's triumph would have meant Giovanni's success, and his success, her own. Now each day brought greater desolation to the city she had loved and with every bursting meteor that shattered the pine trees her own hopes fell. She was weary and faith soared and sang no more. She had played for a new stake and was losing. Rome still was playing for a high stake, but now the struggle seemed hopeless. On the night of the twentieth outside the walls of the Casa Giacometti, the Italians had won a victory with their bayonets, but by the next day a fiery rain fell thick over the Piazza di Gesu, and a tremendous cannonade announced that the French had made the breach and entered the city.

After that Margaret waited despairingly while day followed day in a week of defeat. First Sterbini, hoping to regain his power, exploited Garibaldi's name in a plot that ended in a fiasco. Then Mazzini quarreled with Garibaldi, who gave up his command, but later returned to his post on the Janiculum. The besieged city seethed with unrest. Each day Margaret heard of another familiar place that had been shelled. Holes had been torn in the Spada; the roof of the Church of San Pietro in Montorio collapsed; in the Piazza di Spagna, where Margaret had walked so often, and on Santo Spirito, bombs had fallen. Over the post office, where she had waited so often for letters from Rieti, the lightning of musketry made fireworks in the air. In her room in the Casa Diez she heard the sound of the storm alarm. At the news that came to her in whispers she grew sick at heart. The French were crushing the batteries with cannon they had stolen from Civita Vecchia. The water supply was cut off. Provisions were seized. As Margaret walked to the hospitals, balls and bombs whizzed and burst near her. While she waited alone in the Casa Diez,

Rome fell, fell amid rain and ruin. Not Garibaldi's sabre, nor all the cries of *Viva l' Italia* could save the city. With butt and bayonet, lance and knife, the French closed in upon the Italians, raked their lines, stormed their defenses. The city she had loved was no more.

XLII

WILL ROGERS, HIS WIFE'S STORY [1]

By

BETTY BLAKE ROGERS

Will Rogers (1879-1935), American humorist and "cowboy philosopher," was one of the most popular Americans and foremost comedians of his time. He began his stage career as a rope-throwing cowboy and gradually developed witty speeches which he gave in a slow, drawling voice. He poked fun at Presidents, Congressmen, and other notables and commented humorously on economic problems and political events. Whether he was on the stage, screen, radio, or writing in his syndicated newspaper column, he chose to express himself in ungrammatical English. He debunked stuffed shirts and unsound ideas with an essentially American humor that made him beloved. Will Rogers was one of America's earliest air enthusiasts and is said to have flown over 500,000 miles before he was killed with Wiley Post in an airplane crash near Point Barrow, Alaska.

Mrs. Rogers has written a lively and entertaining book of her husband's life, from which we have selected some of his delightful humor.

WHERE WILL ROGERS FOUND HUMOR

"I don't make jokes," he said, "I just watch the Government and report the facts and I have never found it necessary to exaggerate."

TO TIP OR NOT TO TIP A SOUP PLATE

At the time John W. Davis ran for the Presidency, Will Rogers wrote in one of his weekly articles: "If Mrs. J. W. Davis gets into the White House, it will have a mistress no titled European visitor can embarrass

[1] Betty Blake Rogers, *Will Rogers*, copyright 1941, used by special permission of the publishers, The Bobbs-Merrill Company, Indianapolis, pp. 184, 224-226.

by doing the right thing first. She will never tip her Soup plate even if she can't get it all." Will's innocent line led to an exchange of articles with Percy Hammond, the late New York dramatic critic, who took occasion to reprove Will on his ignorance.

"For years I have been tipping my Soup plate," wrote Mr. Hammond, "but never until Mr. Rogers instructed me, did I know that I was performing a social error. Consultation with the polished and urbane head waiters of the Middle West, where I spent my boyhood, taught me, I believe to eat soup. . . . It is proper to tip one's plate, provided (and here is the subtlety that escapes Mr. Rogers), provided that one tips one's plate from and not toward. Mr. Rogers might well observe the modesty in such matters that adorns Mr. Tom Mix, his fellow ex-cowman. Mr. Mix, telling of a dinner given in his honor at the Hotel Astor, said, 'I et for two hours and didn't recognize a thing I et except an olive.' "

Percy Hammond was a well-known literary figure, famous as wit and critic. But Will maintained and energetically defended his "soup plate position." New York was delighted with his reply.

"Percy, [Will wrote] you say you learned to eat Soup from a Head Waiter. Well, I admit my ignorance; I never saw a head waiter eat Soup. Down in Oklahoma where I come from, we won't let a head waiter eat at our Table, even if we had a head waiter, which we haven't. If I remember right, I think it was my Mother taught me what little she knew of how I should eat, because if we had had to wait until we sent and got a head waiter to show us, we would have all starved to death.

"And as for your saying that anything of subtlety would escape me, that I also admit. But as for me being too Dumb to get the idea of 'the Soup plate being tipped away and not toward one,' that's not Etiquette, Percy; that's just Self Protection. As bad as you plate tippers want all you can get, you don't want it in your lap."

XLIII

BENJAMIN FRANKLIN [1]

By

CARL VAN DOREN

Carl Van Doren's *Benjamin Franklin*, based upon a decade of exhaustive study and research, is biography in its very finest classical tradition. In this rich and full-bodied book on a great American statesman and philosopher, scholarship is made eminently readable.

Benjamin Franklin (1706-1790) had one of the broadest and most creative minds of his time. Author, philosopher, scientist, inventor, statesman, printer, diplomat, humorist—these were some of the careers in which he engaged with success.

He invented the old-fashioned stove, the lightning rod and bifocal glasses, advocated copper for roofs, was responsible for paving and lighting streets, formed the first fire company and the first American fire insurance company, introduced penny postage and established the dead letter office. He also founded the Philadelphia library and an academy which later became the University of Pennsylvania.

"America's patron saint of common sense," as Franklin has been called, was the only man to sign the Declaration of Independence, the Treaty of Alliance with France, the Treaty of Paris, and the Constitution of the United States.

Franklin's almanac, known as *Poor Richard's Almanac*, was his greatest achievement in journalism and made a fortune for him, as well as fame at home and abroad. The *Almanac* was bought regularly and was carefully read. Its reputation was established with its first number when Franklin was only twenty-six. For over a quarter of a century this publication with its wisdom, wit and useful hints was looked forward to by a large portion of the colonial population, Later Franklin collected many of the best of his maxims and published them as the *Speech of Father Abraham* in the *Almanac* of 1757.

[1] Carl Van Doren, *Benjamin Franklin*, copyright 1938 by Carl Van Doren, by permission of The Viking Press, Inc., New York, pp. 106-115.

In the selection which follows we present Carl Van Doren's illuminating account of the *Almanac*.

THE WIT AND CHARM OF FRANKLIN AS POOR RICHARD

For Franklin 1732 was a busy and crucial year. His *Gazette* was profitable, and he had a hand in other *Gazettes* in South Carolina and Rhode Island. He was printer to Pennsylvania and printer on his own account. Besides the Junto there was the new library. Through the library and the Masons he was widening his acquaintance among Philadelphians more prominent than his Leather Apron friends. At home he had a shop in part of his house, where his wife helped him sell books and stationery and his mother-in-law sold the salves and ointments which she made. On 20 October his son Francis Folger was born. But all these were not enough, nor the letters which Franklin wrote for the *Gazette* that summer as from Anthony Afterwit, Celia Single, Alice Addertongue. He wanted another outlet and another income, and perhaps without realizing it, another character to play. He found them in the almanac which he published for the first time in December, in the character of Poor Richard.

Books might sell, almanacs were sure to. Many households in the colonies had no printed matter besides an almanac, but almost every one of them had that. An almanac had been the first thing printed in Pennsylvania, by William Bradford with Samuel Atkins as editor. Almanacs, pocket-size and paper-bound, calculated the tides and the changes of the moon, and claimed to forecast the weather. Almanacs were calendars. They furnished astrology for those who believed in it. There were sometimes recipes in almanacs, and jokes and poems and maxims and odd facts of many sorts. The skimpy margins of the calendar pages were a diary. Children might learn to read from almanacs. The printer of a successful almanac could make money, and the compiler of it a reputation. Andrew Bradford had long issued the annual *American Almanac* of Titan Leeds. Another son of Daniel Leeds, Felix Leeds, was an almanac-maker too. Keimer had undertaken almanacs. And Franklin himself had published not only Thomas Godfrey's almanac for three years but also John Jerman's for 1731 and 1732.

Almanacs usually appeared in October or November for the following year. Franklin was late with his *Poor Richard, 1733*. The *Gazette* announced it as just published 19 December 1732 at five-pence a copy. Within three weeks there had had to be three impressions, and Richard

Saunders quickly passed all his rival philomaths. The imaginary astrologer probably took his full name from an actual English Richard Saunders, compiler of the *Apollo Anglicanus*, though Denham's account book lists a Philadelphia Richard Saunders as one of the firm's customers. The suggestion of the more common name Poor Richard may have come from the *Poor Robin* almanac which James Franklin was issuing at Newport. The prophecy in the first *Poor Richard* that Titan Leeds would die 17 October 1733 is a deliberate echo of Swift's hoax on John Partridge twenty-five years before—Swift's hoax brought to Pennsylvania and persisted in by Franklin for years. But the essence of Poor Richard, his humorous, homely character, was Franklin's own creation. Here are Richard's opening words: "I might in this place attempt to gain thy favour by declaring that I write almanacs with no other view than that of the public good; but in that I should not be sincere, and men are now-a-days too wise to be deceived by pretences how specious soever. The plain truth of the matter is, I am excessive poor, and my wife, good woman, is, I tell her, excessive proud; she cannot bear, she says, to sit spinning in her shift of tow while I do nothing but gaze at the stars; and has threatened more than once to burn all my books and rattling-traps (as she calls my instruments) if I do not make some profitable use of them for the good of my family. The printer has offered me some considerable share of the profits, and I have thus begun to comply with my dame's desire."

The next year Poor Richard was grateful for the profits he had made. "My wife has been enabled to get a pot of her own, and is no longer obliged to borrow one from a neighbour; nor have we ever since been without something of our own to put in it. She has also got a pair of shoes, two new shifts, and a new warm petticoat; and, for my part, I have bought a second-hand coat, so good that I am now not ashamed to go to town or be seen there. These things have rendered her temper so much more pacific than it used to be that I may say I have slept more, and more quietly, within this last year than in the three foregoing years put together." His verses on feminine idleness in his almanac for 1733 were answered by her verses on masculine worthlessness in the almanac for 1734. The little tiff was kept up between them. In *Poor Richard* for 1738 the preface appeared as by Bridget Saunders, who had scratched out what Richard had written. "Cannot I have a little fault or two but all the country must see it in print?" She had gone through the whole almanac in his absence and had put in better weather "for the goodwomen to dry their clothes in." Nor did she like some of his verses. He himself, he admitted in 1747, did not think too highly of them. "I know as well as thee that I am no poet born; and it is a trade I never learnt, nor indeed could learn." He did not claim infallibility in his weather forecasts. "We modestly desire only the favourable allowance of a day or two before and a day or two after the precise day against which the weather is set." Poor Richard was resentful toward people who said there was no such man as he. "This is not civil treatment, to endeavour to deprive me of my very being and reduce me to a nonentity in the opinion of the public. But so long as I know myself to walk about, eat, drink, and sleep, I am satisfied that there is really such a man as I am." People who began to say, after half a dozen years, that he must have grown rich were equally wrong. His printer "runs away with the greatest part of the profit." He suffered from the jealousy of rival philomaths, and was for ever pestered by persons who wanted private astrological advice from him. "The perpetual teasing of both neighbours and strangers to calculate nativities, give judgments on schemes, erect figures, discover thieves, detect horse-stealers, describe the route of runaways and strayed cattle; the crowd of visitors with a thousand trifling questions: Will my ship return safe? Will my mare win the race? Will her next colt be a pacer? When will my wife die? Who shall be my husband, and how long first? When is the best time to cut hair, trim cocks, or sow salad? These and the like impertinences I have now neither taste nor leisure for. I have had enough of 'em." He preferred to live quietly in the country, telling no one where.

The almanac for 1748 and afterwards was called *Poor Richard Improved*, and was larger than before. It had become an institution. It sold ten thousand copies a year. Franklin in 1757, writing his preface for 1758, skimmed his almanacs for twenty-five years to make up a single harangue which Poor Richard said he had heard an old man deliver at an auction. This is *The Way to Wealth*, which stands with the *Autobiography* as the best and the farthest known of all Franklin's writings, and which has been taken for the essence of his wisdom.

It is not that, and it gives only one aspect of the younger Franklin. Father Abraham at the auction is an old man talking about economy. He has chosen from Poor Richard the sayings which specially prove his point, and left out the rest. Having the last word, he has had almost the only word. *The Way to Wealth* has been endlessly reprinted, while the original almanacs were most of them worn out and thrown away, and the few that have survived are guarded like the bullion they are worth. Everybody knows the Poor Richard that has been saved in Father Abraham's speech. Nobody knows Poor Richard as he was in the racy years which made him known to his contemporaries. Franklin, remembering, said he had filled "all the little spaces" with "proverbial sentences, chiefly such as inculcated industry and frugality, as the means of procuring wealth and thereby securing virtue." Poor Richard for 1739 had put the matter differently. "Be not thou disturbed, O grave and sober reader, if among the many serious sentences in my book thou findest me trifling now and then, and talking idly. In all the dishes I have hitherto cooked for thee, there is solid meat enough for thy money. There are scraps from the table of wisdom that will, if well digested, yield strong nourishment to thy mind. But squeamish stomachs cannot eat without pickles; which, 'tis true, are good for nothing else, but they provoke an appetite."

The earlier Poor Richard was by no means always on the side of calculating prudence. "Never spare the parson's wine nor the baker's pudding" (1733). "Innocence is its own defence" (1733). "As charms are nonsense, nonsense is a charm" (1734). "What one relishes, nourishes" (1734). "He does not possess wealth; it possesses him" (1734). "Avarice and happiness never saw each other. How then should they become acquainted?" (1734). "Poverty wants some things, luxury many things, avarice all things" (1735). "There's more old drunkards than old doctors" (1736). "Wealth is not his that has it, but his that enjoys it" (1736). "He that can take rest is greater than he that can take cities" (1737). "Hast thou virtue? Acquire also the graces and beauties of virtue" (1738).

Poor Richard could say: "Nothing but money is sweeter than honey" (1735), but he spoke of many things besides. "Kings and bears often worry their keepers" (1733). "Hunger never saw bad bread" (1733). "Eat to live, and not live to eat" (1733). "Men and melons are hard to know" (1733). "There is no little enemy" (1733). "He's a fool that makes his doctor his heir" (1733). "The heart of the fool is in his mouth, but the mouth of the wise man is in his heart" (1733). "He that drinks fast pays slow" (1733). "Do good to thy friend to keep him, to thy enemy to gain him" (1734). "Where there's marriage without love there will be love without marriage" (1734). "He that is rich need not live sparingly, and he that can live sparingly need not be rich" (1734). "Approve not of him who commends all you say" (1735). "The family of fools is ancient" (1735). "Look before or you'll find yourself behind" (1735). "A lie stands on one leg, truth on two" (1735). "Sloth and silence are a fool's virtues" (1735). "Deny self for self's sake" (1735). "Opportunity is the great bawd" (1735). "An old young man will be a young old man" (1735). "He is no clown that drives the plough, but he that doth clownish things" (1736). "Now I have a sheep and a cow, everybody bids me good morrow" (1736).

"The rotten apple spoils his companions" (1736). "Fish and visitors stink in three days" (1736). "He that has neither fools nor beggars among his kindred is the son of thunder-gust" (1736). "Admiration [wonder] is the daughter of ignorance" (1736). "Bargaining has neither friends nor relations" (1736). "He that can have patience can have what he will" (1736). "None preaches better than the ant, and she says nothing" (1736). "The absent are never without fault, nor the present without excuse" (1736). "Poverty, poetry, and new titles of honour make men ridiculous" (1736). "A country-man between two lawyers is like a fish between two cats" (1737). "Love and lordship hate companions" (1737). "There are no ugly loves nor handsome prisons" (1737). "The worst wheel of the cart makes the most noise" (1737). "Write with the learned, pronounce with the vulgar" (1738). "If you would not be forgotten as soon as you are dead and rotten, either write things worth reading or do things worth the writing" (1738). "Defer not thy well doing; be not like St. George, who is always a-horseback and never rides on" (1738). "As we must account for every idle word, so we must for every idle silence" (1738). "Fly pleasures and they'll follow you" (1738). "Time is an herb that cures all diseases" (1738). "He that would have a short Lent, let him borrow money to be repaid at Easter" (1738). "Eat to please thyself, but dress to please others" (1738). "The ancients tell us what is best; but we must learn from the moderns what is fittest" (1738).

Poor Richard in these gamy years spoke often of women, tenderly and cynically in turn. "A house without a woman and firelight is like a body without soul or sprite" (1733).

> You cannot pluck roses without fear of thorns,
> Nor enjoy a fair wife without danger of horns (1734).

"Neither a fortress nor a m——d will hold out long after they begin to parley" (1734). "Marry your son when you will, but your daughter when you can" (1734). "A little house well filled, a little field well tilled, and a little wife well willed, are great riches" (1735).

> When ♂ [Mars] and ♀ [Venus] in conjunction lie,
> Then, maids, whate'er is asked of you deny (1735).

"A ship under sail and a big-bellied woman are the handsomest two things that can be seen common" (1735). "Let thy maidservant be faithful, strong, and homely" (1736). "He that takes a wife takes care" (1736). "Why does the blind man's wife paint herself?" (1736). "Keep your eyes wide open before marriage, half shut afterwards" (1738).

These varied sayings run through *Poor Richard* side by side with the stricter—and some of them later—maxims of prudence that Franklin put into Father Abraham's summary. (Those marked with a star are thought to be original with Franklin.) "Fools make feasts, and wise men eat them" (1733). "Early to bed and early to rise makes a man healthy, wealthy, and wise" (1735). "Keep thy shop, and thy shop will keep thee" (1735). "God helps them that help themselves" (1736). "Creditors have better memories than debtors" (1736). *"An empty bag cannot stand upright" (1740). *"The sleeping fox catches no poultry. Up! Up!" (1743). *"If you'd have it done, go; if not, send" (1743). *"Experience keeps a dear school, yet fools will learn in no other" (1743). *"The used key is always bright" (1744). "When the well's dry, we know the worth of water" (1746). "For want of a nail the shoe is lost; for want of a shoe the horse is lost; for want of a horse the rider is lost" (1752). "In the affairs of this world, men are saved not by faith but by the want of it" (1754). *"Three removes is as bad as a fire." (1758).

Poor Richard took wisdom and wit where he could find them: from Dryden, Pope, Prior, Gay, Swift, Bacon, La Rochefoucauld, Rabelais, and many other known masters. There are sayings in Latin, Spanish, French, German, and Welsh. The rustic philosopher drew also on the stream of popular adages, whether already gathered into printed collections or still only current in ordinary speech. In this profusion and uncertainty of sources Poor Richard never hesitated to rework his texts to suit his purpose and his audience. Whatever passed through Franklin's mind brought away some of its qualities and its flavour. Writing, he thought, should be "smooth, clear, and short." The Scottish proverb: "Fat housekeepers make lean executors" he simplified to "A fat kitchen, a lean will" (1733). Another proverb ran in its Scottish version: "A gloved cat was never a good hunter"; and in an English version: "A muffled cat is no good mouser." Franklin sharpened it: "The cat in gloves catches no mice" (1754). To what had been: "Many strokes fell great oaks" Franklin gave a more pointed antithesis: "Little strokes fell great oaks" (1751). "Three may keep counsel if two of them are away" became in his handling more cynical, and plainer, as "Three may keep a secret if two of them are dead" (1735). There was a stock saying: "Good wits jump" which Swift put into the mouth of one of his foolish talkers in *Genteel and Ingenious Conversation*. Franklin laughingly dramatized it: "Great wits jump, says the poet, and hit his head against the post" (1735). "The king's cheese goes half away in parings" was an old fling at the wastefulness of courts. Franklin made another application: "The king's cheese is half wasted in parings;

but no matter, 'tis made of the people's milk" (1735). And in one of his proverbs Franklin, proverbial for prudence, took the imprudent side. An Italian proverb had been translated into English as: "It is better to have an egg today than tomorrow a hen." Thomas Fuller in 1732 had firmly turned it to: "It is better to have a hen tomorrow than an egg today." Franklin turned it back to the spendthrift: "An egg today is better than a hen tomorrow" (1734).

There is one larger example of Franklin's method with his sources. In the almanac for 1739 he gave a *True Prognostication* which came direct from the *Pantagruelian Prognostication* at the end of the Urquhart-Motteux version of Rabelais. Of the eclipses of the year Pantagruel says in a rush of words: "Saturn will be retrograde, Venus direct, Mercury unfixed as quicksilver. . . . For this reason the crabs will go sidelong and the rope-makers backward . . . bacon will run away from pease in Lent; the belly will waddle before; the bum will sit down first; there will be not a bean left in a twelfth-cake, nor an ace in a flush; the dice will not run as you wish, though you cog them . . . brutes shall speak in several places; Shrovetide will have its day . . . such a hurly-burly was never seen since the devil was a little boy; and there will be above seven-and-twenty irregular verbs made this year, if Priscian do not hold them in. If God do not help us, we shall have our hands and hearts full." Poor Richard, writing for cramped pages, had to be brief. Writing for Pennsylvania, he left out the Catholic and medieval touches in Pantagruel, and put American notes in their place. "During the first visible eclipse," he wrote, "Saturn is retrograde; for which reason the crabs will go sidelong and the rope-makers backward. The belly will wag before, and the a—— shall sit down first. Mercury will have his share in these affairs, and so confound the speech of people that when a Pennsylvanian would say *panther* he shall say *painter*. When a New Yorker thinks to say *this* he shall say *diss*. And the people in New England and Cape May will not be able to say *cow* for their lives, but will be forced to say *keow* by a certain involuntary twist in the root of their tongues. No Connecticut man nor Marylander will be able to open his mouth this year but *Sir* shall be the first or the last syllable he pronounces, and sometimes both. Brutes shall speak in many places, and there will be above seven-and-twenty irregular verbs made this year, if grammar don't interpose— Who can help these misfortunes!" And so on through the prognostication, fitting the original to fresh uses.

Franklin, creating the character of Poor Richard, also assumed it, as another role like that of the complete tradesman. The rising philosopher could not be for ever in his leather apron, behind his conscious wheelbarrow. He wanted to speak out. Young, he might not be listened to in his own person. As Poor Richard he had a dramatic licence to speak as he chose. He could pretend to be an astrologer and yet make fun of superstition. He could pretend to be old and wise, packing his almanac with wisdom in the verses and proverbs which were all he had space for. If he laid frequent stress on prudence, that was in part because the folk-wisdom on which he drew is largely prudence, which is the ordinary wisdom of ordinary men. At the same time, Franklin believed in prudence. He was not a mystic but a moralist, and the first law of his nature was order. Order in human life, he held, begins in the daily habits of men looking out for themselves. They must work to be happy, and save to be secure. There were plenty of mysteries about men, but industry and frugality were not mysterious. A man who practised them might go beyond them to more important things, as Franklin aimed to. Industry and frugality were the simple, natural road to freedom.

Franklin could see that the times called for Poor Richard's counsel. Philadelphia had not yet become what he helped to make it. Besides the orderly Quakers and Germans there were many immigrants to that hopeful town who had been misfits in Europe and did not soon adjust themselves in America. They looked for the sudden riches they had been told about. They hunted for buried treasure. Disappointed, they drifted off to the back country or to the West Indies. Because some men profited by speculation, many men speculated, wasting time and money. In the shortage of skilled labour, so much work was badly done that the pride of craftsmanship was lost. People who had had no chance to save in England did not learn to save in Pennsylvania. They waited for miracles. Franklin, bred in settled Boston, felt that Philadelphia must be industrious and frugal before it could be anything else. This middle way was the way of the new world. Few men of privilege had come from Europe to America. They had not needed to emigrate. Few of the helpless European poor had come. They had not been able to. The colonists were "middling people" and they must work and save if they were to survive and prosper. Franklin as Poor Richard was merely insisting that the first thing to build in their house was the plain foundation. But with how much wit and charm he insisted!

XLIV

NOAH WEBSTER, SCHOOLMASTER TO AMERICA[1]

By

HARRY R. WARFEL

Harry Warfel's biography of Noah Webster, the great American lexicographer and journalist, is a well-balanced and important contribution to America's cultural and educational history.

Noah Webster (1758-1843) was the son of a Connecticut farmer who mortgaged his farm to send Noah to Yale. After graduation he taught school, studied law and was admitted to the bar. In 1783-85 he published *A Grammatical Institute of the English Language* in three parts—a spelling book, a grammar, and a reader. This was the first American work of its kind, and it soon found a place in the schools of the United States. While Webster worked on his dictionary, the famous spelling book was the principal source of income for his family. Before 1861 the sale of the spelling book had reached more than a million copies a year.

The American Dictionary, which came out in 1828, over a quarter of a century after it was first announced, contained 12,000 words and from 30,000 to 40,000 definitions that had not appeared in any previous dictionary.

Harry Warfel has chosen the following passage from his biography because he believes "the brief character sketch here set down adequately points up the main features" of Noah Webster.

HE MADE WORDS MARCH LIKE WARRIORS AGAINST IGNORANCE

On his seventieth birthday, October 16, 1828, Noah Webster lifted his eyes from the last proof sheet of the scholarly Introduction to his Diction-

[1] Harry R. Warfel, *Noah Webster, Schoolmaster to America*, by permission of The Macmillan Company, publishers, New York, 1936, pp. 1-4.

ary. Slowly he wiped the ink from the quill, laid it down, and methodically capped the inkwell. His moist eyes blinked. He turned to his wife and colleague, caught her hands. Together they knelt by the desk and prayed tremblingly in giving thanks to God for His providence in sustaining them through their long labor. Since June 4, 1800, when the project was first publicly announced, Webster had dandled his book on his knee to the tune of a public lullaby of jeers, insults, and misrepresentation. Every opprobrious epithet in the vocabularies of calumny and abuse had been showered upon him. Undeterred by it, he had completed single-handed America's first monumental work of scholarship. *An American Dictionary of the English Language* was immediately acclaimed, in England and Germany as well as in America, the best work of its kind ever prepared.

Today, *Webster* and *dictionary* are synonymous terms in our language. No tribute can surpass this one.

Yet, curiously enough, although the name *Webster* is on the tip of every person's tongue who wants to consult that indispensable reference book, the dictionary, few can give the lexicographer's first name. When asked the question, the average informed person looks blank a moment, then hesitantly ventures, 'Daniel, I guess.' Thus Noah Webster, who eminently deserves a niche in the Hall of Fame, not only is not memorialized in that pantheon, but has suffered an even worse fate: his name has coalesced with that of the famous orator and statesman who was not even his kinsman.

Like Dr. Samuel Johnson, whose dictionary lost ground as Webster's gained, Noah Webster was more than a 'harmless drudge,' a writer of definitions. Before announcing his dictionary at the age of forty-two, Noah Webster had become the pivotal figure in American education and literature. As the author of a series of primary school textbooks and as the expounder of a nationalistic theory of education, he had become the young nation's first schoolmaster. As an itinerant propagandist for a Constitution, he had done more than any other single individual to prepare a climate of opinion in which a Constitutional Convention could be successful. As a clear-visioned economist, a humanitarian, a magazine and newspaper editor, a historical scholar, and a moralist, he ceaselessly drove his pen in furthering the best interests of his country. Although he completed the Dictionary in 1828, he never surrendered work until death called him in his eighty-fifth year, May 28, 1843.

Something of the many-sided intellectual quality of Benjamin Franklin reappeared in Webster. Both possessed astonishing versatility and delved into every area of knowledge, leaving marks of influence in almost every field of activity developed in their times. It was fitting that Franklin, in his old age, befriended the young schoolmaster and tutored him in simplified spelling. But Webster, unlike Franklin, did not permanently slough off the iron mantle of New England Calvinism. And Webster never sought or obtained high political position. Essentially a scholar and publicist, Webster wielded his pen as a weapon in the perennial warfare against social injustice, scientific error, mental torpor, and national instability. Early in life he called himself The Prompter, the man who sits behind the scenes to correct errors or assist the memory.

Webster became our greatest schoolmaster. He passed successively from the desk of a Connecticut log schoolhouse to the lecture platform, to the editorial chair, and finally to the home library table as the arbiter of every English-speaking reader's and writer's diction. His schoolbooks were carried from the hills of New England across the Alleghenies; his were among the first books printed in every new settlement. Across the prairies and over the Rocky Mountains his carefully marshaled columns of words marched like warriors against the ignorance that tended to disrupt the primitive society of thinly spread and localized culture of America. Dialect variation disappeared from our writing and spelling, and to his blue-backed Speller, of which nearly one hundred million copies were sold before it went out of general use, America owes its remarkable uniformity of language. No other book, the Bible excepted, has strained so many heads, or done so much good. It taught millions to read, and not one to sin. And today the monolithic 'Webster' on every schoolteacher's desk, on the reference tables of libraries, at the elbow of the justice, and on the study table of the scholar, bears silent testimony to Noah Webster's enduring labors and superb genius.

Patient, indefatigable laborer for American cultural advancement that Webster was, he yet never won the warm personal sympathy of his countrymen. A pugnaciousness in propagating his own strongly phrased ideas, a gesture many people considered egotistic, rendered Webster socially unattractive. His tall, spare, Yankee form stiffened under opposition. His massive head grew rigidly upright in an inflexible ambition to do good. The mountainous forehead, crowned with a forest of autumn-tinted hair, sloped to beetling crags of eyebrows. Deep set, as in a cave, small gray eyes flashed lightning warnings of intense mental operations. A massive square jaw and a jutting nose persuaded opponents that here was one endowed by nature to hold his own against any and all opposition. The narrow, thin line of lips held taut a tongue ever ready to castigate error. 'If my name is a terror to evildoers,' Webster once wrote, 'mention it.' In this respect, too, Webster was the typical schoolmaster, the man who is more concerned to have lessons well learned than to secure the adulation of shirking, fawning ignorance.

XLV

FIVE AND TEN: THE FABULOUS LIFE OF F. W. WOOLWORTH [1]

By

JOHN K. WINKLER

Frank W. Woolworth (1852-1919) and the world-famous "Five and Tens" are inseparable, and thus this book is the biography of both. The story is exciting and reveals the history of Mr. Woolworth's struggles and the growth of this widely known business. The passage given here shows some of the difficulties the business had in its earlier days.

THREE OUT OF FIVE FAILED

Woolworth's first venture was a failure. It soon would be a question of either closing his little store or having creditors do it for him.

The latter alternative was intolerable. He would close the store himself. But then—what next? Should he return to Watertown, tail between his legs, and beg back his old job of Moore & Smith? Or should he struggle on with his pet ambition to become an independent merchant?

It was a tough problem for a young man of twenty-seven, in debt and with a wife and child to look after. He pondered the situation during many a wakeful night in his Utica boarding house. Upon his decision depended his whole future and that of his little family.

The more he thought, the more he became convinced that his failure in Utica was due not to himself or to his idea, but mainly due to the poor location of his store and Utica itself, where trading was generally slack at the time. However, he did see one handicap in the five-cent idea—merchandise to sell at that figure was extremely limited. If he could increase

[1] John K. Winkler, *Five and Ten: The Fabulous Life of F. W. Woolworth*, New York: Robert M. McBride & Company, 1940, pp. 49-54, 57.

the figure to ten cents the range would be much wider. Surely there were other communities that would appreciate inexpensive goods. If he could find one, he would choose his location more carefully and he was certain he would succeed. And find such a town he would, before resigning himself to clerking for some other man for the rest of his life.

Accordingly, on May 28, he drew $30 from the bank and set out on another scouting expedition. This trip had a more direct objective than his journey of four months before. For a friend in whom he had confidence had given such a glowing account of Lancaster, Pennsylvania, a live, growing city inhabited largely by thrifty Pennsylvania Dutch, that he determined to survey that city at once. . . .

"I reached Lancaster about dusk on a train from Philadelphia," recalled Woolworth forty years later. "As it happened, this was the very best time I could have arrived, for I saw Lancaster when it was at its best for my purpose. I was amazed as I walked up from the depot to see the crowds on the streets. I had never seen anything like it. The sidewalks were jammed with people, the stores were filled with customers, lights were blazing, and there was an amazing air of business and prosperity. In size, the town did not differ greatly from Utica, but the part of it in which I now found myself was radically different from the part of Utica where my store was located. Right away, I felt that Lancaster was the place for me.

"After spending a couple of hours walking around the business part of the city, and getting my supper in a cheap restaurant, I found a hotel—a vile old one it was, too—where I got lodgings for fifty cents. Early next morning I started out to find a vacant store, and at Number 170 North Queen street I found one that promised to meet my requirements. After concluding arrangements for the place, I took the first train for Utica, arriving there almost stranded financially, but with my hopes renewed and my purpose strong."

There was still the problem of getting out of Utica with clean heels, and of obtaining sufficient cash or credit to stock the new store. Fortunately, there was enough cash in the bank to pay the Utica bills; and Moore & Smith, in response to a glowing letter from Woolworth, offered him additional credit up to $300. For William H. Moore it was bread cast upon the waters. . . .

Woolworth locked his door in Utica on June 11, and opened his modest Lancaster location exactly ten days later. The date, June 21, 1879, marks the launching of the first successful (and what is now the oldest) five-and-ten-cent store in the world. Also, it was the first store to deal exclusively in five-*and-ten*-cent merchandise. Although Woolworth retained for a time the Great Five Cent Store sign, other signs over the 14-foot Lancaster front read: "5 and 10 Cent Store" and "Woolworth's 5 and 10 cent store."

On opening day, the Lancaster store carried $410 worth of stock—the left-over Utica goods plus Moore & Smith's new shipment. Thirty per cent of the stock was sold the first day, and Woolworth felt he had a winner. At once he began to plan expansion. . . .

The Lancaster store continued to prove highly popular with the Pennsylvania Dutch housewives, and Proprietor Woolworth fondled his expansion ideas. He kept his overhead expenses to a minimum, watching his clerks like a hawk for breakage and theft, working them long hours and at low wages. He figured expenses to the penny. Packages were wrapped in old newspapers which he bought at two cents a pound from a local newspaper and lugged to the store on his shoulders. Standard wrapping paper still cost eight cents a pound.

"Mr. Woolworth sat on the platform of a winding stairway at the back of the store, guarding the sales box and watching the clerks at work," says Mrs. Susan Kane of Lancaster, only surviving member of Woolworth's original sales force. "There were three of us and we were paid $1.50 a week. We were not assigned to any particular one of the counters, which lined the large center aisle, but just followed the customers around. After we made a sale we walked back to Mr. Woolworth to get change. He entered each sale on a tablet and added up at night. Our best sellers were tinware, toys, washbasins, wash towels, handkerchiefs and ribbons."

The result of the proprietor's economies and careful management soon showed in a fattening bank balance; and early in July Woolworth wrote his brother in Watertown that he had taken a store in Harrisburg, thirty-five miles from Lancaster. . . .

The Harrisburg store was a repetition of the Utica experiment. Opening July 19, the tiny emporium enjoyed a first day's sale of $85.41; and for several weeks kept up a good pace. Then came a steady decline, broken only by a sales revival during Christmas week. Finally, in March, 1880, Woolworth decided to give it up and seek a new pasture. . . .

For his new location, Woolworth settled upon York, Pennsylvania, and opened there April 3, 1880. . . .

The York store, too, was tiny with pocket-size show windows, and, like Utica and Harrisburg it started out with a flourish. . . .

When sales evaporated to a rock-bottom low of $3.05 on June 25, Woolworth decided to add York to his other defeats.

"In my three months in York, we sold about $1,000 worth of goods," recalls C. S. Woolworth. "Our net profit was exactly $36. We shut up shop in York the last day in June, shipped what stock we had there to Lancaster and I went to work in the Lancaster store. But we had no thought of resting on our oars. In our spare time that summer we traveled all over the surrounding territory, looking for another good location, and finally decided to make our next bid in Scranton, Pa. The Scranton store became the second oldest five-and-ten-cent in the world and Scranton was a good choice for me. I've been here ever since." . . .

"By the end of 1880 I was so rich that I decided to take the first vacation I had ever enjoyed," Frank Woolworth reminisced years later when his stores numbered hundreds. "I was worth $2,000, which looked bigger to me then than $20,000,000 would now. In fact, I felt quite as rich then as I do now because I had the consciousness and satisfaction of having made a success in business."

XLVI

LORDS OF THE LEVEE [1]

By

LLOYD WENDT AND HERMAN KOGAN

Bathhouse John Coughlin and Hinky Dink Kenna, political bosses of Chicago's First Ward, in which the levee was located in the 1880's and 1890's, are the "lords" of this candidly written book. The authors vividly portray the lives and activities of these "lords of the levee" as they played their part in the conduct of municipal government in a great city. The story is as exciting as fiction, as full of suspense and violence as a murder mystery, and yet is a valuable study of the problems of local government. Through its pages stride the fantastic Bathhouse John (nicknamed "Bathhouse" because he was at one time a rubber in a Turkish bath) accompanied by the diminutive, but shrewd and able political adviser, Hinky Dink Kenna, once a bootblack, but in this story a prosperous saloon-keeper (the nickname "Hinky Dink" having been received because of his small stature).

The authors describe the passage which they have selected from their fascinating story as follows: "It deals with the First Ward election of 1894, when Bathhouse John made his first bid for re-election. His foe was Billy Skakel, the fierce Civil War veteran, who once had supported Coughlin but, because Bathhouse balked Skakel's attempts to get a free hand in running bucket shops in the ward, now tried to unseat our Hero. The election was a terrific, violent, brawling affair and, in its violence and vote thievery and strategy, pretty well set the pattern for future voting days in the First (and other) wards."

"WE'RE GOIN' PLACES, YOU AN' ME"

Three weeks to the day after Stead's account of civic rottenness burst upon the city, the top Democrats of the First Ward shuffled to the bar of

[1] Lloyd Wendt and Herman Kogan, *Lords of the Levee*, copyright 1943, used by special permission of the publishers, The Bobbs-Merrill Company, Indianapolis, pp. 97-108.

Mike Kenna's saloon for a political conference. They gulped their beer and gorged themselves on the free lunch and discoursed, meanwhile, in subdued tones. Then at a shout from Tom McNally they left and trooped to a meeting hall at 224 West Van Buren Street, around the corner from Hinky Dink's, to name the aldermanic candidate for the coming term.

Here they fretted and stamped about. Finally Bathhouse John rolled in and there was a great cheer. Then, to begin the briefest political convention in Chicago's history, Johnny Morris leaped to a chair.

"Johnny Coughlin!" he yelled. "Johnny Coughlin! It's Johnny Coughlin we want for alderman again!"

Others joined in the cry and The Bath grinned and waved his hands above his head. Tom McNally, serving as chairman, rapped with his gavel, a bung starter he had picked up at Hinky Dink's, and Morris formally and with great dignity placed Coughlin's name before the assemblage.

"Any further nominations?" asked McNally.

There were none. McNally whacked the gavel once again. The meeting was adjourned and the delegates filed out hastily, still calling, "Hurray for Johnny Coughlin! Hurray for Bathhouse John!"

Again Bathhouse waved his hands and shouted his thanks; then he strode off with McNally and Hinky Dink to a hack stand.

The *Herald* reporter present returned to his office and wrote for the morning's edition:

John J. Coughlin was renominated for the council last night by the Democratic convention of the First Ward. The convention session lasted only a few minutes as the delegates were in a hurry to get away to attend a prize fight.

Two of the leading members of First Ward Democracy were absent from the gathering. Sol van Praag and Billy Skakel had sulked at Billy Boyle's, telling all who paused at their table of their intention to put an end to the political career of Bathhouse John.

Skakel's hatred stemmed from the early days of the young alderman's term, when, with the sanction and protection of Coughlin, Prince Hal Varnell had opened two bucket shops, one at 126 West Washington Street, and another at 116 West Monroe Street, which had cut heavily into the monopoly enjoyed by Skakel with his four similar establishments.[2]

[2] Skakel's operators daily drafted a list of stock quotations presumably based on bona fide trading in western mining shares. Actually, the quotations were completely fictitious. They were listed on a huge blackboard every fifteen minutes and the bucket-shop players bet on their ability to guess whether the next figures would be higher or lower. Since about 300 deals in each of five stocks were "quoted," there were 1,500 chances for action each day and the house took twenty-five cents for each two dollars played.

Coughlin had ignored Skakel's demand that he call on the authorities to stop Varnell, and The Clock, who was far from being the most even-tempered man in the First Ward, thenceforth had regarded The Bath as a mortal foe. Van Praag's interest in defeating Coughlin was more impersonal, but no less impelling, for he envisioned himself and Skakel, rather than Bathhouse John and Hinky Dink, as the fit rulers of the flourishing realm of gambling houses, saloons and bagnios.

Early on the morning following the nominating convention Skakel summoned the newspaper reporters.

"Coughlin's no good," he bellowed. "I asked him to do a few t'ings fer me an' he never done them. He never done a t'ing fer th' party. I'm runnin'. I'm gonna smash him. That bathhouse rubber ain't gonna never be alderman no more. I'll beat that dirty bum!"

With their Carter H. Harrison Club of the First Ward as a nucleus Skakel and van Praag formed the Independent Democratic party and began working with a fury that sent The Bath running fretfully from McNally to Morris to Kenna.

McNally and Morris were as glum as Coughlin, but Hinky Dink's gimlet eyes blinked rapidly and his jaw set. "We ain't gonna be beat by that Billy Skakel, boys," he assured them. "He won't win."

Skakel scoffed at the midget Hink and boasted of his huge campaign fund. He blandly admitted that he was making offers of five dollars a vote where that kind of money was needed, and he told delighted newspapermen: "We're gonna spend money like water. We got plenty."

The political reporters, coming away from the thronged meetings of the Carter H. Harrison Club of the First Ward with the shouts of the Skakel enthusiasts still pounding in their ears, convinced themselves that Coughlin's aldermanic career was approaching its finish.

One newspaper, the *Herald*, even predicted that The Bath would garner fewer votes than the First Ward's Republican candidate, J. Irving Pearce, the mild-mannered owner of the Sherman House. The *Herald's* political editor forecast:

Alderman Coughlin is apparently hopelessly beaten. As matters now stand, he will do no better than third at the finish.

All the other publications, and notably *Mixed Drinks: The Saloon Keeper's Journal*, were voluble in their praise of Bathhouse John's foe. In a front-page column, adjoining one offering a prize rum-drink recipe, that periodical impressively characterized Skakel as

. . . the patriotic soldier who fought to preserve the union and who is now one of the most progressive business lights of our proud Chicago. His election will crush the most infamous autocratic rule that is now threatening to disrupt the Democratic party.

Coughlin paid close heed to the newspapers and what he read appalled him. Refusing to be cheered by Kenna's calm insistence that Skakel would not win, Coughlin hustled to Mayor Hopkins to plead for help. The mayor called Skakel to his office.

"Billy," he said, "I'm asking you to get out of the race. You're hurting the party."

"Nuthin' doin'," retorted Skakel. "I'm th' next boss in the First Ward an' you might as well know it now."

The much-disturbed Bathhouse then sought aid from his attorneys, and Moses Salomon, the erudite state senator from Chicago's First District, plunged into his law books. A week before election day he came forward with a device which he thought might thwart the gambler. He had uncovered a city law which barred any man convicted of a crime from municipal office. Skakel, it was promptly recalled, had been arrested a few years back for gambling and had been fined.

Coughlin and Salomon rushed to the election board, bearing a petition for the erasure of Skakel's name from the ballot. Without granting Skakel a hearing the Hopkins-controlled board, after solemnly considering the charges, held the petition to be legal and proper, and ordered the deletion of Skakel's name.

The action enraged the Skakelites. It was adjudged a blow below the belt. "That fat bathhouse rubber!" blubbered Billy The Clock. "He'll never be alderman again. Sure, I'm a gambler. I don't deny that. But I'm a better man than Bathhouse was or ever will be. I never took a bribe! What can Bathhouse say about that, eh?"

"He never had the chance," countered Bathhouse John. But his seeming blitheness did not reflect the general gloom in his camp over the possibility of his defeat. The election-board trick was not well taken in the First Ward, where men were sensitive concerning their pasts and where political ethics demanded that no public display be made of a man's relations with the police department. Faithful supporters of Coughlin were alienated. Big Sandy Walters was the first to leave.

After a tussle with his conscience, Walters sought out Coughlin in the campaign headquarters and lamented: "Johnny, I didn't ever t'ink you'd do a t'ing like dat, tell on a guy what got t'rowed in th' bink. I ain't wid you no more. Billy an' Sol, they're gonna finish you off. Billy'll be back on th' sheet t'morrow, an' we're gonna give you a trimmin'."

And on the next morning a battery of seven attorneys, including young Clarence Darrow, appeared before County Judge Frank Scales with Skakel and van Praag and a throng of subordinates in the rear. The striking of Skakel's name from the ballot, argued the legal staff, had been improper, illegal, and unconstitutional.

"Yeh, Judge," the gambler chimed in. "It was unfair. Sure I was convicted for gamblin', judge. But it was only a small fine. It really didn't amount to nothin'."

Judge Scales, a virtuous Republican, nodded sympathetically. "Since when," he demanded, "is a man deprived of the right to serve the people merely because of some forgotten misdemeanor? I believe the election board has overstepped its authority. The petition of Mr. Skakel is granted and the board of election commissioners is restrained from removing his name from the ballot."

The Skakel followers greeted this decision with joyous acclamations. They hoisted Billy to their shoulders and carried him in triumph to the street. Coughlin followers spied the procession and hastened to report to Bathhouse John, who morosely complained that it was a trick of the Republican party. He moped about headquarters until the exasperated Hinky Dink finally exclaimed: "Cut it out, John. That Skakel ain't gonna get elected. Don't be a pansy."

While Bathhouse John had been seeking to destroy Skakel before the board of election commissioners, Hinky Dink, with a fine distaste for the involved legal processes, had been more practical. He had evolved an elaborate plan for the re-election of his bulky friend, a plan born as he observed the hungry shuffling before his free lunch counter in the winter of '93.

He knew humans, this little Hinky Dink, and he readily perceived that the favors he had done for the thousands of bums and tramps and respectable homeless men could be easily returned in the field of political action at the cost of no more than the slight effort of balloting. Moreover, the men whose votes were solicited would be grateful and flattered, for they were thereby given standing in the community. Hinky Dink had a simple and basic political philosophy: favors and benevolence produced votes; organization brought them out. While Bathhouse John had been running from Mayor Hopkins to the election board, from adviser to adviser, Hinky Dink had been busily at work, perfecting his organization, issuing calls to the sans-culottes, putting his theories to practical test.

Into the ward from all parts of the city had poured the grateful dregs. They were housed and fed and supplied with plenty of beer. They scorned the glib Skakel promises of five dollars a vote on election day for the snug security of a sawdust-covered floor, fifty cents for their vote, and all the sausages, bread, cheese and lager they could hold. Into The Bath's own precinct Kenna piled 300 additional voters to be registered. Some slept in Coughlin's bathhouse, on the benches or in the steam rooms. Precinct captains like Mike Lawler and Joe Friedman rounded up hundreds of others and transformed their saloons into lodging houses. Cheap hotels, flop joints, deserted buildings, brothels, saloons, empty warehouses, even railroad freight stations—these were the forts where Hinky Dink marshaled the Coughlin voting forces, to await the time when they should march out in the interests of their benefactor. When registration day was over, The First Ward had 8,397 voters on the books—almost twice the number that had balloted in the previous mayoralty election. Skakel howled to the election board, but his protests were ignored.

There was more to Kenna's plan than the mere colonization of voters. He advised Coughlin, as election day approached, to pay another visit to Mayor Hopkins. "The mayor oughta be reminded how we helped him in the election," he suggested. This Coughlin hastened to do, and on the afternoon preceding the election the mayor made his final appeal to Skakel.

"NO!" Billy roared.

Mayor Hopkins shrugged. "There might be a lot of trouble tomorrow, Billy, and I might not be responsible."

Shortly after Skakel departed, Captain Jack Hartnett, head of the First District police, conferred briefly with Mayor Hopkins. That night, at the Harrison Street police station, Lieutenant Charles Holden summoned a group of stalwarts slated for election detail in the First Ward.

"Listen, boys," said the lieutenant, "I don't want you to be taking any part in this election, but the man who always looks out for the First Ward police over there in the city hall needs our help."

The squads went to work that very night. Men wearing Skakel buttons were heaved into cells. Saloonkeepers who displayed Skakel campaign pictures were forced to close promptly at midnight. Equipment in gaming houses owned by pro-Skakel gamblers was confiscated and destroyed. Into the south end of the ward, the district of colored voters hostile to Bathhouse John for aiding in the defense of Policeman Tom Kinsella who had killed a Negro several months back, went plain-clothes detectives.

"Either you line up behind the Bathhouse," they told the crapgame operators, barrelhouse proprietors and panders, "or you get closed up."

While the police were doing their share to create a Coughlin victory, Kenna sought to assure himself further that his loyal voters would go unmolested to the polls the following morning. Besting van Praag, who had a similar idea, by only a few hours, Kenna acquired the services of the dread Quincy Street gang, composed of some of the toughest strong-arm men, bouncers and rowdies in the First Ward. These hoodlums, led by Johnny Dee, a professional slugger, were directed to serve as a roving squad for the protection of Coughlin voters. The police, Dee was informed, would be looking the other way should self-defense entail the application of billies, blackjacks or brass knuckles on bellicose Skakelites.

Shortly after dawn on election day, an hour before the polls were to open, a carriage rolled away from the saloon headquarters of the Quincy Street gang. Aboard were Dee and his brother Dave, a State Street saloon bouncer; Louis Rabshaw, a punchdrunk prizefighter; Jack McCarthy, gambler and slugger; Thomas Kerwin, a big-muscled bridge tender; and Thomas Hanon, a neighborhood tough. Through the precincts the carriage whirled, its occupants on the lookout for anyone wearing a Skakel button or daring to hoist a Skakel banner.

"Coughlin's men," read a report later in the *Tribune*, "went after Skakelites like hungry hyenas in a traveling circus at an evening meal of raw steak. Nowhere was any man wearing a Skakel badge safe from the onslaught of the Quincy Street boys and their cohorts."

The first of the many encounters occurred in the McCoy Hotel on Clark Street, owned by Colonel William McCoy, a friend of Bathhouse John and a rabid Irish patriot.[3] At the entrance Dee's men perceived five Skakelites, doubtlessly bent on evil, for McCoy was a vociferous Coughlin backer.

The carriage halted and Dee and the others leaped out after the Skakel men, who fled into the hotel lobby. Clubs and blackjacks began swinging, furniture was overturned, and a banister crashed to the floor. Colonel McCoy appeared, glanced quickly at the damage, and with an awful cry of rage joined in the fight. Some combatants drew revolvers, and bullets smashed into the gleaming woodwork. In ten minutes the quintet of Skakelites lay in a semi-conscious state on the floor while Dee's gang

[3] Years later McCoy was forced to sell the hotel, and the new owner called it The Victoria, after the Queen of England. This latter humiliation, it was said, hastened Colonel McCoy's death.

kicked them. When the police finally arrived, they glanced at the two sets of badge-wearers, seized the Skakelites and dumped them into the waiting patrol wagon. The Quincy Street Boys moved on.

At a polling place in the Fifth Precinct Rabshaw, eager to display the fistic talents that had brought him indifferent success in the ring, challenged the wearer of a Skakel button. The Skakelite was Solly Smith, who, unfortunately for Rabshaw, was a professional fighter himself. He knocked out his assailant with a single punch. The rest of the gang was about to beat Smith to insensibility when a policeman appeared and took him to jail.

As the voting began, the battle grew wild throughout the First. In the Sixteenth Precinct Toots Marshall, a Coughlin worker, and Sam Phelps, both colored, met and drew pistols. After blazing away for a few minutes both were wounded severely and were hauled away to the Bridewell hospital. In other sections of the ward each time the carriage of the Quincy Street Boys passed a wagon carrying Skakel supporters there was a furious exchange of revolver fire and the terrified pedestrians raced for safe cover.

The members of the Kenna army of floaters were roused from their sawdust beds, and they, along with ordinary citizens courageous enough to venture into the streets, hastened to the polls to exercise their democratic privilege. Lesser members of the Quincy Street gang, traveling in groups of four or five, came out to afford them protection. They prowled the streets, chasing Skakelites into hiding or into the safety of the police stations. Some of the men in the flying squads bore six-shooters, others baseball bats, and they used both frequently. Early in the afternoon one squad of the gang drew up to Hinky Dink's establishment, beat a colored Skakel watcher unconscious and handed him over to the police. Another Negro Skakelite known as Jumbo fled into the saloon, followed by the Quincy Streeters. He ran about in circles, jumped on the bar, broke several bottles, and finally sped back to the street, straight for a near-by police squad. The police clubbed him down and hauled Jumbo to the Harrison Street station, where he was charged with disturbing the peace.

Despite the terrible beatings and the odds against them the Skakel men were not weaklings. One group invaded Hinky Dink's saloon in a surprise onslaught and smashed beer barrels and whisky bottles. Coughlin sluggers came to the rescue and by late afternoon the floor was a foamy sea of beer and liquor. Skakel himself came to the saloon to plead with Hinky Dink for a respite from the slaughter. There was a grim silence when the gambler was blocked at the door by a drunken Quincy Street braggart named Pinky Kerwin, brother of Thomas. The two men eyed each other.

"I licked fifteen men today," sneered Kerwin.

"You touch me," stormed Skakel, "an' you'll die in that swill."

Kerwin backed away and Skakel was permitted to enter. Hinky Dink was elsewhere in the ward, however, and not only did the attempted armistice fail but in every precinct the fighting grew even more desperate. In the saloons those bouncers not yet enlisted for active street battle were kept busy chucking the demonstrative Skakel men into the gutters. In one Clark Street polling place five Quincy Street Boys were beset by a pair of Irishmen named Joe Kelly and Tom Connors. Both were good fighting men, but the gang's fury sent Kelly reeling into the street with a shattered jaw, and Connors against a doorpost, his skull split open. At the Eleventh Precinct polls on Harrison Street twelve Skakel men were arrested after a free-for-all.

Even after the polls closed the struggle continued. A quartet of Negro brothel bouncers named Butterface Jones, Make A Fuss Wilson, Sporting Billy Johnson, and Slick Sam Phillips had been armed by the Coughlin hoodlums with guns and baseball bats in addition to their usual razors. In Harmon Court, just off State Street, during the late-afternoon rush hour these worthies encountered a Skakel gang led by Fighting Billy Marshall, a notorious tough. The voting was over, but blood was hot. The two gangs charged. A crowd collected and soon grew to 3,000 persons. Slick Sam and Marshall began shooting at once while the others engaged with ball bats in hand-to-hand fighting. For blocks along State Street the cable cars were stalled while the rival gangsters beat, cut and shot at one another. A policeman fought his way through the throng, but was unable to halt the battle and turned in a riot call. Three squads of police responded and rushed into the crowd, clubbing indiscriminately. They provided the colored fighters a needed respite, and soon Marshall and his gang lay inert on the cobblestones. They were dumped into the patrol wagon and hauled off to jail, but the wounded Slick Sam was placed in another wagon and taken to the county hospital.

This was the final battle of the day except for minor barroom brawls. By evening, while election judges and clerks were busily tallying the votes, the newspapers made up casualty lists. They discovered that forty Skakel men had been wounded, two of them critically, and hundreds were in cells. Only six men in the Coughlin camp had been seriously injured; none had been arrested.

And out of the brawling and shooting and rioting and fighting, Alderman Coughlin emerged the victor. He collected 2,671 votes while Pearce ran second with 1,261 and Skakel trailed third with 1,046. Whether the rest of the 8,379 registered voters were some of Kenna's floaters who failed to do their duty or duly qualified First Ward residents who feared to visit the polling places, no one, not even the astute Hinky Dink, could determine.

Chicago, accustomed to violent election days, generally agreed that the carnage in the First Ward had exceeded all previous horrors. The *Tribune's* comment summed up the general feeling:

There have been elections in Chicago and there have been elections, but yesterday's fight between the followers of Bathhouse John and Billy Skakel was a world beater. Clubs were trump, and the police carried the clubs. Bathhouse John's election was secured by methods which would have disgraced even the worst river parishes of Louisiana.

The men of the Civic Federation and the Union League Club shook their heads and deplored "the grossness and illegality of yesterday's election in the First Ward." Mayor Hopkins was attacked and accused of ordering the partisan conduct of the police, and although he was firm in his denials, few believed him. Even gang aldermen in other wards shuddered and looked upon Bathhouse John as some sort of wild man.

But Alderman Coughlin was unmoved by the horrified criticism of press and pulpit. He had been re-elected. There were great days in store for him, he told his followers, and he hugged little Hinky Dink in a maudlin display of gratitude.

"You're a great little guy, Mike, you're a great little guy," chortled The Bath, his eyes filled with tears. "We're goin' places, you an' me."

Kenna was not one to become emotional, but he smiled wryly once or twice and slapped Coughlin's ample back. "We'll see, John," he answered. "You're in again; now get goin' in the council."

XLVII

LORD MACAULAY: VICTORIAN LIBERAL [1]

By

RICHMOND CROOM BEATTY

In this intelligent study, erudition and a stimulating style of writing make the story of Thomas Babington Macaulay, Victorian scholar, English statesman, reformer, historian and essayist, genuinely remunerative.

Macaulay (1800-1859) was one of the most widely read essayists of his time. It is said that from the age of three he read constantly and could memorize without effort the books he read. Thackeray declared of Macaulay, "He reads twenty books to write a sentence." His *Lays of Ancient Rome* was published in 1842. One of the *Lays*, "Horatius at the Bridge," is known by almost every child. His greatest work was his *History of England*, and it had a sale in the United States which it is said was exceeded only by that of the Bible. During his service for a number of years in Parliament, he was an eloquent debater and a strong Whig. Because of the self-assurance with which he asserted his viewpoints, Lord Melbourne once said of him, "I wish I were as cocksure of any one thing as Macaulay is of everything."

The passage from Richmond Beatty's book gives the frequently discussed and challenging opinions which Macaulay expressed on the Constitution of the United States and the fate he believed would befall this country.

"I AM OF A VERY DIFFERENT OPINION"

Never in his entire career did Macaulay write a more stimulating series of letters than when, in reply to the entreaties of the American biographer, H. S. Randall, he set forth his opinions on the subject of the Constitution of the United States and the fate that would probably befall this country, once its frontier lands had all been claimed and settled. One might add

[1] Richmond Croom Beatty, *Lord Macaulay: Victorian Liberal*, copyright 1938 by the University of Oklahoma Press, Norman, pp. 364-372.

that he never appeared more courteous than when he made these comments, more considerate of an opposite point of view, or more fully the scholar-gentleman who felt that good breeding should prevail, no matter how fundamentally gentlemen disagreed about principles. Randall had sent Macaulay, in January, 1857, an autograph of Washington. He had remarked, in sending it, that the first president had been exalted by most of his countrymen into a god, while Jefferson, the great democrat, was regarded merely as Washington's foil. This was news to Macaulay. But he felt bound to trust it, because Randall was at work upon a life of Jefferson and therefore should know. Yet what made the statement hard to believe was the fact that nineteenth century America was becoming increasingly democratic, seemed more and more to be falling in line with the ideals which Jefferson had cherished for it. Macaulay confessed his astonishment at this fact, and added that, personally, he had never cared for Mr. Jefferson's views. It was this last remark that brought on the two really valuable letters which followed. Randall asked him for his frank opinion of the American form of government. And he got it.

"You are surprised to learn that I have not a high opinion of Mr. Jefferson," Macaulay wrote, "and I am surprised at your surprise. I am certain that I never wrote a line, and that I never, in Parliament, in conversation, or even on the hustings—a place where it is the fashion to court the populace—uttered a word indicating an opinion that the supreme authority in a state ought to be intrusted to the majority of citizens told by the head; in other words, to the poorest and most ignorant part of society. I have long been convinced that institutions purely democratic must, sooner or later, destroy liberty or civilization, or both. In Europe, where the population is dense, the effect of such institutions would be almost instantaneous. What happened lately in France is an example. In 1848 a pure democracy was established there. During a short time there was reason to expect a general spoliation, a national bankruptcy, a new partition of the soil, a maximum of prices, a ruinous load of taxation laid on the rich for the purpose of supporting the poor in idleness. Such a system would, in twenty years, have made France as poor and barbarous as the France of the Carlovingians. Happily the danger was averted; and now there is a despotism, a silent tribune, an enslaved press. Liberty is gone, but civilization has been saved.

"I have not the smallest doubt that if we had a purely democratic government here the effect would be the same. Either the poor would plunder the rich, and civilization would perish; or order and prosperity would be saved by a strong military government, and liberty would perish.

You may think that your country enjoys an exemption from these evils. I will frankly own to you that I am of a very different opinion. Your fate I believe to be certain, though it is deferred by a physical cause. As long as you have a boundless extent of fertile and unoccupied land, your laboring population will be far more at ease than the laboring population of the Old World, and, while this is the case, the Jefferson politics may continue to exist without causing any fatal calamity. But the time will come when New England will be as thickly peopled as old England. Wages will be as low, and will fluctuate as much with you as with us. You will have your Manchesters and Birminghams, and in those Manchesters and Birminghams hundreds of thousands of artisans will assuredly be sometimes out of work. Then your institutions will be fairly brought to the test. Distress everywhere makes the laborer mutinous and discontented, and inclines him to listen with eagerness to agitators who tell him that it is a monstrous iniquity that one man should have a million, while another cannot get a full meal. In bad years there is plenty of grumbling here; and sometimes a little rioting. But it matters little. For here the sufferers are not the rulers. The supreme power is in the hands of a class, numerous indeed, but select; of an educated class; of a class which is, and knows itself to be, deeply interested in the security of property and the maintenance of order. Accordingly, the malcontents are firmly yet gently restrained. The bad time is got over without robbing the wealthy to relieve the indigent. The springs of national prosperity soon begin to flow again; work is plentiful, wages rise, and all is tranquillity and cheerfulness. I have seen England pass three or four times through such critical seasons as I have described. Through such seasons the United States will have to pass in the course of the next century, if not this.

"How will you pass through them? I heartily wish you a good deliverance. But my reason and my wishes are at war, and I can not help foreboding the worst. It is quite plain that your Government will never be able to restrain a distressed and discontented majority. For with you the majority is the Government, and has the rich, who are always a minority, absolutely at its mercy. The day will come when in the State of New York a multitude of people, none of whom has had more than half a breakfast, or expects to have more than half a dinner, will choose a Legislature. Is it possible to doubt what sort of a Legislature will be chosen? On one side is a statesman preaching patience, respect for vested rights, strict observance of public faith. On the other is a demagogue ranting about the tyranny of capitalists and usurers, and asking why any body should be permitted to drink champagne and to ride in a carriage, while thousands of honest folks are in want of necessaries. Which of the two candidates is likely to be preferred by a working-man who hears his children cry for more bread? I seriously apprehend that you will, in some such season of adversity as I have described, do things which will prevent prosperity from returning; that you will act like people who should in a year of scarcity devour all the seed-corn, and thus make the next a year not of scarcity, but of absolute famine. There will be, I fear, spoliation. The spoliation will increase the distress. The distress will produce fresh spoliation. There is nothing to stop you. Your Constitution is all sail and no anchor.

"As I said before, when a society has entered on this downward progress, either civilization or liberty must perish. Either some Caesar or Napoleon will seize the reins of government with a strong hand, or your republic will be as fearfully plundered and laid waste by barbarians in the twentieth century as the Roman Empire was in the fifth; with this difference, that the Huns and Vandals who ravaged the Roman Empire came from without and that your Huns and Vandals will have been engendered within your own country by your own institutions.

"Thinking thus, of course I can not reckon Jefferson among the benefactors of mankind. I readily admit that his intentions were good, and his abilities considerable. Odious stories have been circulated about his private life; but I do not know on what evidence those stories rest, and I think it probable that they are false, or monstrously exaggerated. I have no doubt that I shall derive both pleasure and information from your account of him."

The famous Whig's strictures and predictions proved by no means comforting to Mr. Randall. In October, 1858, Macaulay received from him a copy of his biography of Jefferson, accompanied by a letter which contained several objections to them. Macaulay replied with uncommon patience. He had noted, he said, Mr. Randall's dissent "from some opinions which I have long held firmly but which I should never have obtruded on you except at your own earnest request, and which I have no wish to defend against your objections. If you can derive any comfort as to the future destinies of your country from your conviction that a benevolent Creator will never suffer more human beings to be born than can live in plenty, it is a comfort of which I should be sorry to deprive you. By the same process of reasoning one may arrive at many very agreeable conclusions, such as that there is no cholera, no malaria, no yellow fever, no negro slavery in the world. Unfortunately for me, perhaps, I learned from Lord Bacon a method of investigating truth diametrically opposite to that which you appear to follow. I am perfectly aware of the immense progress which your country has made, and is making, in population and wealth. I know that the laborer with you has large wages, abundant food, and the means of giving some education to his children. But I see no reason for attributing these things to the policy of Jefferson. I see no reason to believe that your progress would have been less rapid, that your laboring people would have been worse fed, or clothed, or taught, if your government had been conducted on the principles of Washington and Hamilton. Nay, you will, I am sure, acknowledge that the progress which you have been making ever since the middle of the seventeenth century, and that the blessings, which you now enjoy, were enjoyed by your forefathers who were loyal subjects of the kings of England. The contrast between the laborer of New York and the laborer of Europe is not stronger now than it was when New York was governed by noblemen and gentlemen commissioned under the English great seal. And there are at this moment dependencies of the English crown in which all the phenomena which you attribute to purely democratical institutions may be seen in the highest perfection. The colony of Victoria, in Australia, was planted only twenty years ago. The population is now, I suppose near a million. The revenue is enormous, near five millions sterling, and raised without any murmuring. The wages of labor are higher than they are even with you. Immense sums are expended on education. And this is a province governed by the delegate of an hereditary sovereign.

"It therefore seems to me quite clear that the facts which you cite to prove the excellence of purely democratic institutions ought to be ascribed not to those institutions, but to causes which operated in America long before your Declaration of Independence, and which are still operating in many parts of the British Empire. You will perceive, therefore, that I do not propose, as you thought to sacrifice the interests of the present generation to those of remote generations. It would, indeed, be absurd in a nation to part with institutions to which it is indebted for immense present prosperity from an apprehension that, after the lapse of a century, those institutions may be found to produce mischief. But I do not admit that the prosperity which your country enjoys arises from those parts of your polity which may be called, in an especial manner, Jeffersonian. Those parts of your polity have already produced bad effects, and will, unless I am greatly mistaken, produce fatal effects if they shall last till North America has two hundred inhabitants to the square mile."

These citations comprise the substance of Macaulay's remarks. Randall attempted to draw him out further, but to no purpose. He had said his say, and that was the end of it. Perhaps it is still too early to attempt to estimate the truth of his gloomy forebodings about America; for the possibility of two hundred inhabitants to the square mile here is, fortunately, still remote. Yet this much is at least apparent: Macaulay to the last thought of society in terms of static and distinct classes. There was the lower class, then the middle class of property and respectability, and there was, finally, the aristocracy at the top. This last group, the nobility, could never quite be trusted, he felt, since its position depended upon inheritance instead of natural merit. But the peculiar genius of the English people sprang from the fact that it was possible for members of the middle class to rise to positions of authority. This was eminently sensible, he believed. It was also safe—safe because from birth this class had been taught to respect the rights of property. Those who composed it were at heart conservative.

Actually, of course, his idea of the middle class was an abstraction as intangible as any he had ever despised in Plato. There was no line which divided these respectable burghers from the great chaotic group beneath them. Englishmen might make all the distinctions they could think of: they might partition off their ale houses into two or three neat sections forever. They might stretch their ropes between the twelfth and thirteenth rows of seats at their theaters until Doomsday. Or they could demand that one pay a ten pound property tax to the State before he should be allowed the ballot. It did not matter; it was not by these means that one could distinguish with blind certainty the men of prudence and judgment from the fomentors of revolution. For all such discriminations followed purely economic lines; and with the rise of a system of generally accessible public education, they were already, in Macaulay's day, becoming meaningless. It was fortunately conceivable, in other words, that even from the lowest classes a statesman might arise—like Alexander Hamilton or Herbert Hoover, for instance—who would be in his ways of thought as conservative as Lord Eldon, certainly as conservative as Lord Grey or Lord Macaulay.

Again, he seems to have grievously underestimated the resourcefulness of which the American type of capitalist is capable. Men of the Jay Gould, Jay Cooke, or John D. Rockefeller the Elder type had not yet appeared in this country, nor had the Fourteenth Amendment, which sanctified their corporations by rendering them practically immune to restraint, appeared either. In short, Macaulay had no prevision of the America we know—an America in which the plutocratic, or capitalist class—through its instruments of propaganda, the press and the radio, and through its threat of unemployment—is able to control with reasonable effectiveness those "lower orders" from which he feared so much mischief.

He failed likewise, it seems, to reckon with Jefferson's well known observation that if the majority of citizens should ever come to be deprived of real property—of land—the democracy in which he believed would probably cease to work. And as for the revolution which, Macaulay predicted, would occur when economic conditions became unsupportable in America—such upheavals, as he himself was well aware, have a way of coming regardless of whether "the people" are already in power. One had occurred in France a few years before his birth, while that country was ruled by a despot. The test, on this point, will perhaps always be whether the governing authority is sufficiently considerate of what is demanded by those who are governed.

It is probably inadvisable to consider more closely the relation of Macaulay's views to the present political scene in this country. He could not know that scene—would scarcely, one feels, have wished to know it any too well! And yet it might be added that out of our own conflict between the Conservatives, the New Deal, and the more extreme Labor reformers of the United States (all of them alike in having had parallels in Macaulay's day) may come within the next decade the fulfillment or the refutation of his prophecy. The issue, moreover, will likely be decided upon fundamentally moral grounds. It will be the issue of whether the almost endless opportunity for the amassing of fortunes which this country offered resourceful men during the past century prove finally, through the greed which it engendered, a barrier against all reasonable compromise between warring factions. Certainly it is true that no greater temptation to acquire material wealth has ever been presented a nation equipped with modern industrial instruments. If failure attends the efforts of those who would adjust the ambitions of these hostile interests, Macaulay's prediction will in spirit have come true. A great adventure in government will have been tried, and, at length, superseded.

XLVIII

L. EMMETT HOLT, PIONEER OF A CHILDREN'S CENTURY[1]

By

R. L. DUFFUS AND L. EMMETT HOLT, JR.

Luther Emmett Holt (1855-1924) was the outstanding pioneer in American pediatrics. Dr. Holt was known to thousands of American mothers as the author of *The Care and Feeding of Children.* Robert L. Duffus and Luther E. Holt, himself a pediatrician and a son of Dr. Holt, have not only written the interesting, human story of a delightful personality, but they have also filled the biography with a splendid account of the history from about 1880 to 1924 of pediatric practice and the record of American medicine in its progress in protecting the health of children.

THE AWAKENING OF THE SCIENCE OF MEDICINE

Surgery in New York City in 1880 was barely emerging from the dark ages. Lister's first paper was published in 1867, but it had taken the better part of a decade for his views to obtain a foothold on the other side of the Atlantic. In Bellevue [Hospital] as late as 1871, 22 per cent of all open wounds developed erysipelas, and 40 to 60 per cent of all amputations terminated fatally, usually from pyemia. In the forties, Semmelweiss in Vienna and Oliver Wendell Holmes in Boston had first preached the doctrine of aseptic obstetrics, but as late as 1872 in Bellevue puerperal fever killed one in ten women who underwent childbirth. It was only in the later seventies that more than a handful of mothers were able to thank the author of "The Chambered Nautilus" for life and health. In 1879 had occurred that dramatic scene in the Paris Academy of Medicine when

[1] R. L. Duffus and L. Emmett Holt, Jr., *L. Emmett Holt, Pioneer of a Children's Century,* New York: D. Appleton-Century Company, Inc., 1940, pp. 1-4, 49-50.

Pasteur had interrupted a discussion on the causes of puerperal fever by declaring that puerperal fever was of bacterial origin and was carried by doctors and nurses. To the speaker's retort that he feared the strange microbe would never be found Pasteur stepped to the blackboard and drawing what we now know as the streptococcus, said, "*Voici la figure*." During Emmett Holt's service at Bellevue only one case of appendicitis was diagnosed. The others were called colic, or otherwise described in general terms, and treated medically; and the patients, when soothing potions failed, were gathered to their fathers. . . .

When Luther Emmett Holt took his degree in medicine in 1880, one out of every four babies born in New York City died before the end of its first year. Some cities were worse off than New York, some country districts and small towns better off, but the ratio was representative. The babies of the poor and ignorant in overcrowded tenement districts, and those unfortunate enough to be in institutions had far less chance of survival. Poorly fed and poorly nourished, they fell an easy prey to infections of all kinds, and every summer with as much certainty as the upward curve in the thermometer came the sharp increase in the death rate caused by diarrheal disorders.

There had been, it is true, some improvement over conditions in the eighteenth century, when from 90 to 99 per cent of infants admitted to foundling institutions died, and when Malthus could truthfully say that the surest way of checking the growth of the population was to multiply infant hospitals and asylums. But the improvement had not gone far.

Pediatrics, that branch of medicine dealing with the care and diseases of children, did not exist as a recognized field of endeavor in the United States. The care of the sick child was in the hands of the obstetrician or the practitioner of internal medicine whose interest was chiefly in adults. The training of the doctor in this field consisted of a few casual lectures on children sandwiched into the course on obstetrics. One or two physicians had interested themselves in children and had written treatises on the subject, but they had not penetrated far, nor had their influence been widespread. Medicine as a whole was static. It embraced a body of knowledge handed down from generation to generation which few sought to challenge or to enlarge. The care of the child was not regarded as the province of the physician. It was the undisputed domain of the mother and grandmother, and here again the traditions were passed along from one generation to the next.

In 1924 at the time of Dr. Holt's death a vastly different picture presented itself. Information on infant care and hygiene—based on the best medical knowledge—was the property of practically every educated mother, and much had been done to educate children themselves in matters of health. Medicine had become a dynamic science. Disease was being studied by doctors everywhere—at the bedside, in clinics, in laboratories. Medical knowledge was expanding with unbelievable rapidity. And the diseases of children had assumed a place of major importance. Practitioners engaging in this specialty were to be found in every corner of the country. Full professors of pediatrics giving extensive courses were to be found in practically all medical schools. University departments of pediatrics and research institutes were springing up in the leading medical centers with staffs of workers devoting themselves to the study of disease in childhood, and numerous scientific societies and several special journals had been created to diffuse the new knowledge in this branch of medicine. The results were depicted by that infallible score-board, the infant mortality rate. Down it had come steadily, year by year, to less than one third of the previous figure.

The period between 1880 and 1924 saw the awakening of the science of medicine. It was a period of increasing social consciousness which permitted great advances in public health. In this renaissance it is hardly thinkable that the infant and child could have escaped. Such a development can not, however, be considered apart from the individuals who brought it to pass. Certainly no one person could take the credit for such an achievement. It was the product of many workers on many different fronts, of many leaders and a large army of followers. Yet if one individual were to be singled out as typifying America's accomplishment in those years in saving the lives of her children, that individual would be Emmett Holt. His contribution was not that of the great investigator whose discoveries are epoch-making. He was not of the mighty tribe of Lister, Pasteur, or Koch. Nor was he unique in possessing those traits of character and intellect which make for the highest skill in the practice of medicine. His outstanding contribution was, as he once expressed it, to be a "middleman" of science—one who formed a link between the producer, the research worker in the laboratory, and the ultimate consumer, who might be the practising physician, the health worker, or the public. His function was to translate the new knowledge into practical results and to diffuse those results far and wide. He was above all an educator.

Thrown by a fortunate chance, at the beginning of his career, into intimate contact with one or two spirits who were sowing the first seeds of the newer medical science in this country, Holt followed its growth eagerly and grew with it, and saw to it that it spread to his chosen field. In the combined effort to cultivate that field, an effort which succeeded within one brief generation in converting the field from a barren pasture with only a few blades of grass to a fertile domain producing bumper crops, he was a leading spirit—in time the outstanding leader. He obtained for his specialty a secure place in the sun, and through his own efforts the crops from that field were distributed to all in the land.

XLIX

WOODROW WILSON: LIFE AND LETTERS[1]

By

RAY STANNARD BAKER

In a notable eight-volume work, Ray Stannard Baker has told with clarity and intelligence the significant story of Woodrow Wilson (1856-1924) and his time, his objectives and his accomplishments. There is available in this study a large store of authentic material for biographers and historical students of generations to come who will wish to interpret in even more elaborate detail the life of one of the most interesting figures of modern times.

The selection chosen for this anthology describes one of the most unusual political conventions in American history. Mr. Baker has written us, "I suppose the convention was the freest and in some ways the most important of any in our history." The Republican party meeting in June, 1912, had split with the nomination of Taft and with Theodore Roosevelt leading a revolt from the convention. On June 25 the Democratic party convened in Baltimore, a convention which lasted until July 2 and was marked by intense bitterness between the conservative and progressive elements of the party.

WHEN WOODROW WILSON BECAME THE DEMOCRATIC NOMINEE FOR PRESIDENT OF THE UNITED STATES

Ten days before the Baltimore convention was scheduled to meet, Wilson and his family arrived at the Governor's Cottage at Sea Girt, New Jersey.

"Here we are at Sea Girt. We came down yesterday: the house was ready for us; it did not take long to unpack the trunks; and so we already feel very much at home again. The day is gray and drizzly; the sea makes a dismal voice across the bleak camp ground in front of us; we have had to light a fire in the huge fireplace to keep our spirits (and our tempera-

[1] Ray Stannard Baker, *Woodrow Wilson: Life and Letters*, copyright 1931, reprinted by permission of Doubleday, Doran & Company, Inc., New York, III, 332-362.

ture) up; but here we are a home group with that within us that can defy the depressing influences of the weather. What we now look forward to with not a little dread are the possibilities of the next fortnight in politics. I was saying at breakfast this morning, 'Two weeks from to-day we shall either have this sweet Sunday calm again or an army of reporters camped on the lawn and an all-day reception.' 'Which would you rather have?' Nellie asked. 'Need you ask?' I exclaimed; and that is the way I feel. Now that the *possibility* is immediately at hand (it is no more than a possibility, as things stand) I find myself dreading it and wishing most devoutly that I may escape. Not that I dread what would be really big and essential and worth while in the whole thing, but all that would go with [it]—all that is *non*-essential, *not* of the *business*, merely distracting and exhausting and hateful without counting,—the excessive *personal* tax of a campaign. May the Lord have mercy on me! My heart is not faint, but my taste and my preference for what is genuine and at the opposite pole from mere personal notoriety revolts at the thought of what I may be in for! . . .

"I am well (I do not count a teasing sick headache!) and underneath, deep down, my soul is quiet."[2] . . .

It was by no means a calm and peaceful week. The reverberations of the mighty conflict at Chicago, where the Republican convention was in session, broke the quiet of Sea Girt. McAdoo, who was at the scene of battle, was reporting directly to Wilson. Bryan, also at Chicago, never for a moment allowed the Democratic situation or the Democratic candidates to escape him. Playing the part momentarily of a newspaper correspondent, he was observing narrowly the methods pursued by the Republican "stand-patters" in dealing with their own revolting progressives. It was not unedifying to watch Roosevelt and LaFollette, each bitterly hostile to the other, borne down in common ruin beneath the ruthless "steam roller" of an organization completely dominated by the "interests."

Bryan knew well what a powerful influence the Republican convention might exert on the coming Democratic convention. If Taft won, and Roosevelt bolted, Democratic success depended upon the nomination of a real progressive.

"If the Democrats are guilty of the criminal folly of nominating a reactionary, they will supply Mr. Roosevelt with the one thing needful in case he becomes an independent candidate, namely, an issue, and with two reactionaries running for President he might win and thus entrench himself in power."[3] . . .

[2] Woodrow Wilson to Mary A. Hulbert, June 17, 1912.

[3] From Bryan's dispatch to the afternoon newspapers, June 21, 1912.

On Saturday the 22nd, the Republicans at Chicago adjourned, having nominated Taft. Roosevelt, raging with indignation, was branding the leaders as thieves and scoundrels, and still worse, "reactionaries"! Plans were forming for a new party. "We stand at Armageddon and battle for the Lord."

"The Republicans," wrote Wilson, "have met,—and done their worst; and now the Democrats are to meet and ——?"

On Tuesday the 25th their cohorts descended upon Baltimore. Tammany, led by Boss Murphy and accompanied by Judge Parker and August Belmont, came in a special train with colours flying and a band playing. Thomas Fortune Ryan, the symbol to the Progressives of all that was terrifying in "Wall Street," was there in his special car.[4] It was understood that he carried Virginia safely stowed away in his pocket. Bryan had come on from Chicago, still a busy correspondent, and, with Mrs. Bryan, was at the Belvedere Hotel. Clark, pacing his office at the Capitol, forty miles away at Washington, was in constant and close communication with his managers on the floor of the convention. Underwood, also at Washington, remained quietly at his work. Harmon was at home in Ohio. . . .

The flag-decorated armoury, with the portrait of the patron saint of the party, "WHO NEVER SOLD THE TRUTH TO SERVE THE HOUR," was packed to the roof.

The fine old Cardinal of Baltimore, serene-faced, robed in scarlet, with a skullcap covering his silvery locks, stood with raised hand:

"Let the light of Thy divine wisdom direct the deliberations of this convention. . ."

Just behind Cardinal Gibbons, ready for the fray, sat William J. Bryan. No sooner had Norman E. Mack, the presiding officer, announced that he had been instructed to submit the name of Alton B. Parker for temporary chairman than Bryan went into action. A wave of tumultuous cheering swept the vast gathering. To hundreds of those present he was still "the great Commoner," the "peerless leader." The New York delegation, a solid block in the centre of the floor, sat grimly silent.

The Commoner's face was pale. "His heavy black brows were contracted over his piercing eyes. His hawk nose had an extra downward twist. His lipless mouth was like a thin dagger-slit across his broad face. He held his head erect. . . . The grizzled fringe of his dark hair was ruffled and moist

[4] "For the first time one of the great money kings of America has appeared in person at a national political convention to carry on the fight for the money interests." (Baltimore *Sun.*)

with persperation. He made a fine figure, standing up there, in an old dark sack suit, with a low collar and white string tie. . . ."[5]

He motioned for silence, but the cheers kept up. Then the band began to play. Bryan sat down and fanned himself with a big palm leaf. When the cheering subsided, he began in measured tones his arraignment of Judge Parker, and nominated Senator John W. Kern of Indiana for temporary chairman to oppose him. Kern was Bryan's trusted friend. He had been the candidate for vice-president when Bryan himself ran for the presidency in 1908:

"I appeal to you: Let the commencement of this convention be such a commencement that the Democrats of this country may raise their heads among their fellows and say, 'The Democratic party is true to the people. You cannot frighten it with your Ryans nor buy it with your Belmonts.' "[6]

Bedlam broke loose when Bryan sat down. Hisses and catcalls were intermingled with vociferous cheering.

Senator Kern offered to withdraw his name if Parker would withdraw his. Parker's substantial figure, "elegantly attired," sitting with the New York delegation, did not stir. The old organization felt confident that it could dominate the convention. Let Bryan rant and Kern bargain!

Kern then electrified the convention by nominating Bryan himself for temporary chairman. The old Cardinal who less than an hour before had prayed for peace and concord in the proceedings of the convention, gathered his scarlet cloak about his shoulders and left a hall seething with bitterness and strife.

When the vote was taken, the assurance of the old organization was confirmed. Parker received 579 votes Bryan 508. The "stand-patters" were apparently in control. . . .

If the conservatives—and indeed the Clark managers—were jubilant, Bryan only became more determined. . . .

The next step in the strategy of the progressives was to develop their real strength in the convention itself.

"The present issue here has been sharply defined as one between William J. Bryan and Thomas F. Ryan. . . . The bulk of the delegates here are plain people from the hills. There is no doubt where their sympathies lie. As usual, however, many of them owe allegiance to 'leaders' and are members of state delegations bound by the unit rule."[7]

[5] New York *World*, June 26, 1912.
[6] *Official Report of the Proceedings of the Democratic National Convention*, p. 6.
[7] New York *Evening Post*, June 25, 1912.

Few of the old timers thought that the unit rule, hoary tradition of the party, confirmed by seventy-six years of usage, could be modified. The progressives, however, made a strong appeal to the rules committee, arguing the manifest injustice of forcing delegates elected by districts favourable to Wilson to vote, under a unit rule imposed by a state convention, for Harmon or Clark or some other candidate in whom they did not believe. When the rules committee refused to act, they carried the fight to the floor, on a resolution introduced by Congressman Henry of Texas. The principal champion of the revolt was Newton D. Baker, "a young man with a clean-cut intellectual face," one of the nineteen delegates of Ohio who was himself a strong Wilson supporter, bound under the unit rule to vote for Harmon. . . .

Baker's speech was superb, arousing the convention to a high pitch of enthusiasm. In the midst of it a chance reference to Wilson touched off the fireworks. A demonstration broke loose which lasted for thirty-three minutes—an evidence of the spontaneous ardour of the Wilson support, as surprising as it was unexpected. When the vote was announced, it was a clear progressive victory, 565½ to 492⅓, and the Wilson and Bryan followers literally swept over the convention, carrying everything before them in their enthusiasm.

Wilson himself, sitting quietly with his family at Sea Girt, was called on the long-distance telephone. The news was elating. It indicated that the chances of an outright conservative candidate like Harmon or Underwood were growing dimmer: but the great problem still remained—who was to be the chosen progressive? Clark, Wilson, Bryan? . . .

Bryan was nothing if not audacious. He did not wait for the opposition to move. He forced the fighting. He came into the convention the next day, Thursday, carrying in his hand one of the most astonishing resolutions ever introduced in a national convention. . . .

Bryan rose in his place and asked unanimous consent to present a resolution for immediate consideration. By this time he had become the storm centre of the convention.

"What is the resolution?" yelled a number of delegates.

"My resolution is as follows:

" '*Resolved*, That in this crisis in our party's career and in our country's history this convention sends greeting to the people of the United States, and assures them that the party of Jefferson and of Jackson is still the champion of popular government and equality before the law. As proof of our fidelity to the people, we hereby declare ourselves opposed to the nomination of any candidate for President who is the representative of or under obligation to J. Pierpont Morgan, Thomas F. Ryan, August Belmont, or any other member of the privilege-hunting and favour-seeking class.

"'*Be it further resolved*, That we demand the withdrawal from this convention of any delegate or delegates constituting or representing the above-named interests."[8]

For a moment the convention was stunned into silence. Here was a proposal to turn out of the convention several of the most notable delegates: one at least from the powerful New York delegation, August Belmont; one from the Virginia delegation, Thomas F. Ryan; both sitting in their places on the floor. Ryan rose to leave the hall, but the Virginians held him back.

Pandemonium broke loose. Scores of delegates leaped to their feet demanding recognition. Others stood on chairs to yell defiance at the Commoner. The sergeant-at-arms and the police were unable to quell the disturbance. Bryan himself stood immovable before the storm. . . .

After a heated debate, in which it was argued that the convention had no right to expel delegates chosen by sovereign states, Bryan withdrew the latter part of his resolution: but he obstinately refused to withdraw the whole of it.

"'If thy right hand offend thee, cut it off' . . . if it is worth while to cut off the right hand to save the body, it is worth while to cut off Morgan, Ryan, and Belmont to save the Democratic party."[9]

Demanding a record vote, Bryan was in a strong strategic position, for any delegate voting "nay" was in effect declaring that he favoured the nomination of a candidate favourable to "the privilege-hunting and favour-seeking class."

It was a brilliant stroke, even New York and Virginia joining in support of the resolution. As the vote was being taken, Boss Murphy leaned over to Belmont and said:

"August, listen and hear yourself vote yourself out of the convention."

The resolution carried by a vote of 883 to 201½. It accomplished the result that Bryan primarily had in mind: the vivid dramatization for the people of the nation of the lines of conflict and the forces engaged in the convention. Christian was winning over Apollyon!

It was now near midnight and hot in the teeming armoury, but a Democratic convention, once launched, regards time and weather no more than principalities and powers. Nominations were called for and

[8] *Official Report of the Proceedings of the Democratic National Convention*, p. 129.

[9] *Official Report of the Proceedings of the Democratic National Convention*, p. 136.

the speeches presenting the various candidates continued until breakfast-time the next morning.

Oscar W. Underwood, the "favourite son" of Alabama, was the first candidate to be named—in a strong address by his friend Senator Bankhead. He was cheered for twenty-six minutes. Senator James A. Reed nominated his fellow Missourian, the "houn' dawg candidate," Champ Clark. The barometer of applause rose to an hour and five minutes. A tremendous demonstration! Connecticut then offered her much esteemed Governor, Simeon E. Baldwin; and at the ripe hour of 2:15 in the morning, Delaware yielding to New Jersey, Judge Wescott stepped forward to present the name of Woodrow Wilson. . . .

He was not allowed to proceed at once. The crowd, the galleries especially, could not wait to express their enthusiasm for Wilson. The applause was tumultuous and uncontrollable.

Judge Wescott's magnificent voice carried to the uttermost parts of the vast auditorium:

"The Democratic party is commissioned to carry on a great constructive programme, having for its end a complete restoration of the doctrine of equal rights and equal opportunity. . . . Providence has given us, in the exalted character of New Jersey's Executive, the mental and moral equipment to accomplish this reincarnation of Democracy. . . .

"He has been in political life less than two years. He has had no organization of the usual sort; only a practical ideal, the reëstablishment of equal opportunity. The logic of events points to him. . . . Every crisis evolves its master. Time and circumstance have evolved the immortal Governor of New Jersey. . . .

". . . New Jersey appreciates . . . the honour . . . of placing before this convention as a candidate for the presidency of the United States the seer and philosopher of Princeton, the Princeton schoolmaster, Woodrow Wilson."[10]

The demonstration which followed Wescott's nomination speech exceeded that of any other candidate. Wilson's friends were determined to out-yell and out-march the Clark forces, and they cheered and paraded for an hour and a quarter. A delegation appeared at the head of the parade with a huge portrait of Wilson:

"We want Wilson, we want Wilson."

Day was breaking, but Governor Marshall of Indiana and Governor Harmon of Ohio had yet to be nominated: and there was a drum fire of briefer seconding speeches. . . . It was about seven o'clock in the morning

[10] *Official Report of the Proceedings of the Democratic National Convention*, pp. 160, 161.

when the first ballot was taken. Clark was decidedly in the lead. The ninety votes of New York went to Governor Harmon. Underwood had the support of the Old South:

Clark	440½
Wilson	324
Harmon	148
Underwood	117½
Marshall	31
Baldwin	22
Sulzer	2
Bryan	1[11]

. . . .

The fourth day of the convention (Friday) was devoted wholly to balloting. It was not until the roll was called for the tenth time that the "underground work" which had been going on among the managers bore dramatic fruit. When New York was called, Boss Murphy, arising slowly, startled the convention by delivering his entire delegation to Champ Clark.

It was a tremendous moment. Everyone present knew the significance of the change. It meant that Champ Clark would carry a majority of the convention. "The fight is over," roared a Clark enthusiast. The Missouri delegation arose as one man and began a parade around the hall. Banner after banner joined in the procession. The demonstration lasted for an hour or more. A stampede was in the making. Not for sixty-eight years, since Van Buren was nominated at Baltimore in 1844, had any Democratic candidate who received a majority of the votes in the convention failed to win two thirds and the nomination. Well might Clark's friends consider that the battle was won. And Tammany Hall had won it!

Bryan had been absent during the vote. He had been worn out by the strain of two conventions. He entered at the height of the demonstration, his tall form shouldering its way through the seething marchers. When he learned what had happened he rose in his place, crying out:

"A progressive candidate must not be besmirched by New York's vote". . . .

The issue hung in the balance. A stampede might easily have followed if the states on the roll next after New York had not been among Wilson's strongest supporters. When Oklahoma was called, a Clark member, hoping to break the solid Wilson vote, demanded that the delegation be

[11] *Official Report of the Proceedings of the Democratic National Convention*, p. 196.

polled. "Alfalfa Bill" Murray was instantly on his feet. Alfalfa Bill was lanky and collarless, wore "galluses" and a bandana handkerchief. He could roar like the bull of Bashan. Upon this occasion he not only roared but waved his arms. He had no objection to a poll, but ". . . we do insist we shall not join Tammany in making the nomination."[12]

He was greeted with tremendous applause: the Wilson and Bryan men went wild: Alfalfa Bill had struck the keynote of the hour.

There was no stampede, but the result of the ballot showed that Clark had eleven more than a majority. Wilson's lines, however, had held firm: he lost only two votes from the former ballot. The vote stood:

Clark	556
Wilson	350½
Underwood	117½
Marshall	31
Harmon	31
Kern	1
Bryan	1[13]

Early Saturday morning McCombs called Wilson on the telephone. McCombs was utterly discouraged, and they discussed a message from Wilson releasing his delegates. McCombs thought it would be "a good thing to have in hand." McCombs also wanted instructions as to whom, when the break came, Wilson would turn his strength. He suggested Underwood, but Wilson felt that he had no right to express a preference.

When the Governor left the telephone, tears stood in Mrs. Wilson's eyes. . . .

Later on Saturday morning—the lowest ebb of the convention so far as Wilson was concerned—McAdoo went to call on McCombs, and found him in a state of great dejection. A fatigued mind in a sickly and worn-out body! He had quite lost his head.

"The jig's up," said McCombs. "Clark will be nominated. All my work has been for nothing."

McAdoo was dumbfounded. "Do you mean that you are giving up the fight?"

McCombs said, "It is hopeless. Clark has a majority of the convention and no candidate has ever received a majority without being nominated."

McAdoo replied, "You are all wrong. Wilson is stronger now than he was last night. Under the two-thirds rule Clark can never win."

[12] *Official Report of the Proceedings of the Democratic National Convention*, p. 220.
[13] *Ibid.*

"Why, Governor Wilson himself has given up."

"What do you mean?"

"I talked to the Governor on the telephone very fully about the situation and told him I thought he ought to release his friends, and the Governor has authorized me to release them. I told the Governor that I would have to have a telegram from him authorizing me to do so as his friends in the convention might not accept my statement."

McAdoo understood McCombs to say that he had such a telegram from the Governor, and he was so "indignant and amazed" that he not only denounced McCombs—"We had some very hot words; so hot, in fact, that I can't put them on paper"—but he rushed to the telephone and urged Wilson, at Sea Girt, not to think for a moment of releasing his friends in the convention; that he was gaining strength all the time; that Clark could never get a two-thirds vote. Wilson responded, according to McAdoo, that he had been acting on McCombs's advice, and authorized McAdoo to tell McCombs not to release his delegates. Upon hearing McAdoo's report, McCombs called Wilson on the telephone to confirm the decision. . . .

Looking back, one is impressed by the hair-trigger chances of that unprecedented convention! A single misstep and Wilson would have lost.

When the convention met on the fifth day, the atmosphere was surcharged with excitement. Would there be a stampede to Clark? Would Wilson retire? What would Bryan do?

Wilson himself had been doing some hard thinking as a result of his consultations with McAdoo, McCombs, Hudspeth, and others. While the thirteenth ballot was being taken, he called McCombs—then in the convention hall—and said he had a message which he wished delivered at once to Mr. Bryan. He had written it out hastily in shorthand and had a copy made on the typewriter—the originals remain among his papers—and asked that it be taken down verbatim:

"It has become evident that the present deadlock is being maintained for the purpose of enabling New York, a delegation controlled by a single group of men, to control the nomination and tie the candidate to itself. In these circumstances it is the imperative duty of each candidate for the nomination to see to it that his own independence is beyond question. I can see no other way to do this than to declare that he will not accept a nomination if it cannot be secured without the aid of that delegation. For myself, I have no hesitation in making that declaration. The freedom of the party and its candidate and the security of the government against private control constitute the supreme consideration."

Such a course as Wilson here recommended would oblige every candidate to declare his position regarding Tammany support. Clark would either have to repudiate Boss Murphy or admit his obligation to him—an embarrassing decision!

Whether it was this message that influenced Bryan in making his devastating announcement after the thirteenth ballot, or whether he was already considering some such course, the strategy seemed to have been in the minds of both men.

While Bryan had been maintaining his personal neutrality as between Clark and Wilson, he had all along been voting, as one of the instructed Nebraska delegation, for Clark. And Clark's managers had been doing their best—now their successful best—to enlist the support of the very interests, Tammany Hall, Belmont, Ryan, which were most repugnant to him. How could he continue to vote for Clark?

The crisis came in the fourteenth ballot. When Nebraska was called, Senator Hitchcock asked that the delegation be polled. Bryan rose in his place and demanded recognition. An expectant convention went quiet.

"THE PRESIDING OFFICER: For what purpose does the gentleman from Nebraska rise?"

"MR. BRYAN, of Nebraska: To explain my vote."[14]

Suspecting trouble, opposition delegates clamoured for "regular order." The chairman ruled that nothing was in order but the calling of the roll. Thereupon Bryan replied:

"As long as Mr. Ryan's agent—as long as New York's ninety votes are recorded for Mr. Clark, I withhold my vote from him and cast it——"[15]

Pandemonium broke loose.

Senator Stone interceded for Bryan and asked that he be heard. The Commoner then read the statement which he had prepared. He reminded the delegates that they had passed his Morgan-Ryan-Belmont resolution by a four-to-one vote and had thereby pledged themselves against the nomination of any man connected with the "privilege-seeking, favour-hunting class."

"The vote of the state of New York in this convention, as cast under the unit rule, does not represent the intelligence, the virtue, the Democracy or the patriotism of the ninety men who are here. It represents the will of one man—Charles F. Murphy—and he represents the influences that dominated the Republican convention at Chicago and are trying to dominate this convention. . . .

[14] *Official Report of the Proceedings of the Democratic National Convention*, p. 232.
[15] *Ibid.*

". . . I shall withhold my vote from Mr. Clark as long as New York's vote is recorded for him. And the position that I take in regard to Mr. Clark, I will take in regard to any other candidate whose name is now or may be before the convention. I shall not be a party to the nomination of any man, no matter who he may be . . . who will not, when elected, be absolutely free to carry out the anti-Morgan-Ryan-Belmont resolution and make his administration reflect the wishes and the hopes of those who believe in a government of the people, by the people, and for the people. . . .

"With the understanding that I shall stand ready to withdraw my vote from the one for whom I am going to cast it whenever New York casts her vote for him, I cast my vote for Nebraska's second choice, Governor Wilson."

It was a thrilling moment. The Wilson supporters broke into wild applause. Nebraska voted twelve for Wilson, four for Clark. While the change in the total vote was inconsequential—Clark lost only one and a half votes and Wilson gained only five—it was nevertheless an epoch-making incident. The Commoner had at last made his decision, placed all his power and influence behind Wilson.

Clark, hearing promptly of Bryan's shift to Wilson, came "in a rage" from Washington to Baltimore. He had been absolutely confident of the nomination. He intended to rise to a question of privilege on the floor of the convention. But the convention adjourned just as he was arriving. Would he have stampeded it if he had walked down the central aisle? He was in an ugly mood, and after long talks with his managers and with Hearst, gave out a statement declaring that the "outrageous aspersion" put upon him by Bryan was "utterly and absolutely false." He demanded "proof or retraction.". . .

Clark had reached his zenith. From that moment onward his vote began to waste away, here a vote, there a delegation. Wilson's supporters took courage. The fight became dogged, unremitting. The ballots crept up into the twenties and thirties and still no decision. Wilson at Sea Girt remarked:

"We have been figuring that at the present rate of gain I will be nominated in 175 more ballots."

June 30th was Sunday, and Wilson, with his family, escaped from the noisy camp at Sea Girt and drove to church at Spring Lake, New Jersey. After the service, the Reverend Dr. James M. Ludlow expressed surprise that the Governor should have come such a distance.

"Why, Doctor," he replied, in tones of deep emotion, "where should a man in my straits be on such a day, except in the House of God? I could not remain at the camp."

But, if the convention was not in session on Sunday, the politicians were busy enough. Wilson's opponents were charging, bitterly, that his managers were "making deals," promising patronage. Some of the accusations were specific: McCombs loved political manipulation! To make it clear that he would be bound by no such "arrangements," Wilson issued a statement:

"Of course I do not know in detail what my friends and supporters are doing, but I am morally certain that they are not making arrangements or attempting to come to an agreement with anybody. I am certain that they are doing nothing more than could be done in full view of the country, and that their only means of getting support is argument. There cannot be any possibility of any trading done in my name; not a single vote can or will be obtained by means of any promise."[16]

Nevertheless a political convention is a political convention. Manipulation, tit-for-tat, is the breath in the nostrils of its impresarios. Wilson might protest. McCombs was on the ground. And McCombs's problem, in luring the shy conservatives to Wilson's support, was Bryan. It had been Bryan from the beginning. Bryan stood like a rock in the way. On Sunday McCombs called Wilson on the telephone and told him that the feeling against Bryan was so intense among many delegates that his nomination depended upon the assurance, which McCombs was eager to give, that Wilson, in the event of his election, would not appoint Bryan Secretary of State.[17]

The Governor declined to make any such commitment.

"I will not bargain for this office. It would be foolish for me at this time to decide upon a cabinet officer, and it would be outrageous to eliminate anybody from consideration now, particularly Mr. Bryan, who has rendered such fine service to the party in all seasons."[18] . . .

It grew clearer every hour to the perspiring delegates at Baltimore that the mighty forces of public opinion were behind Wilson. But it was not until the thirtieth ballot, on the sixth day, that Wilson passed Clark, the vote standing:

Wilson	460
Clark	455

[16] Baltimore *Sun*, June 30, 1912.

[17] Josephus Daniels, in the *Saturday Evening Post*, September 5, 1925.

[18] Joseph P. Tumulty, *Woodrow Wilson As I Know Him*, p. 118, Garden City, New York: Doubleday, Page & Company, 1921.

Underwood	121½
Foss	30
Harmon	19
Kern	2

When the newspaper correspondents, rushing up from their tents at Sea Girt to inform the Governor—"You've passed him, you've passed him"—requested a statement, Wilson remarked:

"You might say that Governor Wilson received the news that Champ Clark had dropped to second place in a riot of silence."

Wilson continued to creep up, slowly, irresistibly. What was needed was the dramatic swing-over of some powerful delegation. And this came in the Tuesday session, the seventh day of the interminable convention. Just before the forty-third ballot got under way, McCombs went over to Roger Sullivan of Illinois:

"Roger, we've got to have Illinois, or I'll withdraw."

It was the irritable plea of a sick man.

"Sit steady, boy," replied the boss. A few minutes later, when his state's name was called, he rose and delivered fifty-eight votes to Governor Wilson.

Illinois was followed by Virginia and West Virginia.

It was the beginning of the end. Wilson had 602 votes, Clark had dwindled to 329. Underwood held 98½. The convention was now in the wildest confusion. When the forty-sixth roll call began, Senator Bankhead withdrew Underwood's candidacy, and Senator Stone released the Clark delegates, but announced that Missouri would cast her last vote for "old Champ Clark." John F. Fitzgerald followed by withdrawing Governor Foss's name, giving the Massachusetts vote to Wilson. Thereupon John J. Fitzgerald of New York moved that Wilson be nominated by acclamation. A wild outburst of cheering arose from every section of the armoury. All the delegates, with the exception of those from Missouri, were on their feet. Bryan had a broad smile on his face. Senator Reed objected to the motion, assuring the convention that, while the Missourians cherished no ill-feeling toward the Governor of New Jersey, they must insist on giving their forty-sixth vote to the Speaker. The Harmon men were then released, the roll proceeded, and Wilson polled 990 votes. Missouri paid its last tribute to Clark.

Stone then moved that the nomination be made unanimous. At 3:30 o'clock in the afternoon, Chairman James pronounced Woodrow Wilson the Democratic nominee for President of the United States.

L

STILL SMALL VOICE[1]

By

AUGUST DERLETH

Zona Gale (1874-1938), winner of the Pulitzer Prize for her *Miss Lulu Bett* and author of *Friendship Village*, *Heart's Kindred*, *Birth*, *Romance Island*, *Mothers of Men*, and many other published works, was a Wisconsin neighbor of August Derleth. His thorough account of her works, particularly the story of how *Birth* was written, makes this biography a valuable contribution. Mr. Derleth believes "that by all means the most significant and important incident in the book is the story of how Zona came to write *Birth*, her finest single work." William Lyon Phelps has described the novel, *Birth*, as "realistic art of a high order." The village scene described in this passage is, in the words of Mr. Derleth, "Zona Gale's Spoon River, her Winesburg, her Gopher Prairie."

ZONA GALE'S BEST NOVEL EMERGES

It was still a decade before *Miss Lulu Bett* when Zona came back to live in Portage, and already then she was at work on a long book, a book she called her first novel, her first real novel, a book which occupied more of her time than any other, one which she rewrote and revised constantly, which she interrupted to put together other books, one to which she invariably returned. She had had such a novel as this one in mind for some time; even in the height of her Friendship Village fame, she did not wish Macmillan to publish one of her books as a full-length novel, but only in the $1.20 size. "I shall like that much better, for it *isn't* a novel—and I want my first novel to be a really truly," she wrote to her mother.

This book would not come as Zona wanted it to come; it would not

[1] August Derleth, *Still Small Voice*, New York: D. Appleton-Century Company, 1940, pp. 118-127.

"jell." She tried repeatedly, wrote entire chapters, tore them up in despair. This was not simply a process which went on for a few months; no, it was a matter of years. It took a surprising and unanticipated occurrence to bring her to the perspective which made possible the complete emergence of Zona Gale from the sentiment which held her still.

When it became evident that the United States was drifting towards participation in the European War, her pacifism came to the fore. She released various strong statements to the press, she made many speeches ardently advocating pacifism, she fought war as much as she could by direct and by oblique attack. She enlisted others in the movement, she sought to link the great names of America's past to the cause. "Of all the things for which I am grateful to Mark Twain," she wrote, "I think that I should set first his incomparable prayer in time of war, written shortly before his death. If there is anyone who has not read the prayer, these are the days in which to read it." She fought for her cause without malice. When William T. Evjue, outspoken fighter for peace in his paper, Madison's *Capital Times*, wrote casually to her after the declaration of war that he felt like taking "the hide off Wilson," Zona replied wearily that however horrified and saddened she was by the war, "I don't want to take the hide off anyone," the kind of letter she would always write, the letter of a woman devoid of malice, with no thought of herself, but always consideration for others. This was typical of her. She had by this time taken possession of Portage, also; her many charities had endeared her; her kindness had given her a higher place than fame might have given her among them; her civic pride and ready interest in local matters lent her stability in the eyes of her fellow-citizens. From the moment that the declaration of war was made, Zona found a subtle but marked change in the attitude of her fellow-citizens; many of them were regarding her pacifistic stand with deep suspicion. She was wounded, certainly; the added indignity of finding herself one day under observation by the Federal secret service might have appealed to her as something out of comic opera, the complexion of which the incident unquestionably had, but it did not. She was shaken; but self-confidence and her confidence in people were shocked. This had the felicitous effect of severing the cords of sentiment which had bound her to the Friendship Village of the years just past. It was not, as several inept critics injudiciously wrote later, that she became disillusioned and depressed about village life; it was not this at all; it was the ability she now had to see her village in its proper perspective. The kind of critical nonsense spouted later about her pessimism and disillusionment is typical of the loose thinking and its product foisted upon a too gullible or too lazy public; the incident of the doubt cast upon her motives by the people she knew and trusted to believe in her implicitly served only to establish in her a firm balance which she never had before. She had suddenly been given insight enough to see both sides of the village street, so to speak, and within a very short time, her experience crystallized all those hitherto formless strivings about her long novel, her "really truly" novel, and she turned away from a new futile preaching of pacifism, not from the pacifistic ideal itself, to go back to her book.

Out of this catharsis emerged *Birth.*

If Zona Gale wrote anything at all that has the mark of greatness upon it, that book is *Birth.* Never with any illusions about her work, she had ability to judge her own writing far better than many another writer; she recognized *Birth* as her best work, and never doubted the wisdom of her choice from among her own books. She was never known to deprecate *Birth,* thought she deprecated others of her books, as, for instance, on the occasion of my visiting her ten years ago and praising *Bridal Pond,* arousing her reply, "Oh, no—it isn't a good book, not at all, not like *Birth!*" and subsequently, in answer to my own quick protest at such deprecation, "It's only that I know how far it is from what it might have been. But in *Birth*—that is different." I understood this very well later. The book *Birth* remains her longest, her best, her truest portrait of village life, her most careful work; this stark, realistic story of Marshall Pitt, an insignificant little man who strove to do his best in his small life but could not sell himself, is a village tragedy of the first water, a human tragedy that is as universal as earth itself. From cover to cover, her characterizations in this book are sharp and true, her examination of village life mature, her outlook balanced; nothing of Friendship Village was permitted in Burage, the Portage of *Birth.* Her Mr. Pitt—humble to a fault, pathetically inarticulate with his longing to rise in the eyes of his fellow-men, demanding sympathy in his utter humanity—is a character who will stand beside any character of Dreiser's, of Masters', of Anderson's or Lewis's or Cather's. The tragedy is unrelieved; no one believed in Pitt's innate fineness, his selfish, thoughtless wife deserted him, his son was ashamed of him, unable to recognize his father's unselfishness; but it is not a drab story, it is not bitter, it is not ironic.

If before this time Zona Gale's villages were credible, recognizable, true, Burage lived, Burage breathed. Between chapters in the book the villagers appear to make small talk with the effect of a Greek chorus; the book is frankly in the Greek tradition. It is not alone in these small pieces but throughout the entire book that the village exists in utmost reality. From the very first sentence: "A day of heat withered Burage," to the last, not a solitary false note is struck in the depiction of life in Burage. It is Burage, and not Friendship Village, which is Zona Gale's Spoon River, her Winesburg, her Gopher Prairie.

The village day went on. Everywhere the invisible ruled. The sign for the Angelus was given from the steeple, and the memorial to a moment—mystic and imperishable—beat in many hearts. The little shops were opened, and out came the humble symbols—cakes, fruit, fabrics. Awnings were lowered, watering-cans made cool the old boards, anaemic little boys drew large mops across the windows. A faint odor of browned crust began to steal from the bakery. The photographer set out on the little "cobbled" shelf before an upper window, his negatives—a bride and groom, an old man who "sat" for the last time to please the children; a naked baby. The doors of the Burage *Weekly* were open, and the smell of wet ink and paper hung in the air. In the cramped Post Office the contents of a lean bag were distributed by the old post-master, as slowly as if the mail were mills of God; dusty, fly-specked little hole, where the state functioned as precisely as under hard wood and marble; and, in their tiny glass coffins, marked with worn red letters, were popped missives of death, of life, of love, of unspeakable commonplace.

Epps, the undertaker, ran round the corner. He was going to make ready for burial the body of Lee Ashe. His body lay at the house of a friend across the alley, and there his funeral would be held, because his own parlor had never been furnished. A freckled, hairy man, this Ashe, who had had a way of button-holing folk and talking close to their faces. When one saw him coming, one crossed the street. He had liked others and no one had liked him. Now there went the undertaker. Men saw the crape and thought: "Well, it would have been easy to talk to him sometimes, after all," and they wondered why Epps didn't get his wife to press out that old crape.

A farm wagon was hitched at the bank-corner, and three angular women crossed to the lawyer's office. "Batten, Attorney-at-Law," the sign said, and their hearts beat as they went up the sunken stair. A square man of their family, a man with lips and eye-balls like puffy plums, sat waiting for them. They all talked at once to Batten who listened with his eyes shut and had occasional twinges of rheumatism and twisted in his chair, held his breath, and emitted it in a whisper. All this was about a line fence which had been discovered to be two feet farther east on the surface of the world than was thought to be true righteousness. The man of puffy plums smashed down his fist. One of the angular women sat tense, with thin lips and tossing head. Outside the earth stretched twelve thousand miles each way from Batten's office, and no one was thinking about it.

All down the little Main Street men came to their work. They thought about the orders they must fill that day, the amounts due them; a train whistled, and they knew that it was ten minutes late; so-and-so's grass needed cutting, they noted; and there was his brother visiting from Seattle, why didn't he do it? Fat geese waddled about a back yard. Somebody had a little tree of crab apples, and the family was gathering them for a jar of marmalade. Locusts sang. It was going to be a hot day. Cans of cream were driven to the creamery. A bill poster put up a terrible warning, calculated to lure: "The Candy Ladies. Come and See." Old Mrs. Jellsie fed the white rooster which her son had sent her a week ago. Little Curt Whitman went by with his red cart. The Messers' baby cried.

Once an excitement was caused by Aden Holder, whose mind was queer, appearing on his front veranda and screaming about the protective tariff. His daughter, with her embroidery in one hand, came and led him away, successfully diverting his attention from national politics by telling him that his custard was ready. Once Aden Holder had been the boss of the County. Now he almost ran to his custard.

This was the day on which Jenny Berry let her mother go to the poor house. By scrubbing and cleaning, Jenny had been able to support both, but she had no one with whom to leave her mother. Alone, the old woman cut off her hair, burned the bed-"clothes," chased chickens, emptied a pot of pickles on the front steps. And no one would care for her. So Jenny stayed at home, and they both came near to starvation. "Take her, then," said Jenny at last. "One hell more won't burn nobody. Me? No, I don't care. And ma don't know enough to care. But if anybody invites me to the missionary circle again, I'll knock the top of their head off."

At the Carters', Josephine Carter had just brought home her young husband to the shabby yellow frame house and to the sloping-roofed room where she had slept since she was a little girl. A great occasion. And yet the low windows of the sloping-roofed home looked no different. Next door the Bennet's new house was going up. Only the two of them, and all that room! They say there'll be windows in the closets. What do they want of a fireplace—can't they afford a furnace? *Both*! Say, where did Sim Bennet get his ideas?

About noon a loose horse appears. She gallops on the brick walks and on the side-walk boards. Everybody who has oats comes running with a hatful of oats. She dodges down an alley. Everybody remembers the Johnson's baby in that block. Whose horse is it? Barney's again. Funny he can't keep his barnyard shut up. There she goes! Her master comes running, the horse takes the bridle, and everybody turns indoors, secretly disappointed.

The Summer afternoon slips through the little village, and is gone. It seems to have touched nothing. A few women water the plants. Ministers go patiently about making expected calls and entering them in the little books. A load of hay comes creaking under the elms. Tillie Paul strolls by with a cake which her mother has baked for somebody. The Youngers are carrying their father's supper down to the shop. Poor Jeff Cribb is out walking up and down the bricks—waiting. Everybody knows for what he waits, walking there every day, coughing. A group of girls in pink and blue and yellow, as yielding as thistledown, go footing home from some errand, manufactured for its own delight. Children pass, singing or quarreling. Garments are gathered in from lines and from grass, and sprinkled. Bennie Jedd drives home his mother's cow.

Six o'clock. Over the golden aisles of the streets, mysterious with maple boughs, once more the Angelus, the bass of the round house whistle, the treble of the brick-yard whistle. Burage breathes deep, all the tension of the day dissolves. A new air permeates the village. It relaxes, expects. It is as if some great brooding, wistful face, so close to all, changes expression; and every one replies. A creative moment, spiritual, tender, human. All Burage either goes home or welcomes home. Meetings, supper, complaints, tenderness, irritations, control. An impressive and spectacular and glorious moment, and a terrible moment. The expansion of human beings in centers carefully contrived. Or the crush of human beings into centers benumbing, crippling. Beings seldom thrilling from creative work, but leaden from toil of rote. The cry of all the world in the throat of people of Burage at six o'clock.

In such well-observed detail is the background of village life woven into the story of Marshall Pitt, a portrait not only recognizable, but sentient with life. The sentimentality of Friendship Village has been given over for the reality of Burage; the partly imaginary, wish-fulfillment characters of those earlier books have given way before the completely credible people of Burage. Against this background the small tragedy of Marshall Pitt moves inexorably forward, the pathetic frustrated drama of Barbara Pitt plays itself to its bitter end, and Jeffrey Pitt emerges as the inevitably weak product of these two. Zona Gale was no longer patently aware only of the pleasant aspects of village life; she had gained sufficient perspective to permit her jibing gently at the "valid etiquette of villages. They will face the facts, the horrors of existence; discuss the details of deaths and births. But at mention of a white starched petticoat they still blush." She could write brief, stark lines such as these: "Barbara's flesh was her true identity, and it was still seeking. . . . Her hold upon the moral life was her understanding of money obligation. . . . Barbara had dreamed of love and beauty, and she had missed both. She sought them. This is the epitaph for every woman who fails."

The manifest care with which this book was written, the record of her tribulations with it are pointed by an amusing, trivial error, a single flaw in the book: a minor character, a Mrs. Granger, who dies on page 209, is found still alive some time later on page 296, and so remains throughout the rest of the novel. The book grew out of her years in Portage, beyond any question; it is the stuff of her own experience; she knew this life, she had seen it lived all around her. The critics received the book with strong praise; it was hailed by *The Atlantic Monthly* and *The Dial*, by *Unity* and *The Outlook* alike; and more than one reviewer struck the two familiar notes: "In scope and purpose this is by all means Miss Gale's best work," from *The Outlook*, and "Time was when she made people too sweet," from the Boston *Herald-Journal*. But from her public and from scattered reviewers throughout the country rose cries of rage. Where were the sweet, sentimental people of that earlier town? Where was Friendship Village? The New York *Sun* answered them: "It is where it ought to be, along with Pelleas and Etarre, way back in the past—an excellent foundation for this superior achievement, which retains all the worth of the others, with a better craftsmanship and a far higher understanding."

The book suffered a fate which many another outstanding novel has suffered; compared to the reception given her previous books by readers, it was neglected. There were two reasons for this: her readers were conditioned to Friendship Village, and unimaginatively expected more sweetness and sentimentality from her, and they were ready to turn away from reality because of the war, for *Birth* appeared in 1918. It was an incident of that war which had helped to bring *Birth* to perfection; it was not unnatural that the same war should be in part responsible for its failure before the public.

LI

CLARENCE DARROW FOR THE DEFENSE [1]

By

IRVING STONE

This biography of Clarence Darrow (1857-1938), American lawyer, reads like a rich adventure story. Darrow wished to be known as a friend of labor and the downtrodden. He was counsel for the defense in many famous trials, including that of Eugene V. Debs in the noted strike case and of the McNamara brothers for the dynamiting of the *Los Angeles Times* Building. He was against capital punishment, and it is of interest to note that none of his clients ever went to the electric chair or the scaffold.

From Irving Stone's informal and fascinating biography, with its many rich incidents and amusing stories, we present several word sketches of Clarence Darrow.

MR. DARROW COMMENTS ON HIS OWN APPEARANCE

At forty Darrow was smooth-faced and hard-stomached. He wore a jaunty black derby on the street; in cool weather his meandering black satin tie was kept within the confines of his vest; his clothing had not yet reached that stage of acute dishabille which occasioned his reply to reporters . . . who were twitting him about his appearance:

"I can't understand why you chaps look so different from me. I have my suits made at the same tailors you do. I pay as much for them. I go to the same stylish shops to buy my haberdashery. The only thing I can figure is maybe you dudes take off your clothes when you go to sleep at night." . . .

[1] Irving Stone, *Clarence Darrow for the Defense*, copyright 1941, reprinted by permission of Doubleday, Doran and Company, Inc., New York, pp. 86, 164-165, 169-170.

NO FURTHER QUESTIONS

He took pleasure in outwitting medical men. In the world-renowned Massie case in Honolulu "a prosecution witness, a doctor, had a reputation for withholding on direct examination just enough facts so that if on cross-examination the examiner sought to bring out anything favorable to the defendant, the doctor still had some undisclosed fact with which to confound the defense. It was evident that this doctor was pulling his punches and waiting to tangle with Mr. Darrow. When Darrow rose he asked amiably:

"'Did you enjoy your trip from Los Angeles, Doctor?'

"'Yes, I did.'

"'Are you being paid for testifying in this case?'

"'Yes, I am.'

"Mr. Darrow turned solemnly to the bench and murmured, 'No further questions.'"

HE STAYS IN NIGHTS NOW

Darrow and a college professor named John had debated frequently, "always kidding each other in a humorous vein on the platform. Darrow knew of the professor's inclination to step out of an evening. After his death Darrow and a friend called to pay their respects to the widow, who had placed her husband's ashes in an urn on the mantelpiece. When she left the living room for an instant Darrow gazed up at the urn.

"'Poor John,' he murmured, 'you'll have to stay in nights now.'"

STOLEN TOO RECENTLY

A good-looking young man came into Darrow's office and asked Darrow to defend him against a charge of robbery. Darrow inquired when he could get a portion of his fee. "I can get some of the money for you tonight," replied the young man. "No-oo," murmured Darrow, "I don't care to accept money that has been stolen—so recently."

HE'S TOO RADICAL

Toward more serious problems he turned an acid irreverence. Invited as a criminologist to address the prisoners of the Cook County jail, he gave them a lecture on Altgeld's revolutionary theory of the economic base of crime. "There is no such thing as crime as the word is generally understood. Nine tenths of you are in jail because you did not have enough money to pay a good lawyer. While some of you men might pick my pocket because that is your trade, when I get outside everybody picks my pocket—by charging me a dollar for something that is worth twenty-five cents. If every man, woman and child in the world had a chance to make a decent, fair, honest living there would be no jails and no lawyers and no courts."

When he had finished a guard asked one of the prisoners what he thought of the speech. "He's too radical," replied the prisoner.

LII

ALFRED I. duPONT: THE FAMILY REBEL[1]

By

MARQUIS JAMES

Marquis James has written this biography on the solid foundation of a wealth of firsthand information and facts. The scholarly and unbiased analysis he has made of his subject, combined with his fascinating way of telling his story, makes this an important contribution to the literature of American industrial history.

Alfred I. duPont (1864-1935) was undoubtedly one of the principal creative figures of modern American industry. Mr. James has shown him as one of the ablest and most illustrious members of the family which established a gun powder plant at Wilmington in the early 1800's. Today E. I. Du Pont De Nemours and Company is a world-known chemical manufacturing corporation producing chemicals, dyes, rayon, plastics, explosives, paints, and many other products. Normally only an insignificant percentage of its income is derived from military sales.

Marquis James has chosen an excerpt which he states "narrates not only the turning point in the life of Alfred I. duPont but of one of America's great industrial organizations as well."

"YOU CERTAINLY COULDN'T RUN THE BUSINESS, COULD YOU?"

The Spanish-American War had interrupted an earnest controversy among the DuPont partners. The decentralizing measures introduced by Eugene had not been sufficient to keep the company abreast of the times. Though still the dominant factor in the explosive field, DuPont no longer ruled with the ease and sureness of Boss Henry's day. Independent

[1] Marquis James, *Alfred I. duPont: The Family Rebel*, copyright 1941, used by special permission of the publishers, The Bobbs-Merrill Company, Indianapolis, pp. 137-158.

and semi-independent concerns, particularly Laflin & Rand, grew stronger. Young, vigorous men were coming up in these companies, and this new blood made itself felt.

Of the four partners who shaped the destinies of DuPont, Francis G. and Doctor Alexis I. were ill from overwork and old beyond their years. Frank, forty-nine and a capital scientific man, had worn himself out with managerial responsibilities for which he was unfitted. His brother, 'Lex, fifty-six, who knew nothing of the technical end of the powder business, was a fair executive in a place where a first-rate one was needed. The head of the firm and third brother, Eugene, fifty-nine, was another example of an A number 1 practical powderman in an executive job over his head. The fourth of the older partners, Colonel Henry Algernon, the best executive of the lot, was weary of powder and expending most of his energies in the bizarre battle with "Gas" Addicks for the senatorship.

That left the two junior partners Charles I. and Alfred, neither of whom had the slightest say in the general affairs of the company. Charley did not mind. In poor health, he was satisfied to drum along as a yard superintendent, which, indeed, represented the level of his capacity. Alfred did mind, and continued to butt his head against a stone wall of conservatism represented in the main by two tired men, Eugene and Frank. Having been properly thanked for his wartime services, the stormy petrel was thrust back into a yard superintendency to catch up on black-powder orders while his elders ran the firm. . . .

On October 23, 1899, the family firm became a corporation under the laws of Delaware. The capitalization, $2,000,000, was a symbol merely, having no reference to the actual worth of the property.

Thus as far as management went the difference between partnership and corporation proved to be that between nip and tuck. Partners, and partners only, became stockholders—the four seniors each owning one-fifth of the shares, as they had done under the partnership, and the juniors each one-tenth. Eugene was, of course, elected president and the three other elder partners became vice-presidents. That left the offices of secretary and of treasurer. They were combined and given to a figurehead, Charles Irénée. Thus an office for every stockholder—except Alfred. He was made a director, with nothing to direct.

What Colonel Henry Algernon saw, Alfred also saw, with much more clarity; the company dying on its feet, of dry rot within. Great oaks in the Brandywine woods sometimes went the same way, looking magnificent to the last. Colonel Henry, whose efforts at reinvigoration had failed, had political aspirations to divert him. . . .

Alfred's chief diversion, music, growing deafness threatened to take away. Threshing about for something to fill a world shrinking under his eyes, he had hit on automobiles. After Pierre had deserted the company, Alfred, too, entertained passing thoughts about throwing up the sponge and going to France to learn to make automobiles. He was sure he could build a better car than any produced in America. Then he thought of his son. There must be something to pass on to him; that had always been the DuPont way. . . . Was not this infant, Alfred Victor, the eldest son of the eldest son of the eldest son of the founder?

The ambition to save the company for coming generations of the clan must have received fresh impetus when Alfred saw one hundred DuPonts gathered about the great table he had built for the family's centennial anniversary dinner. How had the company been kept in the family so long? How had it gained and held leadership of the industry? Simply by training, in a hard school, young DuPonts to fill old DuPonts' shoes. Alfred had no objection to requiring the young men to serve stiff apprenticeships. He himself had served a stiff one, and had profited by it. What he did object to was keeping the young men mere apprentices until their natural powers of expansion had been stunted; or until those too alert to endure the stunting process had been driven away. Seated about him Alfred could have counted ten young cousins, including Pierre and four other sons of the brilliant Lammot duPont, who were making or planning careers outside the company.

To convict them of an error of judgment would have been difficult. What DuPont in his thirties could match the material progress in life of Alfred's old roommate, Coleman, who had spent not a day in the service of the company?

The attractive Coly had come up under different auspices entirely. Leaving M. I. T. he had placed himself in the hands of his uncle, Fred duPont, of Louisville, famous for encouraging young men without pampering them. Coly's first job had been driving a mule underground in a coal mine which the Louisville duPonts owned at Central City, Kentucky. The six-foot-four beginner was popular among his fellow-workmen. He joined their Saturday night drinking bouts and signed with the Knights of Labor, the contemporary union. Step by step Coly rose to be general superintendent, then vice-president of the Kentucky family's Central City Coal & Iron Company. Under his administration Central City grew from a squalid mining hamlet to a brisk little city of seventy-five hundred people, its miners the best-housed and most contented in the region. . . .

When death suddenly took Fred duPont in 1893, the widespread holdings he had created for the Kentucky family might have been thrown in confusion save for three men. Two of them were Tom L. Johnson and Arthur Moxham, whom Fred duPont had befriended as poverty-stricken boys and given opportunities to prove their worth. The third was Thomas Coleman duPont, then twenty-eight years old. Johnson and Moxham were happy to pay their debt to Fred duPont by acting as preceptors to Coly.

Under the guidance of older men, Coleman gradually assumed charge of mining companies, steel mills and street railways. . . . This kept him from home much of the time, and in 1900 Coleman removed his family to Wilmington, renting an unpretentious though roomy brick house at 2023 Delaware Avenue. . . .

Meantime Coleman and his fatherly mentor, Tom Johnson, had taken Pierre under their wings, giving him no cause to regret his decision to leave the powder company. Pierre proved very able, particularly in matters of corporate financing. Johnson made him president of his steel company to liquidate certain valuable holdings, principally real estate, which had not been taken over by the United States Steel Corporation. Pierre also began to learn the street-railway business and was a partner of Coleman in several ventures in that field. The two worked well together, Pierre's caution acting as a counterweight to Coleman's boldness.

The crisis on the Brandywine for which Alfred had so long prepared fell suddenly.

On January 21, 1902, President Eugene duPont failed to appear at his office. He sent word that he was remaining at home to doctor a cold. In three days he had pneumonia. On January 28 he died.

Consternation took the surviving stockholders of the corporation—excepting Alfred. There were hurried, flustered, futile meetings—Alfred, as usual, not in attendance and probably not invited.

Who should succeed to the presidency of the firm?

By seniority the post belonged to Frank duPont, who was ill. . . . Frank regretfully said that his health demanded that he "give up active business," rather than assume new burdens.

Doctor Alexis duPont offered, and truthfully, a similar excuse.

Colonel Henry Algernon eliminated himself on other grounds. The management of his large fortune and politics consumed his energies. A few months off was another election, in which the Colonel hoped to smash "Gas" Addicks and carry off the senatorship.

It is improbable that Secretary-Treasurer Charles I. was ever seriously considered. His health, too, was poor; which made it unnecessary to examine his other qualifications.

It is certain that Alfred was not seriously considered; "too young," said Cousin Frank. Of course the objections to Alfred went deeper than the question of age, as Alfred himself later attested. "[I was] young, aggressive, and not popular. I suppose I was impulsive--and not always polite."

Thus the prediction impulsive Alfred often had made came to pass: the company adrift, its old leader dead without a new one in sight.

Secretly the beaten men came to the painful resolution to sell the company. It fell to Frank duPont to communicate this star-chamber decision to Alfred....

Cousin Frank was brief. There was no one, he said, to carry on. The other stockholders felt it would be best to dispose of the business while a respectable price could be obtained. Laflin & Rand was suggested as a likely purchaser. What did Alfred think about the matter?

For once Alfred curbed his ready tongue, though his brain was reeling. Confess to the world the utter defeat and humiliation of the first industrial family of the United States! Sell the company! Transform a heritage of five generations in the making into a chattel to be exchanged for money! Though for years he had been steeling himself to face this very debacle, with difficulty Alfred kept his thoughts to himself. Knowing his only hope to balk the proposed sacrilege lay in curbing his old fault of antagonizing his elders too directly, Alfred replied briefly that in the circumstances "a disposal of the assets of the company seemed advisable." He could trust himself to say no more. But he acted—quietly slipping away to New York to see bankers about a loan for refinancing the company in case cash were needed to block the proposed sale to Laflin & Rand.

When the conversation with Cousin Frank took place Eugene duPont had been ten days with his ancestors in [the family burying ground in] Sand Hole Woods.

Another doleful week dragged by—the company drifting without a rudder. Swallowing hard, the three senior officers and Charles I. did their best to reconcile themselves to the fate they had pronounced on the company. In private they talked much, by way of self-justification. Frank duPont, who had to unburden himself to someone, had long, distressed conversations with his son, Francis I., the young chemist at Carney's Point. The father excused himself on grounds of health. To accept the presidency and try to carry on would be his death sentence. He said the same applied to Alexis. They were all trapped. To sell was the only way out.

Alfred, too, talked. He had to do something to conceal what was going on in his mind—for Alfred, ordinarily, was not good at the arts of dissimulation. He talked about going to France to learn to manufacture automobiles, and would wax warm as he sketched a glowing future for the motorcar. With everyone screening himself behind an excuse for not taking over the company someone put Alfred on record:

"*You* certainly couldn't run it, could you?"

"No," said Alfred. "Maybe I can push a wheelbarrow; but that's all the sense I have."

When the stockholders met to write the formal obituary of the company, they may or may not have been surprised at the presence of Alfred. It was the first stockholders' meeting he had attended in years. He had come up from the yards in his working clothes, his hands grimy with powder. He sat with his eyes closed, perhaps in order to hear better. He said not a word while Secretary Charles I., in a husky voice, read the minutes of an earlier meeting embodying the decision to sell. One by one the stockholders repeated apologies for the necessity of their course. Twelve million dollars was mentioned as a minimum price. At length Colonel Henry Algernon moved, for the record, that the assets of the company be offered for sale to Laflin & Rand and that Hamilton M. Barksdale be appointed agent to conduct the negotiations.

Opening his eyes, Alfred offered an amendment providing that the business be sold to the highest responsible bidder. Alfred's contribution occasioned some surprise. Who, indeed, could outbid Laflin & Rand? Nevertheless, Colonel Henry accepted the amendment. The question put, and all voting "Aye," the meeting was declared adjourned.

Except for Alfred's seemingly innocuous amendment, a cut-and-dried program had gone through—much to the relief of those who had feared that, despite his assurance to Frank duPont, Alfred might make a scene.

The meeting officially over, Alfred was the first one on his feet. "Gentlemen," he said, "I'll buy the business."

The five others present may have suspected that they, as well as Alfred, were losing their hearing. The yard superintendent set them right:

"Yes, I'll buy the business."

Cousin Frank was the first to find his voice. He told Alfred he could not have the business, adding: "Besides, it's cash, you know."

The bald refusal snapped the taut cords holding Alfred's emotions in check. He forgot to be polite.

"*Why not*?" he demanded. "If you can't run the company, sell it to someone who can!"

When Alfred was excited his voice grew shrill. For three weeks he had been restraining feelings which all but consumed a passionate and outraged nature. Backing away from the conference table, Alfred took his stand against the door, as if to say that no one should leave the room without hearing him. He made an arresting figure: soiled working clothes; musclar form, hard as nails; flashing blue eyes; firm chin with the telltale family cleft; big, imperious DuPont nose dominating a strong, sensitive face, which was flushed and defiant. For an instant he stood there, his eyes searching those of first one cousin, then another. Then words burst forth in a torrent. . . .

By the time Alfred ceased speaking, the blood was returning to the face of one of his five auditors—Colonel Henry. Alfred's fighting words were taking hold of the old soldier. Rising from his chair he put a hand on Alfred's shoulder.

"All right," he said, "I'm with you."

And then to the others:

"Gentlemen, I think I understand Alfred's sentiment in desiring to purchase the business. I wish to say that it has my hearty approval. I shall insist that he be given the first opportunity to acquire the property."

Alfred opened the door and slipped out.

Behind him he left not much agreement with Colonel Henry's high-hearted stand. The impression was that Alfred had just made another of his scenes, rendering a hard thing harder all round. Leaving the meeting, Doctor Alexis duPont put in a telephone call for Hamilton M. Barksdale.

A charming Virginian, H. M. Barksdale was perhaps the ablest man, outside the family, ever associated with a DuPont enterprise. . . . Hastening to the residence of Alexis duPont, the Virginian heard from the lips of that ill and upset man the decision to sell the company. Barksdale was asked to assume the presidency for the purpose of conducting the negotiations. If an acceptable price—$12,000,000—could not be obtained, Barksdale was asked to run the business.

Alexis said that in the opinion of the majority stockholders, Laflin & Rand appeared to be the likeliest prospect as a purchaser. As a sort of afterthought he mentioned that Alfred "desires an opportunity to present a proposition" which "has, of course, been granted." It was obvious that Doctor Alexis did not intend that Alfred's proposal be taken very seriously. He renewed his request that Barksdale take the presidency and make it his first duty to deal with prospective purchasers, whether Alfred or someone else. . . .

"In my opinion," the Virginian told the Doctor, "it would be a great misfortune for the company to place anyone at the head of the concern until you have exhausted all efforts to secure a man of your name to take the helm."

What Alexis had been trying to say all along was that such efforts had already been exhausted. Barksdale was courteous but firm. He could not, he said, "at this time" accept the presidency under the conditions imposed.

This was a real disappointment. Unless Barksdale could be prevailed on to reconsider, or someone else be found, the dispirited old officers themselves would have to deal with the determined Alfred. Moreover, the time was short. Alfred had asked for only a week.

On leaving the dramatic meeting of stockholders Alfred, too, used the telephone. Finding his cousin Coleman at home, he got in his automobile and drove to 2023 Delaware Avenue.

The masterful Coly was a hard man to bowl over. He was used to bowling over the other fellow—and settling on his own terms. He talked in round figures—"never mind the pennies"—and in big figures. He immobilized opposition by the bold, swift, decisive strokes of a financial soldier of fortune enjoying the prestige of victory. Dash, competence and confidence were his weapons. To tear apart and rebuild a rickety corporation, taking for his pay a block of stock on the gamble that the reorganization would be profitable, was all in a day's work for Coly. When a thing failed he dropped it like a hot potato, turning, without repinings to something else; he had lost his time, the others their money. . . .

Of all who bore the DuPont name, and none other had been considered, Coly was Alfred's first choice as an associate in what might prove a desperate throw to save the company for the family. The second choice was quiet, even-tempered, inconspicuous Pierre. Alfred really hoped to get them both. His reasons were characteristic, being both practical and sentimental. Alfred regarded Coleman and Pierre as the ablest of the family's young men. Moreover each was the oldest son of a brother of Alfred's father.

After hearing his old chum's audacious proposal—that the three of them buy the company—Coleman, for once, had nothing to say beyond:

"Al, it's a big thing. I'll have to talk to Elsie."

The idea of the strapping, irresistible Coleman taking counsel with his meek little wife on a question of business hazard would have been incongruous beyond belief to one who did not know that couple very intimately indeed. Elsie duPont could walk under her husband's outstretched arm. Most of her time seemed taken up with her five children. Her intellectual attainments were modest. Yet within her placid being was some resource which supplied her towering husband with strength when he most needed it. . . .

After Alfred had gone, Coleman spoke to Elsie, whose comment was brief:

"You know what it is to be in business with your relatives."

Coleman did know. One of the never-solved problems inherited from his Uncle Fred had been to handle the kinfolk who owned part of some of the enterprises with which he had to do. And, of course, he knew the state of affairs on the Brandywine. Coleman announced a decision:

"I won't go in unless I get a free hand."

That, indeed, had always been for him a *sine qua non* in ordinary business matters.

Coleman rang up Pierre in Lorain, Ohio. He said he would go in with Alfred if Pierre would go in. Pierre promised to come to Wilmington the next day to talk about it.

The three cousins met in the billiard room at Swamp Hall [Alfred's residence]. The conversation lasted until late and resulted in an alliance for the purpose of buying the company. Tactfully Coleman asked for a free hand in the corporate management and for the lion's share of the stock that should be divided among the three purchasers. Alfred offered no objections; Pierre none. Coleman could be a very persuasive asker. . . .

Because of his exclusion from the inner councils [and a constitutional indifference to mere dollar values] Alfred had only an imperfect idea of what the company owned. . . . Never in his life had he seen the inside of one of the company's ledgers. Of course he could compute the amount of profits segregated for dividends—being in receipt of one-tenth of them.

Poring over such sketchy data as Alfred provided, Coleman and Pierre could scarcely believe their eyes. To let this property go out of the family for $12,000,000, or for twice that, would be a crime against DuPonts unborn. Just one hundred years before, Eleuthère Irénée duPont de Nemours had begun the erection of the original brace of wheel mills on the edge of the Brandywine. In all the ups and downs of fortune the company had experienced since that time, it seemed certain that no one DuPont's single act had counted for more than that of Eleuthère's great-grandson, Alfred, when his burning protest had halted the irreparable sale to Laflin & Rand. In doing this, Alfred had scarcely thought of the company in terms of money at all but as a perpetual trust for one generation to protect and hand to the next.

The cousins used only three or four days of the week Alfred had asked for in which to submit a definite proposal. Coleman was selected to present the would-be purchasers' proposition to the family elders. This was a wise choice. . . . Coleman enjoyed a considerable prestige in the family for his successes in the West. Like all successful promoters he knew how to create such prestige. . . . Moreover, Coleman was at home dealing with the baffled officers of corporations in distress. He knew the calm, assured line to take to make them willing, yes, eager, to shift their onerous burdens to his towering shoulders.

In the names of his two cousins and himself, Coleman offered to buy the company. He offered to pay not the minimum of $12,000,000 but more —just how much more he could not at the moment say until an opportunity presented to survey the assets in detail.

A good promoter uses as little cash, especially his own cash, as possible. Coleman proposed that the sellers accept notes, bearing 4 per cent, for their stock, plus a bonus of stock in the new corporation to be chartered to run the business.

"You wouldn't want to cripple our plans by tying up all our cash," said Coleman.

A few days before Alfred duPont had faced these same five men. His stinging words, pouring from an outraged nature, had suited the occasion. In the nick of time the sheer force of their impact had blocked the sale to Laflin & Rand. No less impressive now was the gigantic Coleman. For so large a man Coleman had a small head but his countenance was impressive: square, clefted chin; big nose dominating a vital face. His easy gestures, rich, warm voice and confident words were a tonic for the nerves Alfred had shattered.

The elders thanked their Kentucky cousin. They promised to consider his proposal carefully. Coleman departed knowing that he had made his usual happy impression on a distressed corporation directorate.

The next day Eugene duPont, Jr., confidentially told Pierre that the elders, excepting Doctor Alexis who was too ill, had met and decided to accept the proposition presented by Coleman. Eugene was sure that Alexis, too, would assent. . . .

The cousins had to hustle faster than they expected. Pierre dropped around at the company's office, thinking to have a talk with some of his elders and if possible to obtain an inventory of the firm's assets. Cousin Frank, who had acted as president since the death of Eugene, was preparing to open the morning's mail. He handed the letters to Pierre and began to mention other matters that needed attention at once. The astonished younger man protested that he and his cousins were not prepared to take over; that nothing had been put in writing; that even the amount of the purchase price had not been definitely settled. Frank duPont replied that those were details. The elders had decided to sell. If the younger men were serious in their intention to buy and run the business they might as well begin running it now. After a few words to indicate immediately pressing matters, Cousin Frank took his hat and coat and left.

On March 1, 1902, a week after Cousin Frank had unceremoniously turned over his desk to Pierre duPont, the three cousins formally took charge of the company. The financial arrangements represented a masterpiece of promotion, not one dollar changing hands from purchasers to sellers. Everything was on the cuff, excepting $2,100 Alfred, Coleman and Pierre put up for twenty-one incorporators' shares in the new corporation to acquire the assets of the old one which was dissolved. . . .

A rough survey of assets showed the old company to be worth $24,000,000 plus, or double what it might have been sold for had not Alfred taken the bull by the horns. . . . [For these assets] the old-company stockholders agreed to a price of $15,360,000. Payment was made in the securities of the new company which the three cousins had incorporated: $12,000,000 in 4 per cent purchase-money notes; $3,360,000 in stock.

The new company issued, in all, $12,000,000 worth of 4 per cent notes and 120,000 shares of stock with a par value of $12,000,000. All the notes and 33,600 shares of stock, worth $3,360,000, went to the old-company stockholders and to the estate of the late Eugene duPont. This left 86,400 shares, worth $8,640,000, which Coleman, Alfred and Pierre split among themselves as promoters' profits.

[Of the new company Coleman became president and Pierre treasurer. With the title of vice president and general manager Alfred assumed direct responsibility for the production of powder. His first office was a shack in the yards.]

LIII

J. B. MURPHY, STORMY PETREL OF SURGERY[1]

By

LOYAL DAVIS

Dr. John B. Murphy, famous Chicago surgeon, was born of Irish immigrant parents in Wisconsin in 1857 and died in 1916. He invented the anastomosis button (1892) which simplified the technique of abdominal operations and thus lessened their danger. He gained distinction also as a teacher of surgery and in 1911 was president of the American Medical Association.

From Dr. Loyal Davis' spirited story of the life of Dr. Murphy we present a short but unusual excerpt—a scene as Dr. Murphy nears death and outlines his own autopsy.

"LOOK CAREFULLY AT MY KIDNEYS"

"And now," the dying man said to Dr. Keefe, "get a piece of paper and write down what I dictate, will you please?"

Dr. Keefe wrote:

I want a postmortem made after my death. You will find plaques of calcification in my aorta and destruction of its lining membrane. Those changes have been produced by an infection of long standing somewhere in my body. There are two other points I want checked carefully: my appendix, because I had appendicitis when I was a boy, and when I was in Germany studying I had a kidney infection, so look carefully at my kidneys.

Here was a man more concerned with his autopsy than in living. Had he been given one wish, doubtless he would have wanted to perform the

[1] Loyal Davis, *J. B. Murphy, Stormy Petrel of Surgery*, courtesy of G. P. Putnam's Sons, New York, 1938, p. 301.

autopsy on himself, because there was nothing in this world he wanted so much as to know the causes and effects of his illness, of the disease which was striking him down.

LIV

BEAUREGARD, THE GREAT CREOLE[1]

By

HAMILTON BASSO

Without any doubt Pierre Gustave Toutant Beauregard (1818-1893) of Louisiana, who began the Civil War by firing the first gun at Fort Sumter, was one of the most colorful and romantic figures of that tragic war. Hamilton Basso writes interestingly, entertainingly, and with a remarkable insight into the life of the "Great Creole."

Major Robert Anderson, who was in command at Fort Sumter, had been a former artillery instructor of Beauregard at West Point. Anderson had been so impressed with Beauregard, who finished second in a class of forty-five, that he had kept him on as his assistant for a time.

Just before the scene described in this selection opens, the historical records tell us that General Beauregard had sent a telegram to Secretary of War Walker of the Confederacy at Montgomery, Alabama, advising him that an authorized messenger from Mr. Lincoln had just informed Governor Pickens of South Carolina that provisions were to be sent to Fort Sumter, "peaceably if they could, forcibly if they must." Walker replied, "You will at once demand its evacuation; and if this is refused, proceed in such a manner as you may determine to reduce it." Thus the former student directed the bombardment against the fort in command of his old friend and teacher, and the Civil War began.

THE CIVIL WAR BEGINS

The bombardment of Fort Sumter is put down in the history books as the beginning of the Civil War. It should also be recorded as the kindliest military engagement in history, conducted with the utmost good nature, almost tenderness, on both sides—a pleasant curtain raiser which gave

[1] Hamilton Basso, *Beauregard, The Great Creole*, New York: Charles Scribner's Sons, 1933, pp. 81-84.

no hint of the grimness to follow. Only one man was killed, and he while saluting his flag after the bombardment was over, and all the people had a fine time.

No sooner had Walker's telegram arrived in Charleston when everybody knew the fort was to be assaulted. Some telegraph clerk was a little hero that day. From the telegraph office the news spread over the city and to the surrounding countryside. Aides, soldiers and courtiers hurried through the streets. Cannon creaked and rumbled on their way to the wharves. Drums rolled, bugles sounded, flags appeared from every window. Train after train rolled into the city, each packed with crowds of chattering, excited people singing songs and waving more flags. It was just as though they were going to a fair or a jubilee.

It was rumored that the bombardment was to begin at eight o'clock that night. Why eight o'clock nobody knew. But the rumor persisted and the populace, seeking places of vantage, waited for the bombardment to begin. Eight o'clock came, the guns remained silent. Nine o'clock and still nothing happened. By ten o'clock the crowd began to think that perhaps there wouldn't be any bombardment; and by midnight, with a rain beginning to fall, they were convinced of it.

At half-past four the next morning, April twelfth, [1861], the famous "arching" shell made its historic curve across the bay, burst, and fell into the very centre of the fort. That shell is the most poetic missile ever fired. It fairly drips with sentimentalism. It has been written about as poets might write of a lovely woman. It has been given the grace of Venus, the dignity of Juno, the beauty of Aphrodite. It has been the subject of songs, of sonnets, of odes. It has created a small body of literature all by itself.

"A white smoke floated after it, parted from its utmost curve, and melted in the higher air of heaven, like a departing angel of peace, as the missile sped on its errand of ruin and affright. It was the messenger of war in the cloudless sky of a spring day. Alas, with what fortune was fraught this missile describing its beautiful curve through the balmy air. A moment more, and that air was filled and smitten with the fiery wings of death; the ear was torn by fearful sounds; several miles of batteries were sending forth their wrath at the grim fortress that rose so defiantly from the sea."[2]

Awakened by the explosion, the people tumbled from their beds and hunted for places where they could see better. They climbed upon roofs and steeples, hung from windows, mounted fences and poles. The Battery,

[2] E. A. Pollard, *Life of Jefferson Davis*, p. 110. Philadelphia, 1869.

over-looking the harbor, and the wharves were packed, and the more adventuresome spirits had to be driven from the guns.

Never was there a more non-partisan gathering. A rain of shells fell upon the fort. The audience cheered. The fort replied. The audience cheered again, rousingly, for the men who were doing their best to kill a few of their friends and relatives. Even the soldiers themselves cheered.

"Fort Sumter continued to fire from time to time," Beauregard wrote in his report of the bombardment, "but at long and irregular intervals, amid the dense smoke. Our brave troops, carried away by their enthusiasm, mounted the different batteries and, at every discharge from the fort, cheered the garrison for its pluck and gallantry, and hooted at the fleet lying inactive just outside the bar."[3]

The spectacle continued for two days. On the evening of the thirteenth Anderson, with much of his powder thrown into the sea, with the barracks of the fort burned or burning, with his men, sustained for two days on spoiled rice and spoiled pork, exhausted after forty-eight hours of continuous service at the guns, surrendered.

The next morning, in the ruins of the battered fort, he paraded his men and raised the United States flag to receive the national salute of one hundred rounds permitted by the Confederates. On the fiftieth round Private Daniel Hough's gun burst and he was killed. Five other men were wounded. These were the first casualties of the Civil War.

Beauregard was not present at the ceremony. He sat alone in his room, listening to the bells pealing and the shouts of the crowds as they milled through the streets. It would be an unhonorable thing, he declared, to be present at the humiliation of his friend. He did not enter the fort until Anderson and his command, aboard the steamer *Isabel*, were passing beyond the bar.

[3] Alfred Roman, *Military Operations of General Beauregard*, Vol. I, p. 429. New York, 1884.

LV

GROVER CLEVELAND: A STUDY IN COURAGE [1]

By

ALLAN NEVINS

Allan Nevins is unquestionably one of the most distinguished and most skillful biographers of our time. Consequently, this life of Cleveland is an exhaustive, conscientious work of research, and is intelligently written. It provides not only a commendable study of the courageous Cleveland, but also gives a clear understanding of the pressing political and economic problems of the time.

Among other offices he had held, Grover Cleveland (1837-1908) had been mayor of Buffalo and governor of New York prior to his election as President of the United States on the Democratic ticket in 1884. For two terms—1885 to 1889 and 1893 to 1897—he served as President. His administration marked a great advance in civil service.

In 1890 Congress had passed the Sherman Silver Purchase Act requiring the Treasury to purchase a certain amount of silver bullion monthly. The Treasury paid for the silver in Treasury notes, but the notes were legal tender and were redeemable in gold or silver coin at the discretion of the holder. Many holders asked for gold.

In the summer of 1893 the country suffered from a serious panic, and the government's gold reserve fell below the danger point. The government was actually on the verge of being unable to redeem its notes in gold. Cleveland demanded the repeal of the Sherman Silver Purchase Act, which necessitated the purchase by the government of silver. The notes given for the silver were being presented for payment in gold, in addition to which gold was being exported; the result was a possible exhaustion of the nation's gold reserve.

The bitter political battle which took place for the repeal of the silver legisla-

[1] Allan Nevins, *Grover Cleveland: A Study in Courage*, copyright 1932 by Allan Nevins, reprinted by permission of Dodd, Mead & Company, Inc., New York, pp. 528-547.

tion, in which struggle many of the President's own party opposed him, is vividly described in the passage that follows from Allan Nevins' excellent book.

THE GREAT SILVER BATTLE OF 1893

At this moment, when the curtain was about to rise upon a battle royal in Congress, there occurred one of the dramatic minor episodes of American history. The whole strength of the assault upon the Sherman silver-purchase clauses lay, as everyone realized, in the grim determination of Cleveland's purpose. His weight of character could force enough members of his party into line, and nothing else could. Even temporary incapacitation might be fatal to his aims, while if any accident suddenly removed him from the scene, all would be lost; for the Vice President, Adlai E. Stevenson, would infallibly bring the nation to the silver standard. An unhappier time for the development of a dangerous malady was hardly conceivable. Yet on May 5 Cleveland noticed a rough spot on the roof of his mouth. It gave him increasing discomfort, and on June 18 he had it examined by the White House physician, Dr. O'Reilly. The latter found a malignant growth as large as a quarter of a dollar, extending from the molar teeth to within a third of an inch of the middle line, encroaching on the soft palate, and accompanied by some diseased bone.[2]

In alarm, O'Reilly called Dr. Bryant into consultation, while parts of the tissue were sent to Dr. William H. Welch of Johns Hopkins. They confirmed the diagnosis. "Were it in my mouth," Bryant told the anxious President, "I would have it removed at once." An immediate operation was imperative. Yet it had to be kept a complete secret, for the knowledge that Cleveland's life was in danger would have precipitated a new and far greater panic. The most urgent work on the President's desk was hastily dispatched. Dr. Bryant took complete charge of the case, writing Lamont that he could not assume the responsibility for any delay until even August 1st if the growth progressed as it commonly did in such cases.

A series of notes which he exchanged with the Secretary of War record the progress of his preparedness.[3] On June 20 he wrote that he had obtained the services of Dr. W. W. Keen of Philadelphia, one of the most distinguished medical men in the United States—a surgeon in the Civil War, who had studied abroad, and who had collaborated with Dr. S. Weir Mitchell in various medical writings. On June 26 he added that Com-

[2] W. W. Keen, *The Surgical Operations on President Cleveland*, passim.

[3] Letters in the possession of Miss Lamont.

modore Benedict's yacht *Oneida* would be at the disposal of the President on Wednesday or Thursday of the next week, and "I think our friend should go aboard on Friday night or at all events early Saturday." A general physician, Dr. E. G. Janeway, and an expert dentist, Dr. Ferdinand Hasbrouck, both of New York, had been included in the group. Cleveland was anxious to know whether he could see officers of the government shortly after the operation without revealing what he had been through, and on June 27 Bryant wrote that his appearance would not be abnormal, but that there would be a defect in his speech. The next day he wrote again to insist that "our friend should have a night's rest before the step is taken, and should secure it in the place best intended for the purpose"; and he urged that a Cabinet officer be present at the operation. His anxiety lest something go amiss appears in another note:[4]

> Now, Colonel, if you do not intend that Dr. O'Reilly go along, for politic or other reasons, then you should let me know at once, for I must then find someone else. It is my intention to give the anaesthetic myself until time to begin the operation. I do this because I can thus set the example and also the patient will perhaps regard it with some degree of satisfaction. However, someone must begin when I leave off, and I had assigned Dr. O'Reilly to this duty, as I cannot expect either of the other gentlemen to do this for many good reasons. Telegraph me when you leave.
>
> Do you not think there should be a cipher code, which can be used? It seems to me that this will be especially important in case anything unfavorable happens. If anything "springs a leak" it may not be amiss. . . . Benedict is entering into this matter with earnest and well-directed zeal. Does the wife know about it? I ask because she may write me and I wish to know what to say. Give my regards to the President.

On the rough draft of Cleveland's message summoning the special session is a note in Lamont's hand: "Written the day the President left Washington on account of illness. Mrs. Lamont and I accompanied him to New York in Mr. Frank Thompson's car. The operation was the next day."[5] Cleveland, the Lamonts, and Dr. Bryant arrived in New York late in the evening of June 30, and drove openly to Pier A, where he was taken aboard Commodore Benedict's yacht *Oneida*. Here he found Drs. O'Reilly, Janeway, and Hasbrouck, and Bryant's assistant, Dr. John F. Erdmann. The President seated himself in a deck chair, lit a cigar, and chatted until nearly midnight. Once he burst out, "Oh, Dr. Keen, those

[4] June 20, 1893. Miss Lamont's Letters.
[5] Cleveland Papers.

office-seekers! Those office-seekers! They haunt me in my dreams!" The yacht was kept anchored all night in Bellevue Bay, and Cleveland slept without sedatives.[6] Dr. Bryant warned the medical staff to keep out of sight, lest they be recognized by the internes at Bellevue Hospital.

Next morning newspapers were taken aboard and there was a leisurely breakfast. Meanwhile, the saloon was cleared of everything but the organ, which was fastened down, and the yacht began steaming at half speed up the East River. The anxious Dr. Bryant told the captain, "If you hit a rock, hit it good and hard, so that we'll all go to the bottom!"[7] Cleveland was propped up in a chair against the mast, and the anaesthetic—first nitrous oxide gas, then ether—was given, difficulty being experienced in rendering him unconscious. Though Dr. Janeway's physical examination had revealed nothing wrong, and Cleveland had a strong pulse and little arteriosclerosis, it was the effect of the anaesthetic which Drs. Bryant and Keen chiefly feared. The President was fifty-six years old, very corpulent, with a short, thick neck, and of just the build and age for a stroke of apoplexy; while he was worn out physically and mentally by four months of exhausting labor and of fighting with office-seekers.

Dr. Hasbrouck first extracted the two left upper bicuspid teeth, Dr. Bryant then made the necessary incisions in the roof of the mouth, and the operation began. Dr. Bryant, holding the knife, worked at stop speed, and only thirty-one minutes elapsed after the administration of the ether before they had concluded their task. In that time they removed the entire left upper jaw from the first bicuspid tooth to just beyond the last molar, and took out a part of the palate; this extensive operation being necessary, writes Dr. Keen, "because we found that the antrum—the large hollow cavity in the upper jaw—was partly filled with a gelatinous mass, evidently a sarcoma."[8] Actually, states Dr. Erdmann, it was a carcinoma. No external incision was required, and it was not necessary to touch the orbit or skull-cavity containing the eye-ball; and as a result Cleveland was left with the advantage of a perfectly normal appearance of the eye and the absence of any external scar—a fact which aided greatly in keeping the operation secret. Throughout the operation Cleveland, as Dr. Erdmann states, was kept seated in the chair.

At 1:55 P. M. the operation was completed. "What a sigh of intense relief we surgeons breathed," writes Dr. Keen, "when the patient was once more safe in bed can hardly be imagined!" A small hypodermic injection

[6] W. W. Keen, *The Surgical Operations on President Cleveland*, passim.

[7] Dr. Erdmann furnished the author with many details, Nov. 14, 16, 1931.

[8] W. W. Keen, *The Surgical Operations on President Cleveland.*

of morphine was soon afterward administered. Dr. Erdmann was watching over Cleveland when he woke up. With his mouth filled with cotton, the President dazedly demanded, "Who the hell are you?" Dr. Erdmann satisfied him as to his identity and business, and on being asked where he came from, answered "Chillicothe." "Oh," said Cleveland, "do you know Mr. Nibge there?" "Yes, he's the druggist." "Well, is he so poor that he needs a job from me?" "No," said Dr. Erdmann. "Then he won't get one," growled Cleveland.[9]

The operation was completely successful. On July 3 Cleveland was up and about; and when on July 5 the *Oneida*, after five days of cruising, dropped anchor in Buzzards Bay, he was able to walk from the launch to Gray Gables with little apparent effort. On July 17 there was a second brief operation to remove some suspicious tissue, from which Cleveland quickly recovered. Dr. Keen pronounced him the most docile and courageous patient he ever had the pleasure of attending. So well was the secret kept that for almost two months no outsider learned what had occurred. Charles S. Hamlin went to Gray Gables on July 23 to deliver Cleveland some statistics which Carlisle had prepared on the silver question. "Secretary Lamont and Dr. Bryant were there," he wrote in his diary.[10] "Cleveland appeared not well at all. He had his mouth packed with some kind of bandage. Could not speak distinctly. C. S. H. thinks he had some serious trouble with his mouth. Cleveland looked thoroughly tired out. C. S. H. had a long talk with him on financial subjects." A little earlier Attorney-General Olney had called at Gray Gables on business. He and the other Cabinet members except Lamont knew nothing of the real situation. Cleveland, as he states in his unpublished autobiography, had changed a good deal in appearance and lost much flesh, and his mouth was so stuffed with antiseptic wads that he could hardly enunciate. The first utterance Olney understood was something like "My God, Olney, they nearly killed me!" He talked little, was greatly depressed, and in Olney's opinion behaved and felt as if he would never recover.[11] But his constitution came magnificently to his rescue. Within a short time his wife was complaining to Mrs. Joseph Jefferson that she could do nothing with him—that he overworked on his correspondence, and "this morning when no one noticed he got a peach and ate it. Wouldn't you think a child would have more sense after the narrow escape he had?" On September 1 Dr. Bryant's notes recorded, "All healed."

[9] Dr. Erdmann to author, Nov. 14, 16, 1931.

[10] Hamlin, MS. Diary.

[11] Olney Papers.

Yet the operation left its mark upon him. Not externally, for when Dr. Kasson C. Gibson of New York fitted him with an artificial jaw of vulcanized rubber, his face appeared normal and his speech was unimpaired.[12] But thereafter he was thinner; he could no longer labor for twenty-four hours without showing fatigue; and his even temper more frequently betrayed acerbity. The country gradually learned something of the ordeal he had been through. On August 29 "Holland" (E. J. Edwards) published in the Philadelphia *Press* a circumstantial account of the removal of part of Cleveland's jaw. It was received with general incredulity[13] and denied by men close to Cleveland. At this period, says Dr. Erdmann, he did more lying than in all the rest of his life put together. L. Clarke Davis wrote the press from Marion, Mass., that the story "has a real basis of a toothache," but if it had any other "Mr. Cleveland's closest friends do not know it." He added that "I have seen the President at intervals since he first came to Buzzards Bay this summer, passing hours and days in his company and in the boat fishing with him. I passed all of last Monday with him, fishing, and I have never seen him in better health—never stronger, physically or mentally, and I consider him in both respects the healthiest man I know."[14] Not for almost a quarter century did all the chief facts become known.

Meanwhile, on August 7 Congress had opened. Cleveland, when Olney had first met him, was struggling with his special message, but had written only twenty or thirty lines—the first two paragraphs—and Olney undertook to finish it for him. The belligerent Attorney-General was needlessly offensive in some of his references to the silver men, and unwisely extreme in urging Congress not only to repeal the silver-purchase clauses, but to provide that all outstanding obligations of the government should be payable in gold coin.[15] Cleveland struck out these expressions, and the message in its final form was a notably tactful and moderate document. It had to be, for unless he won a number of silver men temporarily to his side the repeal of the objectionable clauses would be impossible. He began by reviewing briefly the painful business situation, showing that "suddenly financial distrust and fear have sprung up on every side," and declaring

[12] A cast showing the exact nature of the work done is in the library of the New York Academy of Medicine.

[13] See N. Y. *Times*, Sept. 1, 1893. Dr. Erdmann states that Dr. Bryant believed Dr. Hasbrouck responsible for the leak, and that it completely ruptured a close friendship between them. He would never speak to Dr. Hasbrouck again, or write him, and sent him his $250 fee by messenger.

[14] Philadelphia *Public Ledger*, Aug. 31, 1893.

[15] Henry James, *Richard Olney and His Public Service*, pp. 32-35, Boston, 1923.

that all this was principally chargeable to the silver-purchase legislation. Since the passage of this legislation the government had bought more than $147,000,000 worth of silver; many of the notes used in its purchase had been paid in gold; and the prospect loomed up of the entire substitution of silver for the gold in the Treasury. If this happened, the United States would sink to the silver standard, and could no longer claim a place among the nations of the first class. In astonishingly mild and even vague language, he recommended, beyond the repeal of the purchase clauses, "that other legislative action may put beyond all doubt or mistake the intention and the ability of the government to fulfill its pecuniary obligations in money universally recognized by all civilized countries." The word gold, with all its hateful associations to the West, was not mentioned. If Cleveland could do it by temperate language, the road to sound money would be made smooth and easy.

But a new spirit was abroad in the land. The first signs of the fierce frenzy of class and sectional hatred which was to fill the middle nineties were appearing. The poverty of the Western farmer, the sufferings of millions of men, women, and children under the merciless pressure of glutted world markets, financial stringency, and heavy debts, were impelling the prairies to the fiercest revolt of their history. An undeniable element in the agony of the period was the increasing value of money, which made it necessary for the debtor everywhere to pay his obligations in a far dearer dollar than he had received, and which gave the Western producer a diminishing return for his products. Already men were beginning to personify gold and silver, to ascribe all virtues to the one and all dangers and wickedness to the others; to treat one as the salvation of humanity and the other as its destruction. The West and South were being set ablaze by men of utter sincerity and of an ability that deserves respect. Jeremiah Simpson, William A. Peffer, Henry M. Teller, William Jennings Bryan, Ben Tillman, Horace Boies, and James B. Weaver. They set forth many errors and half-truths, but they also stated many truths. Throughout the disaffected sections all party lines were giving way. . . .

Under circumstances less critical and appalling than those of midsummer in 1893 the silver lines would have held firm; but as the country reached the very nadir of financial distress, some members of Congress were shaken in their convictions. . . . During July numerous financial houses were still failing, mines and factories were closing, unemployment was increasing, and the money stringency was growing. On August 1 the savings banks of the country announced they would require sixty days' notice from depositors desiring to withdraw money. Banks in New York

City declined, as a rule, to cash checks except for very small amounts, offering instead certified checks payable through the Clearing House. . . .

In an atmosphere charged with suspense, William L. Wilson rose in the House on August 11 and opened the debate on the administration bill for the repeal of the silver-purchase clauses. This measure was almost identical with a bill which Sherman himself had offered in the preceding Congress. The West Virginia member shortly made a prolonged and able argument for it. When he sat down he was exhausted; he was pale and his hands trembled so violently that after vainly trying to still them he clasped them tight and held them between his knees.[16] Thus commenced one of the most dramatic of all the discussions that the House witnessed between the Civil War and Spanish War. Just fifteen days later ex-Speaker Reed closed the debate for the forces of repeal.[17] Between these two men all the best orators of the House had poured out their views, in the stifling August heat, to crowded galleries and benches of scribbling reporters. . . .

Four great speeches marked the half-month of House debate, and three of them—by Wilson, Bourke Cochran, and Reed—were made on the sound money side; the silverites were outfought, and only two young newcomers, Bryan of Nebraska and Joseph W. Bailey of Texas, who had both arrived in 1891, gave eloquent voice to the West. Wilson, who spoke repeatedly, prepared his speeches with meticulous care and committed them to memory. Marked by close reasoning, fine diction, and a delicate wit, and yet fresh enough not to smell of the lamp, they read better than any others of the day. Bourke Cochran, who spoke extemporaneously, loved a fight against odds. . . . In his hour and a half speech on August 26 he was in his best mood, quoting from Locke and Mill, citing many historical instances and closing with a magniloquent peroration of the sort then fashionable. . . .

Yet the greatest single triumph of the debate was Bryan's. On August 16, a drowsy summer afternoon, he rose to make an address for which he had been preparing for months. . . . An expectant murmur came from the Westerners who had flocked to the galleries. Bryan's masterful pose, his air of a child of fortune, his handsome face and fine square jaw, inspired confidence. . . . On his desk lay the proofs of the speech he had composed, and by it stood a glass of malted extract of beef to fortify his strength. Suddenly, as he looked about him, he decided that his prepared address would not do, turned his notes face downward, and began a wholly new speech. The first ringing tones brought members flocking

[16] Washington *Post*, Aug. 12, 1893.

[17] William A. Robinson, *Thomas B. Reed, Parliamentarian*, 288 ff., New York, 1930.

from the lobbies as if by magic. . . . His argument followed the familiar lines. He contended that there was neither gold enough nor silver enough to form the exclusive basis of the world's supply of specie; that to drive either out of circulation was to contract the currency all over the globe; and that such contraction, in the demonetization of silver, had resulted in augmenting the value of gold, increasing the burden of fixed debts, and lowering the price of the commodities produced by the debtor class. . . . What was most needed was a firm assertion of national purpose. But this, he said, ran counter to the schemes of the capitalist classes and creditors:

> On the one side stand the corporate interests of the United States, the moneyed interests, aggregated wealth and capital, imperious, arrogant, compassionless. . . . On the other side stand an unnumbered throng, those who gave to the Democratic party a name and for whom it has assumed to speak. Work-worn and dust-begrimed, they make their mute appeal, and too often find their cry for help beat in vain against the outer walls, while others, less deserving, gain ready access to legislative halls. . . .

Cleveland was pleased, when the vote was taken on August 28, by the decisiveness of his victory. The Wilson repeal bill passed the House 239 to 108. . . .

Meanwhile, a repeal bill had been introduced in the Senate—where the fight would be grim and close—under encouraging auspices. . . . It was favorably reported by the Finance Committee, the affirmative being taken by Voorhees (the chairman), McPherson, Morrill, Sherman, Allison, and Aldrich, and the negative by Harris, Vance, Vest, Jones of Arkansas, and Jones of Nevada. But for the unexpected vote of the tall "sycamore of the Wabash" it would have been reported unfavorably. Behind his action lay a striking story.

Voorhees, whose long service and sixty-six years alone gave him some title to rank with the sages of the Senate, had fought to the last ditch in opposition to Cleveland's renomination. For nearly two decades he had been an inflationist; his florid eloquence had always been at the service of the silver cause, and this fact was well known when he became head of the Senate Finance Committee early in 1893. Two influences brought about a change of heart. One was the evidence that most Indianians joined with the East in demanding repeal, and the other was Cleveland's use of patronage. Nearly every President for two generations had at some time employed the patronage to reward his supporters or punish his opponents. Pierce, Buchanan, and Lincoln had all done so; Johnson had used it for his Reconstruction measures; and Grant had unblushingly thrust an able man out of his Cabinet in order to use the appointment of a successor to buy votes for his Santo Domingo policy. Most examples of these tactics were unhappy, for they had usually proved ineffective, had demoralized the public service, and had deepened the dissensions within the party. But in 1893 the crisis was great, and Cleveland remarked sardonically that "a man had never yet been hung for breaking the spirit of the law." He no sooner took office than he came to an arrangement with Voorhees, the nature of which is patent from Cleveland's papers. On March 21 an Indianapolis politician, Samuel N. Gold, wrote the President that he was puzzled to know why it was that Voorhees, although recently an anti-Cleveland man, seemed to have complete control of the offices in Indiana. The important appointments had all been of men who were close personal friends of the senior Senator.[18] Two days later a Democratic leader in Fort Wayne wrote to make the same perplexed inquiry. And, dated March 20, there came a significant note from Voorhees himself:[19]

> My dear Mr. President:
>
> I do not feel that the sun ought to go down before I convey to you my earnest and grateful appreciation of your kindness and courtesy today in the appointment of Mr. Bisley. I thank you most sincerely not only for the appointment itself, but also for the exceedingly kind and handsome manner in which it has been made. You have indeed made me very deeply and permanently your debtor, and it will be one of the principal pleasures and purpose of my life, and at every opportunity, to recognize and justify, as far as may be in my power, the generous confidence and friendly regard you have extended to me. Permit me to subscribe myself with the highest respect and esteem, yours faithfully, your friend, D. W. Voorhees.

A pledge of support could go no further! And this support was carefully nursed. . . .

At the beginning of September Cleveland was back in Washington watching the Senate debate. There was a small majority for repeal. But the minority was strong enough to obstruct action indefinitely. The silver leaders, Harris of Tennessee and Teller of Colorado, marshalled their supporters; discussion dragged through the hot September days and into October; finally, in desperation, on October 11 cloture was invoked, and a continuous session began which lasted thirty-eight hours, the defiant silverites then defeating it by forcing an adjournment; and not until October 30 was a final vote reached, and the repeal bill passed. . . .

[18] Cleveland Papers.
[19] Cleveland Papers.

At the last moment there occurred one of those crises which so often tested the courage and resolution of Cleveland—and which always found his strength equal to the tension. On October 20 there arose among the Democratic Senators an irresistible movement to end the fight by compromise. Next day, Saturday the 21st, a letter was addressed to Voorhees, signed by 37 of the 44 Democrats in the Senate, outlining a compromise plan. . . . The Washington *Post* lent prominence to an announcement that the Administration was yielding, its Capitol reporter categorically asserting that President Cleveland had abandoned his original determination to secure unconditional repeal and was willing to accept repeal to take effect on July 1, 1894.

Once more Cleveland was in a position where a man of ordinary strength would have bent to what seemed the inevitable, and accepted half a loaf as better than no bread. But what made him a statesman among politicians was the fact that his strength went far beyond ordinary limits. When Carlisle on Saturday afternoon took the compromise letter out to Woodley, Cleveland's anger was intense. At a Cabinet meeting on Monday, October 23, he smote the table with his fist and declared that he would not yield an inch. Before the gathering broke up Carlisle penned a statement which was at once given to the press associations. "The President," it declared, "adheres to the position that the purchasing clause of the Sherman silver law should be unconditionally repealed. . . . It is not true that Secretary Carlisle is, or has been in favor of the compromise which was subscribed to by a number of the Senators on Saturday. He and the other members of the Cabinet are opposed to the measure." This statement knocked the compromise scheme into smithereens, and the Administration steering committee still led by Voorhees, prepared for another determined effort.[20] . . . From the press of the country—even from organs which were none too friendly toward repeal but which recognized a man when they saw one—came a confused noise of cheering. . . .

The Washington *Post* on October 25, five days after it had hoisted the white flag, declared: "The outcome of the fight is a great personal victory for President Cleveland. This expression was on every lip at the Capitol yesterday as soon as it was thoroughly understood that unconditional repeal was on the road to a vote. Against the most formidable obstacles and in the face of an opposition in his own party which was as large numerically as his own adherence, he has brought the entire Senate to his feet. 'Great is Grover Cleveland,' said Senator Manderson yesterday, 'and

[20] Washington *Post*, Oct. 22, 1893; see also Louisville *Courier-Journal*, October 23, 24.

the Democratic Senate is his prophet.'" Sherman had said that unconditional repeal was impossible; the Washington *Post* had said it; Democrat after Democrat had said it; but Cleveland had proved that it was not so.

The great day came on October 30. The Senate met at 11 A. M. The galleries were jammed and long lines of spectators waited in the lobbies to watch the Senators arrive—Gorman with his clean-shaven face and Prince Albert coat; Teller with his look of a Methodist elder; Peffer with his long whiskers and white chrysanthemum; the venerable Morrill; the resplendently-dressed Wolcott. . . . One after another the silverites, Vest, Wolcott, Jones, Dubois, Stewart, and others, fired their last shots; but their animation was gone, for they were pronouncing funeral orations. Peffer alone showed his usual fire in denouncing "the crowning infamy of the century." The roll was called in impressive silence. The clerk announced that the yeas were 43, the nays 32. Including pairs, the vote was 48 to 37. A moment later the Senate stood adjourned. A few spectators gathered about Voorhees to congratulate him, a knot of employees with mops and brooms took possession of the vacant chamber, and the great silver battle of 1893 had passed into history.[21]

[21] Washington *Post*, Oct. 31, 1893.

LVI

COMMODORE VANDERBILT[1]

By

WHEATON J. LANE

Wheaton J. Lane has written an objective and solid biography of Cornelius Vanderbilt (1794-1877), one of the most colorful figures in the history of American shipping and finance. The emphasis in this work is placed upon those phases of Vanderbilt's life which are important in American economic history of the nineteenth century.

At sixteen, Cornelius Vanderbilt purchased a ferryboat to carry passengers and farm products between Staten Island and New York. Two years later he owned three boats, and then steadily expanded his shipping interests. Before long he became known as the Commodore. Finally he transferred his capital to railroads, becoming president of the New York Central in 1867.

Among Commodore Vanderbilt's public benefactions the most noteworthy was his contribution of $1,000,000 for the establishment of Vanderbilt University at Nashville, Tennessee.

WHAT'S THE USE OF AN EDUCATION?

Commodore Vanderbilt was toying with the idea of a grandiose monument to George Washington in Central Park, one that by its magnificence would also be a monument to himself. Apparently Washington was now his greatest hero, William Henry Harrison having been relegated to a secondary position. But Vanderbilt found no sympathy in his family for the proposed plan.

The Commodore was chatting one night with his new friend [Reverend Charles F. Deems] when the conversation turned to the subject of educa-

[1] Reprinted from *Commodore Vanderbilt*, by Wheaton J. Lane, by permission of and special arrangement with Alfred A. Knopf, Inc., New York, 1942, pp. 315-317.

tion. "I'd give a million dollars today, Doctor," Vanderbilt admitted suddenly, "if I had your education. . . . Folks may say that I don't care about education, but it ain't true; I do. I've been among educated people enough to see its importance. I've been to England, and seen them lords, and other fellows, and knew that I had twice as much brains as they had maybe, and yet I had to keep still, and couldn't say anything through fear of exposing myself."

At this moment Horace F. Clark entered the room, and, overhearing the last few words, made some comment about the Commodore finally admitting the advantages of education.

Vanderbilt was not going to give any ground to his ambitious son-in-law. "I seem to get along better than half of your educated men," he exclaimed testily.

Upon Clark's hurried withdrawal, Deems continued with the conversation and shrewdly made the remark that the Commodore was a great hindrance to education. "Why, don't you see, if you do nothing to promote education, to prove to the world that you believe in it, there isn't a boy in all the land who ever heard of you, but may say, 'What's the use of an education? There's Commodore Vanderbilt; he never had any, and never wanted any, and yet he became the richest man in America.'" With this appeal to the Commodore's vanity, Deems went on to point out that a memorial to Washington could add nothing to the fame of the first President, while money spent on education, or specifically on a university, would do great practical good.

The idea thus put in the Commodore's mind was carefully nurtured by Mrs. Vanderbilt and was soon to bear fruit. . . .

It was shortly after this that Mrs. Vanderbilt invited to her house a clergyman whom she had known in Mobile, Bishop Holland N. McTyeire of the Methodist Episcopal Church, South. McTyeire had been a leader in fighting for such reforms in his organization as "lay representation"; and in recent years he and Landon C. Garland, a former teacher of his, had headed an agitation for a central theological seminary for the entire southern Methodist Church. At the time McTyeire was seeking funds for the Central University at Nashville, Tennessee, recently projected to include such a seminary.

The Commodore, apparently mellowing from his normal feelings about clergymen, took an immediate liking to the Bishop; and their later correspondence, although businesslike enough in regard to official matters, reveals a friendly and sometimes jocular tone. In the spring of 1873 Vanderbilt suddenly made a gift of $500,000 to the Central University;

McTyeire was about to retire one night at the Commodore's when a document was unexpectedly placed in his hands for consideration. The terms of the agreement stipulated that McTyeire should be President of the Board of Trust, should possess a veto power, and should arrange for the physical construction of the University; solicitous for the investment of his gift, the Commodore stated that the Endowment Fund, a part of the general grant, should preferably be kept in first mortgage bonds of the New York Central and Hudson River Railroad.

No doubt McTyeire was impressed by the suddenness of the gift, its size, which at the time was unparalleled, and the confidence placed in his administrative ability. Of course he realized that the way had been prepared by Mrs. Vanderbilt and by Deems, who had stressed the poverty and the war-torn conditions prevailing in the south. Vanderbilt was later to write that he had made the gift in the hope that the new University might "through its influence contribute to strengthening the ties which should exist between all sections of our country."

Through correspondence with Bishop McTyeire, the Commodore closely followed the building of the new institution. Upon hearing of the gift, the Board of Trust had immediately resolved that the "name and style of our corporation" should be changed from Central to Vanderbilt University; no doubt the Commodore was highly pleased at the change in name, but he merely wrote back that a copy of the resolution had been received and was "very satisfactory." As the buildings were erected, it became evident that if the Endowment Fund were to be kept intact, more funds would be needed. Again, Vanderbilt came generously to the rescue and before his death he donated, in installments, another $500,000.

On October 4th, 1875, dedicatory services were held at the new University. Landon C. Garland, McTyeire's old friend, had been elected the first Chancellor, and to him the Bishop delivered the keys of the institution. Four faculties, of liberal arts, law, theology, and medicine, had been formed. Principal speaker of the day was Governor Porter of Tennessee, while the Reverend Charles F. Deems also delivered an address as the representative of the Commodore. The last, unable to attend the exercises, was never to see the University which he founded and which was destined to become one of the great educational institutions of the South. He sent a telegram to McTyeire which was read to the assemblage: "We send greeting to you all. May your institution be ever blessed by the great Governor of all things."

LVII

GLORY-HUNTER, A LIFE OF GENERAL CUSTER [1]

By

FREDERIC F. VAN de WATER

General George Armstrong Custer (1839-1876)—with his relentless pursuit of glory, with the maze of inconsistencies and contradictions in his life, and with his egotism—lives again in this excellent full-length biography. His life is a series of paradoxes. He was a devoted son and husband, but a ruthless commander; he was a slovenly cadet and an insubordinate officer, but a disciplinarian of the first rank with his own troops; his major reason now for fame as a soldier is based upon a defeat as thorough as was ever sustained by United States regulars.

Custer distinguished himself in the Civil War, but in fighting the Indians on the heights above the Little Bighorn river in mountain territory on June 25, 1876, he and 264 men of his center column rode into the midst of the enemy, and the entire command was slaughtered by the Sioux under Sitting Bull. Custer's body was found at the apex of a corpse-littered angle of rout. No one will perhaps ever know the full story of "Custer's last stand," his purpose that day, or the instant and manner of his death, which enigmatic death is perhaps one of the reasons for his continuing fame.

The selection chosen from Mr. Van de Water's authentic life of Custer describes his "unusual" record at the United States Military Academy at West Point.

"AN EXAMPLE TO BE CAREFULLY AVOIDED"

The impartial voice of the Academy records portrays George Armstrong Custer as a slovenly soldier and a deplorable student. For the first twenty

[1] Frederic F. Van de Water, *Glory-Hunter*, copyright 1934, used by special permission of the publishers, The Bobbs-Merrill Company, Indianapolis, pp. 28 and 29, 27.

days of his sojourn at West Point whatever high resolutions he had brought with him appear to have endured. It is not until June twenty-third that the "skin book" in which demerits are listed first cites him. On that date he received two demerits for "not casting eyes to the front after being ordered to do so at parade" and another for being late at parade.

These were drops, heralding downpour. He was an indifferent, a tardy and a clumsy recruit who persistently was punished for slackness in drill, dirty equipment or disordered uniform. One hundred demerits in any six-months period supposedly caused the delinquent's expulsion from the Academy. During his first half-year, Custer ran up one hundred and twenty-nine. This total was reduced to sixty-nine by some unidentified Samaritan.

In the subsequent six months, he had eighty-two demerits, four of these for "tobacco smoke in quarters," though in later years he touched neither tobacco nor liquor. He skated nearer the deadline in 1858 for he had ninety-eight demerits during the first half-year and ninety-four during the second.

Most of his offenses at drill disappear during 1859 and 1860. He has learned the exterior appearance of a soldier. Ineptitude is replaced by a general insurgence and slackness—talking, sitting down on sentry duty, visiting out of hours, room unswept, tablecloth dirty, person slovenly.

On March 18, 1860, he got seven demerits for "room grossly out of order, bed down and floor not swept" and also for "bread, butter, potatoes, plates, knives and forks in qrs." That left the wild colt with one hundred and twenty-nine marks against him, twenty-nine more than enough to insure his expulsion at the term's end. Through the intervention of some unidentified "S. B. H.," thirty of these were removed. Presumably S. B. H. managed to put the fear of God temporarily into Custer's heart, for from March nineteenth to June sixth when the half-year ended, no single demerit was set down against him. When authority was sufficiently severe and impressive, he could always be the model soldier.

The reform was not permanent. In the subsequent six months, he ran up ninety-five demerits, largely for neglect of his person or his studies.

His record was as spectacularly undistinguished in the classroom as elsewhere. He stood fifty-eighth in a class of sixty-five during his first year; fifty-sixth out of fifty-nine at the end of his second and fifty-seventh out of fifty-seven when the third concluded. . . .

"My career as a cadet," he wrote years later, "had but little to recommend it to the study of those who came after me, unless as an example to be carefully avoided."

LVIII

PASCAL, THE LIFE OF GENIUS [1]

By

MORRIS BISHOP

This biography of Blaise Pascal (1623-1662), famous French physicist, mathematician, and religious philosopher, is not a light, superficial study, but a solid and significant work. Every student of science, religious philosophy, and the human mind will find this a valuable book.

Pascal's genius in mathematics is indicated by the fact that before he was sixteen years of age he had completed his *Geometry of Conics*, which may be said to form the basis for the modern treatment of the subject. He opened up the path to the calculus of probabilities, and his experiments provided the first complete demonstration of the barometer.

Often Pascal would sit brooding and meditating. Sometimes he would write down a fragment of his thoughts. Occasionally a servant would do it for him. Thus there accumulated a vast collection of his "thoughts," or as they were known when published, "*Pensées*." These thoughts are a mixture of sophistry and expressions of great profundity. In them Pascal reflects both upon man's grandeur and his misery. "Man," he said, "is made only for infinity." Pascal believed that the only perfect knowledge comes through Christian revelation.

Morris Bishop has chosen from his book the passage, as he describes it, of Pascal's "mystical experience which totally changed the current of his life, and turned him from a scientist to an amateur saint. The episode is dramatic and important."

ON THAT NIGHT GOD CAME

It is a good thing to be wearied and spent by the useless search for the true good, so that one may hold out one's arms to the liberator.

—PENSÉES

[1] Morris Bishop, *Pascal, The Life of Genius*, New York: Reynal and Hitchcock, 1936, reprinted by permission of the publishers, pp. 168-180.

Renunciation, total and sweet.

—THE MEMORIAL

The year 1654 divides Pascal's life in two. Had he died in that year, he would be known to history as a scientist of inconstant genius, cut off before his brilliant promise could be fulfilled. The greater Pascal, the poet and counsellor, was born late in the evening of November 23, 1654.

On that night God came, in fire, and talked to Pascal for the space of two hours. By the grace of that night Pascal was delivered from the bondage of corruption; he put off the old man of flesh and put on the new man of righteousness. He emerged from the fire of that night another creature, assured that he had actually been born again. This new self was sent to the school of the soul; the old self, the Pascal that the world knew, was contemptuously thrown to the world's middens.

Such a mystical experience, and such a revulsion in life, and such a logical acceptance of the consequences of revelation, are not the part of ordinary men. "In a great soul," he has told us, "all is great."

His illumination did not come entirely unheralded. We can see some of the preparation of the old man of the flesh.

We know, from Jacqueline's [his sister] words, that about the end of 1653 he was seized by "a great scorn of the world and an unbearable disgust for all the people who are in it." He sought refuge from his disgust, perhaps from his pain, in furious labor. He carried on his treatises on the equilibrium of liquids and on the weight of the mass of air. He did some of his greatest work in mathematics, especially in the theory of numbers. He offers a bewildering list of the investigations which he proposes or has in hand.

His intense mental toil affected his health, as his physicians, years before, had warned him it would. In his other illnesses he had been cared for with the solicitude of an adoring family. Now servants tended his body, and there was no one at all to conjure away his sick thoughts and feverish emotions. A dreadful solitude occupied his lonely bedroom. His father was dead, Gilberte [another sister] far away in Clermont, and Jacqueline, immured in her convent, was still farther. She scorned him as an apostate from the faith; she thought him damned.

Lacking the comfort of human affection, he turned to the consolers of his philosophical worldly friends. He read Montaigne, and took no ease in his smiling skepticism. He read Epictetus, and found the stoic way of life also vanity, for it demands an inner strength which Pascal could not discover in himself nor in man's nature. He read his Bible and his books of piety, and found in them more grief than consolation, for they told of the search for salvation which he had abandoned, the love of God which he could feel no more.

Perhaps, in his Saint Augustine, he happened on the sentence he had himself quoted, in his letter on the death of his father. There is in each of us a serpent, our nature and sense; an Eve, our concupiscent appetite; and an Adam, reason. God's grace will render Adam victorious. Perhaps Pascal, in the night watches, reflected that his Adam, careless of God's grace, had gone his own proud way and had fallen, tempted by the serpent and by Eve.

What was in his mind? We can classify and measure the atoms in the stars, but we have no spiritual spectroscopy. I do not know what is in the mind of those I know best, nor even what is in my own. When I, or others, would read the soul of a suffering genius across three hundred years, on the most insufficient data, we can claim no great authority for our conclusions. Intuition must guide us, and the intuition of others may accept or reject our own.

In Pascal's contempt of the world was mingled, I suppose, a strain of spite. The prodigy was now a man of thirty; the world had forgotten the prodigy, and rendered only a decent respect to the man of science. But a prodigy cannot forget the adulation rendered him in his formative years. It remains to torment him with a sense of unfillment, of failure.

Pascal had come to know failure. His calculating machine did not sell; his scientific friends, admiring though they were, had no conception of the richness and fecundity and future significance of his mathematical work; court society had received him with polite and curious wonder, never with that surrendering acceptance which appeases ambition. He was forever an outsider in their world. And if he had loved, it was in vain, because the rules of that world were too strong for his genius to break.

"It's the effect of force, not of custom," wrote Pascal, in one of these *pensées* which begin in the middle of his thought. "For those who are capable of inventing are rare; the greater number wish only to follow, and refuse glory to those inventors who seek it by their inventions; and if they persist in trying to obtain glory, and in scorning those who do not invent, the others give them funny names, and would be glad to beat them. So let no one pride himself on his ingenuity, or let him content himself within himself."

Did Pascal, in his mood of disillusionment, doubt God as well as the world? Plenty of the *pensées* express unfaith with profound understanding of the skeptic's state of mind. On this evidence the unbelievers have claimed him for their own, and unjustly, for these fragments are probably the utterances of characters in a spiritual drama, and are doomed to prompt annihilation by the faith. There is, in fact, no proof that Pascal ever doubted the existence of the Christian God. His agony proceeded from his sense that the Christian God had abandoned him, as he abandoned the futile worldlings whom Pascal had recently honored and prized.

Looking at himself with the clarity of fever's interims, he was filled with dismay. He recognized clearly all his shortcomings, his sins. "If one does not know himself to be full of pride, ambition, concupiscence, weakness, pettiness, injustice, one is very blind. And if, knowing this, a man does not desire to be delivered, what can one say of him?" Most of all he was amazed and horrified at his apathy, that "strange repose" of his spirit, balanced between the two eternities, between hell and heaven. When later he came to write his *Apology*, he planned it chiefly as an attack on this dreadful apathy of man.

Although he recognized well his strange repose, the mere recognition brought him no release. The cheerful confidence of grace which he had once possessed had now vanished. He had lost everything, even the ardor for salvation, even the love of God. "It is a horrible thing," he says, "to feel everything one possesses slip away."

This is the state of dryness, *sécheresse*, *siccitas*, familiar to the mystics. One feels all communication with God suppressed; one's soul is powerless to receive the divine love which one knows to exist. Pascal had once congratulated himself on his lack of dryness, in a letter to Gilberte: "If [God] interrupts however little [his mercy], dryness necessarily supervenes." Now God had interrupted his mercy, and Pascal had wandered somehow into a desert, peopled only by the mirages of grace.

He was afraid. "The eternal silence of these infinite spaces terrifies me." In all these infinite spaces he could find no God.

In September, 1654, he visited Jacqueline in her convent. She describes his state of mind in a letter to Gilberte, written in the following January: "On this visit he opened himself to me in a pitiful way, admitting to me that in the midst of his occupations, which were great, and among all the things which should contribute to make him love the world, and to which he was outwardly much attached, he was so impelled to quit all that, both by an extreme aversion from the follies and beguilements of the world and by the continual reproach of his conscience, that he found himself detached from all things in a way that he had never been before, nor anything like it; but [he admitted] that also he was in such a great abandonment on God's part that he felt no attraction in that direction; that nevertheless he urged himself with all his power, but that he felt very much that it was his reason and his own mind that were exciting him to what he knew to be the best thing, rather than the movement of God's spirit, and that in the detachment from all things in which he found himself, if he had had the same feelings for God as previously, he thought he could have undertaken anything, and that he must have been bound by horrible attachments in those times to resist the grace which God gave him and the impulses he sent."

Blaise returned again and again to the convent. Jacqueline was wise in the ways of the repentant soul; her pious zeal was informed by understanding of her brother's spirit. She knew the teaching of the saints: that spiritual distress is itself a manifestation of grace, a step in the search for God. The soul must be cleansed of its attachment to the world, and made ready for its new occupant. It must die to the past before coming to the new life. Life is death, and death life; this is the old antinomy, the inescapable paradox of Christianity.

THE ECSTACY

A few days after Pascal's death, a manservant, arranging his clothes, noticed a curious bulge in his doublet. Opening the lining, he withdrew a folded parchment, written in Pascal's hand. Within the parchment was a scribbled sheet of paper, containing the words of the parchment, with some variations. These documents were the record of his mystical illumination, his two hours in the presence of God. For eight years he had worn them as an amulet, hiding them in his coat, sewing and unsewing them at need. It was his precious secret, his protection, his memorial of the coming of grace.

The scribbled paper remains, one of the treasures of the Bibliothèque Nationale in Paris. The parchment has disappeared, but we possess a fair copy of it, made by Pascal's nephew, reproducing the arrangement of the original.

It is reasonable to suppose that the sheet of paper contains the original notes of Pascal's mystical experience, written immediately after the ecstacy, and that the parchment was his permanent record, made at leisure, with certain changes prompted by reflection.

At top of the sheet of paper stands a cross.

Below:

The year of grace 1654,

Monday, 23 November, day of Saint Clement, pope and martyr, and of others in the martyrology.

Eve of Saint Chrysogonus, martyr, and others,

From about half past ten in the evening until about half past twelve,

...FIRE...

God of Abraham, God of Isaac, God of Jacob, not of the philosophers and scholars.

Certitude, certitude, feeling, joy, peace.

God of Jesus Christ.

Deum meum et Deum vestrum.

Thy God will be my God.

Forgetfulness of the world and of everything, except GOD.

He is to be found only by the ways taught in the Gospel. *Greatness* of the human soul.

O righteous Father, the world hath not known thee, but I have known thee.

Joy, joy, joy, tears of joy.

I have been separated from him.

Dereliquerunt me fontem aquae vivae.

My God, wilt thou forsake me?

Let me not be separated from him eternally.

This is the eternal life, that they know thee as the only true God, and the one whom thou hast sent, Jesus Christ.

Jesus Christ,

Jesus Christ.

I have been separated from him; I have fled him, renounced him, crucified him,

Let me never be separated from him.

He is preserved only by the ways taught in the Gospel.

Renunciation, total and sweet.

The paper sheet ends here. The parchment copy adds the lines:

Total submission to Jesus Christ and to my director.

Eternally in joy for a day's trial on earth.

Non obliviscar sermones tuos. Amen.

We may easily go astray in the interpretation of these notes on the night of illumination. They were intended, not as a record, for surely Pascal had no such need, but as something sacred, partaking of the holiness of the experience that prompted them. They were meant for no human eyes, not for ours, not for the analysis of any literary man. We must go cautiously in attempting to see what Pascal saw when he fingered the amulet in the seam of his coat.

But we can, perhaps, understand a little by the method of scientists and literary scholars alike, that of subdivision, classification, and comparison.

The Memorial falls naturally into three parts: first, a mental disturbance accompanied by an impression, visual or figurative, of fire; second, the coming of a mystic grace, God made manifest to the mind; third, the transports and tears of the grateful object of grace. The concluding phrases of the parchment copy, which are in a different rhythm, may be taken as a later addition.

"Fire!" he cries. Was his experience properly a vision, in that he saw flame, as Moses saw the burning bush? No, probably Pascal saw no actual fire, say the doctors; probably the word is a figure for the blazing fervor which possessed him. Fire is the inevitable metaphor for ardor; "the Lord thy God is a consuming fire;" "my heart was hot within me, while I was musing the fire burned," says the Psalmist. Saint Francis of Assisi had an *incendium mentis* on perceiving the winged seraph. The imagery of light and heat is almost universal among the illuminates, as the very derivation of their name suggests.

The imagery of heat has its physiological accompaniment, I would not say cause. Bergson notes that in extreme joy, our perceptions have a quality comparable to light and heat. This quality is the product of the arterial dilation accompanying the emotion.

The comparison with the experience of others is, in the end, not very helpful. We conclude that Pascal saw only a figurative fire, simply because that seems more natural. He had no need of the gross symbols that bring understanding to the simple; he had no need even of words. Like Saint Ambrose, he might have prayed: "Let thy good Spirit enter into my heart and there be heard without utterance, and without the sound of words speak all truth."

The thought of fire suggests God speaking from the burning bush. On that occasion God said: "I am the God of Abraham, the God of Isaac, the God of Jacob." Pascal sets down the words, adding, "not of the philosophers and scholars." In one of his own *pensées* he provides the scholium: "The God of Abraham, the God of Isaac, the God of Jacob, the God of Christians, is a God of love and consolation; he is a God who fills the soul and heart of those whom he possesses, he is a God who makes them feel inwardly their wretchedness and his infinite mercy; who unites with them in the depths of their soul, filling it with humility, joy, confidence, love, who renders them incapable of any other purpose but himself."

The words are of capital importance. They mark the end of his search for understanding by way of science, mathematics, and philosophy. He comprehends now that in seeking understanding, knowledge, he had been, in fact, seeking the peace of certitude, and the only certitude is God. And God, himself the sum of understanding and all knowledge, now puts an end to the search. God reveals himself to be a God of love, consolation, and infinite mercy, not a God of justice. This is an entirely Christian idea, not in the philosophers, not in the Old Testament.

The thought of the Memorial progresses by lyric leaps. One may distinguish alternately ejaculations expressing direct experience: Fire! Certitude! and phrases of reflection, interpretations of the emotions according to Christian theology.

Now an ejaculation: Certitude, certitude, feeling, joy, peace.

The long-sought sign has been granted him. He has found certitude for his intellect, feeling, peace, and joy for his heart. Certitude, clearly, not that God *is,* but that he is *mine*, and that the discovery of him is the only end of our search. There had been no doubt of God's existence in Pascal's mind, only the doubt that God had distinguished him to be a vessel of his grace.

Certitude! The word and the thought recur forever in Pascal's scientific work and in the *pensées*. Indeed, the whole intellectual life of Pascal has been studied with "the conquest of certitude" for its theme.

With "certitude" the vision proper seems to fade. Pascal's mind is free to recognize the inflowing of grace, and to draw from it lessons for his soul's direction. He makes his pledge to God, his promise to forget all that is not God. And he recognizes that God is to be attained by way of the Gospel, and by way of God's mediator, Jesus Christ.

Here is a momentous discovery. Hitherto Pascal had been implicitly a Cartesian in his conception of the grounds of knowledge. He had admitted the metaphysical proofs of God, and had suggested that reason, well conducted, might give proofs of Christianity's truths. But in the world he had learned the importance of the heart, even in the organization of thought. He found that the heart too must be converted. And now he discovered that only Jesus Christ can convert the heart.

Pascal's religion was compounded of the fear of God and the love of Jesus. He had no cult for the saints, and merely a courteous regard for the Virgin, whom he mentions only two or three times, perfunctorily. But from the day of the Memorial to his death, his heart was filled with passionate love for his Saviour. . . .

We return to the Memorial. "Greatness of the human soul!" cries Pascal. Is this pride in man, the arrogance of mortality? Surely Pascal did not mean it so. (And yet mysticism has been called a monument of human pride, in its assumption of superiority to the universe.) Pascal's note preserved only the memory of glory, his gladness that his human soul could touch infinity, converse with God.

"O righteous Father," he continues, "the world hath not known thee, but I have known thee." In this phrase and in that preceding, he preserves the two essential ideas of Jesus: the paternity of God, and the value of the human soul. Neither of these ideas is significant in Judaism or in Greek philosophy.

Overcome by his emotion, Pascal breaks down in joy, in tears of joy.

Here begins the third part of the Memorial, the transports and tears. Pascal's joy brings an immediate sense of his unworthiness of joy, a period of self-examination, a feeling of sin, a kind of anguish. He wrote, later, in a letter to Mlle de Roannez, which seems like a commentary on his Memorial, that the Christian partakes of a joy incomprehensible to the world. But "it is the joy of having found God that is the origin of the sadness at having offended him and [the origin] of all the change of one's life. . . . The worldly have their sadness without this joy, and the Christians have this joy mingled with sadness for having followed other pleasures."

So sadness follows, the consciousness of unworthiness, of sin. Pascal bewails his past separation from God; he pleads with Jesus not to forsake him. He invokes the name of his Mediator. He breathes repentance and love. He has abandoned ideas and thoughts to dwell upon the person of his Saviour.

Again he reflects that Jesus is to be preserved only by the Gospel, by the same way that the Father was to be found. He concludes with the promise: Renunciation, total and sweet.

The flame dies, and Pascal gazes wondering about his familiar room. His body is chilled and numb. He looks at his watch; it is half-past twelve.

VISION OR HALLUCINATION?

It seems a little indecent to inquire into the nature of this experience, to analyze the secret Memorial, to peep through the keyhole at Pascal's interview with God. One can imagine his horror at the thought of the profane throng taking their turn outside his door, diagnosing his ravishment as the hallucination of hysteria, even as incipient insanity. His anguish would not have been diminished by the other file of affectionate emotionalists, who find delicious moments in mysticism as in table-tipping and in ouija-board writing.

The dead have no privacy. The remnants of their souls are on display, for all to see. From the remnants and fragments we reconstruct their souls, as does the paleontologist in his museum. They must be tolerant, if each reconstruction resembles a little the reconstructor, as every portrait is in a way the portrait of the artist, as even a photograph has something in it of the photographer.

Thus our judgment of Pascal's experience is a judgment of ourselves. To Voltaire and the *philosophes* of the eighteenth century it was a manifestation of religious dementia; to positivistic physicians of the nineteenth century it was the first symptom of a progressive epileptoid deterioration of the brain; to the psychologist it is an abnormal psycho-pathological state, a form, perhaps, of self-hypnosis; to the religious it is the direct revelation of God.

To the abrupt question "what was it?" I dare give no answer. No method of interpretation of spiritual experience seems to me solid and secure. The systems of orthodoxy are undermined, and the unorthodox, quarreling among themselves, have created no system that works better, in the given case, than the one they demolish.

One may describe Pascal's rapture in entirely rational, physical terms:

Pascal had been brooding for a year on the failure of human certitude and on the futility of his own ambitions. His ill-health had distorted his view of reality, and had encouraged abnormal feverish fantasies. He had abandoned the everyday activity of social life to seek, in dangerous solitary meditation, a philosophy of existence. He recognized, however, as he told Jacqueline, that it was his own mind, not the impulse of God, that was directing his search. His state of desire was in itself a state of mental and emotional excitement. Desire provoked its satisfaction, hyperesthesia induced a complaisant hallucination.

The difficulty with the rational description is that it stops short at the most interesting moment. We must be satisfied with the word "hallucination," with a physiological description of the accompanying nervous phenomena, and with a cross-reference to other great abnormals. The religious description at least goes farther. It accepts the physiology without cavil, and introduces God by way of explanation. "From the movement of my heart I recognized the presence of God," says Saint Bernard. The mystic's recognition of God is as clear, as natural and factual, as our recognition of a neighbor's face. We may say, indeed: "There is no personal god, intervening in human affairs; hence he does not appear to mystic or non-mystic; hence the visionary is deceived by the fumes of his own disordered imagination." This is a reasonable belief; but to hold it we are rejecting specific testimonies on the basis of an *a priori* theory. In doing so, we are a little unscientific, for the testimonies of the seers of God are innumerable. We had better grant that the mystics have a uniformity of delusion on which a science may be built, though it be a science of folly.

Pascal was following the Mystic Way, a well trodden and well marked road. It has five sections: the first is the awakening or conversion, the second is purgation, the third illumination, the fourth the dark night of the soul, and the fifth is union. Pascal had been passing through his purgation, in which the soul learns to hate itself, to destroy or submerge the ego. Thus Saint Catherine tells us to dig up the root of self-love with the knife of self-hatred. This self-annihilation is a part of most systems of religious perfections, from Buddhism to Communism.

Pascal's ecstacy was illuminative, not unitive. In illumination the individuality remains separate and intact; in the unitive life it is merged with deity.

Pascal never reached the unitive stage. His life was too busy, too filled with warfare. Not until his last illness did he succeed in abandoning the world, and in annihilating his selfhood. Indeed, it has been noted that even in his Memorial he is less concerned with God than with himself. And God, also, seems mightily concerned with Pascal, with his certitude, joy, and reassurance.

His illumination was not, then, the complete experience of the mystic adept. In the unitive ecstacy, the mystic falls into a sort of catalepsy or trance. "Although this ecstacy lasts but a short time, the bones of the body seem to be broken by it," says Saint Theresa. Such visions are very brief, seldom persisting more than half an hour. But in Pascal's case the experience occupied two hours; his thoughts apparently remained entirely coherent and lucid throughout. It was not a Vision nor a Voice but a Grace, says the Abbé Brémond. It was an assurance of the remission of sins, the assurance of salvation, in the Protestant sense. The idea was already a familiar one to Pascal, for Jansenism pictured the coming of grace very much as did Calvin.

Such was the great experience of the night of the twenty-third of November. I cannot tell you if it was God who visited Pascal in his house in the rue Beaubourg. But the important thing, for one whose concern is with the mind of Pascal, is that he believed it to be God. He had a mystic revelation, something outside the order of the universe. He was secure, with the impregnable assurance of the mystic. You can never prove anything to a mystic. He smiles, and says: "Ah, but something happened to me, something which human language has no words to describe, something which human proofs do not touch. I was there; I know. You cannot argue with God, any more than you can argue with the universe." His position is impregnable. His world has more dimensions than ours, and we can never understand his definition of those dimensions.

LIX

LIFE AND TIMES OF PIETER STUYVESANT [1]

By

HENDRIK VAN LOON

Peter Stuyvesant (1592-1672) was the Dutch director-general of New Amsterdam. He had served in the West Indies before arriving in New Amsterdam (later New York) on May 11, 1647, to become director there for the Dutch West India Company. In his earlier military service he had lost a leg and thereafter wore a wooden leg ornamented with silver bands.

In March, 1664, Charles II gave to his brother, the duke of York, the land between the Connecticut river and Delaware bay, and Colonel Richard Nicolls with a fleet of four ships and perhaps 300 or 400 men was sent out to take possession. The Gentlemen XIX (the College of Nineteen which acted as an executive for the Dutch West India Company) informed Director Stuyvesant in New Amsterdam that the expedition was being sent solely against New England, and thus no preparation was made for defense until just before the fleet arrived.

This selection from Hendrik Van Loon's book describes in the author's novel and unusual style how a sad experience in Dutch colonization came to its unavoidable end. Here we see old Stubborn Pete stumping around on his wooden leg in a vain effort to arouse his colonists to defend their homes against the fleet of Colonel Nicolls.

THE LAST OF THE DUTCH STRONGHOLDS IN AMERICA

The English and Dutch colonists in America were . . . informed as early as the middle of the year 1659 . . . that the King, in an outburst of great generosity, had bestowed the central part of the northern American continent upon his beloved brother James, Duke of York, who had fled to

[1] Hendrik Van Loon, *Life and Times of Pieter Stuyvesant*, New York: Henry Holt & Company, copyright 1928 by Hendrik Willem Van Loon, pp. 310-319.

Holland after the collapse of the royalist cause and who with his well-known Roman tendencies had not been happy in that stronghold of Dr. Calvin.

When however attempts were made to verify these rumors in London, they were violently denied. The Gentlemen XIX, who had undertaken to make this investigation, assured their Director in the New Netherlands that he need lose no sleep on that account. Stuyvesant, however, an honest Frisian and therefore by nature suspicious, refused to be reassured. He was passing through the most difficult part of his career. America was doing all sorts of queer things to his erstwhile obedient subjects. First they had wanted to be independent. . . . And now many of them were beginning to say that they did not care whether they were ruled by the King of England or by the Board of Directors of the Dutch West India Company, that they never meant to go back to Holland anyway, that the New World was their home and that the Old World meant nothing in their lives and the West India Company which had neglected them for so many years meant less than nothing. And if this sounded like sedition, the Lord General had better make the best of it! . . . . .

All this was very sad but in the year 1666 there was just exactly one person who continued to uphold the cause of the mother country and he did not even have two good legs to stand upon. Only when bands of irregular troops from the east were beginning to invade the Dutch part of Long Island in the spring of 1665 and were threatening to plunder Nieuw Amsterdam and kill all the Dutch, could the town councillors be aroused from their lethargy and be forced to take some action. They grudingly agreed to meet the Director and discuss plans for the defense of the city. But there was the ever-present problem of financing the enterprise. The Burgomasters thought that it could be done if the Lord General would ask the Gentlemen XIX to give the city a monopoly of the ale-house business. In that way the city would be able to raise enough money to surround the entire lower part of the island with walls.

Lord help us! this is not a very edifying page in the history of our civic past.

But it was only a beginning and worse was to follow. . . . .

And the few belated and panic-stricken measures taken on the morning of the twenty-eighth of August of the year 1664, when four British men-of-war suddenly entered New York harbor and dropped anchor before Nyack were what one might call the reflex action of an organism that had ceased to lead an independent existence.

The only person who upon that occasion was really serious in his defiance of the English demand for an immediate surrender was old Stubborn Pete. Far and wide he sent his messengers and called upon all the able-bodied men of the entire colony to hasten to Nieuw Amsterdam and defend the "key to their own homesteads." A sheer waste of time and energy, for no one came. . . .

Then he counted his own soldiers and inspected his military town guard and made an inventory of his cannon and his gun-powder and found that he could hope to last exactly three hours against the forces of Richard Nicolls' well-equipped squadron.

In this emergency he resorted to his old and trusted tactics of putting up a bold front and scowling like a whole regiment of dragoons and he despatched a very high-handed letter to the English commander and wished to be informed what this unwonted display of force in the colony of a friendly nation might mean.

Nicolls answered briefly that he had come by order of His Majesty the King of England and of His Majesty's brother, the Duke of York, and that he was there to take possession of "what belonged by right to the British crown"—the colony known thus far (and erroneously) as the New Netherlands.

It was a polite note, so damnably polite that it was insulting and furthermore it left no loophole for doubt.

Nevertheless, the Lord General decided to try once more and early the next day a committee of citizens were sent down the bay to confer with the invaders and ask for verbal explanations.

On Saturday, the thirtieth of August of the year 1664, these delegates reported to a hastily gathered assembly of notables that to tell the truth, they had not got very far with the Englishman. He had been very agreeable but he had repeated his request for an unconditional and immediate surrender of the town in the same words as he had used in his answer to the Lord General. When they had asked him to explain by what right or under what treaty he had fallen upon a peaceful nation, Colonel Nicolls had briefly stated that he had come to America to obey orders but not to enter into a debate and that "if anybody wished to argue the case, he had better do so before His Majesty, the King of England, who happened to be living in London."

That was not exactly what one would call a satisfactory answer, but another day had been gained and as the English seemed to be making no preparations to put their troops on shore, Stuyvesant decided to use the next few days for a terrific display of energy. Hoping against hope, the old fellow thought that the sight of hundreds of men busily engaged on the bulwarks, hauling guns from one place to another, filling wheelbarrows with dirt, would discourage his enemies sufficiently to make them go back to Boston. Meanwhile he meant to keep the courage of his people high by telling them of a letter of explanation which Colonel Nicolls had promised to the delegation of burghers on the previous day, which had not yet arrived but which no doubt would put everything in a new light.

As a matter of fact, that letter was already in his pocket. It contained the promise that the rights of all the colonists would be most carefully respected, but that in case of a refusal to surrender the town and the fort, those who opposed His Majesty's just demands would be treated with the utmost severity and would experience all the miseries connected with warfare.

Stuyvesant knew his people. He knew them only too well. Their present luke-warm ardour (kept alive by his story about the "temporary nature" of the English visit) would evaporate the moment they knew that the English meant business and would open fire unless they were given the keys to the city. He therefore decided to keep the contents of the supplementary letter of Colonel Nicolls a secret and fight the thing out. But the Burgomasters of Nieuw Amsterdam knew of the arrival of the document and when the English ships approached the town, landed troops on Long Island and on Governor's Island and during the dark of night actually passed the fort, they hinted that the time had come for surrender.

On the second of September two committees were again sent to the English commander to ask him in the name of the civil authorities of Nieuw Amsterdam what would be the best policy for the citizens of the town to follow. On Wednesday, the third, they reported that their visit had been a very unsatisfactory one. . . .

When urged at least to tell the committee whether he intended to open fire on the town, he had hinted that the first attack would probably occur on Thursday next unless a white flag hoisted on the walls of the fort told him that his wishes had been complied with, in which case the people of Nieuw Amsterdam would find him to be a man of a mild and kindly disposition.

When this answer became known all over the town, it was useless for the Director to try any further defense. Already in the night of the first of September he had sent a message through Hell Gate (which as yet was unoccupied) to inform the Gentlemen XIX of what had happened. This document (which, by the way, never reached Holland) was a sort of last will and testament.

"Long Island is lost," he wrote, "and Nieuw Amsterdam itself has been called upon to surrender. We have no soldiers, we have no gunpowder, we are short of food. Furthermore the citizens are completely disheartened. They cannot see that there is the slightest chance of relief in the case of a siege and if the island falls into the hands of the invaders, they fear for the lives of themselves and their wives and their children. It is clearly apparent that this town cannot possibly hope to hold out for more than a very few days." And he ends his letter by telling the Gentlemen XIX of the hatred for the Company, of which he had heard a great deal these last four days. But what else could they expect, as "every suggestion for improvement made either by himself or by others had been disregarded and left unanswered"? . . .

On the fifth of September, a committee composed of a representative of the Lord General and delegates from the town of Nieuw Amsterdam held a final session with Colonel Nicolls on Long Island near the ferry to Brooklyn. They carried a power of attorney which allowed them to discuss the full details of the forthcoming surrender.

On Sunday the seventh, after the regular afternoon meeting, the twenty-three articles of surrender were read to the assembled magistrates and to as many soldiers and citizens as could crowd into the church.

On Monday, the eighth of September of the year 1664, Pieter Stuyvesant signed a proclamation in which he acknowledged the fact that he had accepted the act of surrender, which by this time was known to all the people.

It was the last time an official document was dated from the Fort of Amsterdam. As for the Director—he slowly hobbled out of the disreputable old fortress and marching at the head of his handful of soldiers, he led them to the *Gideon* which was to carry them back to Holland.

When he returned, the Dutch flag had been hauled down and the English flag had been run up.

Three weeks later the last of the Dutch strongholds in America was occupied by the troops of Nicolls and a sad experiment in colonization had come to its unavoidable end.

LX

BEYOND DAMASCUS, A BIOGRAPHY OF PAUL[1]

By

F. A. SPENCER

Floyd Spencer's partly fictionized biography of the great apostle Paul is interesting reading because of its dramatic quality and lively style.

Paul was probably born within a few years of the beginning of the Christian era. He was taught by Gamaliel, one of the most learned rabbis of his time, and studied the Old Testament and the strict Jewish faith and traditions. While Paul was following his studies, Jesus lived and died. It is doubtful whether he ever saw Jesus.

Sometime later Paul was a consenting witness as Stephen, the first Christian martyr, was stoned to death. The great change in Paul's life came when he was about thirty-two years old, and as he was on the road to Damascus to persecute any members of the new faith he might find there. In a vision he saw Jesus and heard him ask "Why persecutest thou me?" After this vision his whole life changed. Jesus was no longer the justly crucified leader of a heretical religious movement, but the Holy Messiah. He then began to travel widely, preaching that Jesus was the Messiah. It was at the Church of Antioch in Syria where Paul preached for many months that the name *Christian* was first given to the disciples. As a result of his faith, Paul suffered imprisonment and persecution. Paul, more perhaps than anyone else in history, through his missionary journeys organizing churches in various countries, made Christianity a world religion. His epistles or letters to his friends and various churches form a considerable part of the New Testament.

It was probably about 64 or 65 A.D. that the great Apostle Paul, one of the most striking personalities in history, was executed by Nero, as described in the following selection.

[1] F. A. Spencer, *Beyond Damascus, a Biography of Paul,* New York: Harper & Brothers, 1934, pp. 411-414.

I HAVE FINISHED MY COURSE

It is in the month of November. A chill, drenching rain falls steadily on the pavement of the Forum, so near and yet so unattainably far from the state prison where Paul is confined, waiting his second trial. *Why* does not Timothy come with the cloak? It is cold, cold. Too cold for manuscripts and parchments. Will God, will Nero be merciful? Ah, what matter! Better to be at home with Christ than in exile here.

Then one day the rumor flies around in prison that Nero has returned. He has arrived from Greece. The rumor goes below into the condemned hold, the Tullianum, among the prisoners waiting there in piles of bones that would bear white witness, if the darkness were not too black, how many have starved here before they could be executed. But hope is not extinct even in the Tullianum and still less in the prison above. Flushed with the success of his easy athletic victories, Nero will surely be lenient to a poor Jew, guilty of no treason against the government.

But *will* he? Too well he remembers his favorite concubine who (ill chance the day) met Paul before he was confined to prison, the stubborn concubine who embraced the Nazarene religion and refused from that day forth to share Nero's bed....

There comes finally a day toward the close of November when Paul is made ready for an audience with Nero. Freed of vermin and filth, he is ushered into the divine presence. So this, this is the savior of the world....

Do Nero's misted blue eyes look forward to the day, not a year later, when, shivering and pale and clad only in a ragged cloak and tunic, he will take refuge in the villa of his freedman Phaon outside Rome? Does the little doll-image given him by a plebeian friend as protection against plots tell Nero that in a few months he will be lying cold and half-naked and hungry on an old pallet-cot? Does he know that he will die, whimpering "What an artist perishes in me"? The timorous, sensual face, the spotted body, noisome now as a tomb, are ready for death, but the spirit of Nero is grotesquely unready, afraid.

But Nero is thinking now of his choice concubine who has never slept in his bed since that unhappy day when she met the bald, wiry apostle with the prying, pointed beard. He stirs restlessly as Alexander the coppersmith and others make their charges.

Sedition. Member of the cursed sect of the Nazarenes. Guilty of the fire and disaster in the sacred Center of the Earth, the City of Rome. Worthy of torture by the claws of wild beasts. Worthy of the pitch-smeared jacket and the torch. Worthy . . .

Nero yawns. What are these idle political quibbles, these futile religious arguments . . . ? The emperor sits bolt upright. "Death by the sword."

Soldiers escort Paul from the palace of Nero through the Forum. This time Paul is not to know the comparative comfort of the upper prison. He must be confined in the dungeon, the Tullianum, awaiting execution ten days later. A small circle of light appears. The prisoners below blink stupidly, rats scamper away, as Paul is lowered on a rope into the mire. There is nothing now that Timothy can do, if indeed he has come in time, to comfort the apostle. There is small chance that the emperor will grant a pardon.

The tenth day arrives. No word from the emperor. Again the rope is lowered. Reeking with vermin as of old, his garments in mere rags, his face cruelly bitten by rats, drawn with hunger, Paul is hoisted up to the clear air of the prison.

With a sympathetic centurion in charge, the little cortège of disciples, hooting pagans, clanking soldiery, move down the Sacred Way, around the Palatine, the Aventine, and out by the Ostian Gate to the harbor road.

Past the pyramid tomb of Cestius on the right. A mile and a quarter down the Ostian Way, southwest of the city. The morning light, shining for a moment through the rain, touches the arms of the soldiers, gleams over marble palaces on the hills of Rome, rests on the face of Paul, now that of a man, now that of an angel.

Left, right, left, right—down the Ostian Way to the new Ardeatine Road. Along this for three-quarters of a mile. And then into a little lane which leads directly to a natural amphitheater, hill-girt, tree-clad.

Not unkindly the centurion asks, "Any last request?" Paul kneels and prays for the churches, for his friends, for Peter being crucified head downward this very day; he prays for his own soul, now soon to be at home with Christ.

He kneels. The light gleams one brief instant on the descending sword of the executioner. The head of Paul, persecutor and bully, Paul the least of the apostles, Paul the greatest of heretics and sinners and boldest of ministers, rolls on the ground. And where it touches the earth, three fountains, Healing Waters, spring up.

Not even death can separate Paul from the love of Christ and of the Christians. His body, lash-embroidered, stone-bruised with the stigmata of Christ, is thrown into a charnel-pit. But it is soon rescued by Lucina, a devout lady, who buries it in her own garden.

Now he rests in a subterranean chamber, if legend be true, in the Church of St. Paul Outside the Walls. Eighty pillars of granite, presents all of kings, deck the nave under which after a lapse of nearly nineteen hundred years he still patiently waits the coming of Christ.

He lies outside the walls of Rome and outside the true love of the church. Misunderstood in later ages as during his own life, respected but never truly loved, Paul has been the unwilling father of many a theological monstrosity, of blood-lustful persecutors who owed nothing to him but their blind courage and uninformed zeal for liberty, crusaders with drums and tramplings set against the foes of Christ (that is to say of men who differed from them in doctrine). . . .

Everything that Paul hoped for has apparently remained only a hope. Christ remains aloof, serene in the heavens. The Judgment Day has not yet come. The world still longs for bread and games and war more than spiritual salvation. Millions of pagans still remain unconverted. The church itself is split into hundreds of warring sects, grotesquely united only to suppress the human freedom for which Paul fought. The world wags on much as it has always done, giving and robbing, loving and fighting.

Thinking moderns have discarded the panoply of first-century magic and theology in which Paul clothed the human teacher of Galilee. Often, without trying to understand the language of the first century, Paul's natural medium of expression, they have denounced the Tarsian as a perverter of Christ. Yet still they dream that the world may be saved from ultimate destruction by an universal brotherhood, knowing not a barrier of race or sex or social condition, a dream which would have died in Judæa had not a Jew of Tarsus seen a vision on the road to Damascus.

INDEX

Actress, 70-77
Advice, 176-177
Airplane, 38, 213-217
Alexander, Holmes, 171
Alexander the Great, 250-251
Armstrong, Margaret, 70
Arnold, H. H., 42
Arnold, Julian B., 143
Author, 198-203, 265-267, 336-342
Autopsy, 357-358
Aviation, 38-47, 213-217
Aviator, 137

Baker, Ray Stannard, 322
Barton, Clara, 178-185
Baseball, 64-69
Basso, Hamilton, 359
Beaconsfield, Earl of, 121-133
Beauregard, Pierre Gustave Toutant, 24, 359-361
Beatty, Richmond C., 311
Biddle, Francis, 35
Billings, Frank, 222-225
Birth, the book, 336-342
Bishop, Morris, 379
Blindness, 138-142
Bolívar, Simon, 186-189
Bonaparte, Napoleon, 84-95
Books, 143-145
Brooks, Van Wyck, 198
Brooks, William E., 78
Brothers, 84-95
Bryan, William J., 322-335
Buck, Pearl S., 226
Burr, Aaron, 163-170, 171-173
Business, 297-300, 346-356

Canby, Henry Seidel, 102
Carlota [Marie Carlota Amélie], 268-275
Carnegie, Andrew, 145-146
Caxton, William, 143-145
Cemetery, 159
Character, 78, 130-131, 155-157
Children, 318-321
China, 226-236
Chinese, 174-177, 226-236
Choice, 322-335
Christianity, 379-390, 396-399
Churchill, Winston, 82-83
Civil disobedience, 102-107
Civil War, 1, 21, 78, 155-157, 218-221, 359-361
Clapesattle, Helen, 96
Cleveland, Grover, 362-373
Clothes, 343
Coercion, 84-95
Cohen, Lester, 38
Columbus, Christopher, 239-249
Conceit, 238
Confederacy, 21-34, 155-157
Confucius, 174-177
Congress, 362-373
Conqueror, 250-251
Conquest, 84-95
Coolidge, Calvin, 108-120
Constitution, 311-317
Coughlin, John, 301-310
Courage, 64-69, 226-236, 362-373, 396-399
Court Martial, 38
Creditors, 290
Cross-examination, 224-225, 344
Crow, Carl, 174
Crucified, 266-267
Cummings, Lewis V., 250
Custer, George Armstrong, 377-378
Cynic, 273

Darrow, Clarence, 343-345

Davenport, Marcia, 252
Davis, Jefferson, 155-157
Davis, Loyal, 357
Dead, 224-225
Death, 36, 67-69, 115-120, 158, 160, 163-170, 171-173, 186-189, 226-236, 250-251, 267, 269-275, 357-358, 396-399
Decision, 21, 322-335
Democracy, 311-317
Democrats, 322-335, 362-373
Derleth, August, 336
Destiny, 152-240
Detail, 82-83
Determination, 125
Dickens, Charles, 138-142
Dictionary, 293-296
Discoverer, 239-249
Discovery, 239-249
Disraeli, Benjamin, 121-133
Divorce, 84-95
Doctor, 96-101, 222-225, 318-321, 357-358, 363-367
Dooley, Martin, 237-238
Doolittle, James H., 46-47
Douglas, Stephen A., 218-221
Duel, 163-170
Duffus, R. L., 318
Dunlap, Orrin E., 147
Dunne, Finley Peter, 237-238
duPont, Alfred I., 346-356
Du Pont De Nemours, E. I., and Company, 346-356

Economy, 108-120
Edison, Thomas A., 190-197
Editorial, 204-212
Education, 374-376
Einstein, Albert, 134-137
Election, 301-310
Electricity, 147-154, 190-197
Ellis, Elmer, 237
Emerson, Ralph W., 102, 198-203
Empire, 250-251
End, 65-67
Enemy, 288
Epigrams, 158-162, 174-177, 238, 267
Execution, 269-275, 396-399
Explorer, 239-249
Essayist, 198-203
Estate, 156-157
Everett, Edward, 2-4, 12, 18
Eyes, 138

Failure, 297
Faith, 226-236, 396-399
Fighting Angel, 226-236
Financier, 163-170
Fools, 162
Forbes, Esther, 48
Franklin, Benjamin, 284-292
Freeman, Douglas Southall, 21
Friend, 288
Friendship, 218-221
Fuller, Margaret, 276-281
Funeral, 115-120
Futility, 186-189

Gale, Zona, 336-342
Gandhi, Mohandas K., 102, 105, 107, 135
Garbedian, H. Gordon, 134
Gauvreau, Emile, 38
Gehrig, Lou, 64-69
Genius, 134-137, 252, 264
Gettysburg Address, 1-20
Giovanni, Don, 252-263
Gladstone, William E., 121-133
Gold, 362-373
God, 11, 81, 131, 160, 173, 264, 379-390
Government, 311-317
Graham, Frank, 64
Grant, Ulysses S., 78-81

Hamilton, Alexander, 163-172
Harding, Bertita, 268
Heine, Heinrich, 158-162
Holmes, Oliver Wendell, 35-37
Holt, L. Emmett, 318-321
Holt, L. Emmett, Jr., 318
Honeymoon, 113
Honor, 163-170
Hughes, Rupert, 62
Humanity, 134-137
Humility, 264
Humor, 82-83, 114, 158-162, 177, 224-225, 237-238, 265-266, 282-283, 343-345

Incredible, 152
Indians, 244-248
Industrious, 190-197
Inspiration, 198-203, 379-390
Inventor, 147-154, 190-197
Italy, 276-281

James, Marquis, 346
Jefferson, Thomas, 19, 171, 311-317

Jesus Christ, 135, 160-161, 266-267, 379-390, 396-399
Journalism, 204-212, 237
Juárez, Benito Pablo, 269-275
Juliet, 70

Kansas, 204-212
Kemble, Fanny, 70-77
Kindness, 62-63
Kogan, Herman, 301
Kung, Master, 174-177

Lamp, 190-197
Lane, Wheaton J., 374
Latin America, 186-189, 268-275
Leacock, Stephen, 138
Learning, 161
Lee, Robert E., 21-34, 78-81
Levine, Isaac Don, 213
Life, 36
Lincoln, Abraham, 1-20, 155-156, 218-221, 359
Lords of the Levee, 301-310
Loth, David, 163
Ludwig, Emil, 84

MacArthur, Douglas, 45-46
Macaulay, Thomas B., 311-317
McElroy, Robert, 155
Mack, Connie, 64
Marconi, Guglielmo, 147-154
Marriage, 84-95, 108-115, 288-289
Maurois, André, 121
Maximilian [Ferdinand Maximilian Joseph], 268-275
Maxims, 288-291
Mayo, Charles, 96-101
Mayo, William, 96-101
Medicine, 96-101, 222-225, 318-321, 357-358
Memory, 252, 260
Merchant, 297-300
Mexico, 268-275
Missionary, 226-236
Mitchell, William, 38-47, 213-217
Modesty, 134-137
Moir, Phyllis, 82
Money, 288-291
More, Louis T., 264
Morison, Samuel Eliot, 239
Mozart, Wolfgang, 252-263
Municipal government, 301-310
Murphy, John B., 99, 357-358

Music, 252-263
Musician, 252-263

Nerney, Mary Childs, 190
Nero, 396-399
Nevins, Allan, 362
New Deal, 317
Newton, Isaac, 264
Nolan, Jeannette Covert, 218
Nomination, 322-335

Opera, 252-263
Operation, 363-367

Painter, 265-266
Paradox, 158-162, 377-388
Pascal, Blaise, 379-390
Patience, 190-197, 289
Paul the apostle, 396-399
Pearl Harbor, 39
Pediatrics, 318-321
Perfection, 198-203
Persecution, 396-399
Persistence, 190-197, 199
Perspective, 238
Planning, 82-83
Poet, 158-162, 198-203
Politics, 108-120, 204-212, 301-310, 322-335, 362-373
Poole, Ernest, 222
Poor Richard's Almanac, 284-292
Popular government, 311-317
Poverty, 288-289
Prayer, 11, 173
Preacher, 226-236
Presidents, 1-20, 108-120, 322-335, 362-373,
Prime Minister, 82-83, 121-133
Printing, 143-145
Prophecy, 311-317
Puritan, 108

Radical, 344-345
Record, 65-67
Red Cross, 178-185
Religion, 226-236, 379-390, 396-399
Repartee, 265-266
Resistance, 102-107
Retailer, 297-300
Revere, Paul, 48-61
Revolutionary War, 48, 62
Rich, Everett, 204
Rogers, Betty Blake, 282
Rogers, Will, 46, 282-283

Rome, 276-281

Sadness, 33, 67-69, 115-120
San Salvador, 243
Sandburg, Carl, 1
Sandwich, 83
Scarlet Fever, 222-224
Schoolmaster, 293-296
Science, 134-137
Scientist, 134-137, 147-154, 264, 379
Silver, 362-373
Soldier, 21-47, 78-81, 84-95, 186-189, 213-217, 250-251
Soup, 282-283
Speech, 14, 121-133
Spelling, 295
Spencer, F. A., 396
Steel, 145-146
Stern, Madeleine B., 276
Stevens, Thaddeus, 7
Stone, Irving, 343
Stuyvesant, Pieter, 391-395
Success, 76-77, 262-263
Surgery, 96-101, 222-225, 357-358, 363-367
Surrender, 78-81

Tact, 62
Telegraphy, 147-154
Temptation, 155-156
Test, 152
Theater, 70
Thoreau, Henry David, 102-107
Thrift, 108-120
Treaty of Geneva, 178-185
Tumor, 96-97, 100
Twain, Mark, 140-141

United States, fate of, 311-317
United States Military Academy, 377
Untermeyer, Louis, 158

Vanderbilt, Cornelius, 374-376
Vanderbilt University, 374-376
Van de Water, F. F., 377
Van Doren, Carl, 284
Van Loon, Hendrik, 391
Victory, 81
Village Life, 339-341
Vision of God, 379-390

Walden Pond, 102
Warfel, Harry R., 293
Washington, George, 62-63
Wealth, 288
Webster, Noah, 293-296
Weight, 237
Wendt, Lloyd, 301
Whistler, J. M., 265-266
White, William Allen, 108, 204-212
Wilde, Oscar, 265-267
Williams, Blanche Colton, 178
Wilson, Woodrow, 322-335
Winkler, John K., 297
Winwar, Frances, 265
Wireless, 147-154
Wit, 158-162, 265-266, 282-283, 343-345
Woolworth, F. W., 97-300
Work, 190-197, 293-296
World War I., 213-217

Ybarra, T. R., 186
Youth, 70